BILL REID

BILL REID

THE
MAKING
OF AN
INDIAN

MARIA TIPPETT

RANDOM HOUSE CANADA

Copyright © 2003 Maria Tippett

All rights reserved under International and Pan-American Copyright Conventions. No part of this book may be reproduced in any form or by any electronic or mechanical means, including information storage and retrieval systems, without permission in writing from the publisher, except by a reviewer, who may quote brief passages in a review. Published in 2003 by Random House Canada, a division of Random House of Canada Limited, Toronto. Distributed in Canada by Random House of Canada Limited.

www.randomhouse.ca

National Library of Canada Cataloguing in Publication

Tippett, Maria, 1944–
    Bill Reid : the making of an Indian / Maria Tippett.

Includes bibliographical references and index.
ISBN 0-679-31089-4

1. Reid, Bill, 1920–1998.   2. Haida sculpture.   3. Native art—Canada—History—20th century.   4. Sculptors—Canada—Biography.   I. Title.

NB249.R44T56 2003   730'.92   C2003-903059-8

Front cover image: Bill Reid's carving, *Wolf Feast Dish*, 1970. UBC Museum of Anthropology, A9325.

Back cover image: Bill Reid and *Raven and the First Men*. Bill McLennan, UBC Museum of Anthropology, Nb1.481.

Design by Daniel Cullen

Printed in the United States of America

10 9 8 7 6 5 4 3 2 1

For the Master

CONTENTS

List of Illustrations   ix

Preface   1

Part I – A MIXED HERITAGE

CHAPTER 1 - Beginnings   11

CHAPTER 2 - Sophie's Story   27

CHAPTER 3 - Coming of Age   43

CHAPTER 4 - "This Is Bill Reid Speaking"   57

Part II – SALVAGING A CAREER

CHAPTER 5 - Back on the Coast   73

CHAPTER 6 - A Dying Art?   87

CHAPTER 7 - Urban Indian   105

CHAPTER 8 - Form Over Function   123

CHAPTER 9 - Return of the Raven   137

CHAPTER 10 - Setbacks   153

Part III – BITTER HARVEST

CHAPTER 11 - Becoming an Indian   179

CHAPTER 12 - The Best and Worst of Times   201

CHAPTER 13 - Big Is Beautiful   217

CHAPTER 14 - Bill Reid™   235

CHAPTER 15 - Things Fall Apart   253

Epilogue - Farewell   271

Acknowledgements   281

Endnotes   285

Selected Bibliography   311

Index   321

List of illustrations

p. 7   *Loo Taas*, accompanied by *Loo Plex*, carrying Bill Reid's ashes to the island of Tanu. Courtesy of the author.

p. 11   Tanu, 1897. Royal British Columbia Museum, No. PN5652.

p. 18   Skidegate, 1878. Canadian Museum of Civilization, CMC No. 255.

p. 19   Haidas in Skidegate, 1895. UBC Museum of Anthropology, from Gibbert Album, United Church of Canada Archives.

p. 21   Charles Gladstone, 1947. Canadian Museum of Civilization, CMC No. 102054.

p. 24   *Thunderbird and Whale*, argillite, Charles Edenshaw. Canadian Museum of Civilization, CMC No. 72-16818.

p. 24   *Carving on Cedar of Dogfish*, Charles Gladstone. Canadian Museum of Civilization, CMC No. J-241.

p. 27   Graduating Class of 1918, Victoria Normal School. University of Victoria Archives, image number 040200.

p. 43   Skidegate, 1941. National Archives of Canada, No. PA-112851.

p. 46   Basement of Victoria's Provincial Museum, n.d. Royal British Columbia Museum, No. PN11896

p. 51   Bill Reid as a student at Victoria High School. Victoria High School Archives.

p. 57   Bill Reid announcing at CBC, circa 1952. Canadian Broadcasting Corporation.

p. 62   Ryersonia Yearbook, 1951. Ryerson University Archives.

p. 66   Alice Ravenhill's chart. Royal British Columbia Museum, No. PN21630.

p. 67   *The Woman in the Moon*, brooch, circa 1950. UBC Museum of Anthropology, Nb1.688.

p. 68   *Killer Whale Earrings*, silver, 1955. UBC Museum of Anthropology, Nb1.709 a-b.

p. 68   *Eagle Brooch*, gold, 1955. UBC Museum of Anthropology, Nb1.703.

p. 74   *Beaver Bracelet*, circa 1953. UBC Museum of Anthropology, Nb1.743.

p. 74   *Sdast'aas, Two Bears Bracelet*, Charles Gladstone, 1951. UBC Museum of Anthropology, Nb1.749.

p. 76   Ellen Neel and family carving a totem pole. Vancouver Public Library, image number 62667.

p. 87   Charles Edenshaw. Canadian Museum of Civilization, CMC No. 88926.

p. 89   *Hummingbird Bracelet,* Charles Edenshaw. Royal British Columbia Museum, No. CPN9523.

p. 92   Sawing argillite at Slate Chuck Creek, 1954. Royal British Columbia Museum, No. PN5331

p. 93   Salvaging operations at Tanu, 1954. Royal British Columbia Museum, No. PN13975-B.

p. 95   Reid and Wilson Duff at Ninstints, 1957. Royal British Columbia Museum, No. PN7433.

p. 98   Mungo Martin in the Thunderbird Park carving shed. Royal British Columbia Museum, No. PN2041.

p. 105   Bill Reid carving at UBC's Totem Park. Vancouver Public Library.

p. 111   *Dogfish Gold Brooch,* circa 1959. UBC Museum of Anthropology, A1499.

p. 112   Silver earrings, circa 1961. UBC Museum of Anthropology, Nb1.708.

p. 117   Bill Reid (left) and Douglas Cranmer (right) carving at UBC. Vancouver Public Library, image numbers 39374 and 44650.

p. 119   Poles and houses outside the Museum of Anthropology. Les Baszo, *The Province,* M1626B1.

p. 120   *Sea Wolf Sculpture,* 1962. UBC Museum of Anthropology, A50029

p. 123   Silver box, bear and human design. UBC Museum of Anthropology, A1502.

p. 125   *Killer Whale and Raven* platter. UBC Museum of Anthropology, Nb1.748.

p. 126   Panel pipe, argillite, 1963. UBC Museum of Anthropology, A2552.

p. 130   *Gold Eagle Box.* UBC Museum of Anthropology, Nb1.717.

p. 137   Robert Davidson. Courtesy of Robert Davidson.

p. 143   Reid carving pair of oak doors, 1966. Ray Allen, *Vancouver Sun.*

p. 144   Bill Reid with bentwood dish. Ross Kenward, *The Province,* E91-5, 25-179.

p. 145   (top) Bracelet, Wolf, gold, 1962. UBC Museum of Anthropology, Nb1.719.

p. 145   (middle) Bracelet, Dogfish, silver, circa 1961. UBC Museum of Anthropology, Nb1.707.

p. 145   (bottom) Bracelet, Grizzly Bear, gold, 1960. UBC Museum of Anthropology, Nb1.702.

p. 155   Illustration by Art Price. Arthur Price frontispiece, from *Indian Carvers in Argillite* by Dr. Marius Barbeau, courtesy of Arthur Price.

p. 160   Reid and his grandson, Oliver Tanu Lusignan. Ted Grant, Ryerson University Archives.

p. 162   Reid on the roof of his apartment in Montreal, 1970. Private Collection.

p. 165   Sherry Grauer in Montreal, 1970. Private Collection.

p. 171   *Wolf Feast Dish,* 1970. UBC Museum of Anthropology, A9325.

p. 172   Mask, Woman, 1970. UBC Museum of Anthropology, A2617.

p. 173   Bill Reid, Robert Davidson and Mayor Jean Drapeau, Montreal, 1970. *La Presse.*

p. 174   Examples of Peter Page's jewellery, circa 1970. Courtesy of Peter Page

p. 179   Reid polishing a bracelet. Randy Thomas, *Vancouver Sun.*

p. 185   *Discovering Mankind,* argillite chest, Charles Edenshaw. Royal British Columbia Museum, No. CPN10622.

p. 187   *Raven Discovering Mankind in a Clamshell,* 1970. UBC Museum of Anthropology, Nb1.488.

p. 201   Reid carving pole on Queen Charlotte Islands. Royal British Columbia Museum, No. PN13706.

p. 211   Skidegate pole. Royal British Columbia Museum, No. PN13707.

p. 217   Bill and Martine Reid, Granville Island. Ted Grant, Ryerson University Archives.

p. 220   Gold brooch, frog, 1971. UBC Museum of Anthropology, A9349.

p. 226   *Raven and the First Men* on display at the Museum of Anthropology. Les Bazso, *The Province.*

p. 229   Reid and *Raven and the First Men.* Bill McLennan, UBC Museum of Anthropology, Nb1.481

p. 232   *Chief of the Undersea World,* 1984. Ted Grant, Ryerson University Archives.

p. 233   *Mythic Messengers,* bronze relief. Wayne Leidenfrost, *The Province.*

p. 235   Reid at home. Deni Eagland, *Vancouver Sun.*

p. 237   Reid with Barbara Shelly. Ian Smith, *Vancouver Sun.*

p. 238   Reid with students in Granville Island studio, with *Phyllidula, the Shape of Frogs to Come.* Ted Grant, Ryerson University Archives.

p. 242   Launch of *Loo Taas* at Expo 86. *The Province.*

p. 247   Reid pulling down Canadian flag in Paris, 1989. *Vancouver Sun.*

p. 249   *The Spirit of Haida Gwaii. Vancouver Sun.*

p. 250   Reid's assistants working on *The Spirit of Haida Gwaii.* Ian Lindsay, *Vancouver Sun.*

p. 253   Bill and Martine, 1997. *Vancouver Sun.*

p. 257   Reid carving top of box, 1985. Ted Grant, Ryerson University Archives.

p. 266   Protesting against logging of Lyell Island, 1987. Ralph Bower, *Vancouver Sun.*

p. 271   Reid's ashes being carried into the Great Hall at the Museum of Anthropology. Steve Bosch, *Vancouver Sun.*

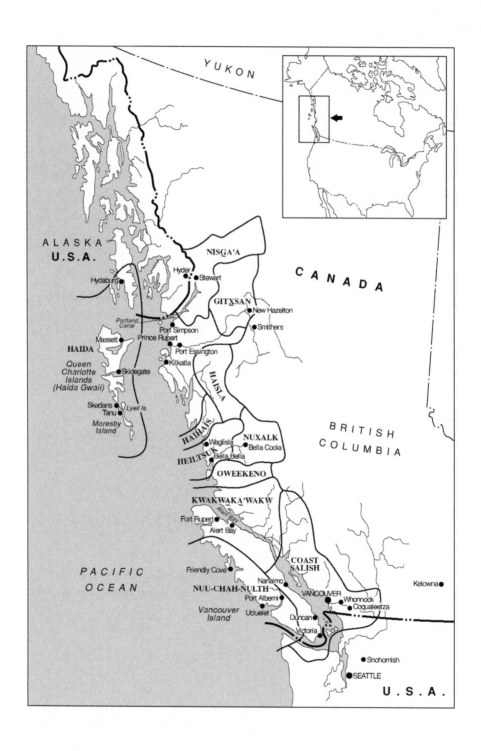

Preface

The last time I saw Bill Reid was in 1994. My book, *Between Two Cultures: A Photographer among the Inuit,* had just been published and I was speaking to a group of businessmen on the top floor of the Hotel Vancouver. Accompanied by his wife Martine, Bill sat close to the lecture podium. I knew who Bill Reid was — I had heard him give a lecture at the University of British Columbia in the late 1970s. During his talk, Bill had worn his knowledge of Haida art and culture lightly. I had been impressed by his modesty, manifested in his attempt to diminish the role he had played in what many people have called the revival of Northwest Coast Native art. Yet it was obvious to me that beneath his offhand manner lay a breadth of knowledge about and a commitment to Native art and culture. I did not see Bill Reid again until a mutual friend invited me to dine with him in the summer of 1990. By this time he had overseen the carving of *Raven and the First Men,* launched his canoe *Loo Taas,* and was in the midst of his largest commission, *The Spirit of Haida Gwaii.*

Long before I embarked on my research for this book, I knew that Bill Reid was not the sole architect of the so-called renaissance of contemporary Native art. As a cultural historian, I suspected that his public persona as a Haida Indian was as much a product of journalists, art patrons, museum curators, and others associated with the non-Native establishment as of Bill Reid himself. At the same time, I had been bowled over by works like *Raven and the First Men*. What other sculpture in the history of public art in Vancouver has so excited schoolchildren that they shout, as they enter the Museum of Anthropology: "Where's Bill Reid's raven?" Or prompts adults to compare *Raven and the First Men* with Michelangelo's *Pietà*, seen on their summer vacation in Rome?

I also knew that Bill Reid was not the only major figure in the history of post–World War II Northwest Coast Native art. During the mid-1950s I had observed the Kwakwaka'wakw artist Mungo Martin (Nakapenkum) both restoring and creating totem poles in the carving shed adjacent to the Provincial Museum in Victoria. As an even younger child, I had attended a pot-latch in the Coast Salish community house at Cowichan Bay on the southeast coast of Vancouver Island. The cedar-scented smoke, the masks and rattles, and the mournful song of the elders, who had beat out the steps for the dancers on their drums, had left no doubt in my childhood mind that Indian culture was very much alive.

These early experiences, along with my later contact, during the course of researching my biography of Emily Carr, with the Gitxsan and Nisga'a peoples living on the Nass and Skeena rivers, with the Nuu-chah-nulth in Ucluelet, and with the Haida on the Queen Charlotte Islands, made me ques-tion the prominent role that Bill occupied in the story of Northwest Coast art. I began to wonder if "revival" and "renaissance" were the right words to describe the process, and whether "continuation" would not have been a more accurate word when talking about what took place in British Columbia dur-ing the 1950s and 1960s.

I would like to have had Bill's response to my lecture on Inuit photography that autumn day in 1994. After all, the central theme of my talk — the ways in which photographic images of indigenous peoples have been used by non-Natives — was of interest to Bill Reid. He did say something when, at the end of my lecture, I walked over to where he was sitting. I bent my head close to his, trying to understand. Bill repeated his effort. But it was no use. Whatever he was struggling to say was incomprehensible to me, as it was to Martine Reid. Parkinson's is a cruel disease; it not only erodes mobility, it robs its victim of speech. The sonorous baritone voice that had brought the evening news to thousands of Canadians across the country had been reduced to a rasping, unintelligible whisper.

I did not think much about Bill Reid again until the spring of 1998. Opening my e-mail one morning in my college rooms at Cambridge University, I was confronted with a number of messages from friends. They all informed me that Bill Reid had succumbed to his long battle with Parkinson's disease on March 13.

Three days after his death, *Globe and Mail* writer Miro Cernetig set the stage for the accolades that followed. Reid had saved "an artistic tradition that was in danger of being lost."[1] The *Vancouver Sun* told its readers how Reid had done this. He had transformed Vancouver's public space by creating monumental sculptures like the *Killer Whale* at the Vancouver Aquarium, *The Jade Canoe* at the Vancouver Airport, and *Raven and the First Men* at the Museum of Anthropology. He had trained a host of younger Native artists, of whom Robert Davidson was the best known. And he had rescued Native art from extinction and thereby restored "a feeling of pride to Native communities up and down the Pacific coast."[2]

A week later, news of Bill's death made it to the obituary pages of the *New York Times*.[3] He was newsworthy in the American press because in the autumn of 1991, one of Bill's best-known works, *The Spirit of Haida Gwaii*, also known as *The Black Canoe*, had been installed at the entrance of the Canadian Embassy in Washington, D.C. In Britain, *The Times* took longer to acknowledge the artist's death. But when it did on April 11, the editor of the "morgue" gave Reid the lion's share of the obituary page. Four photographs accompanied a lengthy text that noted the salient features of Reid's life: study at London's Central School of Art and Design, salvaging and recreating Haida totem poles, and protesting against the logging of Lyell Island on the Queen Charlotte Islands. Few Canadians — dead or alive — have been given so much coverage in a British newspaper.[4]

Reading the obituaries and the tributes made me feel increasingly uneasy about the reporting in the press. Much of it was inaccurate. Writing in the *Globe and Mail*, David Silcox mistakenly credited Bill with being the first artist within living memory to raise a large totem pole and to carve a dugout canoe.[5] Virtually every other reporter ignored the earlier achievements of artists such as Mungo Martin and his wife, Abayah; Jimmy Seaweed; Ellen Neel; John Cross; Claude Davidson; and many others who were active long before Bill Reid appeared on the scene. The public was being given a skewed sense of the past.

Much was left unsaid. No one mentioned the extent to which Bill's work drew on western aesthetics. No one adequately explained why Bill and his work meant so much to the Canadian people. Or how he came to play such a pivotal role in the Native art world. Or how he got to where he was by the end of his life. Or why he was not accepted into the Native and non-Native establishments earlier in his career. Or, finally, why his acceptance in and discovery by the Native and non-Native communities become a major theme in Bill Reid's story of struggle.

As I sifted through the obituaries, I wondered why so many people, from collectors, museum curators, gallery dealers, art critics, and Native rights activists to the public in general, had exaggerated the uniqueness of Bill Reid and misrepresented his achievements in ways that revealed more about themselves than about the artist. Was it simply economics? For surely the value of Bill's work had increased now that he was dead. Did his journey of self-discovery resonate with a society whose identity has always been in a constant state of becoming? What was the evocative power of Bill's art: the exquisitely crafted gold bracelets and boxes, the massive totem poles and canoes, the argillite carvings, the prints and his writings? What was the secret to the way Bill projected himself — his charisma, his partial Native ancestry, and his heroic struggle against a debilitating disease? Whatever it was that made the Canadian public mourn the death of and celebrate the life of Bill Reid, I was intrigued.

When I returned to Canada in June 1998 at the end of the academic year, I made it my business to find out who this man really was and why he and his art had caused so many people to mourn his passing. A flyer issued by the Museum of Anthropology, announcing its acquisition of Bill Reid's papers, gave me some hope. The announcement appeared to indicate that his archive would be made accessible to scholars. When I asked to consult the collection, however, an archivist told me that his heirs had withdrawn it from the museum.

My next step was to approach Bill's heirs. Peggy Kennedy, Bill's only surviving sibling, was generous with her memories. Over lunch, Bill's wife, Martine Reid, shared her memories of the last difficult years of his life. She also kindly invited my husband, Peter Clarke, and me to his forthcoming burial at Tanu, on the Queen Charlotte Islands.

Unlike Emily Carr, Bill never kept a journal or wrote at length about his formative years. And unlike F.H. Varley, whose biography I have also written, Bill preferred the telephone to the letter as a means of keeping in touch with his friends. Bill did comment on his emergence as an artist in numerous interviews and in one short autobiographical piece of writing. But his references to his ancestral link to Haida culture, via his mother's family, were infrequent and inconsistent. Little wonder that those writing on Bill Reid during his lifetime unwittingly propagated his own versions of his life, in ways as derivative as they were incoherent.

In fact, by the time Bill died, his autobiographical accounts had acquired authority through repetition. This, of course, is how legends are made. This is also why biographers become unpopular when they challenge the received wisdom. Few people want to know about the dark side of their heroes' lives. Many prefer to cling to a romantic mythical story.

Since I was unable to rely on Bill's personal archive, I was thrown back on to my skills and training as a historian. Routing out archival sources yielded some wonderful surprises. I found a commonplace book belonging to Bill's grandmother, Josephine, dating from 1888; I discovered the school register from the Coqualeetza Industrial Institute where Bill's mother, Sophie, spent the formative years of her life; I located a collection of love letters written to the woman who broke Bill's heart; I was shown the drawings of a jeweller who helped make and design Bill's early work; I obtained documentation concerning the trial in which Bill was accused of smuggling jewellery into the United States. All these sources, along with the recollections of many Native artists — some captured through the interviewing skills of Beverley Berger — helped me to put Bill Reid into the historical context of Native art.

The study of Bill's carvings and jewellery was better served by writers during his lifetime. In 1986, Karen Duffek provided a brilliant essay on his early work for the catalogue *Bill Reid: Beyond the Essential Form* that accompanied his solo exhibition at the Museum of Anthropology. During the same year, Doris Shadbolt presented a large collection of Bill's work in her beautifully illustrated book *Bill Reid*. These two publications, along with the writings of scholars of the calibre of Michael Ames, Douglas Cole, George MacDonald, Bill McLennan, Bill Holm, Steven Brown, Robin K. Wright, and Aldona Jonaitis, exponentially expanded my knowledge of contemporary Northwest Coast Native art.

Inevitably, then, my work offers a challenge to Bill's autobiographical self, which he consciously or unconsciously often misrepresented. None of this should detract from his reputation as an artist. His work is there for all to see. Showing Bill to possess an elusive personality that changed like the raven's disguises throughout his career makes his achievements all the more interesting and significant. His sensitivity to his Native ancestry was nothing if not complex and ambiguous: variously a burden, an embarrassment, and an inspiration. His tendency to manic depression and, in his latter years, his affliction with Parkinson's disease not only spurred him on to striking accomplishments, but they ultimately made his life a nightmare.

My investigation of how Bill Reid achieved what he did while battling these constraints began in the summer of 1998, when Peter Clarke and I boarded an old fishing boat in Skidegate. With the rest of the burial party, we were soon sailing alongside the canoe that Bill and his assistants had carved in the mid-1980s. The *Loo Taas* was carrying Bill's ashes to the island of Tanu, where his grandmother Josephine Ellsworth was born in 1868 and where his ashes were to be interred the following day. I had begun my book — and, rare for a biographer, I was myself making an appearance, albeit a small walk-on part at the end of the story.

❧

Bill Reid was not a religious person. Near the end of his life he often referred to himself as an existentialist. (He liked the idea of keeping intellectual company with the French novelist Albert Camus.) He did not, therefore, want a burial in either the Native or non-Native tradition. He told Gary Edenshaw (Guujaaw) to "haul his body onto a boat, weight it down with a heavy chain and drop it to a sandy West Coast ocean bottom, where it would become food

Loo Taas, accompanied by Loo Plex,
carrying Bill Reid's ashes to the island of Tanu

for the crabs." Then he hoped that his friends would hold a party a few days later at the same beach and feast on the crabs.[6]

This did not happen. But there was a party to mark his burial. It began in Skidegate on July 3, 1998. At 5:00 P.M. in the evening of that bright warm day, Bill's ashes were carried into the community hall, where five hundred people had gathered to remember his life; to eat venison stew, herring roe on kelp, and two-layered cakes; and to dance and sing in his honour. The "doings" associated with Bill's burial ended two days later.

Bill Reid had already been cremated and his ashes placed in a cardboard box. The box was placed in a replica (made by the Kwakwaka'wakw artist Richard Sumner) of the Haida feast dish that Bill had admired in New York while doing research for the *Arts of the Raven* exhibition in 1967. The replica was placed in a large cedar chest that Don Yeomans had carved and painted for the occasion. In preparation for the long journey to Tanu, where Bill's ashes were to be interred, Yeomans's box was strapped to a palanquin then placed on *Loo Taas*. The following morning, accompanied by the *Loo Plex* and a flotilla of well-wishers, the *Loo Taas* was paddled and towed fifty kilometres down the coast to Skedans. After an evening of feasting and singing on the beach, the revellers were awakened in the early hours of July 4 by a fierce storm. The following morning the sea was still rough, and some of the revellers' stomachs, including my own, still churned. The canoes had to be towed on the final leg of their journey south.

The weary travellers were greeted several hours later on Tanu Island by the Haida Gwaii Watchmen, by a group of elders who had been flown in by helicopter, and by members of the Canadian Coast Guard and the RCMP. When everyone had assembled on the beach, the paddlers, who included Bill's grandchildren, Walker and Tyson Brown, raised the palanquin bearing Yeomans's chest and, to the beat of Guujaaw's drumming and chanting, led the procession to a quiet glade on a small promontory of land jutting out to sea. The mourners formed a crescent on one side of the open grave. Then Dempsey Collison, Chief Chee-Xial, spoke. He apologized for not having carried out Bill's whimsical burial wish. But he and the other Haida had done their best to follow the instructions set out in Bill's will. He then thanked Bill for devoting his life to Haida art and, after scattering a few ashes around the grave pit and into the nearby forest, he sealed the rest in Yeomans's box. The box was placed in the open grave next to a headstone engraved with Bill's wolf crest and with the words "In memory of Iljuwas, Yalth-Sgwansang." Then a shovel was passed from one mourner to another. When the box had disappeared under the soft earth, one of the elders wiped the headstone with a red cloth, and the mourners walked in silence down the path that led back to the beach. Bill Reid's story thus ended in the place where his grandmother Josephine Ellsworth had been born.

PART I

A MIXED HERITAGE

CHAPTER I

Beginnings

Tanu, 1897

Josephine Ellsworth (Elljuuwaas), Bill Reid's maternal grandmother, was born in the village of Tanu (T'anuu) on the east coast of Haida Gwaii.[1] At the time of her birth in 1868, Tanu boasted sixteen large cedar-plank dwellings, over thirty totem poles, and canoes measuring up to seventeen metres in length. On a small island between Logan and Richardson inlets off the coast of Moresby Island, Tanu, or Eelgrass Town, was the third-largest Haida settlement during most of the nineteenth century, after Skidegate (hlragilda) and Masset (radraci7waas) to the north. The village straddled both sides of a blunt rocky point and was dominated by yellow and red cedars, Norway and Sitka spruce, and western hemlock. On the migration route of trumpeter swans, harlequin and wood ducks, and Steller's jays, and permanent home to majestic eagles and metallic-sounding ravens, Tanu, like all the villages on the Queen Charlotte Islands, was never quiet.

Bill Reid liked to think that his grandmother, Josephine, lived according to Haida tradition but that her daughter, Sophie, thought it was sinful and debased to be an Indian. In fact, according to Bill Reid, his mother Sophie never fully believed herself to be Haida. "She saw herself as a blond, blue-eyed European who was stolen by bad fairies and dumped on the doorstep of some very aristocratic Haida family."[2]

Sophie transferred this apparent ambiguity about her Native heritage to her son. Throughout his career, Bill Reid gave conflicting accounts of how he was introduced to Native culture. Sometimes he claimed that his grandfather, Charles Gladstone, had instructed him in the lore, history, and tradition of the Haida people when he was in his early teens. At other times he insisted that he had learned nothing from his grandfather because the man spoke little English; instead, his interest in Haida culture had arisen from his discovery of "primitive" African sculpture through the paintings of Picasso. This line of thinking was inconsistent with Reid's claim, elsewhere, that he had been introduced to Haida art as a child by seeing the gold and silver Native bracelets worn by his mother and her sisters and that a visit to his grandfather Charles at the age of thirteen had made him determined to become a jeweller when he grew up.

Bill Reid was equally ambiguous about the discovery of his Native ancestry. Sometimes he claimed that he had been unaware of being anything other than an average Caucasian North American until he was in his early teens. At other times he pushed the date forward and insisted that he did not know he was Native, had never met his grandmother or visited Haida Gwaii, and did not meet his grandfather until he was an adult. Reid could refer to himself as a Haida prince and as a WASP with equal firmness. He could view weather-silvered totem poles in Tanu or Skedans with as much intensity as he read the writings of Shakespeare and listened to the music of Mozart. And he identified less with his Haida contemporaries than with the landscape of Haida Gwaii and with the carvings and paintings created by a long-dead generation of artists.

The multiple identities that Bill Reid created for himself and his mother make him an unreliable narrator of his own past. Thus any understanding of why Reid thought the way he did must come from other sources.

Preserved in the archives of the Museum of Anthropology a floor below the concrete and glass galleries displaying totem poles, bentwood boxes, and feast dishes is an exercise book. At first glance it is little different from the scribblers in which Euro-Canadian women wrote recipes, poems, prayers, and household hints. Closer scrutiny, however, reveals that, remarkably enough, the book belonged to a Haida woman.[3] Even more remarkable, the woman who recorded and allowed others to record poems, drafts of letters, and prayers in her little book was Josephine Ellsworth.

Bill Reid's grandmother made the first dated entry in her scribbler in 1888, a few years after leaving Tanu, where she had lived, just as her grandson Bill claimed, according to Haida tradition. Until her mid-teens, Josephine had a strong sense of belonging to one of the two moieties, or clans, to which every Haida belonged. She knew not only that she belonged to the Raven moiety (st'langng 'laanaas) and not to the Eagle moiety (sdasta.aas), but that her family possessed the right to display crests representing creatures belonging to the natural, imagined, and mythological worlds. The wolf design, along with several other animal motifs that declared the family's lineage, status, and wealth, was carved onto storage, cooking, and serving utensils and onto ceremonial objects. Crests were also painted onto objects ranging from Josephine's cedar-bark hat to what is the Native artist's largest "canvas": the ten-metre-long surface covering the front of her cedar-plank house.

During Josephine's youth, Chief Gitkun presided over the potlatches and feasts that mourned the dead, named the children, and transferred rights and privileges from the dead to the living. Her elders sang the songs that told of the division of the world into three zones — the sky world, the earth world, and the underworld — and from the mythical creatures who moved from one realm to the other. The village orators recited hundreds of place names, hundreds of people's names, and hundreds of biological names, and told hundreds of stories recounting the history of Josephine's people. The dancers provided a visual confirmation of the social and spiritual order by displaying their ceremonial regalia during their dramatic re-enactments of the myths associated with real and imagined creatures. There were few ceremonies in the summer. Josephine and her sister, Fanny, helped the women dry salmon, halibut, and seaweed. While the men fished or travelled in their huge canoes to the mainland coast to trade with the Tsimshian and Tlingit, the women gathered berries and wove watertight baskets from the strong supple roots of the spruce tree.

In 1878 the young geologist George Dawson, who worked for the Geological Survey of Canada, sailed into Laskeek Bay off Tanu Island. Five years later, when Josephine was fifteen, two American collectors, James G. Swan and James Deans, visited her village during their trip to Haida Gwaii. Josephine witnessed the removal of ceremonial objects by these and other itinerant collectors, and she saw the Indian Reserve Commissioner, Peter O'Reilly, lay a boundary around the village in accordance with the 1871 Joint Commission for the Settlement of Indian Reserves in British Columbia. Shortly after O'Reilly left, Reverend Thomas Crosby's seventy-one-foot steamboat, *The Glad Tidings,* pulled into Laskeek Bay. The arrival of Crosby's floating mission from the mainland coast foreshadowed the demoralization and the physical relocation of Josephine's people.

The autobiographies of the Reverends Thomas Crosby and W.H. Collison give self-serving accounts of their encounters with the Haida, whom they considered to be uncouth savages. According to their versions, the inhabitants of Tanu and Skidegate asked them to establish a Methodist mission on Haida Gwaii. The people of Tanu knew about the prosperous white settlement that had grown up around Fort Simpson and the Anglican Church Missionary Society's model Native village — it had a church, a hospital, and an industrial school — at Metlakatla on the mainland coast. They also knew that the people living at the north end of Haida Gwaii in Masset had acquired modern amenities when the Anglicans established a mission there in 1876. Whether this made the people of Tanu and Skidegate urge the missionaries to do the same in their area is not known. What is known, however, is that the Anglicans could not afford to set up a second mission on the Queen Charlotte Islands, so the Methodists stepped in.

In 1883 the lay preacher George Robinson established a mission in Skidegate. This introduction reinforced the proselytizing activities that Thomas Crosby had carried out from the deck of his floating mission a few years earlier. It also saw the clergy try to persuade the people living in the villages south of Skidegate to move there. Tanu's residents were reluctant to join their long-time rivals in Skidegate. But they did agree to move farther north. In 1884 the first group of villagers relocated to the abandoned Qadasgu on the north shore of Louise Island at the mouth of Church Creek on Cumshewa Inlet. Before Josephine joined the exodus north a year later, she helped collect the remains of the dead from the burial boxes on the mortuary columns and from the burial houses. Then she watched the men of the village dig a large pit near the beach. It was here that over fifty members of Josephine's village came to rest in a mass grave.

When the trader John Work and his crew aboard the *Lama* had dropped anchor off Tanu Island in 1835, they had counted forty large cedar-plank houses and 545 people. By the time Josephine Ellsworth was born thirty-three years later, Tanu's population had fallen to fewer than one hundred inhabitants. The roofs of the unoccupied cedar-plank dwellings had collapsed. The totem poles were leaning drunk-sick towards the ground or had toppled over and were being reclaimed by moss, salal, and salmonberry bushes. And more people were dying.

There had been no signs of illness among the Haida when the first European, the Spaniard Juan Hernández Pérez, anchored the *Santiago* off the south coast of Haida Gwaii in 1774. Likewise, the explorer and fur trader Captain George Dixon, who named the islands after his ship, which took its name from Queen Charlotte, the wife of mad King George III, was pleased to note that the Indians were free from disease a few years later. In 1788, however, Captain James Colnett told a different story. Sailing along the east coast of the Queen Charlotte Islands on the *Prince of Wales,* he encountered corpses and abandoned villages. Moreover, those who had survived their encounter with the first deadly wave of smallpox the previous year were so altered that Colnett hardly recognized them. By the time Captain Charles Bishop arrived on the Queen Charlotte Islands in 1795, things were worse. The disease, he observed from the deck of the *Ruby*, was "raging among them."[4]

From roughly 10,000 when Pérez made landfall at Dadens in 1774, the population of Haida Gwaii fell to 6,693 by 1835 and to 1,244 by 1870. When Josephine was in her teens, it dropped to a pitiful 800. The smallpox epidemic of the 1780s had accounted for the initial deaths. Tuberculosis, whooping cough, measles, and, once the Haida began visiting the newly established Fort Victoria in the middle decades of the nineteenth century, venereal disease and alcohol accounted for the rest. Many Europeans believed that the Haida people would die out. Yet not every Haida succumbed to their encounter with non-Native diseases. And not every government official, entrepreneur, and missionary who visited the Queen Charlotte Islands during the nineteenth century was successful in obliterating the cultural and social traditions of the people who survived.

In May 1885, just after relocating to New Klew, Josephine married the Haida William Wilson. They lived in a single-family, cottage-style dwelling, not in a large communal house. They attended prayer meetings and church services rather than potlatches and feasts. And, by joining a few other adults and children in the village at school, they turned their backs on the way that the Haida were taught — informally and by example. "We are at school every day," a copy of a letter in Josephine's scribbler proudly informed the missionary's wife, Mrs. Hopkins, "and getting on pretty well." It was thus while living in New Klew that Josephine learned how to speak and write English by memorizing passages from the scriptures and by singing hymns. It was in this same village that she and William were baptized. The church did not have a monopoly on good behaviour, though. Haida children were instructed by their elders in proper speech and etiquette. This made it easy for Josephine and William to transfer their Native beliefs and practices to their newfound religion.

Josephine and William Wilson were exemplary Christians. They attended church on a regular basis. They learned hymns by heart and sang carols — "Hark the Herald Angels Sing" was a favourite. They could recite many passages from the Bible. And they actively proselytized among their friends. Josephine took the moral high ground when she told Elizabeth Grey that she had been living in sin. And William commiserated with a man whose "bad" wife had not returned from a visit to Victoria. They also befriended every Methodist clergyman and his family who visited the Queen Charlotte Islands. And when the missionaries left, Josephine's and William's writing skills were sufficient, as copies of correspondence in her scribbler show, to enable them to keep in touch by letter.

While Josephine and William appear to have been willing converts, not every Haida was convinced that medical assistance and education went hand in hand with God. Some did not like living in single-family dwellings. Others rebelled at the prohibition, on threat of a jail sentence, of partaking in winter ceremonies and the carving and raising of totem poles. Living conditions in New Klew were hardly conducive to good health, and there was much illness resulting in many deaths. Despite the positive tone of the entries in Josephine's scribbler, her father was very ill in 1888. And by the end of that year he was dead. Josephine's father was not the Ellsworth family's only casualty. In the early years of the next century, Josephine's sister, Fanny, succumbed to illness, leaving Josephine to look after the orphaned children. By this time Josephine and William had put aside their antipathy to the people of Skidegate and moved to Haida Gwaii's second largest village.

Unlike New Klew, Skidegate was a long-settled Haida community. When Josephine and William moved into a single-family dwelling on the mud flats below the church, the school, and the mission house, Skidegate was well on its way to becoming a model Methodist settlement. Reverend A.N. Miller, who had replaced Reverend Hopkins during the summer of 1888, held weekly services and prayer meetings. He organized a Native brass band that serenaded the villagers on the Sabbath. He taught children and adults alike in the one-room, lean-to school that was added to the mission house. And he encouraged the newcomers to abandon their traditional clothing, their communal houses, and their ceremonies.

The move to Skidegate gave Josephine and William more than white friends, white housing, and a larger dose of white religion. With the emergence of fish canneries and lumber mills on the mainland coast and the establishment of a fish-oil plant near Skidegate, many of the displaced Haida from New Gold Harbour, Skedans, Ninstints, and Tanu were well poised to

Skidegate, 1878

enter the cash economy. The Haida had no difficulty adapting their traditional skills to these new industries. Canoe carvers became boat builders and carpenters; fishermen became gill netters and seine-boat operators. William Wilson himself became a commercial fisherman. He probably supplied fish to Skidegate's fish-oil plant and Josephine may very well have worked in the plant alongside the other Native women who extracted oil — to be used in making soap — from the livers of dogfish. A few Native women worked as housekeepers for the small number of white residents. This is the kind of work to which Josephine turned her hand in 1890 when William Wilson died.

When Josephine Wilson became a widow at the age of twenty-two, she moved in with the Tennant family, who lived at Skidegate Landing. Robert Tennant ran the oil works as well as a clam cannery, a general store, and the post office. He and his wife were known to be demanding employers. Yet there is no evidence that Josephine was unhappy working for the Tennants. She had a chance to improve her English. She learned how to cook and sew according to Mrs. Tennant's exacting standards. In fact, she must have been an accomplished seamstress because she made clothing for the preacher's wife, Mrs. Miller. However hard Josephine worked after William died, she made a point of keeping in touch with her relatives in New Klew. "I am going to clue this fall," she wrote to her cousin, "if the canoe ever here again." She also contemplated a marriage proposal and enjoyed at least one romantic liaison.

After waiting a year following William Wilson's death, in accordance with Haida custom, James Watson of New Gold Harbour proposed to Josephine. Though Watson was the chief of his village, Josephine was not sufficiently impressed to accept his offer. Her letters of rejection, recorded in her scribbler, show her to have been strong-willed and of an independent mind. "You speak of asking my friends and getting their consent," she told Watson, "this is quite unnecessary, if I wanted to marry a man I would do so without asking them." James Watson made a second proposal and Josephine refused him again. This time she hoped that her refusal would stop him "from giving any further annoyance."

Josephine could afford to decline the first offer of marriage. She was young and, according to her future granddaughter, Margaret Reid, she was beautiful. She had no dependants. She had a good job. And she had friends in both the white and Native communities. It was no doubt while Josephine

The Haida, Skidegate, 1895

was working for the Tennant family that she met another suitor, the young Norwegian Fillip Jacobsen.

Jacobsen had come to British Columbia in 1884 at the request of his brother, Johan Adrian, who had been collecting ethnographic material on the Northwest Coast since 1881. A year after Fillip's arrival, the two brothers had amassed three tons of artifacts destined for the Royal Museum of Ethnology in Berlin. Pillaging Native artifacts from the coastal villages of British Columbia was not Fillip Jacobsen's only activity. He recorded myths among the Bella Coola (Nuxalk) and, on the instruction of a well-known zoo keeper in Hamburg, he persuaded nine Natives from the coastal village of Bella Coola to accompany him to Germany. During 1885–86, the nine Nuxalk men sang and danced before appreciative audiences in Hamburg, Leipzig, Dresden, and Cologne, among other cities. When the Bella Coola performed in Berlin, they sparked the interest of one young scholar: the ethnologist Franz Boas, whose writings on Northwest Coast Natives would inspire Bill Reid many years later. In 1886 Fillip Jacobsen saw to it that the nine Nuxalk men were safely returned to their village. Before marrying a woman of Norwegian ancestry and settling in Bella Coola, Jacobsen spent several more years collecting Northwest Coast Native artifacts for museums throughout Canada and the United States.

It was while Jacobsen was on one of his collecting trips to the Queen Charlotte Islands in the early 1890s that he met and became romantically involved with the recently widowed Josephine Wilson. The couple's relationship, which could not have lasted long, ended on a sour note. A copy of a letter in Josephine's scribbler suggests that Jacobsen later accused his former belle of being "a bad woman." Josephine insisted, in response to his accusation, that she had not wanted him: "It was you that wanted me." She also told Jacobsen that if she had wanted to be "a bad woman," she would not have worked hard in order to buy herself European clothing. Jacobsen made at least two attempts at a reconciliation. But Josephine could not be swayed. Jacobsen had challenged her good name, and she did not want to see him again.

Little more is known of what happened between Josephine and Fillip. Had Bill Reid's mother, Sophie, been the product of this union, she might have had good reason to think of herself as less than fully Haida. But the fact is Sophie was born eight months after her mother married her second husband, Charles Gladstone.[5] Moreover, Jacobsen's annoyance, so evident in Josephine's reception of his churlish letter, may very well have arisen from his discovery that, during his absence from Haida Gwaii, the woman whom he had taken to be his sweetheart had become involved with another man.

∾∾∾

Charles Gladstone, who was known variously as Sdast'aas or Hai'mas, not only had an English name; according to Bill Reid, he was notable for his blue eyes and fair skin. As an adult, Reid encouraged suggestions that his grandfather had European paternity. Thus his confidante Doris Shadbolt faithfully reported Swiss ancestry at one point, only to change the story later by attributing paternity to "an English aristocrat."[6] Of course, if Bill Reid's fertile but inconsistent speculations were correct, he himself would have been less than half

Charles Gladstone, 1947

Haida. And if Sophie had been Jacobsen's child, this would have made Bill less than one-quarter Haida.

The important point is less about blood than about culture. It is certainly true that many Haida women returned from the annual migration to Victoria carrying the offspring of casual liaisons with European men. But everything we know about the Gladstones suggests they were exactly the kind of moralized, Christianized Haida converts least likely to fall into promiscuity. Charles Gladstone's father, Abraham Gladstone, had been given his name by the Methodist missionary George Robinson, probably in the 1860s when the cult of the British Liberal leader William Gladstone — a special hero to Methodists — was in full spate. That Charlie Gladstone was born in 1872 to a respectable, married couple of unadulterated Haida descent seems overwhelmingly likely. Bill Reid's great-grandfather Abraham came from no farther away than Kiusta (K'yuust'aa) on the north island and belonged to the Sta'stas clan. This was what several members of the Gladstone family believed at the time and what they told the ethnologist Marius Barbeau in 1947, long before more romantic notions of European aristocratic lineage were given currency.

Josephine must have thought that Charles Gladstone was a good catch. He came from a Methodist family. He was an accomplished boat builder and general carpenter. And, after making a trip to Masset in 1897 where he visited his famous uncle-artist Charles Edenshaw, or Edensaw (Da.axiigang), he became a reasonably proficient craftsman in wood, argillite, and his favourite medium, silver.

After contact with the Europeans the Haida had access to more tools and their material culture grew exponentially. As a result of their participation in the marine-based fur trade, they were able to build more totem poles, mortuary columns, and houses. Bracelets and rings, hair ornaments, ear pendants, and nose rings that had been previously fashioned out of copper and iron were now made from the precious trade items. Edenshaw and Gladstone made their bracelets in the same way the artists had during the early years of the century. They hammered gold and silver coins into sheets of metal, then decorated the material with the intricate and rhythmic lines characteristic of Haida design.

Not only did the fur trade give Native artists new materials; it gave them a new clientele. From the moment the first Europeans made landfall on the west coast of North America, they admired and bartered for ethnographic carvings. By the early years of the nineteenth century, Native artists responded to the demand for examples of their material culture. They expanded their repertoire to include napkin rings and brooches, which they sometimes decorated with the American eagle or with European motifs. By the middle of the nineteenth century, what many non-Natives pejoratively called "curios" or "artificial curiosities" became more than "tourist" souvenirs. Native carvings and baskets were a distinctive and almost compulsory feature of the Canadian display booth at international fairs such as London's Great Exhibition in 1851. By the 1870s curios were exhibited in the foyers of Victoria's best hotels, and, as a result of the collecting activities of the Jacobsen brothers and others, they were displayed in the glass cases of museums around the world. By the turn of the century, the purchase and sometimes theft of ethnographic material from Native Indians living on the west coast had reached a point where there were more artifacts outside British Columbia than in it.

Today we call cedar-bark hats and baskets "art"; likewise, wooden masks and rattles, argillite totem poles, canoes, and pipes (that cannot be smoked). We buy these items in galleries and museums, not alongside sailing ships or on the docks of remote northern outposts. But in Charles Edenshaw's day, he travelled to Port Simpson along the mainland coast or went down to Victoria to sell what he called his Victoria carvings. Visiting anthropologists bought the diminutive totem poles and houses that he had fashioned out of soft black shale or argillite. And he also produced works for the Haida community.

Edenshaw was a master of any medium in which he chose to work. His designs on precious metal, wood, and argillite were both structured and organic. His knowledge of space and balance, of tension and release was so finely tuned that every motif he painted, carved, or engraved possessed an energy that resembled a tightly coiled spring. Though Tom Price, John Cross, John Robson, and a few others produced equally admirable work, much of which has been attributed to Edenshaw, it is his name that early twentieth-century anthropologists singled out.

Charles Edenshaw had several students but he must have favoured his sister's son, because Charles Gladstone inherited his carving tools when

left: Thunderbird and Whale, *Charles Edenshaw;*
right: Carving on Cedar of Dogfish, *Charles Gladstone*

Edenshaw died in 1920. However much potential Gladstone might have shown his uncle, he was by far the inferior artist. A comparison of the motifs on Edenshaw's *Thunderbird and Whale* argillite carving with Gladstone's *Carving on Cedar of Dogfish* shows that the younger man was no innovator.[7] Preparatory drawings for Gladstone's argillite carvings, wood panels, and silver bracelets indicate that he had an unsteady hand. His work was not improved by his lack of imagination. Conversely, Edenshaw knew, as every great Native artist before him had known, how to push the limits of the design while adhering to the traditional vocabulary of Native art. This is what gave his work a sense of surprise. And this is what enabled him to expand his repertoire of motifs. Gladstone had only one thing in common with his uncle. Like Edenshaw, he was determined to pass on what he had learned to the next generation of artists. Even so, whenever he tried to do this, he lost his temper.

Charles Gladstone learned more from Charles Edenshaw than how to transform silver coins into bracelets. On his visits to Masset, where his uncle had relocated from Skidegate as a child, Gladstone saw the walls of Edenshaw's bedroom papered with reproductions from *The Illustrated London News*. He met Edenshaw's schoolteacher cousin, Henry (gyaa whlans), who could quote Shakespeare and Goethe with equal skill. And he became acquainted with the ethnologists and museum officials for whom Edenshaw produced work.

Josephine no doubt relished the contact with the westernized Edenshaw family. Following her marriage to Charles Gladstone, she maintained her links with the Tennant family and with the Methodist Church. She became a prominent member of the Women's Missionary Society, an organization that brought women together to sing, pray, and sew. In 1920 Josephine became its vice-president and, a few years later, she was elected president. When Josephine and Charles had children — they produced six between 1895 and 1912, of whom Bill's mother Sophie was the first — they saw to it that all were baptized. And when Sophie, Irene, Eleanor, William, Ernie, and Percy reached school age, they all attended the Methodist day school in Skidegate. Convinced that European ways were superior to Native traditions, Josephine and Charles also joined a number of Native families in Skidegate who sent their children to the church-run Indian residential school in southern British Columbia. Sophie, Eleanor, and Percy, along with the Gladstones's ward, Mabel Crosby, were all enrolled in the Coqualeetza Industrial Institute for ten months of the year.

Josephine and Charlie's children would thus become more white and less Haida. In so doing, they would take the process of acculturation, begun by their parents, a stage further. So they were not, as their nephew Bill Reid liked to think, the first generation of the Gladstone family to plant their feet, albeit uncertainly, between two cultures.

CHAPTER 2

Sophie's Story

Graduating Class of 1918,
Sophie Gladstone in first row, second from right

It is a long way from the Queen Charlotte Islands to the Fraser Valley in southern British Columbia. In 1905, getting to the Conqualeetza Industrial Institute from Skidegate entailed sailing across the rough waters of Hecate Strait to settlements at the mouth of the Nass and Skeena rivers on the mainland coast, then heading south to Vancouver, then up the Fraser River to Sardis. The journey took ten days in all.

Sophie, now ten years old, did not make this daunting journey alone; she was accompanied by two other girls from Skidegate, Ellen Collison and Rebecca Wesley. And when she arrived at the Indian residential school, her cousins Margaret and William Gladstone and Emma and Barney Cross were already there. And before the school year began, more familiar faces appeared with the arrival of two other girls from Skidegate, Mabel Crosby and Ethel Calder.

Situated on the south side of the Fraser River in the lush Chilliwack Valley, the Coqualeetza Industrial Institute was flanked on two sides by the magnificent coastal range. The year Sophie enrolled, sixty-two boys and twenty-nine girls made up the student body. They all lived in an imposing three-storey brick dormitory and were taught by eight demanding teachers who devoted a great deal of their time to religious instruction. Sophie Gladstone began her day kneeling beside her bed in the dormitory. After morning prayers, but before breakfast, she sang a hymn with the others, then listened to a reading from the Bible. During the day, her lessons always commenced with a prayer. And in the evenings she and the other children recited a passage from the Bible before singing more hymns. According to Reverend Joseph Hall, who was the principal during Sophie's tenure at the school, this strict regime was intended to boost the morale of the students.

It was not all religion, though. The children spent the morning in classroom studies and the afternoon engaged in practical work. The boys learned how to make shoes, to farm, and to repair machinery. The girls learned how to sew, cook, bake, and launder. All these tasks helped run the institute. In this way the children contributed directly to their keep.

Many of the students, who ranged in age from three to twenty-four, were lonely. They missed their families. They were weary from the long hours of manual labour. And many were bewildered by the relentless religious instruction. When Sophie's younger brother Percy left the institute, he had grave doubts about Christianity. Masset-born Claude Davidson missed speaking Haida. "If you were caught using your own language," he recalled, "you would get a whipping."[1] Illness was a further cause of distress for the children. During Sophie's six and a half years at the institute, her cousin Barney Cross and her friend Ethel Calder died of consumption. Her parents' niece and ward, Mabel Crosby, contracted the same disease. Learning of her illness in October 1911, Josephine and Charles Gladstone made the long journey south to Sardis. Though they took the sick child back to Skidegate, their efforts were in vain. Within a few years Mabel was dead.

Sophie remained at the school twice as long as her friends from Skidegate. She was better equipped to prolong her education because she had arrived with more schooling and with a better knowledge of English. Josephine and Charles had made Sophie attend the school in Skidegate on a regular basis. When they went fishing or when Charles took a carpentry job away from home, Sophie boarded with the Freeman family. By the time she arrived in Sardis, Sophie was proficient in English and had passed the fourth grade. This accomplishment made her a prime candidate for a privilege that the institute's teachers bestowed on only a small number of children: all-day schooling. The increase in classroom time did not, however, prevent Sophie from improving her sewing skills, initially taught to her by Josephine. Or from learning how to play the piano.

By the time Sophie left the Coqualeetza Industrial Institute at the age of sixteen, she was an accomplished seamstress, knew how to play the piano, and, most important of all, had a taste for study. Like most of the children who had been taught on a full-time basis, she proceeded to the high school in the nearby town of Chilliwack. After matriculating three years later, she followed the example of her cousin, Margaret Gladstone, who had obtained a teaching position at a Native school after she left Sardis in 1907. In 1914, at the age of eighteen, Sophie accompanied Skidegate's residents to the canneries on the mainland coast and taught there for the summer. She continued her peripatetic life, travelling south to the small town of Snohomish in the state of Washington, where she worked in a hospital. Four years later, she took up residence in Victoria, where she enrolled in the newly founded Normal School. It took Sophie just over a year to qualify as a teacher.

In January 1919 the twenty-three year old Sophie Gladstone was offered a teaching position in a white school located in the town of New Hazelton (Gitanmaax). Joining two other teachers, she taught a wide range of subjects — writing, diction, arithmetic, music, Canadian history, and geography — to twenty-one pupils. At one hundred dollars a month, the job paid relatively well. Moreover, teaching white rather than Native students put an extra twenty dollars a month into Sophie's pocket.

The town where Sophie Gladstone took up her teaching position was remote — it lay 187 miles inland from the coast. Named after the hazel bushes that grew along the banks of the nearby Skeena River, New Hazelton was in a state of transition. The old town had been a distribution point for trekkers on their way to the nearby goldfields. It then became a supply centre for fur traders, railway workers, and ranchers, and a jumping-off point for a transient, largely male, population, who were on their way to the silver-and copper-mining communities to the north. When Sophie arrived in 1919, New Hazelton had a population of eight hundred, a commercial centre comprising three square-fronted banks and hotels, a drugstore, a hospital, a school, and two churches, of Methodist and Anglican denomination. Although New Hazelton had all the trappings of a town, it lacked such basic amenities as a sewage system and running water. And with the post–World War I economic slump in full swing, it did not look as though things were going to get any better.

Not everyone wanted to return to the boom-and-bust era that had characterized the Klondike gold rush in the 1890s. Many people were consciously inventing new traditions, albeit within the framework of the British Empire. Some settlers were even incorporating — or, as we would say today, appropriating — Native culture into their identity. For example, when a stone artifact was discovered near New Hazelton in 1919 and ethnologists in Ottawa requested it for their museum, a correspondent for the local paper suggested that it could form a basis for their own museum. "There are now a large number of valuable Indian curios in this district," it was claimed, "and a very creditable start could be made."[2]

In spite of the rest of the town's interest in Native artifacts and culture, Sophie had nothing to do with the nearby Gitx̱san village of Kitwankul (Gitanyow) whose inhabitants, according to one local historian, "were not very well disposed to the white man."[3] She found friends in the white community. The pioneer owners of the general store and post office, R.S. Sargent and his wife, became close friends. There was also an American, called Reid; tall and blond, he was her senior by thirteen years. Sophie's assimilation into the dominant Euro-Canadian community was completed when, less than a year after arriving in New Hazelton, she married William "Billy" Reid.

Reid epitomized many white males in northern British Columbia. He was single. He was a passionate hunter and fisherman. And he was from somewhere else. Born in 1882 to Charles Reid and Pauline Newman, young William had left his native Michigan while still in his teens. Although he never saw his parents again, he did keep in touch by corresponding with his mother — a German-speaking Pole — in her native language. Any other vestige of his central-European and Scottish-American heritage was largely forgotten once he left home.

Billy Reid arrived in northern British Columbia during World War I. He settled initially in the town of Smithers, where he was allegedly involved in the hotel business. A ranching and mining community to the south of New Hazelton, Smithers was a rough place to live and an even rougher place in which to run a hotel. (These establishments generally existed for the purpose of selling the volatile combination of alcohol and sex.) It is clear that, along with almost every other northern resident, Reid was an avid speculator — in liquor as well as in gold and silver. Because the prohibition law was openly flouted and probably unenforceable, rum-running was easy. Several articles from the region's local newspapers darkly hint that Reid's business interests, which saw him travel to Smithers, Telkwa, and New Hazelton at regular intervals, ran more towards the illicit alcohol trade than the hotel business. It is likely that when he met Sophie Gladstone in 1919 Reid was speculating in mining shares and contemplating making a career for himself in the hotel business. But his full-time job was rum-running.

There was nothing unusual about a white man courting a Native woman. During the first three-quarters of the nineteenth century, Hudson's Bay Company factors, fur traders, miners, and settlers frequently formed liaisons with women of Native ancestry. British Columbia's first governor, Sir James Douglas, had taken Amelia Connally, the daughter of a Hudson's Bay Company chief factor and a Coast Salish woman, for his wife. It was only when white women immigrated to British Columbia in large numbers towards the end of the nineteenth century that it became sinful, in the view of many, to consort with a Native woman.

Settlers living in rural areas of British Columbia where white women continued to be in short supply were less judgmental about country marriages. Native women who had been educated in the residential school system were exemplary homemakers. Once they entered white society, they usually severed connections with their Native relations. Contrary to popular belief, it was not the white male who was in danger of being short-changed in a mixed marriage, but the Native woman.

The usual story, as noted earlier, is that Sophie Gladstone turned her back on her Native ancestry when she married William Reid on May 19, 1919. It was also thought that this transition was easy because she did not look Native. It is true that school, work, and travel in the white community had given Sophie manners and speech that made her little different from most Euro-Canadian women. Yet a photograph of Sophie surrounded by her fellow graduands at the Normal School in Victoria leaves no doubt that she had Native blood flowing in her veins. As the Haida scholar Marcia Crosby put it years later, Sophie looked Haida "even though she didn't want to."[4]

Although Sophie clearly wanted to live and work as a white woman, she did not renounce her family in order to do so. Following her marriage to Billy Reid, she maintained contact with her many brothers and sisters and with her parents. Sometimes Sophie's family visited her in New Hazelton. At other times she took the stern-wheeler down the Skeena River to Prince Rupert, and from there sailed on the overnight boat to Skidegate. When she had children, she saw to it that at least one of them was baptized in the Methodist Church in Skidegate. As well as remaining in touch with her siblings and with the village of Skidegate, Sophie continued to wear silver bracelets that her father, Charlie Gladstone, and John Cross had made for her. And, while Sophie would never publicly admit to doing something so Indian, her daughter Peggy remembers her mother weaving a tiny basket out of grass.

However strong Sophie's cultural links were with her Native past, the act of marrying William Reid took the acculturation process, begun by her parents in the 1880s, one stage further. She lost her Native status, forfeiting her right to claim federal assistance. She renounced her membership in the

Skidegate band, and with it her right to live on the reserve. This was an enormous price to pay for marriage to a rum-runner — if things went wrong in her new life with Billy Reid, she could not live in the village that, during the formative early years of her life, had been home.

This was the sort of risk that Sophie Gladstone and every other Native woman took when they married outside the Native community. Indeed, federal laws still define who is Native and who is not. Though Sophie was Haida, once she married Billy, she was technically no longer an Indian; she was white.

☙⚬☙

For most women schoolteachers who taught during the early decades of the twentieth century, teaching was a stop-gap between Normal School and marriage. When Sophie Gladstone married in 1919, she quit her teaching job at the end of the school year. A few months later, now heavy with child, she took the Grand Trunk Pacific Railway to Prince Rupert, then boarded a Canadian Pacific steamer bound for Victoria. Though she made the nine-hundred-kilometre voyage down the coast to Victoria alone, she was among friends once she got there. She picked up with women she had known while studying at the Normal School and with the Tennant family, who had employed her mother in Skidegate in the 1890s. Friends therefore surrounded Sophie Reid when she gave birth to her first child. Her son, William Ronald, was born on January 12, 1920.

During Sophie's confinement in Victoria, Billy Reid was busy. He had moved to the northwest corner of the province where he was in the process of buying a hotel. The small town of Stewart lay at the head of a seventy-mile-long canal bounded on both sides by a wall of steep mountains. The area surrounding it and the neighbouring town of Hyder — which straddled the Canadian-Alaskan border — was barely accessible. The prospectors who had opened up the area at the turn of the century had crossed the rugged landscape by packhorse. Two decades later, a three-kilometre dirt track connected Hyder to Stewart until steps were taken, in 1929, to join the two settlements with a proper road.

When Billy Reid arrived in what is known as the Cassiar District in 1919, silver, copper, and gold mines such as the Big Missouri, Silverado, and Premier were returning large profits to their investors. The ore was extracted well above the treeline at the five- to eight-thousand-foot levels. It was arduous work. The miners lived in flimsy wooden shacks that clung to precipitous mountain slopes. When they came down to Stewart and Hyder, they wanted a drink and a good time.

Reid offered everyone who visited the Cassiar District — investors, engineers, surveyors, and miners — a bed, plenty of alcohol, and amusement in a number of hotels under his proprietorship. From 1919 to 1924 he operated a hotel in Stewart. In 1925 he opened a second hotel, The Alaskan, in Hyder and acquired a third, the Hotel Keith in Stewart. According to an advertisement in the *Portland Canal News*, the Hotel Keith was "thoroughly modern." It provided its guests with steam heating, electric lights, and baths. And best of all, "the Convenient Hotel," as Reid called it, was just a three-minute walk from the town's lifeline to the rest of the province: the wharf.[5]

Reid took advantage of his location on the Canadian-Alaskan border and made a respectable income. The repeal of British Columbia's prohibition act in 1920 coincided with the implementation, the same year, of the Volstead Act in the United States. Thus while miners were denied alcohol in "dry" Alaska, they could cross the border and drink legally in Stewart or in the Canadian side of Hyder. In 1924 things were even better for hotel owners than they had been in 1920. That year the province's beer-by-the-glass legislation allowed hotelkeepers like Reid to operate beer parlours and to open ladies' and escorts' lounges.

Sophie remained in Victoria while Billy was establishing himself in Stewart. In 1921 she gave birth to her second child, Margaret, whom the family called Peggy. Just before this, Sophie had invited Leah Alfonsine Delcusse Brown to join them. "Gogga," as the children liked to call her, delivered the baby. Peggy, who looked after Leah in her old age, recalled, "She was the first person I saw in my life and I was the last person she saw when she died."[6] A trained nurse from Lille in France, Leah Delcusse had moved as a young woman to England where she became an ardent anglophile and a fierce supporter of the Church of England. From there she travelled to Canada. Initially she worked in a hospital in Alberta, then she moved to the Queen Charlotte Islands, where she delivered babies and met and married a Mr. Brown. It was on one of Sophie Reid's visits to her family there that she became acquainted with the recently widowed Mrs. Brown. By the early 1920s, Gogga was installed in the Reid household as a nanny, nurse, housekeeper, and cook.

Mrs. Brown was more than a helpmate for Sophie and the children. Her strong commitment to the Anglican faith prompted Sophie to leave the Methodist church of her childhood and join the congregation of Christ Church Cathedral in Victoria. More significantly, Mrs. Brown's dislike of Billy Reid fuelled Sophie's growing discontent with her husband.

Though Billy made frequent visits to the capital city during his wife's residence there in the early 1920s, he preferred to reside in northern British Columbia. Like many men who lived on the edge of organized society, he was happiest inhabiting the margins of the floating frontier world, not living in a town that one writer described as "a kind of sublimated England."[7] Not only was Victoria too genteel for Billy Reid, its citizens openly disapproved of mixed marriages. Victoria was also too far from the American border to allow Reid to take financial advantage of the liquor laws. Making the point that he wanted to raise his children in the Cassiar District, he purchased a substantial residence there in 1921.

A former brothel, the house that Billy Reid bought for Sophie clung to the side of a steep slope overlooking the town. Unlike the Hotel Keith, it did not have an indoor toilet. Moreover, the steps leading up to the front porch were treacherous. (In the summer they were covered with slippery green moss and in the winter with ice and snow.) Nevertheless it was the most handsome residence in town. It had a wraparound porch, a sewing room for Sophie, and a view of Hyder's buildings that marched over the tidal mud flats on wooden pilings. Avid gardeners, Sophie and Billy soon had sweet peas and climbing nasturtiums growing up trellises in front of the house. They planted strawberries and raspberry bushes in the back garden. (Over fifty years later when their son, Bill, visited Hyder, the house had been demolished but the now wild strawberry and raspberry plants were still bearing fruit.)

Although Hyder and Stewart were geographically remote, they were not entirely cut off from the more populated areas of British Columbia and Alaska. Daily sailings from Stewart's wharf connected residents with Prince Rupert, the Queen Charlotte Islands, and other points up and down the coast. There was a weekly newspaper, an opera house, a radio station, and an outfitter named H. Zeffer who stocked whipcords and English tweeds. And there was just enough local talent to allow Sophie's young children to take dancing and music lessons once a week.

With Mrs. Brown to look after her small children, Sophie was free to socialize with the wives of the banker and the newspaper editor. She also had time not only to make clothes for her children but to earn a little money on the side by sewing for others too. Although Billy Reid's position as the owner of up to three hotels at a time put Sophie at the high end of the social scale in Hyder, she never warmed to the place. The long dark winters were bleak. Snow began falling in September and bare patches of earth did not appear again until June. There was a dearth of culture. And, above all, Sophie found herself living with an increasingly difficult husband.

Billy Reid was a rolling stone who had chosen, maybe wrongly, to marry. He spent too much time in his saloon talking with his friend, the flamboyant Black Jack MacDonald, and socializing in the demimonde of gambling, drinking, amusement, and casual sex that the bordello culture of his hotel catered to. He drank too much and played too many poker games. And, as Sophie knew too well, all of this meant that he preferred to be with his chums in whichever hotel he happened to own, rather than in the parlour with his wife and children. Unhappy in her marriage, unable to sustain a bourgeois lifestyle on the frontier, Sophie Reid, Leah Brown, and the two children moved back to Victoria in 1923.

⤜◦⤛

Sophie Reid knew better than anyone else that having a Native for a mother in Victoria would be of no advantage to her children. The Coast Salish Natives had been moved from the Songhees Indian Reserve in the Inner Harbour of the city to the suburb of Esquimalt in 1911. The few who stayed behind were associated, in the minds of the city's white residents, with beer parlours and drunkenness, prostitution and jail. Sophie also knew that it was little better to be of mixed race. During the middle of the nineteenth century, white commentators believed that "half-breeds" possessed "the vices of both races."[8] By the 1920s most continued to believe that the children of mixed-race marriages fared worse than those of full-blood because they had no place in either the white or Native sphere.

Because most of Victoria's citizens preferred their Indians to be untainted by white blood, confined to reserves, and living well beyond the city limits, Sophie did everything she could to hide her Native ancestry. She resided in the middle-class district of James Bay. The Medina Street house was near the Dallas Road cliffs overlooking the Strait of Juan de Fuca and within walking distance of Beacon Hill Park and the centre of town. She dressed her children in formal clothing of her own design. (Young Bill wore white gloves.) And she enrolled her children in Miss Carr's school for infants. "I must have been three," Peggy recalled, "and I sat down at the desk with everyone else and she put things on the board and told us to copy them." Alice Carr was annoyed when the young child was unable to copy the work into her exercise book. It is not surprising that the nursery teacher showed herself, in Peggy's words, to be "a mean thing." And that Alice's artist sister, Emily, whom the Reid children saw sketching in Beacon Hill Park, made a more favourable impression on them.

Although Billy Reid continued to feel out of place in Victoria, he made regular visits to his family. Peggy remembers how her tall and jovial father accompanied her to Alice Carr's school. But Billy Reid was caught in a dilemma — he could not settle to life in the city but he wanted to have his children and his wife close at hand. So in 1926 he persuaded Sophie — and Mrs. Brown — to return to Hyder.

Peggy's memories of the next six and a half years in Hyder are not unpleasant. The half-hour walk to the one-room schoolhouse took her and Bill along a wooden sidewalk, past the town's library and general store, past the place where the prostitutes hung out, past the place where the yelping sleigh dogs were tethered, and past the stone hovel where the shoe-repair man lived. In the winter Peggy and Bill rode home from school on the back of the snowplough. When the snow thawed in the spring, they walked home from school through a forest of scrub willow, aspen, and spruce. During the long summer holidays, the children explored the hills lying behind the family home. This was where they picked wild blueberries, thimbleberries, and huckleberries, where they swam in a makeshift swimming pool, and where the whole family sometimes gathered for a picnic. At the beginning of July, the children attended the annual Dominion Day Celebration with its bun-eating contest, pillow fights, and tug-of-war.

Unlike Peggy, Bill never chose to recall his childhood in such detail. The six years — from the age of six to twelve — that he lived in Hyder following the family's return from Victoria were, he felt, best forgotten. For one thing, he was living in closer proximity to his father, whom he felt did not like him. Although he could admire the way his father wore his clothes, Bill's overall impression was that Billy Reid was weak and blustery — yet as hard as a rock. Even when he became an adult, Bill insisted that his father had "had little or no influence" on his life.[9]

Added to his estrangement from Billy Reid was the young boy's inability to make close friends. "Anybody who smelled weakness," he later recalled, "jumped all over me."[10] The first time this happened was shortly after he had started school. Twins boys from Stewart who had been expelled from the elementary school there were forced to ride two and a half miles on horseback in order to attend school in Hyder. When they entered the schoolyard, they would seek out their victim. Most often it was Bill. They "used to beat him," Peggy recalled, "they'd take the horse whip to him." Bill "was a sort of quiet introverted boy," she continued, "who didn't always go out and make friends easily." Things did not improve until Bill was transferred, at the age of eleven, to the much larger elementary school in Stewart. It had three rooms and twice as many pupils as the school in Hyder. It offered grade seven and, most important of all for Bill, did not have the disruptive twins among its ranks. In this new environment Bill made rapid progress with his studies, discovering that with a little effort he could be at the top end of the class.

Bill was an introspective and shy child; he was also a "fiddler." Peggy remembers her brother always making little things. He would smash a light bulb, extract the wire filaments, and then make tiny winged insects by bending the wire into various shapes. He transformed his mother's empty thread spools into military tanks. He carved a Viking ship and a smaller Arab dhow out of wood. He also made a miniature tea set for his sister. Carved out of blackboard chalk, then decorated with his mother's nail polish, the tea set was so small and fragile that Peggy kept it in a matchbox. Bill found that chalk was such a good medium for carving that the first totem pole he ever made was fashioned out of blackboard chalk. Bill's fingers were never still. But it was ironically Sophie's third and last child, Robert, who was apparently the artist in the family.

Born in 1928, the fair-headed child quickly became the apple of his mother's eye. Bill's junior by eight years, Robert seemed the most artistically minded and creatively gifted member of the family. While his older brother transformed wood, chalk, and wire into boats, tanks, and cups and saucers, young Robert began to draw as soon as he was old enough to hold a pencil. "He couldn't sit still," Peggy recalled, "his little fingers would go for a pencil." In fact Robert would draw so intensely he would go white in the face. His artistic ability won him praise not only from his sister — the young child received much attention from his elder brother. On several occasions Bill encouraged Robert's talent by striking a pose for the young child to sketch. (His usual was a cowpuncher cooking up a meal over a campfire.) Thus from the early 1930s it was Robert, not Bill, who was designated to become an artist.

On the evening of December 7, 1932, the fortunes of the Reid family radically changed. That night a fire swept through Stewart. Residents in Hyder saw the glare but could do nothing to stop the distant flames from spreading. The town's buildings were made of wood and it had been a dry winter. By morning the Stewart Cafe, the Northern Drug Company, the Stewart News office, the Hotel Stewart, and almost every commercial building in town, with the remarkable exception of Billy Reid's Hotel Keith, had been reduced to cinders. The tragedy made William Reid the sole hotel proprietor in town. But the town was in ruins. The country was in the middle of an economic depression with twenty-eight percent of the workforce unemployed. If things were not bad enough, the United States had lifted the Volstead Act the previous year, thereby eliminating the advantage Reid had enjoyed by operating one of the few "wet" hotels in the region. Now fifty, Billy kept the Hotel Keith going for a few months after the fire, then declared bankruptcy. He moved into a rooming house in Stewart, where he lived for the rest of his life.

As though anticipating disaster, Sophie Reid had moved to Victoria that summer along with her three children, now aged twelve, eleven, and four. Once again, Leah Brown accompanied them. Sophie had never been happy living in the frontier community. In addition, she wanted to give her eldest son a better education than that offered by the Superior School in Stewart —

Bill was due to enter the one-room high school, which taught grades eight to eleven. Above all, her marriage had not improved since returning north.

Marrying Billy was the price that Sophie Gladstone had paid to become white, which, as her son Bill recalled, "shows you how badly she wanted to escape."[11] Her marriage had helped her to mask her Native ethnicity and thereby given her status in the white frontier town of Hyder. But the reality of whom she had married set in when Sophie discovered that she had tied herself to a man who felt most at home in the tavern, who drank too much, and who had gambled away whatever profit he had made during the prosperous years of prohibition. Billy had clearly made Sophie a better lover than husband. The pairing of the Native schoolteacher and the American hotelkeeper might have provided the plot for a good romance novel, but it was not a stable foundation for marriage.

Before the fire swept through Stewart in 1932, Billy had occasionally slipped a fifty-dollar bill into a letter to Sophie. After the fire, Sophie was forced to become the sole breadwinner for her children. Though she was qualified to teach school, two things were against her. First, her teaching experience had been limited to six months — and that was more than ten years before. And second, any employer in the school system would know that she was of Native ancestry. Sophie was left with one choice: to turn her hand to a skill that she had practised throughout her life — dressmaking.

Sophie initially ran her dressmaking business from the James Bay home that Billy Reid had bought for her in 1921. Then, in order to increase her income, she rented out the second floor of the house and moved her business to the third floor of an office building on View Street in the heart of the city. It was not the best year to be setting up a dressmaking business. Custom-made ball gowns and smartly tailored suits were considered to be expendable luxuries during the Depression. Consequently, in 1935 Sophie was forced to sell the Medina Street house and move the family into rented accommodation. The Belle Apartments on unfashionable Cook Street put Sophie farther from her dressmaking premises in the centre of town and farther from the middle-class suburb of James Bay. As a single parent, an urban Haida, and the victim of a depressed economy, Sophie found her social standing had plummeted like the shares on the stock market. Suddenly she was sewing garments for the very women whose lives she wished to emulate.

Beset by worries about money and disappointed by the failure of her marriage to Billy Reid, Sophie found herself occupying a middle ground between the Native and non-Native worlds. On the one hand, she gained moral support through her continuing contact with her Native siblings, especially Eleanor. But on the other, her success as a seamstress in the white world demanded she hide the fact that she was Native. This situation created a kind of cultural schizophrenia that Sophie was determined to spare her children.

There was a cruel irony in Sophie and Billy's story. She was defensively conscious of her Native ethnicity and craved the bourgeois ideal. He was totally indifferent to his whiteness, his class, and the bourgeois values to which his wife aspired. Moreover, while Sophie made every effort to teach her children white middle-class values, their role models for success did not come from their unsuccessful father, but from her Haida relatives. Sophie's brother, Percy Gladstone, would become the first Native in British Columbia to graduate from the University of British Columbia with a Master of Arts degree in economics. (Peggy, who got a Ph.D. in psychology from London University, followed her uncle's example.) Sophie's sister Eleanor — or Ella as everyone called her — finished her studies at Columbia Business College, then became an accountant for a hardware store in Vancouver. Sophie's sister-in-law, the wife of Ernie Gladstone, was a nurse. Sophie's father, Charles Gladstone, was a well-respected slate carver, jewellery maker, and boat builder. And there was the successful dressmaking career of Sophie herself.

Sophie Reid became the most sought-after seamstress in town. Seeing the high standards she imposed on every garment she made had an immense effect on her eldest child. "Whatever I learned about design," Bill Reid later recalled, "I learned from her."[12] This was not the only thing he got from his mother. Sophie knew that the success of her business depended on three things: keeping abreast of the latest trends by studying fashion magazines and by visiting the city's most expensive dress shops, using the best fabrics to hand, and ensuring that every garment she produced was well-made. Sophie's standards would become her son's credo when, twenty years later, he became a professional jeweller.

After Sophie and the children settled in Victoria in 1932, a few letters went back and forth between Stewart and Victoria. But Billy never again visited Victoria, where his wife brought up their growing family alone.

CHAPTER 3

Coming of Age

Skidegate, 1941

Bill Reid did not know when he left Hyder in the summer of 1932 that he would never see his father again. Nor did he appreciate the significance of stopping in Skidegate on his way to Victoria.

This was not the first time that Bill had been in his mother's village. When he was three, and Peggy was one and a half years old, Sophie had taken them to

Skidegate on the overnight steamer, the SS *Prince John*. Despite Sophie's new interest in the Church of England, she had baptized Peggy at Skidegate's Methodist church. Bill and Peggy had met their grandparents, Josephine and Charles Gladstone, possibly for the first time. A photograph of a thickly moustached Charles Gladstone embracing a curly-headed jovial child dressed in a sailor shirt and short pants commemorates Bill's visit to his grandfather in 1923.

Peggy encountered her grandparents again when she was nine years old. Josephine and Charles had anchored their fishing boat in the coastal town of Prince Rupert for the summer. Sophie's sister Irene, who was visiting Hyder at the time, took her niece to Prince Rupert on her return journey to the Queen Charlotte Islands. Sophie had prepared her daughter for the meeting by telling her that Josephine was tall and beautiful. She probably also told the child that her grandmother spoke English. Yet the person nine-year-old Peggy encountered on the wharf at Prince Rupert did not match her mother's description. "This huge woman was sitting there and she wouldn't speak English — either she couldn't or she wouldn't but she didn't anyway." Though "scared stiff" of her grandmother, Peggy warmed to Charles Gladstone: "He was lovely and he made an effort to speak English to me."

There was never any doubt during Peggy's childhood about her ancestry. She remembered her mother's arms covered in silver and gold Haida bracelets. She remembered frequent visits from her mother's Haida relatives. And although Peggy might not have known that her mother belonged to the Raven side of the Haida people, she did know that she was Native. "I knew my father was partly Scotch in the same way," she recalled.

Like his sister, Bill remembered the constant stream of Haida visitors during his childhood in Hyder. He also remembered the blue oblong trade beads that his grandmother, Josephine Gladstone, sent to the family in a shoebox before she died in the early 1930s. And he remembered his mother's arms adorned with Haida jewellery. "That's where I got the idea to start this whole business in jewellery," he recalled in 1974, "because my mother had one gold bracelet made by John Cross."[1]

Bill also linked his 1932 visit to Skidegate to the beginning of his interest in Native art. "I didn't learn anything directly from him," he later recalled of his meeting with his grandfather, but "got sort of interested in it."[2] Native children learned by observing their elders, and twelve-year-old Bill, who was already a fiddler, spent a good deal of time hanging around his grandfather's work-shed. This is how Charles Gladstone had learned from Charles Edenshaw. Now Bill watched his grandfather engraving silver bracelets and carving the soft black stone that he had quarried from the argillite deposit at Slate Chuck Mountain, which rose above Skidegate Inlet. He saw, and probably even held, the delicate bone-handled tools that Charles Edenshaw had bequeathed to Charlie Gladstone and that Gladstone would one day bequeath to him.

Bill was exposed to not only his grandfather's handiwork, but the carvings and jewellery of Tom Moody, Moses Jones, Luke Watson, John Marks, Jim Mackay, and John Cross. He also saw the three remaining totem poles that stood on the crescent-shaped beach near his grandfather's work-shed. He met two of his three uncles, William and Ernie, who were fishermen and boat builders. He talked to several elders in the village, including the white-haired, pipe-smoking carver Henry Young, who told him stories about the various figures he carved on the totem poles. And he met Chief Solomon Wilson, who recounted the story of the first European sailing vessel that was sighted by a Haida. Everything the twelve-year-old boy saw and heard on this trip made a lasting impression. It reinforced the fact that he had Native blood in his veins. He told a reporter twenty years later that it made him decide to become an Indian carver and jeweller when he grew up.[3]

⌒⌒⌒

Far from the popular belief that Native culture was rapidly dying out, Bill knew, as a result of his visit to Skidegate, that it was very much alive. He saw how Charles Gladstone and other Native artists in Skidegate were supplementing their incomes by selling their work through white middlemen such as George Cunningham in Port Essington and the head logger in Skidegate, Tom Kelly. He might have even heard that the demand for Native art was so great that Japanese craftsmen were making a healthy profit by producing miniature replicas of Kwakwaka'wakw totem poles and canoes.

When Bill arrived with his family in Victoria following his visit to Skidegate, he must have seen hundreds of Native handicrafts crammed into the windows of curio shops clustered at the top end of one of Victoria's busiest

Basement of Victoria's Provincial Museum

thoroughfares: Government Street. And when Mrs. Brown took him and Peggy to the Provincial Museum shortly after he arrived in the city, he would have seen even more. But what he saw in the museum was different from what he had seen in Skidegate and in the souvenir shops on Government Street. Many of the items in the museum had been produced for utilitarian and ceremonial use as well as for trade. This gave them an authenticity lacking in the made-for-tourists curios produced by Bill's grandfather.

Victoria's Provincial Museum of Natural History was an exciting place to visit. In the imposing entrance hall stood a stuffed cougar, a brown bear, a variety of birds, a moose, and a house post from the village of Skidegate. Around the mezzanine, overlooking the entrance, were glass-topped cases containing blue-winged moths, amber-coloured butterflies, and splayed insects of every variety. And confined in the basement, like delinquent children standing face-to-the-wall at the back of a classroom, were the Native artifacts.

Bill found every linguistic group in the province represented. Some of the artifacts had been bequeathed to the museum. But most of them had been collected — or stolen — during the early years of the century by a handful of amateur enthusiasts, professional anthropologists, and the museum's first curator, C.F. Newcombe. The subterranean rooms housing the artifacts were ill-lit and low-ceilinged. Rattles, baskets, jewellery, and stone hammers were crowded into dusty glass cabinets. Paddles, masks, and cedar-bark clothing jostled for space on the walls and on the long tables. Some of the masks — *Chief of the Undersea, Black Man of the Woods, Conceited Woman,* and *Nightmare Bringer* — were finely carved portraits representing creatures from the real and mythical worlds.

There were no dioramas, films, or piped-in melodies, as you would find in today's museums. Moreover, none of the carvings bore the names of the artists who had created them. And, while the creatures that were carved, engraved, or painted onto wood, silver, and cedar bark could be identified, the meanings that had changed as they were handed from one generation to the next were gone. Even so, any twelve-year-old-boy with an interest in his province would have found the work on display and the maze of rooms housing it enchanting. The carvings, weavings, and jewellery evoked the Northwest Coast's primordial forests and the indigenous people who had inhabited the land and shore before the arrival of the Europeans. Unlike western art, Native art was romantically believed to be a product of a direct and untainted artistic expression wrought by anonymous artists who had lived at a time when it was neither illegal nor irreligious to make carvings and to hold ceremonies. The absence in the museum of any work by a contemporary Native artist inevitably reinforced the belief that traditional Native art was a thing of the past. The fact that a few Native artists were still producing ceremonial and utilitarian objects in addition to the familiar souvenir carvings and weavings passed most by.

How far did young Bill comprehend the popular distinction between the "authentic" carvings in the museum and the work that his grandfather was producing for the tourist trade? How much was he aware of the way in which the white community had appropriated Native art for its own use?

Students at the School of Handicraft and Design in Victoria had long been applying Native motifs to their handicrafts. Native designs were used for club logos and in advertising. Totem poles were erected in the city's parks to attract the tourists. Native carvings were deemed to be the most suitable gift for visiting dignitaries. Finally, the material and oral cultural of Northwest Coast Indians was providing non-Native writers, painters, and musicians across the country with themes for their work.

During the early years of the century, Picasso, Matisse, and Apollinaire had based their modernist paintings on African and Oceanic masks and sculpture. By the 1920s Canadian artists recognized that Northwest Coast art had much in common with modern symbolist art. And, since it was wrongly thought that the younger generation of Natives in British Columbia possessed neither the ability nor the inclination to carry on the work of their forefathers, their art and their culture became fair game for everyone else. During Bill Reid's boyhood, A.Y. Jackson, Edwin Holgate, Annie Savage, and other artists from eastern Canada used Native themes for their work. Novelists — Ralph Connor in *The Gaspards of Pine Croft* (1923), Frances Herrings in *In the Pathless West* (1904), and A.M. Stephens in *Kingdom of the Sun* (1928) — made Native-white relations the central theme of their works. Composers of the stature of Leo Smith and Ernest MacMillan transcribed Native songs into European notation. And the Toronto choreographer Boris Volkoff, whose ballet company competed in the dance section of the 1936 Olympic Games in Berlin, borrowed Native masks from Ottawa's Victoria Memorial Museum in order to give their west coast Indian ballet, *Mon-Ka-Ta*, authenticity.

One artist in particular had long been making the Native motif her own. When Bill arrived in Victoria in 1932, Emily Carr, who lived a few blocks from his home, had made a second sketching trip to the Queen Charlotte Islands in order to paint the totem poles and had exhibited the results in New York, Washington, D.C., and Toronto as well as Victoria. Like other non-Native artists, Carr felt that Native art was dead and needed salvaging. "I began to realize that these things were passing and I started in earnest to make a collection of paintings," she said of her depictions of totem poles and community houses. She also believed that Native art corroborated the modernist project. "The oldest art in Canada, that of her Native Indians," she wrote in 1929, "is by far the most 'modern' in spirit."[4]

Bill was introduced to Carr's paintings by Jack Shadbolt, his young art teacher, when he entered grade eight at South Park Elementary School. Shadbolt, whom Emily Carr called a know-it-all, was immersed in the work of the Russian artist Wassily Kandinsky and was interested in modern poetry and in the paintings of Picasso. Shadbolt did more than impart his enthusiasm for the European avant-garde to his students. During Bill's first term, Shadbolt joined Carr and other local devotees of avant-garde paint-ing in the "Modern Room" section of the Island Arts and Crafts Society's annual exhibition. He doubtless encouraged his students to see this exhibi-tion at the society's venue, the Crystal Gardens, which was only a few blocks from the school.

Though Bill left no record of his young teacher, Shadbolt never forgot the tall shy boy who sat at the back of the classroom. "I remember this little fellow — he would grow to six foot three — with spectacles sitting quietly in the corner. He had a kind of smile on his face," Shadbolt recalled, and "he was very enigmatic. He would enjoy in his own way, but he would never let on."[5]

One reason why Bill was shy and withdrawn was that he was learning how to identify with his new surroundings by suppressing the fact that he was a northerner and of Native ethnicity. Writing to the president of the University of Victoria to accept an honorary degree many years later, Bill said that he was flattered by the offer because Victoria was his hometown.[6] When he filled out an application form for a Canada Council grant in 1967, he claimed that he had taken all of his schooling in Victoria, forgetting the seven years he had spent in classrooms in northern British Columbia.[7] And when he took friends to his home during his teens, it never occurred to them that the Reid family was anything but white. One of Bill's chums, Sid Baron, never knew that Sophie Reid was Haida. He felt, in retrospect, that "it was almost like they wanted to keep quiet about it."[8]

Bill had much to deal with as a young man. There was the tension between his admiration of Native art and his wish to produce it, on the one hand, and the way in which the white community, on the other, were appro-priating it for their own use. There was the painful process of hiding his Native ethnicity and of transforming himself into a full-blooded non-Native Canadian. There was the financial strain, especially on his mother during the

Depression: custom-made ball gowns, as noted earlier, were expendable luxuries in the 1930s. There was the shame of having a father who never appeared. And, finally, there was the difficulty experienced by all the Reid children of dealing with their mother's frequent bouts of temper.

Sophie Reid clearly lacked the emotional resources to nurture her children. Living in a residential school during the formative years of her life had not taught her how to relate to children in a familial setting. Like many Natives who had gone through the residential school system, she barely knew how to act as a parent. "Mother spent the whole weekend screaming, not just lecturing," Peggy recalled, "but screaming — it seemed like the whole weekend." Robert, then eight, spent a good deal of time in the streets because he thought that nobody cared if he came home. The Reid children began to dread weekends. They transferred what affection they had for their mother to Mrs. Brown. The unhappy household became so distressing for young Robert that when he was once swept out to sea while playing on the beach below the Dallas Road cliffs, he claimed that he didn't really care if he came back.[9]

Given these circumstances, it is not surprising that Bill remembered having "a terrible image" of himself while attending South Park School.[10] Moreover, when he entered Victoria High School at the age of thirteen, he recalled being "a most unenthusiastic student."[11] However unenthusiastic Bill might have been about his studies, the impression he gave to Peggy was that he was smarter and cleverer than she was. Bill's grades certainly bear out his sister's high opinion, for he was consistently ahead of the other students in his class. Indeed, he was so advanced that he took advantage of a new policy that allowed bright and industrious students to complete high school in three rather than four years. He was just sixteen years old when he graduated from Victoria High.

Little is known of these three years that Bill spent at the oldest high school west of the Rocky Mountains. In 1936 he was described by fellow classmates in the graduation yearbook, *The Camosun,* as "well liked by all" and "the tallest member of the class, whose deep whisper is heard from the back of the room."[12] Bill had conquered his inability to make friends: he was well liked. However, he was no extrovert. He never participated in sports or ran for the high school's student council or joined any clubs. But he did form a friendship with his art teacher, Earl "Bunny" Clarke, who had exhibited with Jack

Bill Reid as a student at Victoria High School

Shadbolt and Emily Carr in the Arts and Crafts Society's Modern Room and aspired to become a full-time sculptor. Bill also related to another teacher. The attractive Latin instructor, nicknamed Lola by the students, would sit on her desk at the front of the classroom and tantalize the male students by displaying her silk stockings and more leg than was considered polite.

After graduating from Victoria High School in 1936, Bill recalled spending a year in bed. Though he claims he did not rise until three every afternoon, he helped with the household chores, did most of the shopping, and cooked the evening meal. And he must have had some sort of job because by the end of the year he had enough money to pay $108 for his tuition fees at Victoria College.

∾∾

Craigdarroch Castle was an amazing venue for a college. The mansion had been constructed for a coal baron, the Honourable Robert Dunsmuir, in the late 1880s. It had well-tended gardens and, despite being surrounded by a twenty-foot-high stone wall, the upper floors of the building offered splendid views of the city, the Strait of Juan de Fuca, and the Olympic Mountains. The Dunsmuir mansion also possessed one of the finest collections of art nouveau stained-glass windows in North America. The palatial building had been a military hospital at the end of World War I, then in 1922 was bought by the province and transformed into a post-secondary institution.

Affiliated with McGill University in Montreal, Victoria College offered its students the first two years of post-secondary instruction in the arts and sciences. If students wanted to complete their B.A. or B.Sc. they had to cross Georgia Strait and enrol in the University of British Columbia. English, a foreign language, biology, and mathematics were compulsory courses. History, economic history, psychology, Greek, and French were electives.

Although the principal, P.H. Elliott, was known for his strict regime — tardy students could enter the classroom only with the permission of the instructor (and a student's attendance was always recorded) — the college's 211 students had a good time. A number of dances were held, often hosted by the lieutenant-governor and his wife. These were stylish affairs. Every ball commenced with a sit-down dinner, then the students danced from nine until two in the morning to the music of Len Acres's ten-piece orchestra. The venues — the Empress Hotel's ballroom, the Crystal Gardens, and the Royal Victoria Yacht Club — were the best in town.

It is not known whether Bill attended any of these events. He must have devoted some time to his studies because, as in high school, he obtained consistently high marks. He did take some time off, however, and became an active member of the Literary Arts Society, which he joined within a week of entering the college. Along with Pierre Berton, the future popularizer of Canadian history, he became a member of the society's executive committee. In this position he could choose and sometimes even introduce the speakers. Not surprisingly, he invited his former art teacher from Victoria High School, Earl Clarke, to speak about contemporary sculpture. And, on one occasion, he mounted the podium himself. On February 3, 1938, Bill gave the Literary Arts Society a talk on "the fantastic, the modern fairy tale exemplified in the tales of Lord Dunsany."[13]

Bill's interest in fantasy and allegory had been nurtured during the year he spent in limbo between high school and college. James Stephens, Roark

Bradford, Vachel Lindsay, and James Branch Cabell, whose writings lay out-side the canon of English literature, were among his favourite authors. These writers were concerned with the romantic and idealistic manifestations of love and with the visions of mystics. They used a simple formula of escape, recovery, and consolation. They made their characters experience the extremes of love and hate; violence and intense beauty; benevolence and malignity. Bill liked the contrast of emotions, the declaratory style, and the flamboyant idiom of their prose. The monstrous, clever, amusing, urbane, and detached central character in James Branch Cabell's novel *Jürgen* became a role model for Bill — "the kind of fellow I would have liked to be."[14] Throughout his life, Bill reread Cabell's novel several times.

Student life at Victoria College offered Bill a contrast to his earlier life in Hyder, Stewart, and Skidegate. It helped him to forget that he was of mixed race and from northern British Columbia. His year there made him into the middle-class non-Native that Sophie hoped he would become. But Native culture did find a place in student life at Victoria College, if only in the appro-priated form. The college's handbook greeted its students with an invented Native welcome: "Kla-How-Yah." And the back page of the college annual, *The Craigdarroch*, carried an advertisement for "that special gift." Native carv-ings in wood, ivory, and silver were available at the Arctic Studio curio shop.

∽∘c∽

Although Bill earned well-above-average grades at Victoria College, he had neither the motivation nor the finances to pursue his studies for a second year. He had probably felt out of place at Victoria College — just as he had felt out of place at South Park School and Victoria High. Living on the sec-ond floor of an apartment at 1021 Cook Street put him at the opposite end of the social scale from most of his fellow students. The city's debutantes and future male aristocracy lived in Rocklands, Oak Bay, and the Uplands, where their mothers did not have to hold down a job in order to keep the family afloat. Though he would always remain proud of having completed one year of advanced study, he did not choose to go on.

As soon as he left Victoria College, Bill sought to expand his knowledge of two things that had interested him throughout his school years: drawing and painting. Victoria was not the best place to do this. In those days it was a cultural backwater. Most of the city's artists, writers, musicians, and actors were amateurs. Their cultural societies and clubs promoted styles and traditions that were long out of fashion elsewhere. Emily Carr was still in Victoria but, by the time Bill left Victoria College, she had suffered her first heart attack and no longer possessed the energy to promote the cause of modern art. This left only a few individuals, such as the artist Allen Edwards, to challenge the conservative patrons and artists who dominated the city's cultural life.

After hearing that Edwards was offering classes in drawing from the nude, Bill enrolled. Offering instruction of this sort in conservative Victoria was a bold move on the art teacher's part. Not surprisingly, someone heard about the "orgy" that was taking place, and two members of the city's police force suddenly took an interest in life drawing. From their vantage point on the fringe of the classroom, they watched Edwards teach his students about human musculature by outlining the muscles on the model's body in charcoal so that by the end of one evening, a fellow student recalled, her body resembled a road map. And if it happened to be raining, she looked badly bruised because water dripped from a leaky skylight and smeared the charcoal all over her body.[15]

It was in Allen Edwards's evening art class that Bill learned the rudiments of the human form. Like every other student in a life drawing class he began by making lightning sketches. This taught him how to summarize, condense, and capture the salient features of the figure with a few deft strokes of the charcoal. Working more slowly, he learned how to make a more finished charcoal drawing in which shading, proportion, gesture — and even the model's character — were carefully noted. Bill developed a superb knowledge of anatomy thanks to Edwards's classes.

One of Bill's fellow students, Sid Baron, remembered seeing the slender young man sitting on the fringe of the life drawing class. Both of them, it turned out, were eighteen years old, footloose, and "crazy" about the swing music of Tommy Dorsey and Benny Goodman — and they became good friends. When they were not sketching, they listened to popular and (sometimes) to classical music on the radio at Sid's home. They took long walks along Victoria's waterfront cliffs. They did a good deal of talking about art, capitalism, and communism. "We were happy, we did a lot of laughing. He had as much of a twisted sense of humour as I have and we used to rub off on each other."[16]

When the two young men met, Sid was interested in abstract painting. Bill was attempting to fashion himself into a modernist, building on what he had learned about contemporary painting in Jack Shadbolt's class, at Victoria High School and, later, as an active participant in the Literary Arts Society at Victoria College. It was probably now that he became interested in African sculpture, initially through looking at reproductions of paintings by Picasso. Here was a prompt to connect the Northwest Coast artifacts he had seen in the Provincial Museum with the curios in the Government Street shops, with the Native carvings, and with Emily Carr's paintings of totem poles and community houses. And he could not have failed to notice the raising, in 1939, of six totem poles on a vacant lot next to the Provincial Museum. But if Bill was thinking about Native art, he said nothing to Sid Baron. The process of re-making himself into a white middle-class boy from Victoria demanded that he keep his interest in Native art and culture to himself.

∽ჿ৻ঽ

Peggy recalled that her brother had a nice voice and enjoyed hearing it. Sid Baron admired Bill Reid's lovely smooth cool voice, too. And, years later, when a Haida elder from Old Masset named Florence Davidson decided to give Bill a name, she chose Kihlguuline, "the one who speaks well."

Ever since learning how to project it from the back of the classroom without raising it, Bill had been fond, even proud, of the sound of his own voice. And when he left Victoria College in the spring of 1938, he put his childhood ambition of becoming a silversmith on the back burner and drifted into what he described as "an unpaid job" with a local radio station as an announcer-operator.[17] Peggy insists her brother would never have worked without being paid.[18] Given the financial circumstances of the Reid family, she is probably right.

At CFCT in Victoria, Bill wrote the commercials, read the news, and spun the records. He learned how to wrap his tongue around difficult-to-pronounce words, how to fill dead air time, and how to sound as if he wasn't reading from the script, so that his voice resembled ordinary conversation. Bill liked working in this blind, non-visual medium. He had a natural aptitude for stimulating the imagination of his listeners so that they heard, saw, touched, smelled, and even tasted whatever he described. He enjoyed giving the community a sense of itself by reporting gossip, sharing confidences, and telling jokes. Many of his friends remember how much he liked to talk. Radio gave Bill an opportunity to air his views without being interrupted. He had the last — if not the only — word. He could be as intimate with his audience as he liked without having to undertake any further obligation or commitment to them. Above all, working as a radio broadcaster in a small provincial capital made Bill a local celebrity.

Bill's big-man-in-town status was not unlike the easy popularity that his father had enjoyed among his hotel clientele in Stewart and Hyder. And when Bill had completed a year at CFCT and began working at stations across the country, his peripatetic life resembled the way his father had lived during the formative years of his life. But Billy Reid was far from his son's mind. In fact, Bill was determined to forget not only that he was the son of a loser but also that he was the son of a Native woman.

CHAPTER 4

"This Is Bill Reid Speaking"

Bill Reid announcing, circa 1952

Bill Reid left Victoria in 1939 to take a job at CKOV in Kelowna, British Columbia. He was a young man on the make. He was infatuated with jazz and with contemporary art. And, above all, he was full of dreams about becoming number one in radio. After spending a year working as a broadcaster in the interior of the province, Reid got a big break. In 1941 he met the country's liveliest man in commercial radio.

Jack Kent Cooke was a dashing figure who possessed an uncanny skill for making money. He acquired radio stations when they were at the bottom of the market then made a fortune by doubling the commercials, cranking up the promotions, and offering his listeners twenty-four-hour-a-day broadcasting with so much wattage that it was like listening to a church bell in a telephone booth.[1] Cooke was both a man's man and a ladies' man. He was also a star-spotter. Lorne Greene — the future Ben Cartwright of the television series *Bonanza* — was launched on his career by Cooke. And so was a young radio announcer from western Canada.

Reid was equally impressed by the flamboyant entrepreneur and the two men soon became fast friends. He began working for Cooke in May 1941 in Rouyn, Quebec. Then he station-hopped across the country, moving to Kirkland Lake, Ontario, to Vancouver, to Toronto, to Windsor, and in 1948 back to Toronto.[2] Reid's eight-year-long employment with Cooke encompassed the last half of World War II. Though poor eyesight kept Reid out of the front line, he claimed to have contributed to the war effort in two ways. First, he helped make Harvard trainers for an airline company in Montreal; while there, he spent a good deal of time carving ornaments on toolboxes.[3] And, second, he was conscripted, in February 1945, into the army as a private. "My military career consisted entirely in starting training programs which were discontinued because various sections of the war fronts became inactive."[4] Discharged in July 1945, Reid never got a posting farther east than Calgary.

Though Reid escaped active war service, he did not escape marriage. While working at Vancouver's CKNX in the early 1940s he became acquainted with the station's receptionist. Mabel (or "Binkie") Van Boyen was stunningly good looking. She was also willing to follow her twenty-four-year-old "radio tramp," as Bill liked to call himself, back and forth across the country.[5] After their marriage in 1944, Binkie continued to work in whichever town Bill happened to be broadcasting from. But since Bill worked in the evening and Binkie worked during the day, they saw little of each other. Although this setup would not appear to make for a good marriage, during the first years things seemed to go well. And things looked even better for the young couple when Bill landed a job in Toronto with the Canadian Broadcasting Corporation (CBC) in 1948.

Thought by many to be the best public broadcasting station in the world at the time, the CBC was only twelve years old when Bill was hired as an announcer. Consciously highbrow and consciously not American, the CBC aimed to make Canadians aware of the society around them and the changes that were taking place in the post-war world. The corporation's management set high standards for its broadcasters. "The Announcer must be a man of wide general culture," the *Handbook for Announcers* noted, "and must by reading, by listening, and by personal contacts, keep himself abreast of developments in music, literature, drama and current affairs."[6] The people who ran the corporation set strict guidelines to help the announcers achieve these goals. Even after Reid had completed several weeks of training in preparation for the new job, the CBC's wordsmith, Steve Brodie, kept him on a tight rein. Brodie corrected Reid's grammatical errors, made foreign words pronounceable, and saw to it that, if the young announcer did not know how to enunciate a word, he consulted either the corporation's handbook or a nearby set of index cards.

When Reid joined the network it had just launched a new and exciting arts program called *Wednesday Night*. It featured talks by notable scholars such as the historian Arnold Toynbee, plays by T.S. Eliot, and classical music. Reid attributed his education as an adult to programs like *Wednesday Night*. Through them, he acquired an eclectic knowledge of music and literature. The only program he made a point of avoiding was the farm report.

However much Reid enjoyed listening to the CBC, he never contributed to its arts programs. He was an artist-manqué, an aficionado of British and American literature. The CBC wanted his voice, not his patchy knowledge of the arts — its National News Service needed more newsreaders. Earl Cameron, who had read the national news during the previous five years, had moved into general broadcasting, and Harry Mannis, who fronted CBC *News Roundup* and *Dominion News,* had taken his place. Reid was brought on board to replace Mannis, and from January 1949 to the spring of 1952, CBC's *Dominion News* and *News Roundup* began with "This is Bill Reid speaking."

Practically everybody in the country listened to *News Roundup,* which followed the evening news. The fifteen-minute-long program dealt with most aspects of Canadian life. During Reid's first year at the CBC there was much to report in Canada. In 1949 there were no fewer than five provincial elections and three national conventions — the CCF, the Liberals, and the Progressive Conservatives — and Newfoundland had joined the country as Canada's tenth province. And thanks to a large network of foreign correspondents — Matthew Halton in London, James Minifie in New York, and Herbert Steinhouse in Paris — Reid kept his listeners informed about what was happening around the world.

Reid's rhythmic and highly declamatory style of speaking was modelled on the most popular voice in the industry, CBS's Lowell Thomas. His rapid, almost urgent, delivery of the news gave the impression — perhaps the illusion — that what he was telling his listeners was not manufactured by some backroom scriptwriter, but was organized by the events themselves. In this sense, everything that Reid said carried authority.

Billy Reid never got a chance to hear his son on national radio. He had died in 1942 in Stewart at age sixty. But Sophie, who had moved her dressmaking business to Vancouver so that she could be closer to Peggy, now a student at the University of British Columbia, and to her sister Eleanor, listened to her son on the radio. So did her relatives on the Queen Charlotte Islands. When they heard Bill reading the evening news, they exclaimed, "That's Sophie Gladstone's boy!" As Skidegate resident Diane Brown recalled, "We were proud of him before he started art."[7] But radio-speak and the kind of English that people spoke in Skidegate were very different. Henry Young was typical of most elders in the village, who could never understand what the CBC's announcers were saying. He could understand the English used on the short-wave radio by the fishermen, but he could not understand a conversation between two high school students. Young's contemporary, Charlie Gladstone, would also have had difficulty comprehending the rapid-fire cadence of his grandson's baritone voice on the radio. Even so, he had the satisfaction of knowing that Bill was on the air.

It took Reid only a few months to discover the disadvantages of working for the country's official radio station. Highly trained news editors prepared his copy as the bulletins came over the wire from the Canadian Press Service. Although Reid reviewed the copy and made suggestions for changes in phrasing before he went on the air, the script was never of his own making. The constraints of reading someone else's script and the intellectual limitations of the job were not the only problems Reid encountered at the CBC. Accuracy was always foremost in a broadcaster's mind. Reid was a perfectionist, and when he got things wrong the blunder was heard across the country. Reid did not possess the confidence or the sense of humour that allowed veteran broadcasters like Knowlton Nash and Lowell Thomas to burst into laughter when they found a news item amusing or when they made an error. From the moment Reid stepped into the broadcasting booth, he was tense. "My anxiety dreams are still about the radio business," he recalled years later. "I have a quarter of an hour of air time to fill and no script."[8]

Although he was not always happy with the limitations imposed on him at the CBC, hosting two programs on a nationwide network was a prominent job for a man of twenty-nine. Being at the centre of attention and in the possession of information that he handed out to thousands of people every night did, however, suit Reid's autodidactic temperament. In spite of his nervousness, this was the kind of role he enjoyed playing, and would continue to enjoy playing throughout his life.

∽∾ᴄᴄᴀ

Working for the CBC from 6:00 P.M. to 1:00 A.M. left Reid with a large part of the day free. One sunny afternoon in September 1949, while spending a few idle hours window-shopping in downtown Toronto, he spotted a notice attached to a fence. It was an advertisement for a jewellery-making course at the Ryerson Institute of Technology. "It was an amazing confluence of circumstances," he told an interviewer in 1985. "I thought they might be able to teach me to make jewelry like my grandfather and John Cross had made for my mother in the Queen Charlottes."[9]

Ryerson's two-year course in the design and making of jewellery was a more ambitious program than Reid was looking for. But the tuition fee was affordable; in addition to an annual fee of twenty-five dollars, students paid only ten dollars for materials. And the courses were offered during the daytime, which suited Reid. In the autumn of 1949 Reid enrolled as a full-time student. Over the next two years he took four courses — from September to January and from February to May.

Ryersonia Yearbook, 1951

During his first year at Ryerson, Reid was introduced to the tools of the jewellery trade. He learned how to make and use hammers and beaders, pushers and punchers, files and fine-toothed saws. He became familiar with the properties of various metals. A troy ounce of gold could be beaten out into a hundred-square-foot sheet. Silver would bend without cracking and, unlike gold, was not unattractive when it was scratched. And platinum was ideal for mounts and almost as malleable as gold. He also learned the difference between soft soldering, whereby two metals were joined by a composite of lead and tin, and hard soldering, which involved joining two perfectly fitting seams. He was taught how to polish a piece of jewellery on a lathe and how to transfer a design onto metal by using tracing paper and a sharp-pointed pencil. He also learned how to chase (the technique known as repoussé). The process involves raising the flat surface of metal into bas-relief by giving it a series of rapid blows from the wrist with the chasing hammer.

When Reid was not at his bench in the school's well-equipped workshop, he and the other students visited the leading jewellery manufacturers in the province. At the Dominion Diamond Company, he watched jewellers transform a diamond in the rough into a highly polished stone. At Harry Winston's, he saw the famous blue Hope diamond. At Canada's largest jewellery manufacturer, Levy Brothers in Hamilton, Reid learned how to set diamonds. And when the class was taken to the Royal Ontario Museum, Reid garnered ideas for his work from the collections of Roman, Chinese, Native American, and African artifacts.

Of particular interest to Reid were four totem poles that stood back-to-back in two stairwells in the east wing of the museum. Three of them — one mortuary and two memorial poles — came from Nisga'a villages along the Nass River. The fourth pole was from Tanu on the Queen Charlotte Islands and had stood in front of an Eagle lineage house during his grandmother's childhood. Ottawa's National Museum ethnologist, Marius Barbeau, had removed it and the other poles in the late 1920s. Under his supervision, they were broken down into segments, then shipped in a boxcar to Toronto where they remained in storage until the museum expanded its premises in 1933 and put them on permanent display.

Although the pole from Tanu was coated in ugly black paint when Reid viewed it — a clumsy preservation attempt by Barbeau — and showed signs of damage — the result of its long journey to Toronto — all of its original features were visible. As Reid climbed the staircase to the third floor, he saw the beaver sitting at the base of the pole, and emerging from it a human head with long slim-fingered hands. Poised midway up the column, and visible from the second floor, was a sensitively carved frog. And when he reached the top of the staircase, Reid saw three human figures supported by his (and his grandmother's) family crest, the raven, crowning the pole. These figures were close enough for Reid to touch. All of them would find their way into his jewellery and into the pole he would carve in Skidegate many years later.

Reid was also exposed to Native jewellery during his early years in Toronto. On one of his walks around Toronto, he noticed a pair of gold bracelets in the window of an antique shop. They were displayed with a label identifying them as "genuine antique Inca bracelets." Noting their similarity to the bracelets his mother wore, Reid felt they were probably the work of a Haida artist. At sixty dollars each they were too expensive for him — or for anybody else — to purchase. Several months passed during which Reid made a daily pilgrimage to the window of the antique shop. "I finally couldn't stand it any longer," he told a reporter in 1953. "I knew that they'd eventually be melted down for gold. I told myself that in another ten years I'd never miss the hundred and twenty dollars." Reid entered the shop determined to make his extravagant purchase. The price tag had fallen off one of the bracelets, and when the shopkeeper took the pair out of the window, he looked at the single price tag and, much to Reid's surprise, asked for sixty dollars. "I didn't say a thing," Reid recalled. "I just paid the sixty dollars and got out of there at a fast trot."[10] Although Reid did not realize it at the time, he had just acquired two 22-carat gold bracelets — one with a dogfish and the other with an eagle motif — that had been made by Charles Gladstone's uncle, Charles Edenshaw.

☙✌❧

Reid encountered a friendly atmosphere at the School of Jewellery Arts. P.W. "Jimmy" Green, who headed the jewellery department, entertained Reid and his fellow students in his home. He found his students apprenticeships or jobs. (Green could do this because the jewellery trade had been supporting the program — the only one of its kind in the country — since its inception in 1946.) Green also encouraged his students to exhibit their work. During Reid's second term at the school, Green arranged for him and two other students, Pat Patterson and George Moore, to exhibit their work. In January 1950, the young men presented three pieces of sterling silver — a pendant and two brooches — in a display case before two thousand members of the Canadian Jewellers Association at the Royal York Hotel in Toronto.

Reid was fortunate in being able to study under Jimmy Green. Before joining Ryerson in 1948, Green had spent almost twenty years at Toronto's Platinum Art Company and T. Eaton Company's jewellery department. Though he was well qualified to give his students a sound grounding in jewellery-making techniques, he thought that jewellery design, as Reid remembered, "began and ended with Queen Mary's time — all hearts and flowers and bowknots."[11] Reid was prompted to fondly mock his teacher because he knew that jewellery design had undergone a radical change since Jimmy Green had apprenticed in London's Soho district.

Following World War II, many jewellers or "studio goldsmiths," as they became known, had revelled in the technical aspects of jewellery-making.

A simple clasp became a challenge for the jeweller rather than a burden. Non-traditional materials became more popular than precious metals. This was because teachers such as a former member of Germany's Bauhaus, László Moholy-Nagy, who taught at the School of Design in Chicago, were encouraging their students to work in plastic, stainless steel, and other non-precious materials. Post-war jewellery-making also changed when American and European exhibitions of ethnographic art and the popularity of southwest Native American silver jewellery prompted jewellers to incorporate ethnographic motifs into their work. For example, a jeweller at Cartier produced a Sioux-head tie clip. And the American jeweller Earl Pardon adapted African and Oceanic motifs to his jewellery design.

From reading books and magazines and from talking to other students, Reid also knew that visual artists such as the British painter Alan Davie and the German-American émigré Max Ernst were designing and making jewellery. And that New York's Museum of Modern Art had admitted jewellery to its exhibition rooms in 1946. By the 1950s jewellery was considered a wearable art form; some people even referred to it as miniature sculpture.

Not only did Reid become aware of the convergence of jewellery-making with both high art and ethnographic artifacts, he was also introduced to the work of Margaret de Patta, whose adaptation of Constructivist sculpture gave her a niche in the history of twentieth-century American jewellery. Reid liked the way de Patta's transparent stones seemed to float above a fragile metal structure. He admired the sense of rhythm she gave to every piece of jewellery she designed. Over the next two decades Reid adapted many of de Patta's stylistic devices to his own work.

Three discoveries Bill made in these years re-ignited his childhood interest in Native jewellery and later influenced his approach to contemporary painting: the example of de Patta's modernist jewellery, the recognition that the jeweller was a fine artist, and the understanding that it was valid for contemporary jewellers to incorporate ethnographic motifs into their work.

～∽✑

The first piece of jewellery that Reid made at Ryerson was a ring for Sophie Reid. Of rather conventional design, it was fashioned out of white gold and set with a ruby and two diamonds. He also made several free-form pieces of jewellery that probably owed their debt to the work of de Patta. Only occasionally during these years did Reid adapt Northwest Coast Native motifs to his jewellery. On one of these occasions, when Jimmy Green saw Reid copying Native designs onto small pieces of tracing paper, he asked him what he was doing. Reid told Green that he was from a tribe of Haida Indians and he wanted to adapt motifs from their art to his jewellery. Green did not know very much about Native art, but he knew that Reid was very adept and a quick learner, so he showed him how to transfer his drawings onto metal.[12]

Reid was aware that he had to master the vocabulary of Haida art before he could do two things: adapt its intricate designs to any given space and create his own designs within the Native idiom. This is what he was trying to do when Green observed him fashioning Native motifs into triangles and circles. Working in pen and ink or with a soft-leaded pencil, Reid was teaching himself how to control the subtle changes in the width and direction of the formline

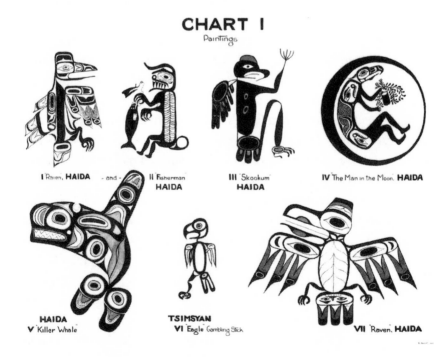

Alice Ravenhill's chart

that underlies the structure of every motif. He was also attempting to understand the rudiments of another powerful design element — the ovoid. He wanted to make it appear so tense that it looked as though it could spring apart. And he was learning how the tertiary and background areas of a design could be filled with cross-hatching or with solid colour, or left blank so they could function as negative space.

Reid's first drawings, which are housed in the archives of the Museum of Anthropology at the University of British Columbia, were tentative and awkward. They show that he had much to learn. How, for example, to distort, dissect, and abstract an animal or mythical creature so that it could be adapted to any space. How to maintain the overall symmetry of a work while maintaining the characteristics of the figure depicted. How to reconcile the restraint, fundamental to all Native design, with the sense of monumentality. And, finally, how to give his work the sense of movement and fluidity so well realized in de Patta's jewellery.

The Woman in the Moon, *circa 1950*

Reid began teaching himself to do all these things by studying the Native designs reproduced in Robert Bruce Inverarity's seminal 1950 work, *Art of the Northwest Coast Indians,* and in Alice Ravenhill's *A Corner Stone of Canadian Culture: An Outline of the Arts and Crafts of the Indian Tribes of British Columbia* (1944). For example, a tattoo drawing illustrated in Ravenhill's book inspired Reid's *The Woman in the Moon* brooch.[13] Under Jimmy Green's supervision, Reid copied the motif onto paper. He reduced the tattoo to less than one-half its original size and reversed the ground so that the negative image became a positive one. He transferred his drawing onto a thin sheet of silver and brought the surface of the design to a high polish before cutting it out of the silver sheet. Reid then "sweated" the fragment onto a piece of oxidized silver, added a clasp to the unpolished back, and the brooch was complete.

Killer Whale Earrings, *1955*

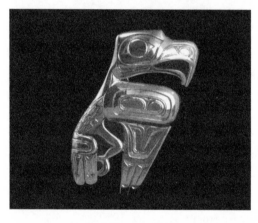

Eagle Brooch, *1955*

Reid adapted other tattoo drawings — originally produced in 1905 by John Wi'ha and Charles Edenshaw for the anthropologist John Swanton — to his jewellery. For example, a tattoo drawing of a killer whale became the motif for Reid's *Killer Whale Earrings*.[14] This time Reid avoided the difficulty of fitting the image onto a predetermined space by cutting out the incised profile of the whale then attaching it to a triangular surface of his own making. The result was not entirely satisfactory because the earrings were representative neither of contemporary nor of Native jewellery, but stood somewhere between the two genres. Reid avoided the problem of adapting a motif to the dimensions of a preconceived ground in yet another way. After extracting the figure from the sheet of silver, as in his *Eagle Brooch* (1955), he simply left the bird in profile.[15]

ᏨᎦᎡ

These early experiments revealed to Reid the flexibility of Northwest Coast design. He could adapt a motif to a free-standing object or fit an abstracted design onto a flat surface. Above all, he could apply contemporary forms and modern techniques to traditional Native art. But on a personal level, what was really going on here? What prompted Reid to tell Jimmy Green that he was Haida when only a few years earlier he had kept his Native ancestry from his best friend? And why did he tell a colleague at the CBC that he should be producing programs on Native Indians?

Something had clearly happened between Reid's departure from Victoria in 1939 and his employment at the CBC a decade later. It was not just the physical distance between Bill and his mother that made the once shy and withdrawn boy who had tried so hard to be fully white not only admit that he was a Native, but boast about it.

Bill Reid's successful career as a radio broadcaster had given him the confidence he previously lacked. His exposure to the artifacts in the Royal Ontario Museum, the purchase of two gold bracelets, along with an undocumented visit to his grandfather in 1948, had awakened memories of his boyhood experience in Skidegate and his wish to produce jewellery in the Native tradition. All these things prompted Reid to do something different from his fellow students at Ryerson by using motifs he felt he had an inherited right to use.

When Reid took the job at the CBC in 1948, he had hoped to make broadcasting his career. And although he later complained that he did not have a chance "playing in a game with the big bugs," becoming a first-class broadcaster was still very much his goal. This was certainly the image that Reid projected to the editor of *Ryersonia* who described him as a family man who indulged in jewellery-making as a hobby. While Reid would claim, years later, that his ambition at this time was "to become the greatest contemporary jewelry-maker in the world," according to his entry in the 1951 edition of *Ryersonia,* he wanted "to reach the top at the CBC."[16]

Reid's entry in *Ryersonia* characterized him as a family man and the father of one child, Amanda, who was born in 1950. But all was not well in the Reid household. According to one of Bill's old friends, Binkie did not share her husband's "interest in things cerebral or artistic."[17] Then there was their different work schedules — Binkie still worked in the day and Bill in the evening. They did meet for dinner, but Bill's absence almost every evening must have put an understandable strain on the marriage.[18]

Unhappy in his life with Binkie and unfulfilled by his broadcasting job at the CBC, Reid was also uncertain whether he would become anything more than a hobby jeweller. He did not, for example, complete the two-year course of study at Ryerson. In the spring of 1951, a few months before graduation, he took an apprenticeship with Jimmy Green's former employer, the Platinum Art Company. Owing to a drop in sales, however, Reid was laid off.

With his apprenticeship brought to an abrupt end some time in 1951, Reid became increasingly restless. That restlessness prompted him to make a short trip to Vancouver. It was a seminal trip. First, he discovered that the CBC needed someone to read the local evening news and to host a new program, *A Man and His Music*. Second, a short visit to Skidegate reinforced his 1948 observation that his grandfather, Charles Gladstone, was among the last generation of Haida silversmiths. And third, when Reid showed his grandfather what he had been doing at Ryerson, Gladstone, who knew good workmanship when he saw it, was impressed.

Reid's access to power tools and to new jewellery-making techniques had allowed him to do things that were beyond his grandfather's technical ability. No wonder Reid returned to Toronto convinced that it was up to him to carry on an artistic tradition that would vanish with his grandfather's death. And no wonder Charles Gladstone became his mentor over the next few years. Given Reid's long-standing interest in things Native and given his new-found willingness to admit that he was Native, he knew it was time for him to go home.

PART II

SALVAGING A CAREER

CHAPTER 5

Back on the Coast

In the summer of 1953 a reporter for the *Vancouver Sun* walked into the basement workshop of Reid's home on Granville Street in downtown Vancouver. Bill had been living in the city for just over a year.[1] After spending the first few weeks in Vancouver with his now married sister, Peggy Kennedy, and her family, Binkie, Bill, and Amanda had moved into a home of their own. This is where Rhodi Lake, the reporter, found him: huddled over his workbench and surrounded by an assortment of files and pliers, with a jeweller's saw and a homemade blowtorch to hand, and, around him, bracelets by Charles Gladstone and John Cross. Reid appeared younger than his thirty-three years; his black hair and hazel eyes made him extremely handsome.

Reid did not hide his Haida ancestry from the *Sun* reporter. He proudly told Lake that he was the grandson of Charles Gladstone who, in his view, was one of the best carvers in Haida Gwaii. He might have even shown Lake the recently made silver *Beaver Bracelet* that had been inspired by Gladstone's *Sdast'aas, Two Bears Bracelet*.[2] Reid made it clear, however, that he wanted to do more than simply copy the work of the previous generation of artists. He told Lake that he wanted to apply the principles of contemporary jewellery-making to Haida art. And he wanted to do this in order to cultivate a

Beaver Bracelet, *circa 1953*   Sdast'aas, Two Bears Bracelet,
                                      Charles Gladstone, 1951

twentieth-century audience for his work.[3] Thus, even though Reid was still very much under the influence of his grandfather and dependent on the motifs that he found in publications by Ravenhill and Inverarity, he was determined to bring Haida art into the world of contemporary jewellery. This was a goal from which Reid never departed.

A lot had to happen before the non-Native public would accept Native art on its own terms — or, more precisely, on the terms that Reid would establish for it. Yet it would be wrong to think that no one else but Bill Reid was trying to create an appreciative audience for Native art and culture at this time. Since well before World War II, a number of non-Native organizations had put on exhibitions of children's Native art, encouraged the production of Native handicrafts, sponsored public lectures, and given scholarships to promising young Native students. Alice Ravenhill's British Columbia Indian Arts and

Welfare Society and Anthony Welsh's Okanagan Society for the Revival of Indian Arts and Crafts had even asked the federal government to acknowledge the rich heritage of Native people and to investigate the dire social and economic conditions under which most Natives lived. From the perspective of the twenty-first century, the efforts of these genteel do-gooders may seem patronizing and feeble. But an even more concerted effort to address the imbalance between the collection and preservation of museum artifacts and the production of contemporary Native art would do little to make the general public take Natives and their art seriously.

It happened in the spring of 1948, the year that Reid made the short trip from Toronto to Vancouver. That spring, the Conference on Native Indian Affairs was organized by the BC Indian Arts and Welfare Society and the University of British Columbia. Reid did not attend the conference, but he certainly heard about it from his uncle, Percy Gladstone, who was a student at the university. The conference organizers asked people from the private and public sectors to discuss a number of problems relating to the production of Native arts and handicrafts, Native health and welfare, and Native education. They even gave a few representatives of the Native community an opportunity to air their views on these matters. In a brief speech, Percy Gladstone tried to impress on the white participants how important it was to find out what the Natives wanted.[4] And a Kwakwa̱ka̱'wakw artist from Alert Bay who had been selling work from her Totem Art Studios in Stanley Park since moving to Vancouver in 1946 spoke at greater length.

Ellen Neel was well poised to tell the conference participants why and how contemporary Native artists should be supported. "Our art must continue to live," she pleaded, "for not only is it part and parcel of us, but it can be a powerful factor in combining the best part of the Indian culture into the fabric of a truly Canadian art form." Neel took on the curio dealers, whom she felt had cheapened Native carving for their own profit. Then she turned to the subject of contemporary Native artists. They must, she insisted, be allowed to use new and modern techniques, new and modern tools, new and modern materials.[5]

All this would have struck a chord with Bill Reid had he been at the conference. But for the majority of those in attendance, Neel's talk fell on deaf

Ellen Neel and family carving a totem pole

ears. This was because the non-Native educators, social workers, and museum officials, and other non-Native participants, had a different agenda than Ellen Neel. They wanted to salvage Native culture by training a new generation of Native artists through the Indian residential schools. This line of thinking failed to address the irony that, while it was all right to make and sell Native art to tourists, it was illegal — due to the continuing ban of the potlatch — to use it in a ceremonial context. And, above all, it ignored the fact that, despite the missionaries, despite the banning of Native ceremonies, and despite the emergence of the residential schools, Native art, as Ellen Neel made so clear in her talk, was very much alive.

∽∾⌒∾

Reid became "chummy" with Ellen Neel shortly after arriving in Vancouver in 1952.[6] He was impressed by Neel's large output of carvings and silkscreen prints. He marvelled at the various ways in which she promoted Native art to the frequently hostile white community. (Neel lectured to schoolchildren and members of the general public. She encouraged white interest by demonstrating her carving skills at her studio at Stanley Park.) And Reid sympathized with the difficulties Neel encountered trying to earn a living from her work. (Although Neel received many public commissions from the City of Vancouver and from the business sector, people did not always pay on time and sometimes not at all. Her son Bob recalled, "We never ever did make any money. I mean, it was starvation city."[7]) Even though Reid knew that Neel had to produce work for the tourist trade in order to support her family, he was critical of the low standard of her work. In contrast to Neel, Reid was determined to make every item he produced into a work of art. And he could afford to do so because he did not have to produce quickly fashioned made-for-tourists items in order to support his family.

Reid thought that Ellen Neel was the only artist who was keeping Native culture alive when he moved to Vancouver in 1952. But he was wrong. Neel's uncle, Mungo Martin, whom Reid would observe carving at the University of British Columbia, had been making totem poles for the provincial government since the 1930s. The Nanaimo-based silversmith Jimmie John was demonstrating his jewellery-making skills in a department store in Seattle. And, since leaving the Alberni Indian Residential School, the Nuu-chah-nulth artist George Clutesi had been producing canvases and recording the legends of his people in an effort to make the non-Native public understand and appreciate the imaginative and resourceful Native peoples in their midst.

While Reid may very well have known about Clutesi, who had given a series of talks on the CBC, he was unaware of the activities of other Native artists. As a member of the white community, Reid was more in tune with white attitudes. He knew, for example, that a spate of anti-Native articles had appeared in the local press in January and February of 1954. "More Totem Nonsense" was one headline. Totem poles, according to another writer, were "crude monstrosities." The Provincial Museum's plan to establish a living museum of Native art was "out of the question." And a proposal to maintain the totem pole motif on British Columbia's licence plates that was introduced in 1952 was, according to another journalist, evidence that the government had submitted "to cults and fetishes."[8]

Reid challenged this overt display of racism in an open letter to the editor of the *Vancouver Sun*. Published on February 9, 1954, under the title "Totem Pole Is Epic in Carved Wood," Reid hit back in a lengthy peroration. He began by contrasting the imitation totem poles produced in Japan with the magnificent monumental sculptures found in Native villages from Alert Bay to Alaska. Totem poles, Reid told the readers of the *Sun*, were family monuments "illustrating legends of epic proportions, rivalling, and very often having the same origins as those we revere in our early Greek and Biblical literature." He wrote that the public should allow Native Peoples to relearn their pride and skill in "the old arts." And that if Native art forms were allowed to blend with Western art, Canadians would have an art form of their own.

It took Reid fewer than five hundred words to set out a thesis that he would adhere to for the rest of his life. Traditional Northwest Coast art was second to none. The production of contemporary Native art should incorporate elements from European culture. And the combination of Native and non-Native art would give birth to a new art form to which all Canadians could relate. Reid had expressed some of these views to the *Sun* reporter Rhodi Lake a year earlier. But this time the words were all his own. The forceful manner in which he conveyed his ideas about Native art and culture showed Bill Reid's writing at its best.

Reid's appeal for tolerance for and understanding of Native art was not just the result of his friendship with Ellen Neel. He was particularly sensitive about white attitudes towards Northwest Coast culture when he wrote his letter to the editor because he had just returned from Haida Gwaii. In one sense, the visit had been an unhappy one. Charles Gladstone, now in his eighties, had just died. Yet in other ways, the trip was a success. Shortly after returning, Reid told a friend that a revival of interest in carving seemed to be taking place.[9] Tim Pearson had begun to carve "deep" in a manner that would characterize Reid's work a decade later. Arthur Moody was making medallions with raised figures. (He'd also made a ring set with the heart of an Alaskan abalone shell.) Arthur Moody's son, Rufus, along with Louis Collison and Tim Pearson, was producing innovative work too. And, if Reid had travelled to Old Masset to the north of Skidegate, he would have found Robert Davidson Sr. (gannyaa) using illustrations from Marius Barbeau's *Haida Myths Illustrated in Argillite Carvings* as a model for his own argillite carvings.

The local minister, Reverend L. Hooper, was partly responsible for making an elder, George Young, and many other residents in Skidegate believe that their people were going to keep carving the way their fathers did. It was Hooper who had encouraged the men to produce more and more carvings in order to supplement their seasonal incomes. He had found markets for their work and persuaded the men to raise their prices. And, in an effort to keep bootleggers out of the curio market, Hooper had even attempted to get the carvers to form a union.

Not only did Reid look at what was being produced, but he also proudly showed many of the artists he met in Skidegate his own work. By 1954 he had begun to work in carbonaceous shale that he cut, carved, and polished, then rubbed with oil to darken its colour. The artists were intrigued to see how Reid had mounted a piece of argillite onto silver. In spite of being impressed, they felt his asking price for the brooch — one hundred dollars — was too high. "All right for rich people, but not for the 'average' person" was how one elder responded to the extravagant price tag.[10] It would have been impossible for any artist in Skidegate to ask this kind of price for a work that was destined for the souvenir market. Consequently, they did not follow Reid's example. Tim Pearson and his contemporaries in Haida Gwaii continued to price their jewellery at ten or twelve dollars.

Reid's visit to Skidegate was timely. He had recently become involved in an organization founded by former students of the residential school where Sophie Gladstone and two of her siblings had been educated. The members of the Coqualeetza Fellowship raised funds to help support Native men and women who were attending college or university. They also held exhibitions in order to promote a better knowledge and understanding of Native culture among the non-Native community. Reid had learned about the organization from one of its most active members, his aunt, Ella Gladstone. It was Ella who told Reid about the society's plans to hold an exhibition of Native art at the

Vancouver Art Gallery during the summer of 1954. And it was Ella who asked Reid to help her and the fellowship's president mount the *Arts and Handicrafts Show.*

The chair of the three-member exhibition committee was Hattie Fergusson. A Tsimshian from Kitkatla, Fergusson was determined that the show would be organized by the Natives themselves. (Whenever officials at the gallery attempted to interfere, Fergusson told them, in no uncertain terms, to mind their own business.) Although she admitted that she was not very well versed in Native art, she considered herself competent enough to recognize good workmanship when she saw it. And whenever she felt that she was not sufficiently qualified, she assured officials at the Vancouver Art Gallery that there was a man "whose hobby is making Indian bracelets, pins etc." who could advise her.[11] Reid did more than give Hattie Fergusson advice. When he discovered the breadth of activity that was going on in Skidegate during his visit in 1954, he actively sought contributions to the exhibition.

This was not, of course, the first time that the white community had recognized the aesthetic merits of Northwest Coast Native art. As far back as 1897, the German ethnologist Franz Boas had paid tribute to west coast Native art.[12] And long before the Surrealist painter Wolfgang Paalen followed suit, Karl Einstein had suggested in 1915 that "primitive" art should be treated as fine art.[13] Yet west coast Native art did not make its debut as art under Canadian auspices until 1926. That year, westcoast Native carvings were included in an exhibition of Canadian paintings at London's Wembley Exhibition. A year later, a large number of Native carvings and weavings were exhibited alongside the canvases and watercolours of non-Native Canadian artists. This landmark *Exhibition of Canadian West Coast Art: Native and Modern,* at the Victoria Memorial Museum in Ottawa, was mounted some fourteen years before New York's Museum of Modern Art put on its exhibition of Northwest Coast art. The intent of Eric Brown, director of the National Art Gallery, and Marius Barbeau, who organized the Ottawa exhibition, was "to mingle for the first time the art work of the Canadian West Coast tribes with those of our more sophisticated artists in an endeavor to analyze their relationships to one another." Referring to the Native work on display as "primitive and interesting art," the organizers hoped that it would take "a definite place as one of the most valuable of Canada's artistic productions."[14] But this did not happen. Even though Barbeau hoped that the modern work would serve as an interesting background for the Indian art, the paintings of Emily Carr, Edwin Holgate, and A.Y. Jackson stole the show.

Nor was the 1954 exhibition the first time the Vancouver Art Gallery supported non-western art. In 1941 the gallery had put a collection of contemporary and historic Native art, borrowed from Victoria's Provincial Museum, on show. Although the work prompted one critic to note how it resembled "the work of Matisse and Picasso," the exhibition made little impact on the general public.[15] (The work of contemporary Native artists did not appeal to white collectors simply because it was believed any carving that was worth having had to be old and produced by a long-deceased artist.) A year later the Provincial Museum in Victoria began the annual *Exhibition of Modern Indian Arts and Crafts*. Yet more than a decade passed before the Vancouver Art Gallery devoted exhibition space to non-western art again.

The *Arts and Handicrafts Show* was originally conceived as an exhibition of historical work to be compiled from local museums and private collectors. But four months before the opening, the organizing committee decided to include living artists. This decision was no doubt due to the efforts of Ellen Neel and Bill Reid, who had become involved in organizing the show.

The artists who contributed to the exhibition came from as far away as Fort St. James. (Surprisingly, there was no entry representing Reid's recently deceased grandfather, Charles Gladstone, even though his work was now in the hands of Ella Gladstone and of Bill himself.) Many of the contributors had produced their work while they were patients in Native hospitals or while attending residential schools. A few like Ellen Neel, George Clutesi, and the popular young Native artist Judith Morgan were professional artists. Most, however, had produced their work in order to supplement the income from their full-time jobs. Given the part-time status of most of the contributors, Hattie Fergusson predicted that the work would likely fall short of professional standards. In requesting the gallery's support for the exhibition, she had even told one official that "our Indian painters, as you no doubt know, are still amateurish but if we can show the best they can offer, we'd highly appreciate it."[16]

Much of the work on display was not for sale. The Coast Salish Chief Capilano, Mungo Martin, and many others chose to submit ceremonial items. However, works that were available for purchase could be acquired for a modest price. Beautifully woven cedar-bark baskets ranged from fifty cents to twenty dollars. An argillite totem pole was priced far below the most expensive basket. But if you wanted an 18-carat gold bracelet made by Bill Reid, you had to spend seventy dollars. And if you wanted to buy an argillite and silver brooch — probably the work Reid had proudly shown artists in Skidegate — the price was one hundred dollars.

Although Reid was the only artist to exhibit work in gold, he was not the only artist to exhibit jewellery. Two unidentified artists from the Haida and Kwakwaka'wakw Nation exhibited a silver bangle and a silver bracelet. Arthur Moody contributed an argillite medallion with a raised surface that he had shown to Reid in Skidegate. And a Heiltsuk artist from Old Bella Bella ('Qélc) who was identified in the working list of exhibits simply as "George," completed the jewellery section by showing a silver pin decorated with an eagle motif.

The *Arts and Handicrafts Show* opened on the ground floor of the Vancouver Art Gallery on the morning of July 13, 1954. There was no reception. There were no speeches. (A non-Native artist, Mildred Valley Thornton, did give a small reception for some of the participants in her home on Comox Street that evening.) Nor was there a catalogue. Hattie Fergusson was told that it would not sell. She could not even persuade the gallery to produce a list of the contributors with potted biographies. She had also made an unsuccessful attempt to persuade one of the curators at the gallery to write a short essay on the work in the exhibition. "Contrary to what most people think," she told one gallery official after the exhibition had closed, "Indians appreciate practical criticism."[17]

The exhibition received almost no coverage in the press. There was no discussion of the extent to which Bill Reid and the other artists in the exhibition had based their work on illustrations taken from the publications of Alice Ravenhill and Marius Barbeau, as well as other authors. There was no consideration of why artists like Ellen Neel had incorporated themes from western art into their work. Or of the extent to which Reid had introduced contemporary jewellery-making techniques into his work. A reporter for Victoria's *Colonist* newspaper, Miss Dee, did make an appearance. But her interview with Hattie Fergusson did not focus on the work in the exhibition. Miss Dee was only interested in discovering how a group of Native Indians had managed to secure the largest gallery in Vancouver for their work. "We simply asked for it," an annoyed Fergusson told Dee, and the interview ended.

It was not just the lack of media attention that kept the public from beating a path to the Vancouver Art Gallery. Attitudes towards Native art had changed little since the 1948 conference. Many British Columbians still preferred traditional over contemporary Native art because it evoked the indigenous people who had inhabited the province's vast primordial forests long before the arrival of the Europeans. For most people, then, contemporary Northwest Coast Native art contained a dual element of tragedy and irony. At its worst, as the anthropologist George Swinton noted of contemporary Inuit art, it embodied an actual stage of ethnic agony and death. At its best, it spoke to a greater degree of what was than of what is.[18]

The lack of response from the general public made Bill Reid wonder if the effort to mount the show had been worth it. Fergusson, however, was more philosophical: "This sort of thing has to be built up over a period of time," she told one of the officials at the gallery.[19] Indeed, Fergusson asked the Vancouver Art Gallery to allow her committee to mount an exhibition of Native art the following year. Convinced that the exhibition had been a flop, the gallery turned down her request.

During the course of helping to organize the exhibition, Reid had attempted to raise the aesthetic standard of contemporary Native art by suggesting that the committee accept only the best work available. This stand had frequently brought him into conflict with the other two members of the organizing committee. When Ella Gladstone submitted two argillite totem poles that she had brought back from the Queen Charlotte Islands, Reid made it clear that he did not want them in the show. "Reid says that I will be disappointed in [Rufus] Moody's totem because he doesn't think much of it," Fergusson noted. "Miss Gladstone says that if anyone wants an authentic Indian slate carving that is it."[20] (Moody's totem pole remained in the exhibition.) Reid also ran into trouble with Ellen Neel. When he saw the poor quality of her made-for-tourists totems, he cringed. And when Neel asked the committee if she could demonstrate her carving skills during the exhibition, Reid persuaded Fergusson and his aunt to veto her proposal.[21]

Reid did not escape criticism himself. In response to his obvious dislike of so much of the work submitted for consideration in the exhibition, Fergusson complained that he was too much of a perfectionist. She also wondered how he could make the claim that his work was authentic when he had used electric tools to make it. Moreover, although Fergusson considered Ellen and Bill to be the best artists in the exhibition, she told one gallery official that, in her view, Neel was as deceiving to the uninitiated as Reid.[22]

Even so, to Hattie Fergusson the exhibition had been a success because it had got all the participants talking about Native art. Yet the experience of showing their work in an art gallery did not change the way artists produced their work or how the public received it. Most artists continued to make art of varying standards for the tourist trade. This prevented them from amassing a body of work that would inform their future work or serve as an example for the next generation of artists. Moreover, the need to sell everything they produced meant that if a gallery or a museum did offer them a show, they did not have a substantial body of work to exhibit. This, along with the low expectations of the public, prevented Native artists from earning a reasonable living for their work and, above all, from receiving the critical attention and the exposure that their work deserved.

If sales had been better at the *Arts and Handicrafts Show,* things might have been different. But, with few exceptions, the work did not sell. The public balked at paying high prices for work they believed had been produced for the tourist trade. This attitude left Bill Reid out in the cold because his prices were comparatively high. Yet like any jeweller who works with precious metals, he had to recover the cost of his materials. Not surprisingly, he only sold one item: a silver medallion priced at eleven dollars.

Though he must have been disheartened by the public response to his jewellery, Bill Reid could afford to weather any financial loss he might have incurred. Unlike the majority of participants, he did not have to supplement what Hattie Fergusson called his hobby by taking seasonal jobs such as fishing and logging. His position at the CBC as a broadcaster was full-time. There was little chance that he would be laid off or that his salary — enormous compared to most Native incomes — would be reduced to meet economic exigencies.

If anyone benefited from participating in the *Arts and Handicrafts Show,* it was Bill Reid. Although this first attempt to raise contemporary Native art to the standard of fine art and to gain recognition for his own work had failed, the experience had taught him much. By the time the exhibition closed, he knew that if he was going to make a name for himself as a jeweller, it would not be by exhibiting his work alongside men and women who produced work largely destined for the tourist trade. He also knew that the recognition he so badly wanted would come only if he did two things. First, he had to cultivate the museum and art gallery curators, the critics, and the patrons, because these were the people who would exhibit, write about, and buy his work. And second, he had to exhibit his work alongside white artists.

Reid rarely acknowledged his participation in the *Arts and Handicrafts Show.* In retrospect, the exhibition had clearly been a detour on the road to recognition and acceptance by the museum and gallery establishment. It was, therefore, best forgotten.

CHAPTER 6

A Dying Art?

Charles Edenshaw

Bill Reid had an instinct for making friends with the right people. Well before the opening of the *Arts and Handicrafts Show*, he had begun to make contact with the museum sector of the white community in Vancouver. At the University of British Columbia he visited the modest display of Native artifacts housed in the basement of the library. It was here that he met and befriended the museum's curator, Audrey Hawthorn, whose anthropologist husband, Harry, had set up the Department of Anthropology in 1947.

Hawthorn's first impression of Reid was that he was a "very pleasant soft-spoken young man." She was therefore surprised to discover that he was the host of one of the CBC's most popular programs, *A Man and His Music*. She was even more surprised when Reid revealed that he was the grandson of her friend Charles Gladstone and the nephew of Percy Gladstone, who had been among Harry Hawthorn's first contingent of anthropology students.

Reid established his credentials as a jeweller on that first meeting. He told Audrey Hawthorn that he had just graduated from Ryerson, where he had taken a course in engraving. Then he showed her three pieces of jewellery. Two of them were medallion pins fashioned, according to Hawthorn, in the art deco style. A third piece, *The Woman in the Moon*, was the brooch that Reid had based on a tattoo drawing by the Haida artist John Wi'ha. Hawthorn liked the brooch better than the modern jewellery and bought it for twenty-five dollars. And before Reid left the museum, she offered him some advice: stick to Northwest Coast themes.

Hawthorn recalled that she could never have predicted that the un-prepossessing, soft-spoken, and somewhat shy man who had shown her his jewellery on their first meeting would become "a permanent fixture" in the museum.[1] Yet she must have sensed that making jewellery was more than a hobby for Reid, because when she heard that the Canadian Authors Association was looking for someone to produce a medallion for the winner of the Canadian Biographical Award, she recommended Bill Reid. The commission was right up his alley. The association did not want to commission the usual run-of-the-mill medallion embossed with elaborate crests and Latin mottoes. They wanted something different, something that reflected the Canadian experience. This is how they came up with the idea of having their medallion decorated with "an authentic B.C. Indian design." According to Rhodi Lake, who wrote about the commission in the *Sun*, this is what Reid gave them when he produced "a delicately designed and crafted piece of jewelry engraved with a design of the Great Tyee Raven."[2]

Reid not only received his first commission and got to know Harry and Audrey Hawthorn during his first year back on the west coast, but he also began working his way through the literature devoted to Native art and culture. In the books and periodicals written by the National Museum of Canada ethnologist Marius Barbeau, he read about Haida totem poles, Haida argillite carvings, and Haida engravings. Though Reid would later agree with the next generation of anthropologists that the works of Barbeau, Ravenhill, and Inverarity were not great examples of scholarship, he was nevertheless chuffed to find the work of Charles Gladstone, and many of the other artists he had met in Skidegate, featured in their books. He recalled spending hours poring over illustrations of their work in an effort to "unlock the secrets of the ovoids, formlines, etc."[3]

In 1955 Bill Reid's reading expanded to include the recently published work of another writer on Northwest Coast Native art. Franz Boas's book *Primitive Art* offered Reid the most sophisticated discussion on the meaning and form of Northwest Coast Native art to date. The book also gave a lot of space to the work of the artist under whom Reid's grandfather had apprenticed. Reid not only studied the illustrations of Edenshaw's work in *Primitive Art* but, as he later admitted, "I just blatantly copied Edenshaw's designs."[4]

Reid sought to imbue his own work with the exuberant quality of Edenshaw's tense, clean, elegant, and rhythmic lines. He tried to make his

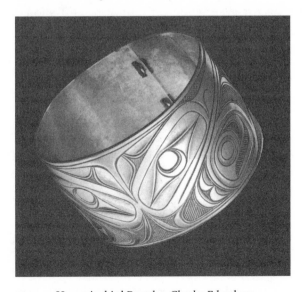

Hummingbird Bracelet, *Charles Edenshaw*

figures appear equally lifelike so that it would seem as though they were performing the actions associated with the myths and legends they represented.
None of these things were easy for Reid to do. A quick glance at Edenshaw's
Hummingbird Bracelet shows how brilliantly he could adapt a motif to any
given space. The crudely rendered beaver motif on Reid's *Beaver Bracelet* was,
by contrast to Edenshaw's work, at odds with the contour of the bracelet.[5] It
was years before Reid could transfer the underlying dynamics of Haida art
to his own work.

For Reid, Edenshaw was the linchpin between the anonymous craftsman
and the superstar artist, between the unbending traditionalist and the imaginative creator, and between the popularizer who produced work for the curio
trade and the artist who created ceremonial objects for his own people. Reid's
uncritical admiration made him believe that Edenshaw was the most accomplished Haida artist to date. This was not a fair assessment, for it did not take
into consideration the work of Tom Price and several other Haida artists
whom the anthropologists had left out of their books on Northwest Coast
Native art. Reid also assumed that the essential form of Haida art had
remained largely unchanged until Edenshaw came on the scene. This was
equally wrong. The art form had never stopped evolving. Even so, Reid did
have the best teacher available to him through illustration. Moreover, his
admiration for Charles Edenshaw found him a soulmate at the Provincial
Museum in Victoria.

∾ᴐᴄ∾

Wilson Duff was thinking about writing a monograph on Charles Edenshaw
when Reid met him in the winter of 1953–54. An anthropologist at the museum
in Victoria, he was also planning an expedition to the Queen Charlotte Islands.

Reid knew that Duff had been to Haida Gwaii in the spring of 1953. His
friends in Skidegate had told him how the young anthropologist had made
an inventory of the totem poles that he wanted to move from the deserted
villages of Skedans and Tanu to museums in Victoria and Vancouver. Reid
had also learned how Duff had made a good impression on the Haida by pro-
nouncing their names correctly, discovering who owned the poles, and agree-
ing to pay their owners fifty dollars a section. All this so impressed Reid that

when he heard that Duff was planning another expedition to Haida Gwaii in the spring of 1954, he saw the opportunity of combining his broadcasting skills with his growing knowledge of Haida art. He wrote to Duff asking for details of the expedition. Then he invited himself along.

When Reid decided to link up with Wilson Duff, he became part of a process that was as much about cultural appropriation as it was about preservation. Salvaging Native art for display in non-Native museums was motivated by the long-held belief that immediate action was crucial, because civilization was pushing indigenous peoples to the wall by destroying their artistic culture and sometimes by destroying the Native peoples themselves. Throughout the nineteenth and early twentieth centuries, most Canadian museums had been happy to let other people collect and preserve the Natives' heritage for them. And it was not until 1927 that an amendment was added to the Indian Act that made it illegal for anyone to remove artifacts from reserves without first getting the government's consent. But, sadly, the amendment was not enforced. Native artifacts from British Columbia continued to fill the storage vaults and display cases of museums around the world.

Marius Barbeau sought to reverse this process. On a visit to the University of British Columbia in 1947, he suggested that a number of totem poles be removed from the remote villages along the coast and displayed in Totem Park at the University of British Columbia and in Thunderbird Park adjacent to the Provincial Museum in Victoria. Cognizant of the extensive totem pole restoration and preservation scheme undertaken by the Alaskan government's forestry service branch from 1938 to 1942 among the Tlingit, a group of academics, including Hunter Lewis, Kenneth Caple, and Harry and Audrey Hawthorn, launched a restoration and reproduction program. In 1953 this group joined forces with the museum and industry — H.R. MacMillan, Walter C. Koerner, Powell River Lumber Company, BC Packers Ltd., Flavelle Lumber Company, and Union Steamships — to form the Totem Pole Preservation Committee. The expedition that Bill Reid was about to join was under the aegis of this nascent committee.

Before leaving for the Queen Charlotte Islands in the late spring of 1954, Reid told his radio listeners that his participation in the expedition had two goals. First, he would be able to help rescue a number of totem poles that were

Sawing argillite at Slate Chuck Creek

in danger of disintegrating. And, second, he would "see something of the old way of life, even its ruins, before even these were gone."[6] When Reid arrived in Skidegate a few weeks later, Duff had hired Jimmy Jones, the son of the hereditary chief of Tanu, to skipper the *Seiner II* and taken on five other residents of Skidegate — Albert Jones, Roy Jones, Clarence Jones, James Wilson, and Allan Young — to help remove the poles.

It was a seminal trip for Reid. Sailing south of Skidegate for the first time, he discovered Skedans to be one of the loveliest places he had ever seen. He never forgot the desolate beauty of the poles that stood or lay among the ruins of the abandoned villages of Skedans and, farther south, of Tanu. Nor did he forget how difficult it had been to extract a hundred-year-old pole from a tangle of salal and salmonberry. Or how the crew had struggled to lower an unwieldy waterlogged pole to the ground, sawn it into sections, and dragged it over boulders to the shore where it was crated then floated to a nearby navy vessel for transportation south.

The trip was not over when Reid sailed north to Skidegate. Accompanied by Wilson, he climbed up the mountain that rose behind Skidegate to the deposit of argillite at Slate Chuck Creek. A photograph shows Reid sawing a piece of argillite in preparation for taking it on the steep climb down the mountain. As he already suffered from back problems, it is unlikely he carried out the argillite on his back.

Before the poles were delivered to the provincial and university museums, a newspaper article appeared in the press. Reid was not mentioned but Duff and his crew were praised for saving "the last six salvageable totem poles" from the isolated villages of Skedans and Tanu.[7] Ironically, while the expedition was being hailed a success, the unsuccessful *Arts and Handicrafts Show* had just opened at the Vancouver Art Gallery. But unlike the salvage operation at Tanu and Skedans, the exhibition was not deemed to be a newsworthy item.

Before the expedition, Reid already possessed enormous respect for Duff. After living and working with him for three weeks his respect knew no bounds. This was because Duff reinforced Reid's belief that although the art was dead, the memory was dead, and the way of life was dead, the art was worth salvaging. Moreover, Duff agreed with Reid that the most outstanding artist was Reid's new mentor, Charles Edenshaw. But there were other reasons

Salvaging operations at Tanu, 1954

why the two men got on so well during their first and subsequent expeditions to the Queen Charlotte Islands. They were comfortable sharing rather long periods of silence. And they had discussed their depressive tendencies. During the trip Duff had helped Reid out when he was suffering from the malady that eventually caused his own death. Reid had welcomed Duff's sympathetic company and tried to reciprocate.[8]

Before leaving for Haida Gwaii, Reid had blithely promised to bring the anthropologist "fabulous wealth and fame" by making him the star of a series of radio programs based on their expedition.[9] When Duff and Reid returned to Vancouver, Reid stuck to his promise. But Duff wasn't interested in becoming a radio star. Swamped with work, he suggested that Reid should make the programs himself. Reid jumped at the opportunity, gladly accepting Duff's official report of the expedition and his offer of help.

Duff was generous. He answered Reid's questions, which ranged from topics such as the role of a Haida chief to the perceived Polynesian origin of the Haida people. Duff also helped him to sort out the difference between what Reid called the public's romantic view of the Indian and the "distressing ordinariness of the people."[10] Answering Reid's probing questions was hardly a burden for the busy anthropologist. Indeed, after receiving a letter from Reid, Wilson was intellectually stimulated for days.

The process of transforming information from Wilson Duff's notebook accounts of the expedition into radio-speak was equally exciting for Bill Reid. Duff's lively prose gave Reid the heroic style that matched the way he read the news on the CBC. "We weren't too late," Reid said of the expedition. "Everywhere there was a wealth of wonderful detail, powerful wings and feathers, huge impassive eyes, little crouching figures. The jungle growth of the North Pacific had almost reclaimed some of the poles, crawling over them and splitting them with its roots."[11] Reid cleverly relayed the exuberance that Duff had confined to his notebook during the trip to a wider audience. Although it was Reid who wrote, produced, and narrated the account of the expedition to Skedans and Tanu, the words and phrases were more Wilson Duff than Bill Reid.

Reid joined Wilson Duff on two further expeditions to Haida Gwaii. The first, in June 1956, was for the purpose of surveying the poles at Ninstints

Reid (far left) and Wilson Duff (far right) at Ninstints, 1957.

(Sgangwaii'llnagaay) in the southern archipelago of Haida Gwaii. The second, a year later, was to remove the poles from Ninstints. The 1957 expedition, known as the Ninstints Recovery Expedition, was a major operation. Besides Reid, there were four anthropologists, two cameramen, and four Native helpers and navigators from Skidegate. As before, Reid did not provide the muscle that felled, dismembered, crated, then floated the poles to a nearby vessel for shipment south. Nor did he make sketches of the poles before they were toppled to the ground; that was left to the expedition's official artist, the Provincial Museum employee John Smyly. Reid was on the Ninstints Recovery Expedition in his capacity as a broadcaster. A photographic record of the expedition shows him, wearing a checkered shirt, standing with one hand on his hip or both hands in his pockets. From beneath the brim of his baseball cap, he appears to be unscrambling the figures on the poles and relating them to the legends that he had read in the books by Boas and Barbeau. In this sense he was more of an observer than anything else.

When the results of the Ninstints Recovery Expedition were published, Reid put his newly discovered vocation as a writer and producer to use once again. With Duff's lyrical style of writing very much in mind, Reid wrote, then produced and narrated the script for the CBC film *Totems.* He also made a watered-down film about the same trip for the Recreation and Conservation Branch of the provincial government. *The Silent Ones* was completed in 1961. In both films Reid mourned the demise of Native culture and the passing of "a fine looking people with pride in their race and lineage." He praised the salvage operation, repeating, "We weren't too late." And he gave his narrative a sense of drama by giving the real and mythical figures depicted on the poles human characteristics. The poles were "impossible giants" who had resisted being cut down. They had "impassive eyes" that had "kept watch" over the eleven-member crew when they had sat out a two-day rainstorm in their soggy tents.[12]

ᕗᑐᐧᑐ

The relocation of totem poles from distant Native villages to urban settings reached a peak in the summer of 1957. But so-called salvage operations like the Ninstints Recovery Expedition did not end when the poles reached the University of British Columbia and the Provincial Museum. Many of the poles had been damaged during their journey south or while being felled or sawn into sections in preparation for transport. This meant that most were unsuitable for exhibition out of doors. Since few museum interiors could accommodate more than one or two large-scale carvings, many of the salvaged poles ended up in sheds where they continued to rot.

University of British Columbia academics turned to Ellen Neel for help in 1949. That year she agreed to restore a number of Kwakwaka'wakw poles, including one that had been carved by her grandfather and teacher, Charlie James (Yakuglas). The work, which was carried out at the University of British Columbia's Totem Park, was strenuous. It interfered with the souvenir business Neel had established at her carving shed in Stanley Park. After working at the university for several months, she had asked her uncle, Mungo Martin, for help.

Restoring the poles for outdoor display at Totem Park proved almost as difficult for Mungo Martin as it had been for Ellen Neel. Though Martin did his best, most of the poles were beyond repair. As Bill Reid would observe a few years later, it quickly became apparent that it wasn't a very successful venture on the university's part. Yet the university academics were convinced that Martin's skills as an artist working in the old tradition could be put to use. They also felt that if he made new poles or copied old ones it would be faster and cheaper than repairing the salvaged poles. Martin agreed to make two new poles for Totem Park and was hired at carpenter's wages ($2.70 an hour). The result was two forty-foot poles in which Martin incorporated his family's crest figures.

Hiring Neel, then Martin, signalled that the university was willing to make room for an activity in which Kwakwa̱ka̱'wakw artists like Mungo Martin and others had been engaged since well before World War II. Bringing Native artists to work in the city not only reversed the policy of keeping them as far away as possible from the urban centres, it was also the first step in making room in the museum for Natives as artists in their own right. But the university should not be given credit for instigating the revival of Native art. What they did was follow Ellen Neel's example of moving the activity from the village to the city.

The university got more than two new poles for Totem Park when they brought Mungo Martin and his wife, Abayah, to Vancouver from Fort Rupert. Fluent in Kwakwa̱ka̱'wakw and cognizant of the meaning of everything they carved or wove, the Martins linked museum officials and the public who came to watch them work with the past. As Mungo Martin often said, "Nobody knows now, only me."[13] Using their contacts in the villages of Alert Bay and Fort Rupert, the Martins helped museum officials to identify the objects they had stored in their vaults and to collect more. Mungo also told Audrey and Harry Hawthorn what not to collect. If "the owner had no right to it and was selling someone else's property," or "it did not belong in the inherited myth but had simply been 'invented' by somebody," Mungo was quick to point this out to Audrey Hawthorn.[14] Abayah Martin introduced her son-in-law, the artist Daniel Cranmer (Pelnagwela Wakas), to the Hawthorns. He sold artifacts to the museum too. And when Cranmer came down from Alert Bay to lecture to students in Harry Hawthorn's anthropology class in 1949, he also brought his son, Doug Cranmer, who, a decade later, became Bill Reid's assistant.

Mungo Martin in the Thunderbird Park carving shed

When Bill Reid made his short visit to Vancouver in 1951, he had seen Abayah Martin weaving on an upright loom and Mungo Martin, now in his early sixties, carving totem poles in the shed. Reid had watched Martin drawing, chipping, and sawing his poles, and he heard him singing songs about the figures he was carving. By the time Reid took up permanent residence in Vancouver the following year, Abayah and Mungo Martin were living in Victoria.

Wilson Duff had employed Martin, his son David, and Henry Hunt to restore and copy a few of the salvaged poles. He had also commissioned them to build a large plank house in Thunderbird Park adjacent to the museum. In order to celebrate the completion of the community house in December 1953, Martin hosted the first legal potlatch since it had been legalized two years earlier. Representatives of twenty-eight tribes came to watch David Martin dance before an open fire, to see the masks and other ceremonial regalia in use, and to hear Mungo Martin and the other elders sing to the steady beat of the drums. The event, which lasted for three days, caught the imagination of the Victoria public, who lined the streets on the last day of the event in an effort to catch a glimpse of the dancing and singing. (It also awakened me, then aged eight, to the mysteries of Native culture.)

Although Bill Reid did not attend Mungo Martin's seminal potlatch, he did keep track of the restoration program at the Provincial Museum. When he heard that Martin had been commissioned to carve a Haida pole for Thunderbird Park in 1955, he asked Harry Hawthorn whether he might be hired to re-create a Haida village at the University of British Columbia. Harry and Audrey Hawthorn told Reid to take his idea to the president of the university, Norman "Larry" MacKenzie, and this is what he did.

Several days later Reid wrote to MacKenzie. It took him eight pages to tell the president why he, rather than anyone else, was qualified to re-create a Haida village at Totem Park. Reid began his masterfully argued proposal with an account of how Native culture had reached a nadir through its encounter with disease and alcohol and why totem poles were decaying in the deserted villages up and down the coast. Reid did praise the salvation efforts of a few devoted members of the Provincial Museum and the university — in which he had, of course, taken part. He acknowledged the hiring of Mungo Martin to reproduce old poles as well as to make new ones. But on the whole, Reid concluded, Native art had been allowed to decay in the deserted villages or been sold to foreign collectors and museums. (Reid pointed out that there were now more artifacts from the Northwest Coast outside of Canada than in it.) And even the restoration program had been a failure. Martin was not only an old man; as a Kwakwa̲ka'wakw he was incapable of working in the Haida style. What he had produced to date had, in Reid's view, "somehow not quite come off."

Having established the demise of Native art and the unsuitability of hiring Mungo Martin to reproduce Haida totem poles, Reid went on to make a number of general points. First, there were no artists capable of producing anything other than second-rate copies of traditional work: "To expect a modern Indian, uneducated either in the patterns of his ancestors or those of today, to recreate what are essentially great artistic achievements, is an empty hope." And, second, Haida art forms were not only superior to those of other Native groups, but closest to classical European art. As a living art form, therefore, the Northwest Coast culture was dead and Native artists would, in

Reid's view, likely "produce nothing more of artistic interest except for the work of a couple of slate carvers and one other individual, myself."[15]

In an effort to convince MacKenzie that he was the best person to direct and partake in the creation of a Haida village, Reid noted the unique circumstances of his birth and training. Though of Haida and Caucasian ancestry, he had been raised in the non-Native world. (He forced this point by telling MacKenzie that he had been unaware of his Native ancestry until he was in his teens.) As a non-Native, Reid continued, he had worked as a broadcaster, during which time he had been a keen student of modern painting and, by association, of "primitive" and Northwest Coast Native art. Thanks to a jewellery-making course at the Ryerson Institute in Toronto, he had become a skilled craftsman. This had enabled him to expand the field of Native jewellery that had been previously restricted to engraved bracelets, simple earrings, and brooches. He had, in fact, been so successful since moving to Vancouver, he had managed to sell everything he produced for very good prices.

All this led Reid to tell MacKenzie that he was wasting his time as a radio announcer. He could give up his job at the CBC and work full-time as a jeweller. But, he continued, there was a much better use of his time: the re-creation from photographs and museum artifacts of some of the finest examples of Haida and Tsimshian art. Reid told MacKenzie that he would not undertake to design a totem pole: "Under no circumstances do I believe I could surpass the best of the old carvers." Yet given enough time, enough money, and enough help from "some talented Indians," Reid was confident that he could reproduce "any Haida carving from a fifty foot totem pole or canoe to the finest slate carving."[16]

In eight pages, Reid had declared the end of Native art and culture through its assimilation into the dominant white community. He had established the superiority of Haida carving over that of any other tribal group. He had dissociated himself from the economic and social disparity experienced by the contemporary Native as well as from the curio maker, and even from his grandfather, Charles Gladstone. Above all, Reid had put himself in a pivotal position. He claimed technical know-how on the one hand and, as a person of Native ancestry, on the other, he claimed to appreciate and respect the art of the Haida people and the right to replicate it.

Reid's proposal did not fall on deaf ears. Less than a year after writing to MacKenzie, Reid was in Victoria, carving on a large scale for the first time. It was Wilson Duff who arranged for Reid to help Mungo Martin, his son David, and Henry Hunt carve a replica of one of the Haida totem poles that he and Reid had removed from Skedans in the summer of 1954.

Reid learned much during his two-week apprenticeship with Mungo Martin in the spring of 1956. The senior carver taught him to make and use a D-edge, an elbow adze, and a curved knife as well as chisels and wedges. He introduced Reid to Doug Cranmer, who became his assistant on the university project a few years later. And Martin's son, David, showed Reid how to transform a shipwright's adze into a wonderful tool by adding a short handle. Reid learned quickly and carved a small figure on the Haida pole that was eventually erected at the Peace Arch near Blaine on the British Columbia–Washington border.

It was a good two weeks for Reid. Back in Vancouver, he told Duff that his study with "Professor M. Martin" had spoiled him completely. Returning to work at the CBC, or even to his jewellery bench, now seemed ridiculous.

Though Reid often claimed that *A Man and His Music* was one of the most diverse and entertaining programs produced in the country, he was carrying out his job with less and less enthusiasm — and showing it. Takao "Tak" Tanabe, a Winnipeg painter newly arrived in Vancouver, lived near the CBC studios and had become friendly with Reid. Tak was on the front line to see how Reid handled his personal and artistic frustration at this time. After spinning his last record for the day, Reid would telephone Tak:

"Hi."

"Is that you, Bill?"

"Yeah."

"Want to come for coffee?"

"Yeah."

"I'll watch for you."

Bill would leave the CBC studios before the last record had finished playing. By this time Tak had made a pot of coffee and was on the lookout for Bill. When Bill's tall lean figure appeared, Tak would throw the front door key out the window for him. Soon the two men would resume their conversation over a cup of coffee:

"How are you, Bill? You sounded rather tired on the radio."

"Well, yeah, I was, you know."

Long pauses would ensue. Then, according to Tak, Bill would ask him for advice before reverting to deep silence again.[17] The problem was simple: Bill was deeply troubled about whether he should jeopardize his good and reliable income by quitting his job at the CBC.

Coping with Reid's mood swings, as Wilson Duff had discovered in 1954, was a burden on many of his male friends. When he was "up," he had an inflated sense of his self-worth, was more talkative than usual, and worked obsessively. When he was down, the opposite was true. According to Jack Shadbolt, who had by now befriended his former student, Reid seemed to have "a deep sadness within himself."[18] In Tak Tanabe's view, Reid was often confused. And the Vancouver writer David Watmough saw how Reid could make enemies with greater facility than he could make friends. Watmough found it difficult to relate Reid's trenchant personality with the soft beauty of his jewellery.[19] Even with those people whom Reid considered to be close friends, there were problems. "He couldn't take a joke about his shirt hanging out or that he was unshaven," recalled George Rammell, a future assistant, who believed this revealed that Reid was deeply insecure.[20]

Why was Reid plagued with apathy, low self-esteem, and outbursts of irritability and bitter remorse? What accounted for the long silences that were a feature of his friendships with Wilson Duff, Tak Tanabe, and others? Was this behaviour new? Or did the manic depression that plagued Reid for most of his adult life begin the year after he graduated from Victoria College, when he spent much of his time in bed?

It was several years before Reid was formally diagnosed with manic-depressive, or bipolar, illness. Yet all the accounts of his abrupt mood changes, his dramatic shifts in sleep patterns, and the rise and decline of his energy suggest that he had been suffering from this malady for some time.[21]

Bill Reid's uncertainty about where he was going as an artist contributed to his low self-esteem. There was his frustration over his job at the CBC, a job he could not afford to relinquish. (He had at least ten years to put in with the network before he would be eligible for a reasonable pension.) He had a wife and, with the "adoption" of the Haida Native Raymond Cross in the early 1950s, he now had two children to support. And things did not look as though they would change — his attempt to persuade Harry Hawthorn to obtain a grant from Walter Koerner for the Haida village project that he had proposed to MacKenzie had failed. "Harry's getting old or something," Reid complained to Wilson Duff in July 1956, "and seems to have given up the idea of getting any money for the university poles."[22]

Reid's spirits rose when he learned that Mungo Martin had been commissioned to carve a pole for Queen Elizabeth to celebrate the province's first one hundred years. He asked Wilson Duff whether he could join the project. "I'm sort of opposed to the whole idea in principle," he told Duff in July 1956, "but if it's going to be done, and it looks as though it is, I'd like to see it done as well as possible anyhow."[23] Reid was not invited to return to Victoria. Though Martin had shown admiration for his skills as a jeweller by purchasing one of his silver bracelets for Abayah, he did not want Reid to help him and his son David carve what would become the province's largest pole to date.

A year later, Reid's hopes for employment on the Haida village project soared again when Harry Hawthorn applied to the newly founded Canada Council for funding. Larry MacKenzie, who was a member of the first adjudication committee, received the university museum's application to train Native artists during the creation of a Haida village for Totem Park. But the proposal was not popular. A few months later, in February 1958, the Canada Council turned down Harry Hawthorn's application "on the grounds that a perpetuation of a dying art does not make sense."[24]

Reid clearly had to look elsewhere if he was going to further his commitment to and involvement in Native art. With the prospects of creating a Haida village gone, it seemed as though his attempt to carve on a grand scale was over.

CHAPTER 7

Urban Indian

Reid carving at Totem Park

After returning from his two-week apprenticeship with Mungo Martin in Victoria, Bill Reid visited the Vancouver Art Gallery. The curators were in the process of organizing a retrospective exhibition of indigenous west coast art and he offered to help. This was the break Reid had been waiting for. From the moment his offer was accepted, he put his mark on the *People of the Potlatch* exhibition. He ensured that the work of Charles Edenshaw, Charlie Gladstone, and John Cross was shown by lending silver and gold bracelets from his mother's and from his own collection.[1] He made his own artistic contribution to the exhibition by covering two large display panels with Native designs copied from Alice Ravenhill's book (these served as a backdrop to one of the showcases). And, when the exhibition opened in mid-April of 1956 Reid gave conducted tours of the ground-floor galleries, gave talks on the radio, and wrote and narrated a film entitled *People of the Potlatch*.

We can get a sense of what Reid might have told the adults and school-children whom he took around the exhibition rooms by looking at his script for *People of the Potlatch*. In it he wrote of the dignity, power, and monumentality of Native carving. He pronounced an abstract design, painted on the sides of a bentwood box, to be a perfect combination of form and decoration. And he ranked the tribal groups according to his aesthetic preference. Kwakwaka'wakw art was emotional and dramatic; Coast Salish art was crude and tentative; Heiltsuk art possessed a moody and austere quality; and the restrained static form of Haida carving gave it great strength. There was nothing new in Reid's partisan preference for Haida art, nor in his treatment of Native carvings as high art. He had expressed these views in his letter to MacKenzie a year earlier and he would continue to express them whenever he got the chance.

People of the Potlatch was different from the *Arts and Handicrafts Show* Reid had helped to organize two years earlier. It was curated by two non-Natives, J.A. Morris and Audrey Hawthorn. It had the full cooperation of the Vancouver Art Gallery and the University of British Columbia. It included no work by a contemporary Native artist. And, in a more fundamental way, unlike the *Arts and Handicrafts Show*, it was a success. An attractive catalogue, along with enthusiastic coverage in the local newspapers and Reid's radio and television progams, brought 10,600 members of the public to the gallery.

In planning *People of the Potlatch* the curators had set out to do two things: first, show the relationship between the social and economic structures of the society and the art forms; and second, treat the objects on display as works of art. These two objectives were not easy to reconcile in one exhibition. Treating the work as art assumed that the public was familiar with the language of abstract expressionist painting, and that they did not have to possess any knowledge of the myths represented by the creatures depicted or have any understanding of the social and economic conditions from which the work had arisen. However, arranging the exhibits according to household activities, tool-making, fishing, and ceremony ensured that the public would view the work in an anthropological rather than artistic context. The exhibition therefore fulfilled neither of the curators' goals. What it did do was to offer a sanitized view of west coast peoples and their art.

Reid was one of the few persons of Native ancestry to attend the opening. The artist Willie Seaweed and the first Native Member of Parliament, Frank Calder, received invitations but chose to attend the Native Brotherhood Convention at Cape Mudge, which was being held at the same time. And although there was no work on show by contemporary Native artists in the main body of the exhibition, Reid and an old friend, the designer Robert Reid, produced a series of promotional engravings. Their rigid geometrical designs were more reminiscent of the motifs on Chilkat blankets and the jewellery of contemporary Mexican artists than of the rhythmic designs painted on Haida cedar-bark hats and bentwood boxes. On sale during the exhibition for two dollars each, the engravings were a bargain. Yet almost no one was tempted enough to buy one.

On the back of his successful contribution to *People of the Potlatch*, Reid was invited, in 1958, to help celebrate the province's centenary by organizing the Native section of an exhibition devoted to British Columbia art. The Vancouver Art Gallery insisted that all ninety-six exhibits for *100 Years of B.C. Art* be selected on the basis of their aesthetic quality. Reid jumped at the opportunity to become familiar with the Native artifacts housed in public and private collections throughout the province. And this is how he became acquainted with the province's major patrons. (The businessman-collector Walter Koerner, whom he met through Koerner's nephew John Koerner and Wilson Duff, would be important to Reid's career at a later date.) It's also how he became familiar with a wide range of artists and styles. Reid also relished the opportunity to contribute an essay on Native art to the catalogue.

The themes running through Reid's short essay would have been familiar to anyone who had seen the film *People of the Potlatch* or had heard him talk about Native art and culture on the radio. Once again, he attributed the decline of Northwest Coast Native culture to the European invasion. And once again he claimed that the best art united excellent workmanship with beautiful design and sacrificed movement and expression for unity and form. Not surprisingly, the artists who produced this kind of work were Haida. The worst Native art, on the other hand, was, Reid wrote, characterized by the "childlike creations" of the Coast Salish and by the "terrifyingly imaginative" art of the Kwakwaka'wakw. In privileging Haida art over the art of other west coast tribes, Reid was attacking the most popular and more familiar art of the Kwakwaka'wakw. And by choosing to display the works in the exhibition as *art*, rather than museum artifacts, Reid was making it clear that anyone who viewed the exhibition did not have to know the myths or the history of Native peoples in order to appreciate the work on show. This was high art, the best of which, in Reid's view, ranked "with that of any fine artist's past or present, anywhere in the world."[2]

Bill Reid gave no place in the exhibition to his own work or to that of any other contemporary Native artist. As he maintained in the catalogue, the small number of Native craftsmen who were working in the Native tradition were incapable, as he had told Larry MacKenzie three years earlier, of producing work that compared with the masterpieces of the past. This line of thinking fit in with Reid's passion for salvage anthropology, the objective of which was to make the white community appreciate the aesthetic merits of traditional Native art, especially that of the Haida people. Since contemporary Native artists had, in Reid's view, little understanding of or interest in their traditional culture, he had taken out of their hands the responsibility for making and exhibiting Native art.

The subtext of Reid's essay for *100 Years of B.C. Art* was clear: collectors, anthropologists, museum and art gallery curators, and publicists — like Bill Reid himself — were better suited to be the caretakers, evaluators, and interpreters of Native culture than were the Natives themselves. Like the Indian agent and the missionary of an earlier era, the museum curator was now the judge of what constituted a proper artifact, a proper price, a proper potlatch, and, by implication, a proper Indian.

Bill Reid must have taken pleasure in the respect that was shown to him by museum and gallery officials, anthropologists, and discerning collectors throughout the province. This attention had come about because he was articulate, he knew what he wanted to say, and, in the view of the Native artist Doreen Jensen, he "was available just at the right time when things were starting to change."[3] But it was not just timing that made Reid a much sought-after commentator on Native art from the mid-1950s. His insistence that Native culture was dead echoed the long-established views of commentators such as Lynn Harrington, who felt that "we can only look at what they produced and perhaps feel a deep regret and maybe a little shame that such a culture should have been allowed to disappear so completely."[4]

Reid's notion that the Haida preferred to look forward instead of back was in tune with white assimilationist thinking.

☙⊘❧

Reid's growing reputation as a publicist, curator, writer, and broadcaster on Northwest Coast art and culture reinforced his feeling that he was wasting his time at the CBC. And yet it was his job there that had given him contacts with the museum and gallery world and that had allowed him to become involved in the making, salvaging, recreation, and promotion of Native art. It was in the CBC's recording studios, located on the sixteenth floor of the Vancouver Hotel, that he had met the literary critic George Woodcock; the well-known Vancouver Island naturalist Roderick Haig-Brown; the newly arrived Vancouver Art Gallery docent, Doris Shadbolt; and the president of the University of British Columbia, Larry MacKenzie. It was there, too, that he had met other cultural figures, including Marius Barbeau, Northrop Frye, and his old Victoria High School principal, Ira Dilworth, who was now director of the CBC in Ontario.

During the decade following Reid's arrival in Vancouver, the city's population had doubled. High-rise buildings had replaced many of the wood-frame houses in the West End. Cedar-clad houses with large picture windows appeared in the forest suburbs to the west and north of the city. In the centre of Vancouver, jazz clubs, theatres, and private art galleries that were willing to take a chance on home-grown modernist painters of the likes of Gordon Smith, Jack Shadbolt, John Koerner, and Tak Tanabe made the director of the National Gallery of Canada claim that there seemed to be "more good artists per square mile in British Columbia than in the rest of the country."[5]

The city's public and private cultural institutions were not alone in celebrating the fine and performing arts. The province's most successful public utility, BC Hydro, commissioned the artist Bert Binning to produce an Oxford-blue and aquamarine logo for the shiny new buses that were replacing their outdated streetcars. Convinced that good design was one solution to the province's social and economic problems, the Vancouver Art Gallery had mounted the seminal *Canadian Design for Living* exhibition in 1953. And when the Federation of Canadian Artists decided to sponsor an exhibition devoted to the province's most accomplished jewellers in the spring of 1955, it was not surprising that the Vancouver Art Gallery gave them a venue.

Bill Reid dominated the Federation of Canadian Artists exhibition by contributing twelve of the thirty-six pieces of handmade jewellery on display. He also charged the highest prices for his work. Moreover, he was the only artist to combine Native motifs with contemporary jewellery-making techniques. And he was alone again in contributing work that had been designed by a fine artist. Reid so impressed the judges that they awarded him a gold star for outstanding craftsmanship and gave him special mention for transforming John Koerner's modernist designs, based on the abacus calculating system, into a stunning ebony and silver bracelet, earrings, and brooch set.

Reid continued to submit his jewellery to exhibitions and craft fairs throughout the 1950s. In 1956 he walked off with a major award at New Brunswick's Handicraft Guild Centennial Exhibition. In May of the following year, he received a prize at the North West Trade Fair in Seattle. He also saw three pieces of his jewellery, decorated with Native motifs, included in the International World's Fair in Brussels.

As early as 1954 Jack Shadbolt had judged Reid to be one of the finest jewellers in the country. What Reid's former teacher called his "costume jewellery" showed how well Native designs could be adapted to contemporary jewellery.[6] Three years later, a reviewer called Reid "the most accomplished jewellery artist and craftsman in British Columbia." Like Shadbolt, who claimed that Reid was the grandson of a Haida chief, the writer for *Western Homes & Living* attributed his "creative spark" to his Native mother, Sophie Gladstone.[7]

Despite the positive reviews, honours, and medals, if Bill Reid was famous in the 1950s, it was not primarily for his own art. Apart from his two weeks with Mungo Martin, he had carved nothing on a large scale. Though he was getting reasonable prices for his jewellery, he was still dependent for inspiration on the work of Charles Edenshaw, of which his *Dogfish Gold Brooch* is the best example.[8] Not surprisingly, by the late 1950s he had become bored

Reid's Dogfish Gold Brooch

working in the Native idiom. In 1957 Reid told a writer for the *Radio Times* that although this period of re-creating Indian handicrafts had been an important and worthwhile stage in his career as a jeweller, he wanted to move into the area of contemporary art.[9] Interviewed a year later by Mary Ann Lash in *Canadian Art*, Reid explained why he had come to this decision. By copying Native designs, he had "reached a dead end for himself at least in Haida jewelry."[10]

Reid's disenchantment with using Native motifs in his jewellery arose from his often-expressed belief that no contemporary Native artist could take the art form beyond the work of Charles Edenshaw or any of the other artists he had put on show in the *People of the Potlatch* and *100 Years of B.C. Art* exhibitions. Reid's wish to join the modernist camp of jewellery makers was also prompted by his exposure to the modern jewellery he was viewing in the craft fairs and, above all, by his encounter with a young jeweller who had recently immigrated to Vancouver from Switzerland.

Reid saw Toni Cavelti's work for the first time in 1956. It was displayed in a window below the city's most avant-garde gallery, the New Design Gallery.

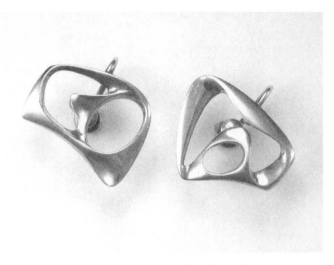

Silver earrings

Cavelti's jewellery ranged from lyrical and organic forms to spiky, linear works that echoed the paintings of the abstract artists who exhibited in the gallery above his shop. Although eleven years younger than Reid, Cavelti had won the Diamonds International Award in New York and had been invited to exhibit in London's prestigious Worshipful Company of Goldsmiths Hall. Convinced that Cavelti had much to teach him, Reid arranged to share work-space in his Burrard Street store. During the ensuing six months, Cavelti helped Reid to construct a perfectly fitting clasp and a necklace that sat per-fectly on the neck of the wearer. Cavelti insists, however, that it was Reid who enriched *his* design skills. Reid did share his small circle of patrons with Cavelti. He introduced him to Jack Shadbolt, Gordon Smith, and other artists in the city. And it was through Reid that Cavelti got to know one of the city's most promising architects, Geoffrey Massey.[11]

It is not surprising that Reid and Cavelti influenced each other's work and formed a life-long friendship. They were both perfectionists; they shared a love of small things; and, above all, they revered the well-made object. But the two men were also different. Cavelti liked to begin early and work a reg-ular day. Having been up late the previous night announcing on the radio, Reid would arrive at Cavelti's shop in the middle of the afternoon, work for a couple of hours, then leave. Reid's attempt to share a bench with Cavelti was short-lived. Within six months, Reid was out and his friend Tak Tanabe was in his place. Cavelti nevertheless left his mark on Reid's work. A pair of beautifully crafted, free-flowing silver earrings, made by Reid in the late 1950s, fulfilled his wish to produce contemporary jewellery, but they owe their inspiration to Cavelti.[12]

Despite his exposure to Cavelti's work, Reid didn't know enough about silver-making techniques to take his work any further. And while he had a large number of friends who were artists, he rarely took an interest in their work. Indeed, Reid's involvement in exhibitions, making films, presenting radio documentaries on Native art and culture, and, when he could find the time, in making jewellery, prompted Toni Cavelti to remark that his friend never gave the impression of being primarily a jeweller, or a carver, or a writer, or a printer, or an intellectual.[13] Reid did not know where he belonged. Although he wanted to work in the contemporary idiom, he had built his reputation at the craft fairs by producing work with Native motifs. This, according to Jack Shadbolt, left him "in a little bit of a philosophic dilemma." He knew that, despite his ability to produce earrings in the modern idiom, he was not a modernist. On the other hand, he knew that he was more than a Native craftsman in the old tradition and more than a curio maker.[14] Above all, as Tak Tanabe recalled, Reid was smart enough and acute enough at this time to know that modern jewellery was not as saleable "as the Indian stuff."[15] So however much Reid wanted to create what he called "original works" in the modern idiom, financial need kept him producing Native work.[16]

During the 1950s Reid was as ambiguous about his relationship with women as he was about his relation to contemporary and Native art. According to one friend, he became increasingly distant from his wife when he discovered that Binkie "was just an ordinary, though attractive, woman without much interest in things cerebral or artistic." Being "a nice person, but dull intellectually" was not enough for Bill. Binkie was aware of Bill's restlessness. (According to Bill's sister Peggy, he was repeatedly unfaithful to his wife.[17]) In fact, she was, the same friend remembered, "going crazy" because she could not figure out why Bill was paying so little attention to her.[18]

Family obligations were not sufficient to keep Bill's relationship with Binkie intact. She obtained a legal separation and moved her daughter, Amanda, and "son," Raymond, to the Queen Charlotte Islands. There she cultivated a friendship that she had earlier established with Bill's Haida cousin, William Stevens. After her divorce from Bill in 1959, Binkie married William.

Though now free to openly pursue his relationships with other women, Bill was not happy with Binkie's move to the Queen Charlotte Islands. After the failure of the *Arts and Handicrafts Show* in 1954, Bill had gone out of his way to dissociate himself from the Native community. He repeatedly told his non-Native friends that, while he admired Native artists from the past, he considered their descendants to be "a bunch of drunks."[19] And while he continued to revere the work of Charles Edenshaw, he felt that contemporary Native artists would do better to learn a trade such as carpentry or mechanics. That his "son" and daughter would be raised in Haida Gwaii could not have pleased him.

～◦⌒◦～

"There was always a charming girl hanging 'round Bill," Tak Tanabe recalled. Reid had no trouble attracting women. He charmed them with his sensuous voice, his non-aggressive laid-back manner, his self-confidence, his philosophical talk, and his good looks. While these attributes might have made him irresistible to most women, they did not make him a constant lover or a faithful husband, as his next wife, Ella Gunn, soon discovered.

Tak Tanabe met Reid's new companion at a party of social workers. Tanabe's former wife, Patricia, was a social worker, and the "blond, tall, and handsome" woman on Reid's arm was in the same profession.[20] Ella Gunn had been married before and that union had produced a daughter. The prospect of having another child to care for was no deterrent and on October 31, 1959 — Reid liked to point out it was Halloween — Ella Gunn became the second Mrs. William Reid. The couple and Ella's pre-teen daughter moved into an apartment in the West End. A few months after their marriage, it became apparent to Reid's friends that he and Gunn were ill-suited. The marriage blew up. And Bill was divorced, for a second time, in 1962. Gunn moved to San Francisco with her daughter, leaving Bill free to embark on a series of relationships with other women.

It was not easy for any female who came within Reid's ambit to put up with his infidelities. Once she discovered how unfaithful her suitor was, she simply pulled out. And there was another problem. Reid's frequent bouts of depression made him difficult to live with, work with, and love. Having an affair — preferably with a WASP — usually brought Reid out of his depression. It also raised his self-worth — for a while. But as soon as he had conquered his new belle, his respect for her vanished, and he set out to find someone else to take her place. His manic-depressive cycle motivated him to work, propelled him into new relationships, then spun him into inertia, self-loathing, and silence.

Dealing with Reid's dramatic mood swings was difficult for all his friends. He nevertheless enjoyed a number of long-term relationships with men. Many of his male companions envied his seemingly easy rapport with women. They were impressed by his silences and, in contrast, by the ease with which he could expound on any topic. Robert Reid enjoyed listening to Bill talk because the things he said were intrinsically interesting. "He wasn't trying to impress you," Robert insisted, "he just had things to say about the things he thought."[21]

With few exceptions, the wives of Reid's male friends were not as enamoured with him as their husbands were. Reid was a man's man — providing his male companion was willing to listen to or tolerate his silences, his mood swings, and his habit of switching from one topic to another in mid-sentence. Conversations with Reid were usually one-sided. If you were not a good listener or not interested in what Reid was saying, you quickly became bored.

Though many of Reid's friends took his interest in Native culture seriously and were willing to sit in companionable silence during his bouts of depression, many considered him to be a dilettante, an experimenter in the idioms of modern and traditional Native art. Creator Reid was not. Salvager, romanticizer, student, and popularizer of traditional west coast Native culture he clearly was. This is where Bill Reid put most of his manic energy during the second half of the 1950s and this is where his reputation lay.

In 1959 Reid's life was given the focus it clearly needed. That February the Canada Council agreed to support the museum's much-revised proposal to build a Haida village on the grounds of the University of British Columbia.

When Harry Hawthorn learned that the Canada Council had finally "yielded to western pressure," he was delighted.[22]

The museum's revised proposal put Reid at the centre of the project. Although his wood-carving experience had been limited to just two weeks, the museum had assured the Canada Council that "his general technical facility and design sense would enable him to carry out this work."[23] Moreover, Reid would have help. The thirty-two-year-old Nimpkish artist Doug Cranmer became a valuable assistant. During his youth Cranmer had watched the carvers Arthur Shaughnessy, Charlie James, and Frank Walker, and after moving to Victoria in the mid-1950s he had been taught by Mungo Martin. Anticipating that the museum's application to the Canada Council would be successful, Reid had telephoned Doug Cranmer in 1958 to ask him if he would join him on the project.

The $15,000 grant, awarded to the university the following year, gave Reid and Cranmer three years in which to duplicate thirty totem poles and house posts. The university agreed to pay for maintenance, accounting, and other services and to supervise the project; the Canada Council would cover the carvers' wages and the cost of their tools and materials. When the news became public, the irony of the Canada Council supporting the re-creation of totem poles that government policy had helped to destroy was not lost on the writer for *Radio Times*: "Bill Reid is assuaging, perhaps, both the white man's burden of guilt and creating a living memory of the arts of the once great nation."[24]

Reid told the story — more than once — of how he learned that the university had been awarded the Canada Council grant. "I read the item about the grant over the air, and after the newscast I phoned Harry. Then I went up to the CBC executive offices and resigned." Reid's story is somewhat telescoped but basically rings true. "It was an amazing act of faith on Hawthorn's part," he continued in his account. "My entire wood-carving career up to then consisted of ten days of partially carving the little man on the pole with Mungo."[25]

Soon after reading the news, Reid presented Harry Hawthorn with a rambling summary of how the project might be realized. The money could be used to duplicate some of the better poles or it could be treated as a first instalment towards the completion of a more ambitious project. The second

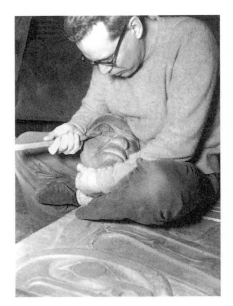

Reid and Douglas Cranmer carving at UBC

option would entail constructing a full-scale house — to double as a theatre-in-the-round — of some forty or fifty square feet, along with a small grave house and a number of poles. Reid suggested two ways in which he and his assistants could make the second option efficient. First, they could have most of the actual work done in the mill. (The carvers would cover the exposed surfaces with adze marks to simulate the real thing after the house had been built.) And second, departing from traditional methods once again, the figures on the totem poles could be roughed out with a power saw. If this procedure were to be followed, it might be best, Reid suggested, to keep tourists and other onlookers away from the site lest they discover that he and his assistants were not using traditional methods.

In the early spring of 1959, Reid resigned from his job at the CBC.[26] He was immediately hired by the university at a salary of $500 a month, plus paid leave. This represented a considerable pay cut. (Reid told a reporter that not only would his annual income fall from $12,000 to $6,000, but he would have to deal with his personal business on his own time.) However great the reduction in salary, Reid got far more than his assistants. On his suggestion they were paid an hourly rate equivalent to the wage of a logger.

Reid would have preferred to work with only Haida artists. In the spring of 1959 he travelled to the Queen Charlotte Islands in search of assistants. But he found only one man: his cousin, Herman Collison, whom he referred to as "an illiterate deaf mute lad of twenty-three." Collison proved to be a good worker, but he possessed no carving skills. Moreover, because promised assistance from the Department of Indian Affairs never came, Collison had to return to the Queen Charlotte Islands after helping to carve only one pole. Although Doug Cranmer was reluctant to carve in the Haida style, he was, in contrast to Collison and Reid himself, a highly skilled carver. And unlike Reid, he did not have to make preparatory drawings. Cranmer could plan everything in his head, "then go ahead and do it."[27]

The first pole that Reid, Cranmer, and Collison carved was a replica of a Haida pole that Reid had seen lying on the floor of the forest at Ninstints and now lay in three decaying fragments at the university's museum. Originally the frontal pole of a community house, the pole was crowned by three watchmen and supported by an eagle, a cormorant, and a thunderbird in a human form. The men began carving a two-thirds replica of this pole in the middle of May 1959. They completed the pole during the first week of August.

It was difficult work. The southern red cedar log that H.R. MacMillan had donated to the university project was too coarse-grained for the demands of fine carving. Reid's patron, Walter Koerner, offered to provide white cedar logs from the Queen Charlotte Islands where, unlike MacMillan, he had logging operations. A strike unfortunately prevented him from doing this immediately. By the time the strike was over and the logs had arrived at the university, the museum had decided that it would be redundant for the carvers to copy another Haida pole. By October 1959, Reid and Cranmer were thus given the freedom to carve a pole of their own design.

The four remaining poles and the double mortuary pole that Reid and Cranmer began to carve were not, therefore, direct copies as originally planned. Rather, they were an amalgamation of whatever crests the two men chose to put together. This marked a departure from traditional Native practices. Most turn-of-the-century Haida artists would never have carved anything but their own crests. Nor would they have sought the assistance of a non-Haida carver. As Reid later admitted, "There were lots of things that happened up there that

Poles and houses outside the Museum of Anthropology

would probably be frowned upon by the people of the past because we included some poles' crests which I suppose would never really be together." Reid felt that he had not done a disservice to the art form because he was working strictly within the stylistic convention of Haida art.[28]

But what, in the end, did Reid and Cranmer create at Totem Park? Certainly not, apart from one work, reproductions of salvaged Haida totem poles. And certainly not totem poles, or grave and community houses that emerged from the history and experiences of the persons for whom they had been carved. Reid and Cranmer produced work that combined figures and other design elements simply because they looked good. This blurring of the distinction between tradition and invention resulted in a modernist adaptation of traditional Haida art.

Working at Totem Park marked an important step in Reid's development as an artist. By combining figures that told no story, by increasing or scaling down figures at will, and by creating work for museum display rather than for ceremony, Reid reinforced his long-held belief that one could and should

Sea Wolf Sculpture, *1962*

approach these works on purely aesthetic grounds. For example, while work-ing at Totem Park he and Cranmer carved *Sea Wolf Sculpture,* a work that was inspired by a memorial figure they had seen in the Provincial Museum.[29] Not satisfied to simply copy the original work, Reid and Cranmer put another whale under the wolf's forepaw and made their carving more naturalistic than the sea wolf in the museum. And, by robbing the original sculpture of its memorial pole plinth, they allowed their sculpture to exist in its own space. While isolating the work from meaning and function clearly put it in a new context, doing so gave the figure the artistic stature that Reid and Cranmer felt it clearly deserved.

Reid often spoke passionately about his tools, most of which he made himself. The curved knife — an adaptation of the traditional Native tool that, unlike a chisel or a mallet, did not chew up green wood — was a favourite. At the same time he appreciated the speed of power tools. It had taken Mungo Martin and his assistants over a week to strip the bark off a log in preparation for carving a pole. The same task had taken Reid and Cranmer a matter of hours. Vancouver's Power Machinery Company, from whom the university purchased its electrical equipment, used this comparison to their advantage: "Do you picture in your mind's eye a noble red man in fur pants and deer-skin, moccasins, hacking at a tree with a stone axe? If so you lose the wampum, friend. To be truthful Bill wears well-cut slacks while plying his ancient craft. Instead of deer-skin moccasins, he wears leather shoes with vinyl soles. And on the day the photographer went around to get Bill's picture carving totems, he found him using — not an ancient stone axe — but a rip-roaring, time-saving PM Canadian chain saw."

When he began the Haida village project, Reid was using a power chain-saw only for bucking. A few weeks into the project, however, he and Cranmer used the chainsaw for all the roughing-out work. This was too much for a Californian film crew who had come to Vancouver to capture Reid on camera. When they heard the buzz of power saw and plane saw, they abandoned the project. (Fortunately for the film crew, they found an artist who was less enamoured with the latest technology. Mungo Martin was making a box without the help of power tools and he became the subject of their film.) The Kwakwaka'wakw chief, Alfred Scow, was equally unimpressed when he visited Reid at the carving shed in Totem Park. To Scow, Reid was still famous for his career in radio. "Why did you leave a good job like that to do this?" "This," Reid replied, "beats working for a living."[30]

Reid revelled in his new job. He liked being out of doors and being his own boss. He enjoyed being surrounded by the weather-silvered totem poles that he and Duff brought to the university from the Queen Charlotte Islands. They evoked the presence of the artists who had carved them. Their frozen stance, which eliminated all movement and expression, made him appreciate what he often referred to as the terrible tension inherent in the most accomplished Haida carvings.

However much Reid had wanted the job, he did not envision carving totem poles and cedar-plank houses for the rest of his life. "It's a never-never land existence spending your time whittling poles and it's not my idea of a permanent occupation," he said. For Reid, carving totem poles was tanta-mount to a contemporary Greek sculptor reproducing statuary in the manner of the ancient Greeks. He was not unappreciative of the experience. Indeed, he hoped to maintain "what is essentially universal and important from this art form and relate it to circumstances of my own century, my own people."[31] But when the Haida village was finished in 1961, he was ready to move in another direction.

Reid had said from the beginning of the project that he was doing the job in order to repay a debt to his ancestors. He had also made it clear that he wanted to return to contemporary jewellery-making. With this in mind, he applied, in 1961, for a Canada Council grant that would allow him to observe and study drawing, craftsmanship, anatomy, and sculpture in Europe. In supporting his application, Harry Hawthorn told the secretary of the Canada Council that "his talent is too big for him to continue to work completely within the existing North West Coast Indian traditions."[32] Had Reid asked for funding to produce totem poles or jewellery decorated with Native motifs, he might, like the artist George Clutesi who worked in the Native idiom, have been successful. While the council was willing to support Native artists, it was not prepared to finance what amounted to Reid's training as a jeweller in the contemporary European tradition.

Although Reid did not receive the grant and had no future prospects of getting a major commission, several things had become clear to him by 1961. Native artists could work within any tribal art form. Native plank houses could be put to non-Native uses, such as a theatre-in-the-round. It was legitimate to scale up small carvings into large monumental works. (This reversed the trend for scaling down totem poles into miniature argillite or wood carvings.) Native art could be produced in the city as well as in distant villages. It was the museum and funding agencies like the Canada Council that would guide, shape, and determine what kind of work would represent contemporary and traditional Native art. And above all, as Reid demonstrated to everyone who worked with him, the Native artist could work to the music of Mozart and treat the museum's curator to a lunch consisting of "a nice group of baskets packed with some cutlery, nice sandwiches with the edges cut off and a bottle of white wine." Audrey Hawthorn recalled that she had never expected to have an "elegant lunch" served to her in the carving shed at Totem Park. But when Bill Reid came onto the scene, this is what she got.[33]

CHAPTER 8

Form Over Function

Silver box, bear and human design

In 1962 it became clear to Reid that he would not receive the funding from the Canada Council that would allow him to study, then pursue, a career as a contemporary jeweller. He therefore put most of his energy into perfecting his jewellery-making skills, adding to his slim knowledge of Haida mythology, and coming to grips with the underlying principles of Haida art.

When Reid set up his jewellery business on a full-time basis in the spring of 1962, he continued to work in silver, and when he could afford it, in gold.

He took enormous pleasure in making the perfectly fitting clasp. In a series of bracelets, produced during the early 1960s, he mimicked the marks left on wood by the blade of the adze by stippling their smooth surface.[1] He also applied his engraving tools to the sides and lids of silver and gold boxes, of which his silver box with a bear and human motif is the best example.[2] All the work that Reid produced during the 1960s demonstrated that he was no longer content simply to copy the work of his mentor, Charles Edenshaw, or of any other artist. As Reid proudly announced in 1965, from now on his designs would remain "within the convention established in Haida art" but, like the combination of figures on the totem poles at the Haida village, they would be "original."[3]

Breaking away from the old forms happened almost by accident. "One day I just did something that didn't relate to the old designs," Reid recalled. "It was quite an amazing experience to look at it and realize that it was not too bad and that I could create, if not new, at least different, interpretations of the old forms."[4] From the early 1960s, Reid knew that working within what he called the "non geometric geometry" of traditional Haida art presented limitations for the artist. The European artist could draw with great sweeping curves; the Native artist had to draw "painfully bit by bit."[5] In 1963 Reid made an argillite panel pipe that incorporated an eagle and a bear prone along the base and a human, a frog, and a killer whale surmounted by a wolf, a raven, and another frog. This, along with other argillite carvings such as the *Killer Whale and Raven* platter, showed the level of originality, dexterity, and sheer virtuosity that Reid was able to achieve at this time.[6] Like his mentor, Charles Edenshaw, Reid was taking the formal and aesthetic components of Haida art to new heights.

Reid did not know many of the stories or myths associated with the creatures he was carving and engraving in argillite and silver. He rationalized this lacuna by claiming that "we don't know the significance of much of the design" and therefore had no hope of getting "back to the genuine stuff."[7] He told his sister, Peggy Kennedy, that he didn't like himself for making what he called "artifakes." Unlike traditional Native carvings, the things that Bill made were, she continued, "just for other people to look at, and he didn't feel it was right."[8]

Killer Whale and Raven *platter*

All this meant that, during the 1960s, Reid's interest in Native art was almost entirely aesthetic or formalist. As one close friend observed, "In the beginning it was just nice designs that he could use."[9] Reid confirmed this view when he told a journalist: "The only criterion must be whether the original Indian designs are being used to create something beautiful."[10]

Bill Reid's obsession with form did allow him to make beautiful, well-crafted objects in the Native idiom. Yet focusing on the look of a work, as I discovered while on a research trip to the west coast of Vancouver Island in 1974, diminished its meaning.

I had come to the Native village near Ucluelet in order to see where Emily Carr had spent a summer during the late nineteenth century with her missionary-sister Elizabeth. The village had, of course, changed since Carr's

Panel pipe, 1963

time. Modest single-family dwellings had replaced massive cedar-plank houses. And the dugout canoes, which Carr had sketched in pen-and-ink and watercolour, had, like any memory of her visit, vanished. While the Nuu-chah-nulth elders appeared to bear little similarity to how Emily Carr had portrayed them, they still possessed a respect for and an interest in Native art. One of the carvings they proudly showed me was a headdress in the shape of a bear's head. It was covered in fur. Thinking the skin to be that of a bear or cougar, I was surprised when the carver told me, "Ladies' coat — Salvation Army." When he sensed my surprise, he continued my lesson in acculturation by revealing the real significance of the carving — its function. "The bear," he said, "dances good."

I did not know that the meaning and function of a work was as important to the Native tradition as its artistic quality — and sometimes more important. I had wrongly chosen to judge the elder's carving according to the aesthetic appeal it had for me. Any other attributes it might have possessed for its owner — prestige or power, physical or spiritual links with an earlier generation, the validation of myths, the distinction of rank, among many other things — had passed me by. I did not even know that there was no word, in any of the Northwest Coast Native languages, equivalent to art or artist.

Doug Cranmer's father, Dan, was worried that the meaning associated with Native art was being lost. When he helped Audrey Hawthorn acquire work for the museum, he insisted it "be real stuff, not imitation." And if she wanted to learn about Native culture, she should, Cranmer told her, attend a potlatch and see for herself.[11]

Meaning was not always uppermost in the minds of the curators who collected Native carvings for their institutions during the 1950s and early 1960s. Audrey Hawthorn based the cash value of an artifact on two things: the age and fineness of the carving and its condition. She discovered the extent to which her criteria were out of sync with Native perceptions when she tried to get an opinion on the artistic merit of a copper — the greatest symbol of wealth among Native Peoples — that the museum had recently acquired. Hawthorn asked an Alert Bay artist, Mr. Johnson, to tell her whether the grizzly bear on the copper was well drawn. Johnson understood Hawthorn's question, but he was less interested in the artistic merit of the copper than in the fact that when he was a child he had seen the copper exchanged for five hundred blankets at a potlatch in Fort Rupert.[12]

Mungo Martin was as concerned as Dan Cranmer that the meaning and function of the objects he had created were dominated by aesthetic not monetary concerns. This is no doubt the reason why he held the elaborate potlatch at Victoria's Thunderbird Park to inaugurate the opening of the Kwakwaka'wakw community house. And why he saw to it that tribes up and down the coast and anthropologists from the Provincial Museum attended the winter ceremony in 1953. What Mungo Martin wanted to do was put the masks, rattles, drums, and other ceremonial objects amid the songs, dramatic re-enactments, movement of the dancers, and flickering light of the fire. His fear that people would not care about the old ways after he had died, and that the art would no longer be used within the ceremonial context, became particularly poignant when his apprentice son drowned in a boating accident. After he had buried David, Mungo Martin handed over his family's dance masks and potlatch regalia to the Provincial Museum.

Martin's own death in 1962 brought the kind of accolades that Bill Reid would receive thirty-six years later. But none of the Natives who attended Martin's magnificent funeral knew the words to the traditional Kwakwaka'wakw mourning song. One of the non-Native mourners, the American Bill Holm, had made a tape recording of Martin singing the required song. Holm produced the tape at the funeral and Mungo Martin sang his own requiem.

∼ɔc⌐ɔ

In 1971 Wilson Duff paid Holm, a Seattle art historian, anthropologist, artist, and museum curator, an enormous compliment when he told a student that Holm "makes better Haida art than any living Haida. He makes better Kwakiutl masks, sings better Kwakiutl songs, and dances better Kwakiutl dances than any Kwakiutl."[13] Not only did Bill Holm dance and sing, he had carved everything from masks and rattles to twenty-foot-long canoes. But it would be for his book *Northwest Coast Indian Art: An Analysis of Form* that Bill Holm would become best known.

By the time *Northwest Coast Indian Art* appeared in 1965, Reid had known its author for a decade.[14] The two men had met at an auction of Native artifacts in Seattle. Reid was not well known at the time, but Holm had heard about him through his friends Mungo Martin and Wilson Duff. Reid had also heard of Holm. By the time they met, the Scandinavian-American's carving skills were legendary among the Native and the non-Native communities of southern British Columbia.

After their initial meeting in Seattle, contact between Reid and Holm was off and on. In 1959 Reid asked Holm to supervise the job on the Haida village project. Although Holm did not take up Reid's offer, the two men subsequently corresponded. Sometimes Holm visited the CBC, where he would marvel at how Reid would slip from music commentator to Northwest Coast art enthusiast without missing a beat. There was always much for the two men to talk about. They had been struggling independently to make sense of what made Northwest Coast art what it was. Shortly after they met, they reinforced each other's findings. Yet it was Holm who was the scholar and Holm who produced a book that would cultivate an appreciation for the art of northern tribes and, by so doing, determine the future development of Native art.

Northwest Coast Indian Art: An Analysis of Form built on earlier attempts made by Franz Boas, Alice Ravenhill, and the German ethnologist Herman Haeberlin to describe the aesthetic principles underlying Northwest Coast art. What Holm did was to create a vocabulary for the design elements found in low-relief carving and two-dimensional painting. Suddenly there was a word for the primary element of Northwest Coast design: the formline. There were words, too, for the ovoids, split U's, and split S's. Holm also wrote intelligently about positive and negative space. He designated primary, secondary, and tertiary areas within any given design. He categorized motifs as configurative, expansive, or distributive. And he produced drawings to illustrate the design units, or elements, that made up Northwest Coast art. Holm's work established the principles of composition that underlay the northern style of Northwest Coast design. Soon after the book's publication, practically every Native carver had a copy of it on the workbench or in the carving shed. As Gitxsan artist Earl Muldoe recalled, Holm's book had "a tremendous impact on a lot of our work."[15]

In 1951 James Houston, a writer, government bureaucrat, and adventurer, produced a manual to show Inuit artists what sort of carvings would be useful and acceptable to the white buyer. The simple line drawings in *Eskimo Handicrafts,* and the carvings that were made by Inuit artists as a result of Houston's illustrations, owed as much to the sculpture of Henry Moore — whose work Houston admired — as to traditional Inuit sculpture.[16] Although Holm's *Northwest Coast Indian Art: An Analysis of Form* was a far more sophisticated study than the manual Houston produced for Baffin Island carvers, it had no less impact on the Native community. It set subsequent standards for the kind of art that Northwest Coast artists would make — and that white patrons would buy. The art should not be bold or garish, like the art of the Kwakwaka'wakw Nation, but simple and sculptural, as seen in the art of the Tsimshian and Haida peoples. And, as with non-representational painting and sculpture, it should elicit an aesthetic response from the viewer. Holm's ideas were derived as much from his knowledge of western graphic design as from his appreciation of Northwest Coast Native art. Wilson Duff's dictum — "When you look at the arts of tribal peoples in situations of acculturation, you should look hard at the dominant culture" — was applicable to Holm's study.[17]

By focusing on the form rather than on the meaning and function of a work of art, Holm had unwittingly undone the efforts of scholars such as Wilson Duff — who, according to Bill Reid, was "trying to uncover the many layers of meaning which he felt surely lay behind the convoluted, complex

Gold Eagle Box

surface patterns of Northwest coast art in all its forms."[18] But Holm's standardization of design and technique, along with his stereotyping of form and
content, left little room for experimentation. Moreover, by basing his analysis
on a small selection of nineteenth-century artifacts produced by northern
artists, Holm had shifted the public's attention away from Kwakwaka'wakw,
Coast Salish, Nuu-chah-nulth, and other tribal groups in central and southern British Columbia. Many of the artists who used Holm's book followed the
examples in it to the letter. "Their work," Doug Cranmer noted, "has come
out all looking the same."[19]

Bill Holm could never have foreseen the enormous impact that a study,
written as an academic exercise for the University of Washington anthropologist Erna Gunther and published several years after its completion, would
have on generations of Native artists. In this sense, an anthropologist of a
later generation was right when he acknowledged the extent to which he and
others in the museum world were helping to manufacture the very artifacts
they were studying.[20]

Holm modestly insists that Bill Reid did not learn anything from
Northwest Coast Indian Art: An Analysis of Form. Indeed, he thanked Reid in

the preface for giving him suggestions and insights. Yet Reid saw things differently. On more than one occasion he acknowledged his debt to what he called Holm's "handy-dandy do-it-yourself Indian art book."[21] Certainly, following the book's publication, the motifs that Reid engraved on his gold and silver jewellery lost their rigidity. And, while Reid was still taking his cue from Charles Edenshaw as demonstrated by comparing his *Gold Eagle Box* with Edenshaw's *Bear Mother* argillite compote dish, he was working in a different material (silver), in a different form (a box), and in a different method (casting).[22] By becoming more receptive to the idea of experimentation, Reid was showing how contemporary jewellery-making techniques could be brought together with traditional Native designs to produce something new and exciting.

Holm's book also prompted Reid to refine his knowledge of the structural elements underlying Northwest Coast Native motifs first presented to him in Franz Boas's *Primitive Art.* But understanding these things was only the first step, according to Reid, in making art. "What happens after that depends on the personality of the artist, the talent and genius — if you want — that he brings to it, the devotion and most of all the emotional energy which he manages to infuse into it." [23] Most important of all, Holm had helped Reid answer a number of rhetorical questions that Wilson Duff had posed in relation to contemporary Northwest Coast art. Was it an art form in search of a reason to justify its own existence? Was it a medium without a message? And if this was the case, was contemporary Northwest Coast art all form with little substance and content? After absorbing Holm's seminal work, Reid was able to answer these questions by replying that "it's very easy and perfectly correct to say, sure, most of it is."[24]

Reid kept the wolf from the door after completing the Haida village by taking on a number of short-term projects. In 1962 he carved a totem pole for the Vancouver Parks Board. (It was a replica of a pole that had been moved from Skedans to Vancouver's Stanley Park in 1936.) A year later, he carved a pole for the London head office of Shell Oil and a bear sculpture for Walter Koerner.[25] Koerner also commissioned Reid to travel to the Queen Charlotte

Islands to look for salvageable totem pole fragments that would be suitable for display in the University of British Columbia's museum. After Reid returned to Vancouver, Wilson Duff and Colin Graham, curator of the Art Gallery of Greater Victoria, invited him to design a memorial plaque to honour Mungo Martin. Responding to their instructions to create something different in concept and form from the work on display in Victoria's Thunderbird Park, Reid submitted drawings, for which he was paid fifty dollars. Due to the theft of the money that had been raised by public subscription for its execution, the silver plaque, based on Reid's design, was not completed until 1966, when it was installed in the Provincial Museum.

Though Reid had left the CBC in 1959, he maintained his connections with the broadcasting industry in order to supplement his precarious income. In June 1962 he contributed to the corporation's two-part *Explorations* television series devoted to the Haida. A year before that, he had written and narrated a radio documentary for the CBC on the history of the Skeena River. In "River of Clouds," Reid brought the recollections of Natives, traders, pioneers, and missionaries together with the sounds of the river. His voice-pictures of the Skeena show his evocative writing, dramatic presentation, and sonorous baritone voice at their best. "At first the river is brown and deep and the reaches are long and patterns of cloud puff and whirl against the dark mountain side," Reid began, "but gravelly streams drain the juices and the sun glimmers on the bends and the islands come — one or two, then ten, twenty, plumed with cotton-wood trees that are sheered like giant hedges, and there the water runs swiftly in cloudy channels."[26] Reid might just as easily have been describing the seventy-mile-long fjord, the Portland Canal, that led to his boyhood town as describing the banks of the Skeena River, where Sophie Gladstone had taught school and met her husband, Billy Reid, in the second decade of the century. It would have been obvious to anyone listening to the program that the narrator had a first-hand acquaintance with the sounds, smells, look, and history of the northern landscape and its people — even though Reid insisted on calling Victoria his hometown.

☙❧

After his divorce from Ella Gunn in 1962, Reid lived a peripatetic life in Vancouver, moving from West Broadway to Burrard Street in the West End, then to a ramshackle building on Dunsmuir, and eventually to 1156 West Pender Street. Here, in a low wood building in the centre of downtown Vancouver that overlooks Stanley Park, Coal Harbour, and Grouse and Hollyburn mountains, Reid's studio and living quarters are still well remembered by a number of people.

Reid believed, as he later wrote, that "if you produce a good product you will find that people appreciate it."[27] Yet, as he told the young art student Einor Vinge, the salesman artist needed to remember that "it isn't how good you are at what you do; it's who you know."[28] Cultivating clients was important, because a jeweller could not sell precious jewellery cheaply. The once shy and withdrawn Reid proved to be a masterful salesman. He made friends with his clients — when he had completed a work, he invited them to his studio. After unveiling a new piece, Reid treated his audience to his own variety of pancakes, fried oysters, and spiked milkshakes, which he mixed in a five-gallon pail and stirred with an electric drill. He entertained his guests with his talk, skipping from one subject to another in mid-sentence, keeping his listeners slightly off-guard. He played Haydn's trumpet concerto, and songs by Bob Dylan and Joan Baez. Audrey Hawthorn felt that visiting Reid in his studio was very much like going to some secret society because the men and women who attended the unveilings wore gorgeous gold and silver medallions, rings, and lapel pins all fashioned by Reid. "Everyone was in a very happy humour," Hawthorn recalled, "because it was obvious [that] Bill was prospering as a new jeweller."[29]

No matter how good a cook, or how charming or challenging a conversationalist, though, Reid was not making the kind of money he had earned as a radio announcer by selling work from his Pender Street studio. In 1962, things did improve when Doug Cranmer opened The Talking Stick, with Peter Scow, the first Native-run craft shop in the province. Reid probably sold his jewellery through this outlet in Vancouver, and in 1965, when Mrs. A.H. Bessie FitzGerald, an entrepreneur involved in the arts, established a third branch of her Victoria-based crafts business in Vancouver, Reid became her star exhibitor.

Begun in 1949 as the Wagon Wheel, re-christened in 1952 as The Quest for Handicraft Ltd., FitzGerald's business provided an outlet for people who worked in both the Native and Euro-Canadian traditions. Trained as an agent for the Canadian Guild of Crafts in Montreal, then employed by the Hudson's Bay Company as a buyer of Inuit art, she was the first person in British Columbia to market "Eskimo" prints. FitzGerald was very demanding of her artists, which kept standards high and earned the store a reputation for stocking "top-quality" all-Canadian products.

Bill Reid respected the high standards that FitzGerald imposed on all her artists. He supplied her with dozens of rings, brooches, and bracelets — all decorated with Native motifs. He also produced more time-consuming items: from silver boxes in two-dimensional relief to six-foot-high totem poles. He made diminutive replicas of large wooden sculptures; he cast cufflinks and earrings from handmade wax models. He decorated non-traditional objects, such as cigarette lighters, with Native motifs. And he even took on less orthodox commissions — for example, he designed chandeliers in a spare modernist style, reminiscent of Toni Cavelti's jewellery, for the Union Club in Victoria.

Most of the work Reid produced for The Quest fell into the category of handicrafts. Unlike his grandfather, Charles Gladstone, he rarely signed his name on these items. Most simply bore the words "Haida Art." Bill usually worked to order, producing only what FitzGerald thought she could sell. "If you'd like to send me a list of stuff you'd like in order of priority," he told her in 1965, "I'll try to follow it in future shipments."[30]

Producing work of respectable quality at a low price is a challenge that every artist who sells his or her work through a craft shop has to deal with. The Quest was not an art gallery, so FitzGerald could not ask art gallery prices. This made things difficult for artists like Bill Reid, for whom labour and materials were often well beyond what the market could bear. Fearing, in retrospect, that the work he produced for The Quest had sometimes been well below his standard, Reid told a friend that he was to flatten anything he came across bearing the words "Haida Art."[31]

However, Reid rarely lowered his standards in order to keep down production costs. "I tried to do it as cheaply as possible, which accounts in part for the technique," he told FitzGerald in 1965. "However it didn't work too well and I realized I'd have to take a loss."[32] On another occasion he felt that the asking price for a silver box — the price was $225 — was more than the handicraft market could bear. He found a solution by offering to split the markup with FitzGerald. "Feel free to make any adjustments," he told FitzGerald in April 1965.[33]

FitzGerald was sometimes tardy in reimbursing Reid for his work. When this happened, he showed that he could be tolerant, if characteristically ironic. "In my chronic hand to mouth existence if my hand is a little slow getting to my mouth I go very hungry and all the little people who depend on me, small struggling firms like the Bank of Montreal, the BC Hydro, the HBC, etc. start sending me even more pitiful appeals than this one," he wrote on one occasion. "I'm in no position to worry too much about terms just now," he continued on a more serious note. "Pay me whatever you think the box is worth if you want it at all."[34] Though payment from FitzGerald for a silver box or a gold brooch sometimes came long after Reid had to meet the cost of labour and materials, she never failed to pay him in the end.

If Bill had been able to sell his work in an art gallery — like the Ojibwa painter Norval Morriseau, who had his first major exhibition in Toronto in the early 1960s, or like the fifty-six-year-old Kwakwaka'wakw artist Henry Speck (Ozistalis), whose work sold at the New Design Gallery in Vancouver — he would have found it easier to keep "the small struggling firms" at bay.[35] Reid was not, however, producing canvases or prints for display in an art gallery. Even if he had been, he could not have passed the "genuine Indian" litmus test that made Torontonians pay enormous sums of money for the work of Morriseau, whom the critics could claim was "by the accident of isolation . . . a painter untouched and uninhibited."[36] Unlike Morriseau, Reid had more than grade four education, and he had not lived in a remote Ontario settlement with no electricity or telephone. Above all, Reid had not been raised on a reserve.

By the late 1960s, thanks largely to Bill Holm, Bill Reid had resolved his creative dilemma better than his commercial quandary. His problem was that he and his work were too sophisticated and too expensive to realize a true profit from craft-shop prices. At the same time, his work was not suitable for exhibition in an art gallery or in a jewellery store. This must have made Reid ask himself: "Am I an artist, a craftsman, or a high-street jeweller?"

CHAPTER 9

Return of the Raven

Robert Davidson

Bill Reid was aware that his success entailed building — and allowing others to build for him — a national reputation as an artist. By the late 1950s, his involvement in exhibitions and television programs had earned him some celebrity as a specialist of Native peoples and their art.

Thanks to Bessie FitzGerald's and Reid's own marketing skills, a small group of collectors were, from the 1960s, committed to buying his work on a regular basis. The making of the Haida village, along with the frequent donation of his work to the University of British Columbia's anthropological museum, made curators there realize that it was not only the Kwakwaka'wakw who were keeping Native art alive, but also the Haida — and one Haida in particular.

Reid was not, of course, the only artist of Haida descent making art. There were many artists of his grandfather's generation still producing work in Skidegate. And there was a younger generation of artists based in Old Masset, of whom Robert Davidson was the most prominent.

Davidson was born in Hydaburg, Alaska, in 1946 but spent his childhood in Old Masset at the northern end of the Queen Charlotte Islands. The great-grandson of Charles Edenshaw, Davidson was more closely related to Edenshaw than Reid was. (Bill Reid was his great-great nephew.) In 1965 Robert Davidson left Haida Gwaii in order to complete his high school education. He arrived in Vancouver with a minor reputation as a carver of small argillite totem poles. When he was seventeen, the National Film Board of Canada had called him one of the Haida Nation's most promising artists in a short documentary devoted to his work, *Haida Carver* (1963).

Reid was curious about the young artist from Old Masset and in 1966 sought him out at Eaton's department store where, in his spare time, Davidson earned extra money by demonstrating his carving skills. Davidson has often recalled his first encounter with Reid. As he was working, he heard a voice at his shoulder. The person speaking to him identified himself as Bill Reid. "I wanted to crawl under the table," Davidson recalled, "I was just so intimidated."[1] Reid invited the young man to drop into his Pender Street studio. Davidson was too shy to take up the invitation, and it was only because of a chance meeting some months later at the funeral of the first minister of Haida ancestry, Reverend Peter Kelly, that Davidson encountered Reid again. This time Reid took the nineteen-year-old artist directly to his studio. Learning of his wish to study art, Reid offered to help him enrol at the Vancouver School of Art. When this proved difficult to arrange, Reid took Davidson on as an apprentice. The Department of Indian Affairs provided grants and subsidies to enable status Natives to further their education.

Davidson applied for a grant to cover his living expenses. He was successful and became Reid's apprentice. After a few months of working with Reid, Davidson moved into the Pender Street apartment-studio. He remained there for one year, then enrolled at the Vancouver School of Art.

Reid often boasted that he was the only person producing Native jewellery at the time. In his contradictory fashion, he also acknowledged the emergence of a new generation of Native artists, though he feared that they were being crowded out by the white artists who were working in the Native idiom. Reid hoped that, by supporting young artists like Robert Davidson, he would raise the standards of contemporary Native art and offer a challenge to white carvers, like his good friend Bill Holm, who seemed to be doing better work than almost anybody else.[2]

Robert Davidson was not Reid's first student. In 1956 he had taken on the Coast Salish Native artist Arnold Phillips as an apprentice. The same year, he had taught an extension course in elementary jewellery-making at the University of British Columbia. Throughout the 1960s, he would offer more courses under the auspices of the Community Arts Council, local elementary and secondary schools, and the Vancouver School of Art. Even though Reid described himself in the Vancouver business directory as a teacher, he never considered himself to be one. In fact, his idea of teaching was to let the student hang around his studio.

This method of learning suited Davidson. He watched Reid make his own tools. He learned how to handle needle-nose pliers, a quarter-inch drill, and a curved knife — all by observing Reid. A few months into his apprenticeship, Reid put him into a separate room and said, "Now design a bracelet." Davidson worked on the silver bracelet for four days, during which Reid made frequent inspections of his work. If the bracelet was more than a sixteenth of an inch out, he sent Davidson back to the bench.

Davidson's apprenticeship was not limited to making jewellery. Reid encouraged him to study the anthropological collections of Northwest Coast art that were housed in the city's museums. He introduced Davidson to the writings of anthropologists such as Franz Boas. He taught him the importance of actively, and even aggressively, promoting his work. Davidson learned how to woo museum curators, gallery dealers, newspaper critics, private collectors, and the public in general. He also learned how to survive in the city. Reid introduced Davidson to fine wine, French cooking, and classical music. By the example of his own life, Reid showed Davidson how it was possible to listen to Mozart, eat good food, and drink fine wine without losing his credibility as a Native artist. This was among Reid's greatest gifts to the many Native artists who came within his ambit: he showed them that it was perfectly legitimate for a Native artist to live in two worlds.

Reid and Davidson were different in many ways. Davidson had started carving totem poles in wood and argillite at the age of thirteen. Reid had not begun making jewellery until he was in his late twenties. Davidson had been taught by Native artists, first by his grandfather, Robert Davidson Sr.; then by his father, Claude; and, shortly before meeting Reid, he had worked with Doug Cranmer. Reid, by contrast, had learned almost everything he knew about Native art from books, from anthropologists, and by looking at the artifacts in local museums.

The two men differed in yet another way: in their relationship to the Queen Charlotte Islands and to the Haida people. Davidson was a status Indian and very much aware of being Native. When, as a child, he had occasion to enter a white home he had always felt dirty, "as if I should take my shoes off and wipe them clean."[3] Reid was certainly not stigmatized by poverty, low educational expectations, poor job prospects, or any of the other problems that status Natives had to face on a daily basis. He had chosen, during his years at the CBC in Toronto, when to identify himself as a Native. He had spent most of his life in cities. And he felt more at home in that world than on the Queen Charlotte Islands. He was known in Skidegate as Sophie Gladstone's son or as the man who had read the news on the radio. In 1963 an anthropologist doing fieldwork in Old Masset told Wilson Duff that Reid was "in bad odour." This was partly because Reid's ancestors came from Old Masset's rival village, Skidegate. But it was largely because they considered him to be white.[4]

No one was in any doubt as to which community Robert Davidson belonged in.

"I feel I come from the reserve situation; I have a fairly good understanding of reserve people who have lived in their homeland and hardships that we've gone through. I'm not saying that Bill didn't go through these hardships. He was different — but there's a definite difference. Bill had a talent and a connection to a broader audience, [and] he had intelligence, working with the media . . . whereas people on a reserve are a lot more sheltered, you know, not so trusting because so much trust has been taken away from us because of all of the broken promises, because of losing so much of our culture and who we are."

Reid's and Davidson's approaches to their work were as different as their experience of Native life. Davidson respected Reid's wish to make beautiful things. By contrast, he was willing to sacrifice beauty if it meant pushing the margins of the traditional Native art form to a new boundary. His delight in experimenting did not make him the lesser artist of the two men. In fact, Davidson eventually became a better designer than Reid. And, although in the future he produced work for the white marketplace, Davidson was staunchly committed to seeing his work used in a ceremonial context. When Davidson later put more and more energy into reviving Haida songs and dances, Reid accused him of "playing Indian."[5]

During the time that Davidson was Reid's student, however, Reid was very solicitous and protective of his young protegé. There were other people who wanted to study with him, but Reid did not find anyone as compatible as Davidson. Feeling the loss of Raymond, who had been officially adopted by William Stevens, Binkie's husband, Reid told Davidson that he wished he were his son (though admittedly Reid subsequently told at least two other young men the same thing).[6]

Throughout his career, Reid formed strong working relationships with younger men. He did not regard them as competitors, still less as equals. He did not allow them to be as talkative as he was. What he wanted were pupils, helpers, and disciples: men who were willing to listen to his lengthy monologues that were inspired by his strong didactic urge. As Robert Bringhurst observed after Reid's death, his friend "knew that he knew a lot of things that other people didn't know and he liked to share them."[7] This is precisely what Reid did with the young male apprentices, assistants, housemates and companions who moved in and out of his life.

∽∘᪶∾

Reid was very busy during the year that he took on Davidson as an apprentice. He was teaching part-time at the Vancouver School of Art. He was in the midst of completing several public commissions associated with the forth-coming centennial celebrations: *Gold Box* for the Indians of Canada Pavilion at Expo 67 in Montreal; *Laminated Cedar Screen* for the new British Columbia Provincial Museum in Victoria; and a jacket design for the book *British Columbia: A Centennial Anthology.*[8] There were also a number of private commissions to be completed — a slate and silver box for the retiring head of the British Broadcasting Corporation and in 1966 a pair of oak doors, with a marine motif, for the home of the collector Lois Spence. There were orders to be filled for Bessie FitzGerald. And, in 1965, there were illustrations to be drawn for Christie Harris's book *Raven's Cry.*

Although reluctant to take on the project, when Reid read Harris's man-uscript dealing with the Edenshaw family, he told the author, "That's not bad. I'll illustrate it."[9] Harris had used two sources in writing her account of the Edenshaw family: information she had absorbed while living in Prince Rupert and the writings of anthropologists. She also admitted to drawing on her vivid imagination — "I make most of my work a little fictional."[10]

The drawings that Reid produced to illustrate Harris's text owed much to the illustrations that the Prairie wood-cut artist Walter J. Phillips had pro-duced for Marius Barbeau's 1928 publication *The Downfall of Temlaham.* Equally helpful to Reid were the printing techniques — the use of a bold out-line and cross-hatching, the juxtaposition of straight and curved lines, and the superimposing of one image on another — that he had acquired during his collaboration, in the 1950s, with the designer Robert Reid. Yet Reid's drawings of Natives presenting gifts to Captain Cook and his montages of swirling canoes are unimaginative. The drawing is stiff. The blending of line and tone is uncertain. And the inclusion of two Iroquois false face masks in a book dealing with the Haida is risible. But most reviewers, such as Jacqueline Hooper of the *Vancouver Sun,* were unaware of these inconsistencies. For Hooper, Reid's illustrations, and indeed all of his work, embodied a great sense of power and beauty.[11]

The most interesting illustration that Reid produced for *Raven's Cry* was a self-portrait.[12] In the foreground lie the tools of the carver's trade: an elbow adze, a wedge, and a curved knife. (Reid did not include the power saw that had been his most valuable tool during the construction of the Haida village.) In the

Reid carving pair of oak doors, 1966

middle ground of the drawing, Reid portrays himself carving a totem pole. Above him are the ghosts of his Haida ancestors and possibly of Edenshaw himself. Superimposed over these ghost-like figures are the totem poles that once dominated the villages in Haida Gwaii. Harris reinforced Reid's visual depiction of his place in the hierarchy of Haida art by including his name in the Edenshaw family tree. She wrote: "The ghost of the greatest of all Haida artists simply moved into his great-grand-nephew's workshop." Reinforcing his ancestral links with Haida Gwaii's most famous artist, Reid wrote towards the end of the book that "Great Uncle Charles is my super-ego."[13]

This was an important claim for Reid to make. The right to become a carver was not entirely based on skill, but on an artist's status in Haida society. Charles Edenshaw's high-ranking position in the community had given him the right to be trained as an artist and initiated into the secret societies.

By establishing his lineage to Edenshaw, Reid was announcing that he had an ancestral right to produce work of equal distinction. Reid thus assuaged his concern about working in an art form that, in his view, had lost most of its meaning and had reached its peak long before he appeared on the scene.

ᑎᔕᐁᔕ

Following the publication of *Raven's Cry,* Reid had a chance to raise his public profile as an expert on Native art once again. In 1967 he became involved in the Vancouver Art Gallery exhibition *Arts of the Raven: Masterworks by the Northwest Coast Indian.* This gave him an opportunity to make a few dollars — he had not received a regular income since completing the Haida village for the University of British Columbia in 1962. It also gave him a chance to travel — he had not done much since moving to Vancouver. And, most important of all, his participation in the exhibition allowed him to exhibit his own work.

In their capacity as consultants for *Arts of the Raven,* Reid and his friends Bill Holm and Wilson Duff chose the work for the exhibition. They travelled throughout North America to visit collections of Northwest Coast art from which they selected masks, rattles, bentwood boxes, pipes, and other items that conformed to their artistic sensibility. At the Smithsonian Institution in

Bill Reid with bentwood dish

Gold and silver bracelets

Washington, D.C., for example, Reid was thrilled to discover a thirty-foot totem pole that had been removed from the village of Tanu. And when he pointed a flashlight at a grimy object housed in a storage vault at the American Museum of Natural History in New York, he found, to his delight, the Alaskan Tlingit bentwood dish that Franz Boas had illustrated and written about in *Primitive Art.*[14]

The late nineteenth-century dish was badly worn and covered with greasy dirt. Reid removed the grime with his handkerchief and exposed the marvellous design. The paint was too faded to be photographed, so Reid made a drawing of the design that covered all four sides of the dish. When he returned to Vancouver, he scaled up his drawing, then transferred it onto four two-metre-high panels. A special room was set aside for the display of the original dish, and Reid's panels were used as a backdrop. During the course of visiting other museums in preparation for *Arts of the Raven,* Reid found more work by this artist. These discoveries convinced Reid that only a small number of artists, such as the anonymous "Master of the Black Field," had produced exceptional work.

Reid did not want to include work by living artists in *Arts of the Raven*, but his fellow curators persuaded him to change his mind. He submitted thirteen works. Among them were pendants, brooches, boxes, and bracelets made out of gold and silver with abalone inlay. A platter, a totem pole, and a panel pipe — all made out of argillite — along with a wolf mask and a large crouching bear made an impressive display of work. Reid demonstrated, in gallery eight which Wilson Duff called "The Art Today," that he was as comfortable working in gold and silver as he was in wood, argillite, and ivory. Above all, Reid showed that he could work on any scale.

Reid commissioned his friends Doug Cranmer and Robert Davidson — whom *Time* magazine called "the most promising young Haida artist in the show" — to produce five works each for "The Art Today" section of the exhibition.[15] Following a visit to the Provincial Museum, he added three more works by the Victoria-based Kwakwaka'wakw artists Tony and Henry Hunt. He also invited Doris Khyber-Gruber, a non-Native weaver of Chilkat blankets, and three American artists — Bill Holm, Don Lelooska Smith, a Cherokee who worked in the Northwest Coast style, and Michael Johnson — to submit work to the contemporary section of the exhibition.

The exhibition was the brainchild of the Vancouver Art Gallery's director, Richard Simms. But it was Jack Shadbolt's wife, Doris, the recently appointed curator, who did most of the work. She had long been interested in the relationship between Native art and contemporary painting. In 1947 she had written in *Canadian Art* that western artists could learn much from the formal organization, the emotional expressiveness, the simplicity of form, and the truth that was to be found in "the untutored naive qualities of primitive art."[16]

By the mid-1960s, Shadbolt no longer referred to Native art as primitive. As she made clear in the foreword to the *Arts of the Raven* catalogue, it was high art not ethnology.[17]

Everyone associated with *Arts of the Raven* shared this view: the exhibits were not to be treated as artifacts, crafts, or tourist curios. They were fine art objects. This is how the organizers encouraged the public to view the exhibition, which took up 12,900 square feet of the gallery's exhibition space and lasted throughout the summer of 1967. This is also how the critics, from the *Vancouver Sun* to the *New York Times*, wrote about the show.[18] And yet the curators did not display the work as fine art. Most of the exhibits were clustered into groups according to type or medium — masks, small sculptures, flat design, and argillite. Some of the work on show was illuminated by shafts of dim light or by flickering shadows. And piped-in music followed the viewer from one gallery to the next. Surely no exhibition of western paintings and sculpture would have been subjected to this kind of *son et lumière.*

The catalogue accompanying the exhibition was almost as impressive as the items on display. In his essay, Bill Holm presented a highly condensed version of his recently published treatise on west coast Native art. Wilson Duff compiled the catalogue entries and wrote two essays. One gave a short history of Native peoples. The other focused on the work of Charles Edenshaw. It was the largest collection of Edenshaw's work exhibited to date. Sixty-six objects including massive house posts, delicate argillite carvings, silver bracelets, and walking sticks — some of which have subsequently been attributed correctly to other artists — dominated the exhibition.

Bill Reid's essay was more personal than the ones by Holm and Duff. In it he established his credentials: "For two decades now I have lived intimately with the strange and beautiful beasts and heroes of Haida mythology, and learned to know them as part of myself, and through their powerful realizations in the high art of the Indian past, perhaps to know something of the people who at one time shared this intimacy." He asked his reader to remember that the faded, and often cracked, works on show were once "objects of bright pride, to be admired in the newness of their crisply carved lines, the powerful flow of sure elegant curves and recesses — and yes, in brightness of fresh paint." They had been created according to rules and conventions so strict that it might seem that any individual expression must be stifled. But, Reid continued, it was the very tension between the rules and the artist's own imagination that produced the latent energy that made every object appear to be inhabiting its own frozen universe.[19]

Reid had never written so evocatively about Native art. Nor had he previously made such public claims for his own understanding of Native art and culture. No one challenged his suggestion that those viewers who possessed a sound comprehension of European art would find a deeper meaning in the art on display than the artists who had created the work. No one asked why

Reid's carvings and jewellery dominated the contemporary section of the show. And no one asked why he had included three non-Native artists in the contemporary section of the exhibition. (Perhaps anticipating trouble, Reid took pains in his essay to establish Bill Holm's right to produce Native art.[20])

By 1967, Mungo Martin and his son David were both dead. Reid's former rival in Vancouver, Ellen Neel, had died a year earlier. But there were living artists whose work Reid chose not to include in "The Art Today" section of the exhibition. Haida artists Pat Dixon, Rufus Moody, and Pat McGuire, who had been working in silver and argillite for over a decade, were not represented. Watson Williams, George Clutesi, Alex Julian, and Raymond and Howard Williams, who had been equally productive, were left out because the exhibition focused largely, though not exclusively, on northern tribes. (These artists belonged to the Nuu-chah-nulth and Coast and Interior Salish Nations in southern British Columbia.) The work of the prominent Kwakwaka'wakw artist, Willie Seaweed, who died a few weeks after the exhibition opened, was excluded from gallery eight for the same reason. However, the work of these, and of many other contemporary Native artists, could be viewed in four venues within walking distance of the Vancouver Art Gallery. Indeed, Jacqueline Hooper made the work shown in these alternative exhibitions the subject of an article in Seattle's *Post-Intelligencer.* While "the culture which produced the master-works of the past may be dead," she wrote in the summer of 1967, "the unique form in Northwest coastal art is very much part of the present, to be repeated and appreciated by all — Indian and non-Indian alike."[21]

When *Arts of the Raven* closed at the end of the summer and the 546 exhibits were returned to their owners, the organizers took a deep bow. They had done something that previous curators at the Vancouver Art Gallery had failed to do. They had convinced the public that work produced by Northwest Coast artists should be treated as works of art, not as museum artifacts or crafts or tourist curios. And they had shown, through the work in gallery eight, that Native art was not dead and had not been completely absorbed into the culture of the dominant white society.

Much of the success of *Arts of the Raven* was due to timing. The exhibition coincided with the hundredth anniversary of Canada's birth. The centennial year 1967 had to be commemorated and, from the Vancouver Art Gallery's point of view, there was no better way to do it than by showing work that would speak to the whole province (and to the whole country). If they had devoted the centennial exhibition to the leading art movement of the day, non-representational painting, it would have been controversial. While some commentators insisted that the visual language of modernist painting had paved the way for the public's appreciation and acceptance of Native artifacts as art, non-representational painting was not a popular art form among the general public. Nor was it indigenous to British Columbia. (Art critics omitted Vancouver from their discussions as to which city, New York or Montreal, had fathered non-representational painting.)

Perhaps the most important factor in the positive reception of *Arts of the Raven* was the political and social climate of the 1960s. There was the example of the American civil rights movement to the south. There was the shocking revelation that thirty-eight percent of Canada's Native population were on relief and that the majority of those who were employed earned less than $2,000 a year. Plays such as George Ryga's *The Ecstasy of Rita Joe* (1966) and exhibitions such as the Native-curated *Indians of Canada* at Expo 67 made Canadians aware of, if not sympathetic to, Native peoples' wish to achieve economic, social, and political parity with the rest of the country. The Native way of life also offered the younger generation of Canadians a challenge to the dominant culture, to technology, and to urbanization. And, finally, the belief that Native peoples lived somehow closer to nature made anthropologists and members of the counter-culture alike admire Native shamanistic beliefs and their intuitive forms of wisdom.

Reid's domination of the contemporary section of the exhibition established his reputation as the leading Native artist in British Columbia. The presentation of his work to the thousands of people who viewed the exhibition created a demand for his work. His role as a consultant had reinforced his acquaintances with local collectors such as Walter Koerner and his brother Otto. At the gala dinner on the opening night, Reid had met the director of the National Gallery of Canada, Jean Sutherland Boggs, Lieutenant-Governor George Pearkes, and the city's mayor, Tom Campbell. And, by the time the exhibition closed, Reid had become better acquainted with Bill Holm, Wilson Duff, Audrey and Harry Hawthorn, and Doris Shadbolt. It struck at least one Native observer that these were very powerful people. As Marcia Crosby later pointed out, "Most aboriginal people didn't circulate in these circles."[22] By the end of 1967, however, Bill Reid clearly did.

∽∘ᗗ

In the process of working with Reid on *Arts of the Raven,* Wilson Duff, who had left the Provincial Museum and joined the faculty of anthropology at the University of British Columbia, suggested that they collaborate on a book dealing with northern Native art. Duff's proposal gave Reid a reason to apply, once again, to the Canada Council for an arts fellowship. Unlike his unsuccessful application six years earlier, this time he hedged his bets by offering to do several things.[23] During the course of his year-long fellowship, he would view and photograph Northwest Coast Native art in museums and galleries throughout Europe. (This would form the basis of the research for the book that he planned to write with Wilson Duff.) And when he was not on the road doing research, he would carry out "experimental and practical" tasks relating to contemporary jewellery-making at London's Central School of Art and Design.

In his application, Reid asked several people to support his claim that, apart from Mungo Martin, he was the most important Native artist in the province. Describing him as "a man of the world," Harry Hawthorn assured the Canada Council that Reid was capable of "searching out examples of Native North West Coast art in European museums." Reid's second referee, Wilson Duff, echoed Hawthorn's praise. To him Reid was an uncommonly perceptive and articulate man whose articles and scripts on Native art commanded a great deal of respect. Reid's third referee, the industrialist Walter Koerner, had helped fund the construction of the Haida village at the University of British Columbia and contributed, with other members of the Koerner family, to the mounting of *Arts of the Raven.* Though unable to comment in detail on the applicant's artistic merits, Koerner could claim with assurance that if the council supported Reid, it would be making an excellent investment in Canadian talent.[24]

Reid's referees had a personal interest in seeing him succeed. Hawthorn and Koerner were important patrons, and Duff was Reid's co-author on the proposed study of Northwest Coast art. Sensing this lack of impartiality, the Canada Council asked the former curator of the Vancouver Art Gallery, R.N. Hume, to assess Reid's application. Hume, who had got to know Reid through both the *Arts and Handicrafts Show* and *People of the Potlatch* exhibitions, was spare in his praise. Though he acknowledged Reid's expertise in the area of Native art, he wondered where his loyalties lay. Was it in the area of anthropology, or design, or art? Had Reid not perhaps spread himself somewhat thinly over these areas? Hume was prepared to support Reid's application only if he promised to adopt a more "singular pursuit into the world of design and craftsmanship."[25] This was a tall order for someone who did not know whether he was a craftsman or a fine artist, whether he preferred to make jewellery in the Native or contemporary idiom, or whether to simply write and talk about Native art.

During Reid's participation in *Arts of the Raven*, the press and the Vancouver Art Gallery had referred to him as a "noted Haida carver."[26] But when he was awarded the $7,000 Canada Council arts fellowship in 1968, this perception of him changed. There were only six senior grant recipients the year Reid received his award. With Fritz Brandtner, Claude Tousignant, Guido Molinari, Alan Jarvis, and Joyce Wieland for company, Reid was no longer just a craftsman, or a working jeweller, or even a Haida carver. He had joined the world of fine art as an artist.

CHAPTER 10

Setbacks

I n the spring of 1968, a local television station in Vancouver made a short documentary film about a red cedar screen that Bill Reid had recently carved for the new Provincial Museum in Victoria.[1] The film crew took a novel approach to the subject. They set the screen in the middle of the forest. Then, as Reid emerged from the tangle of trees and underbrush, the camera began to roll. After being introduced by an off-screen announcer, Reid made a half-hearted attempt to recount the myths associated with the raven, fisherman, bear mother, sea wolf, eagle, and frog, among the other creatures depicted on the screen.[2] "What is it all about?" he asked. "Oh, about the people, about me, a few half-remembered legends — badly transcribed by me into my only language, English. There is an eagle and a frog," he continued, "and there has got to be some story about them but I don't know one." Reid could recall only fragments of the myth relating to the raven who had cuckolded the fisherman. He did, however, know something about the contents of the fisherman's halibut box, which he had placed in the centre of the screen. But he stopped short of relaying the myth. "What else is in the box," Reid joked, "isn't fit for Anglo-Saxon sensibilities."[3]

Reid never told his viewers that the purpose of such screens was to proclaim the history and the inherited crests of a high-ranking chief. To be fair, he had not hidden the fact that the myths associated with the figures linking the oral narrative with the visible world had eluded him and that he was uncertain about the boundaries dividing the human from the animal and spiritual realms in Native mythology.

Few people who saw the film realized that Art Price's drawing illustrated in Marius Barbeau's *Haida Carvers in Argillite* (1957) had inspired Reid's screen. Or that it had been Price, not Reid, who had first made the interlocking figures on a panel pipe fit into a square format. Nor did the announcer disclose the fact that Reid had not been the only artist who had contributed to the work. After roughing out the figures, Reid had arranged for another carver to do the "detailing and finishing" on the screen for him.[4]

This method did not represent a new way of working for Reid. He had watched and helped Mungo Martin and his assistants carve a pole. And he had hired assistants himself on the Haida village project. Several months into Robert Davidson's apprenticeship, Reid had invited the young Haida to help him carve a twelve-foot totem pole. (Reid had carved the raven on the bottom while Davidson carved the killer whale on the top. The finished product, destined for the home of a private collector, was unique because it combined figures that had been carved in very different styles.[5]) It is clear that once Reid had worked out the overall design of a particular work, the process of transforming it into argillite, wood, or metal was sheer drudgery. "The screen, thank God, is nearly finished," he told the art critic David Silcox. "In fact the final form is established, and I've been able to turn it over to a helper for detailing and finishing so I can get on with the few other things I have to do before I leave."[6] Thus well before illness prevented him from executing his own designs, Bill Reid was happy to let someone else do the lion's share of the manual work for him. That his assistant might change the look of the cedar screen did not seem to concern him. Finishing the commission was Reid's goal, and he used every means to meet the designated date of completion.

Reid rarely showed the sort of ambivalence exhibited in the film towards a project. He had been unhappy about many aspects of the Provincial Museum commission. For one thing, he felt that the museum had not paid him enough for the work. The non-Native artist Lionel Thomas

Illustration by Art Price

had received the enormous sum of $80,000 for his work while Reid, along with the twenty-six other artists who were asked to produce work for the new museum, were paid considerably less. Equally disturbing, Reid had underestimated the costs involved in the job. "I made it a lot fancier than it had to be," he told his film audience. He may also have been aggrieved that Thomas's "Hippie Harpooners" — as one critic called the thirty-three-foot-long sculpture portraying eight west coast Natives harpooning a grey whale — was installed in the museum's foyer while his screen was confined to the third floor.[7]

Towards the end of the film, Reid bade farewell to his ancestors and to his production of their art: "There won't be more from me."[8] He told his viewers that the screen was a kind of postscript to what he called all the funny games that he had played as a somewhat Haida artist. This statement has a familiar ring. Although working in the Native style had made him famous and had even allowed him to earn a decent living, the repetitiveness of the work, the lack of context and meaning, and Reid's belief that an earlier generation of artists had done things that were beyond his ability did not make it an alto-gether satisfying activity. "In twenty years, I, with a pretty good increment of intelligence and talent, have perhaps begun to be able to create some good things in the Haida convention," he had told the Provincial Museum curator, Donald Abbott, earlier that year, "only to find that now my only impulse is to give it all up and start over being a citizen of my own country."[9] With $7,000 from the Canada Council in his pocket, Reid must have felt that he could afford to turn his back on Native art.

If Reid had never produced another work in the Native idiom, he would have been remembered as one of the first Native artists to carve an imagina-tive, rather than a traditional, functional, or ceremonial work, for a public institution. Scholars would have congratulated him for having integrated no fewer than fifteen figures into the screen's square format. And the more observant among them would have appreciated the extent to which he had shown that Haida art was as much about the interaction between the figures as about the figures themselves.

By the time the film was aired on Channel 10 in Vancouver, Reid had left British Columbia. (He had hinted to his audience that he would be leaving Canada by saying goodbye to his lost children — a reference to Amanda and Raymond, now living on the Queen Charlotte Islands — to his old loves, and to his hometown, Victoria.) After visiting his brother Robert in Toronto where he was a successful commercial artist, Bill had travelled to London, England. Though still committed to producing the book on Native art with Wilson Duff, he was looking forward to putting all his creative energy into making himself into a jeweller working exclusively in the contemporary European style.

∽◦◦∽

Reid arrived in England in May 1968. He took a room on the sixth floor of a building on Jermyn Street located in the West End of London. It was a splendid location for someone who had never visited Britain's capital. He could walk to all the tourist sites: the Houses of Parliament, Piccadilly Circus, and Buckingham Palace. He had the leafy expanse of St. James's Park at his doorstep. It was a short ride on the underground to London University where his sister, Peggy Kennedy, was studying for a Ph.D. in psychology. (She became a psychologist at London's Hackney Hospital.) And most important of all, it was a ten-minute walk to the Ethnography Department of the British Museum off New Bond Street where Reid would spend many afternoons viewing Northwest Coast Native carvings and jewellery.

Never bashful, Reid spent his first weeks in London introducing himself to the city's leading jewellers and silversmiths. In pursuit of a boyhood interest in silversmithing, he sailed across the Irish Sea and drove to the southeast corner of Ireland. There he visited the Kilkenny Design Workshops, which the Irish government had set up in 1965 in order to improve the standard of industrial design. It took Reid only a few days to realize that any attempt to become as competent as the silversmiths whose work he had viewed in the antique shops along Government Street on his way to Victoria High School as a teenager would, at his age, be a hopeless endeavour. He returned to London where, for the remainder of his year abroad, he studied the latest trends in contemporary European jewellery design and consulted several public collections of Northwest Coast art.

On his way to Ireland, Reid had visited Liverpool in order to view and photograph the Northwest Coast collection housed in the city museum. When he returned to London, he frequently walked from Piccadilly to the British Museum's Ethnography Department. There he saw what Captains James Cook and George Dixon had collected on the Queen Charlotte Islands two hundred years earlier. He photographed these objects, along with a number of Kwakwaka'wakw, Tlinglit, and Tsimshian masks, rattles, storage boxes, and headress frontlets. He also saw an ivory walking stick finial that the museum had attributed to Charles Edenshaw. Photographing and compiling information on some of the oldest Native artifacts that he had ever seen was the first step towards doing research for the book he was writing with Wilson Duff.

༄༅

The arrival in Europe of one of Reid's old friends from Vancouver, the artist Tak Tanabe, interrupted his visits to the British Museum. From mid-August to mid-September 1968, the two men toured the Continent, driving as far south as northern Italy. The trip was mainly for pleasure. Reid did not consult, as he had proposed to do in his grant application, the ethnographic collections of Northwest Coast art held by museums in Frankfurt, Berlin, and Hamburg. However, he later claimed to have visited several collections of historical and contemporary European jewellery.

Tak Tanabe does not remember viewing any of these collections during the course of their Continental tour. What he does remember, however, is how his travelling companion sat in the front seat of the car and whispered into a tape recorder. As they sped through northern Europe, Reid recorded love letters to a young actress whom he had met in Toronto on his way to Europe. Intent on keeping the relationship alive, Reid spent a good deal of time composing oral letters and, at the end of each day's journey, locating a post office so he could mail them to Canada. In this way, Reid's most recent conquest received both a running commentary of the trip and the continued assurance of his love.[10]

After returning to London from his whirlwind tour of the Continent with Tanabe, Reid asked the Canada Council for the second instalment of his grant. He told them why he had been unable to keep to his proposed plan of research. The Russian invasion of Czechoslovakia in August 1968 had prompted him to cancel his trip to the Soviet Union. It would, he reported, have been "extremely distasteful" to visit the Soviet Union while Russian tanks were rolling into Prague. In protest over the invasion, Reid sent his visa back to the Soviet Embassy in London. He also demanded that Soviet officials return the money he had paid them in advance for the trip. Reid thus missed an opportunity to view the Russian Northwest Coast artifacts he had seen illustrated in Erna Sibert and Werner Forman's book, *North American Indian Art* (1967).

Reid felt that his exposure to European jewellery had been more stimulating than if he had moved directly from his workbench in Vancouver to one in London.[11] Yet by the end of his first six months in Europe, Reid had consulted only two of the sixteen ethnographic collections he initially planned to visit. The proposed research program had proven to be a far more ambitious undertaking than he was capable of carrying out.[12] And in addition to this, he had become as disenchanted with researching Native art as he had been with making it.

∽∾◡∾∾

It is only three stops on the London Underground from Piccadilly Circus, where Reid lived, to Holborn Station. From the middle of September until Reid returned to Canada the following summer, he made the fifteen-minute journey to the Central School of Art and Design in Holborn almost every day.

For most of the school's seventy-five-year history, its jewellery instructors had prepared their students for employment in the jewellery and silver-smithing trades located in London's Hatton Garden. Like Reid's former teacher Jimmy Green, the instructors in the jewellery department at the Central had put a greater premium on materials and craftsmanship than on good design. But all this changed in 1961 when the Worshipful Company of Goldsmiths mounted the *International Exhibition of Modern Jewellery 1890–1961*. The exhibition turned jewellery-making on its head. It made the skill and imagination of the jeweller as important as, if not more important than, the material value of the object.

Within four months of occupying a bench at one of England's most prestigious colleges of art, Reid had become infected with the Central School of Art and Design's experimental approach to jewellery-making. The teachers and students alike used non-traditional materials. They borrowed ideas from modernist painters and sculptors. And they treated each piece of jewellery they made as a work of art.

By far the most experimental piece that Reid designed and made during his first months at the Central was a gold and diamond necklace.[13] Composed of white and yellow gold and diamonds, the necklace was later dubbed "a masterpiece of contemporary jewellery" by Toni Cavelti. This was because it

Reid and his grandson, Oliver Tanu Lusignan

sat well on the neck, it moved smoothly, it was flexible, and the clasp, as Cavelti pointed out, "snapped as it should."[14]

Reid's assemblage of shapes and blobs was not unique. The structure or base of his necklace took its inspiration from the miniature pyramids that one student at the Central, Gunilla Treen, had welded together to form a stunning necklace. The delicate gold wire sections that Reid superimposed over the pyramidal base of the necklace had their genesis in the work of one of the school's most imaginative instructors: David Thomas.[15] And the way in which Reid had made his diamonds float over the delicate gold tracery owed a huge debt to his earliest mentor: Margaret de Patta.

Karen Duffek has suggested that it was Reid's understanding of Haida logic that enabled him to bring two complementary forms into one space.[16] It may be equally true that Reid's familiarity with Kwakwaka'wakw transformation masks gave him the idea of inserting a detachable brooch into the front of the necklace. One might also credit the drawings of Thompson River Native necklaces that Reid had seen illustrated in Franz Boas's *Primitive Art* for giving him the design structure of his necklace.

However much Reid's Native sensibility might have been at play when he made the gold and diamond necklace at the Central, the work is firmly rooted in the modern idiom of jewellery-making. Pyramidal forms such as the ones Reid used were popular forms for other jewellers at the school, and they could also be seen in the wall reliefs and abstract sculptures of British and European artists. Reid was very much in tune with this modernist sensibility, and his magnificent necklace was a testament to his engagement with the vocabulary of mid-twentieth-century modern sculpture and jewellery. Reid was so excited by his necklace that he saw it as the first work in an exhibition that would be solely devoted to his contemporary jewellery.

However much Reid was now committed to making jewellery in the modern idiom, though, he could not get Native designs out of his head. Using the repoussé or chasing method, he produced a three-inch-wide gold bracelet with the raven and wolf — his family crests — in half-relief. He also made a gold pipe finial. (This was inspired by the walking stick finial — attributed to Edenshaw — that he had viewed in the British Museum.)

Reid put in regular hours at the bench during his year in London but he also found time to spend many evenings with his sister Peggy and her husband, Stewart Kennedy. He escaped the rain by travelling to Tunisia with Alanis Obomsawin, a Native songwriter and filmmaker from Montreal. And when Sophie Reid came to London to visit her son and daughter, he took her to Paris. There he showed an expatriate British Columbia artist, Joe Plaskett, his "chef d'oeuvre necklace"; he also made time to visit the collection of Fabergé jewellery in the Louvre.[17]

There is no doubt that during his year in England, Bill Reid produced some of his most innovative jewellery. Hobnobbing with the students and instructors at the Central School of Art and Design had improved his jewellery-making techniques and expanded his knowledge of contemporary design. He had also found a way to take what had become repetitious drudgery a stage further. Most important of all, after his year in London, Reid had no doubt in his mind that from now on the objects he created — whether they were worn, or walked around, or paddled in — were works of art.

∽∾

Bill Reid had only enough money to live in England for a year. In the spring of 1969 he returned to Canada, but not to the west coast. He had visited the country's largest city briefly during Expo 67 and had found it a stimulating place to be. The celebration of the Canada's one-hundredth birthday on the Ile Ste-Hélène and Ile Notre Dame in the St. Lawrence River had revitalized the old and new districts of Montreal. The aluminum-and-glass-clad towers in Place Ville Marie and the world's largest underground city beneath Place Bonaventure were evidence of both the city's economic prosperity and post-Duplessis liberalism.

On the roof of his flat in Montreal, 1970

Reid chose to live in Montreal's older quarter, which boasted stone-faced buildings with spacious rooms, mullioned windows, and decorative wrought-iron balconies. The city's old-world cosmopolitan sophistication was not its only attraction for Reid. His old friend from Vancouver, Robert Reid, was an established book designer in the city that now became his home. And one of his most enthusiastic patrons, Adelaide de Menil, lived a few hours' drive away in New York. Her efforts not only promoted Bill Reid's name, but also threatened to compromise it — in ways that are still not entirely clear, but which merit some examination.

The wealthy daughter of John de Menil, co-founder of the Amon Carter Museum of Western Art in Forth Worth, Texas, Adelaide was a well-known collector and photographer of Northwest Coast Native art. Reid had accompanied her and her companion, the anthropologist Edmund Carpenter, on a trip to the Queen Charlotte Islands two years earlier. On that trip, de Menil had taken photographs in preparation for an exhibition and book that she was doing on abandoned Native villages in British Columbia. Now familiar with the more remote villages on the Queen Charlotte Islands, de Menil and Carpenter, accompanied by the American collector Clinton Helvey, made another trip during the late summer of 1968. This time they were looking for more than sites to photograph. On August 29, the Royal Canadian Mounted Police caught them removing three totem poles and a grave marker from the village of Skedans. (Reid had taken them to this village the previous year.) De Menil, Carpenter, and Clinton Helvey were charged, under Section 90 of the Indian Act, with removing artifacts from reserve lands.

Although Bill Reid was not directly implicated in the incident, the American couple gave the residents in Skidegate the impression that, like their friend Bill Reid, they were from Vancouver. During the course of the hearing, which took place in Skidegate immediately after their arrest, Edmund Carpenter claimed that he was operating under a permit from George MacDonald, an archaeologist at the National Museum in Ottawa. Carpenter insisted, moreover, that he did not intend to add the artifacts to his own vast collection of Northwest Coast art, but to give them to a museum so they might be preserved from decay.[18] With the possible (though not proven) involvement of an official from the National Museum, a statement against de Menil and Carpenter would, in the view of the Provincial Museum curator Peter Macnair, be "a black eye for anthropologists."[19] The magistrate, Jack Fraser, dismissed the charges on grounds of intent. But the distraught residents of Skidegate who had attended the hearing were not happy with the magistrate's decision. They insisted that if and when the "salvaged" poles were put on display in the Provincial Museum, they should have a label stating that "the poles had been taken illegally by Americans," then recovered "through the alert efforts of the RCMP."[20]

The incident did not dampen de Menil's or Carpenter's enthusiasm for Northwest Coast art. An exhibition of de Menil's photographs entitled *Out of Silence: Totem Poles of the Northwest Coast* opened at the Harvard Graduate School of Design around the time that Bill Reid was travelling back to North America from his year abroad. De Menil planned to publish the photographs in book form and had asked Wilson Duff to write an essay to accompany them. Duff declined. Then de Menil found someone else: Bill Reid, recently settled in Montreal, was virtually on her doorstep.

Reid's contact with Adelaide de Menil was strictly business; not so with all women. When he arrived in Montreal, he lived initially on Crescent Street with Robert Reid. It was here, at the age of forty-nine, that he met a woman whom he assured was the love of his life.

Sherry Grauer was Reid's junior by some nineteen years but she had the economic security and academic credentials in the visual arts that he lacked. Born in Toronto in 1939, then raised in Vancouver, Grauer had studied French in Switzerland, art history at Wellesley College in Massachusetts, and painting at the Ecole du Louvre in Paris and at the Art Institute in San Francisco. When Grauer met Reid in the summer of 1969, she had been living in Montreal for almost two years.

Grauer already knew who Bill Reid was when she met him at Robert Reid's apartment. She had seen him carving poles for the Haida village project on the University Endowment Lands where she had ridden her horse as a young woman. This was before she became well known for producing work that challenged the traditional art-historical categories of sculpture and painting, representational and abstract art. By 1968, Grauer had embarked on a series of wire-mesh sculptures, one of which, *Dog Face Boy's Picnic,* would

Sherry Grauer in Montreal, 1970

find its way into the permanent collection of the National Gallery of Canada. Grauer's eclectic work was rooted in the landscape surrounding Vancouver yet it also reflected the diverse history of twentieth-century art. A lively woman, well-heeled and attractive, Grauer appreciated Reid's wish "to do international stuff." At the same time she engaged with his interest in Northwest Coast art.

Reid envied Grauer's freedom of expression because, as he told her, "the sort of thing he did required more planning." Her imaginative use of a wide variety of materials, along with her involvement in the hands-on process of making art, loosened up Reid's approach to his own work and thereby expanded his artistic vision.[21] Not long after they met, Bill and Sherry became lovers.

Before Reid moved into Grauer's spacious second-floor apartment on Park Avenue, they took a trip to New York. Reid was anxious to show Tak Tanabe, who was now living there, and his patrons Adelaide de Menil and Edmund Carpenter what he had produced in London. It was supposed to be a short trip: a reunion with old friends, a chance to show off his new woman, and maybe even an opportunity to pick up a jewellery commission. But it turned into a nightmare.

Reid and Grauer arrived at the American border in Utica, New York, at 6:30 P.M. on September 10, 1969. The customs official asked them if they had anything to declare. The answer was no. Seeing a piece of Reid's gold jewellery on the dashboard — a gold bracelet-watch that he had made at the Central in London — the customs official's eyes, according to Grauer, "nearly popped out." He then asked the couple if he could inspect their luggage. His search revealed another piece of jewellery: it was the remarkable gold and diamond necklace that Reid had made in London. Reid was flattered by the customs official's interest in his work. Thinking he would like to see more, Reid naively said, "I have some more jewellery." He then produced a pair of gold cufflinks and a few other pieces of jewellery that he had stored in his shaving kit. Convinced that Reid was embarking on more than a pleasure weekend to New York, the official ushered him into the customs office. Reid was asked to empty his pockets. This disclosed a gold bracelet. (It was in Reid's pocket because he was self-conscious about wearing it with a short-sleeved shirt.) Further inspection of Reid's car revealed an attaché case. It contained even more jewellery. There was the gold finial he had made at the Central and a small silver Haida bracelet that belonged to the New York collector George Terasaki. Expecting to find even more jewellery, the customs officials told Reid to strip and searched his clothing. No other pieces of jewellery were found.

Reid had initially told the customs officials that all the items were his. Further interrogation, however, brought out the truth. He did not own the old silver Haida bracelet but was returning the repaired work to George Terasaki. This, along with a cheque for $1,000 from Adelaide de Menil, aroused further suspicion. More customs officials arrived on the scene and more questions were asked. "Why did you not declare the jewellery before entering the United States?" "Do you intend to sell the jewellery in New York?" "Why did you lie about the silver bracelet?"

The customs officials then withdrew, leaving Reid to watch their animated conversation through the window of the room where he was being detained. When their deliberations ended, they formally charged Reid with "wilfully and knowingly and with the intent to defraud the United States" smuggling jewellery into that country.[22] They read the accused his rights, offered him counsel — which he refused — then allowed him to make one telephone call. Bill called his brother Robert at his home in Toronto. No one answered the telephone. Before being escorted to jail in Albany, Reid asked Grauer for a pencil and paper so he could record his ordeal.

After Reid's arrest, Grauer took a room in a nearby motel. A few days later, she returned to Montreal in order to raise funds for Reid's lawyer. On September 30, twenty days after his arrest, Bill's brother Robert came up with $4,000 for the bail bond. Grauer returned to Albany, then drove back to Montreal. This time Bill was in the passenger's seat.

Reid was right, of course, when he told his interrogators that he and Sherry just wanted to spend a pleasant weekend in New York City. But the customs officials were equally correct in suspecting that the visit was not entirely without an ulterior purpose. When they rifled through Grauer's car, they had found de Menil's photographs, along with several books on Native art, indicating that Reid had begun the research in preparation for his essay. If Reid had not been arrested, he would have proceeded to New York, where he might or might not have sold some of the jewellery to his clients. And he would certainly have discussed his proposed text for de Menil's book. As things turned out, he had spent the next two weeks in jail.

If Reid had been a national figure in 1969, the border-crossing incident would have made the headlines: "RCMP breaks into artist's Montreal apartment on orders from U.S. officials" or "Artist forced to sell his work to American collectors because Canadians aren't interested in buying Native art." Although Bill Reid was not well known in 1969 and his story didn't make the headlines, he did have a few friends in high places to call on for help. The director of the Canada Council, Peter Dwyer, was later in touch with the Canadian consul in New York and Reid's lawyer in order to recover the confiscated jewellery. And others, including the well-known academic administrator Geoffrey Andrew, along with Bill's friend, Robert Reid, acted as character witnesses at his trial.

~~~

Robert Reid remembers that Bill was "really down" during the winter of 1969–70.[23] This was not surprising. Bill was in debt to his brother for $4,000.

He was financially dependent on his lover, Sherry Grauer, with whom he now lived and to whom he owed money for his lawyer's fee. His jewellery, which he considered to be his best to date, was in the hands of the customs officials (and remained there for over a year). He was prohibited from entering the United States, and was thus out of touch with his American patrons. Most serious of all, following his indictment on November 10 and his arraignment three weeks later, Bill faced a trial, the outcome of which could land him in jail for more than twenty days.

A few weeks before the trial began on February 12, Sophie Reid flew to Montreal to offer her support. She was still living in Vancouver, though, at the age of seventy-four, she was no longer earning her living as a dressmaker. Sophie nevertheless led an active life: joining her friends to admire the North Shore mountains which rose above the city, lunching at the genteel Hotel Georgia, and dining with her sister Ella on Friday evenings. The trip to Montreal put a large dent into Sophie's "not-so-big account." It also left her exhausted. But she had no regrets about the expense and the toll the trip had taken on her health. "Thank you dear ones, for the lovely time you showed me," she wrote Bill and Sherry after returning to Vancouver, "I really enjoyed every minute of it."[24]

Less than a month after Sophie Reid had returned to Vancouver, Bill was in court on charges of smuggling goods into the United States. The trial, which took place in Utica, New York, before a predominantly black jury, lasted several days. The case for the defence rested on the claim that jewellery did not have to be declared providing it was for personal use or artistic exhibition. Louis Wolfe established his client's standing as a Native artist and jeweller. He did this by drawing the jury's attention to the items that had been found in Grauer's car at the time of Reid's arrest: the album of photographs taken by de Menil, the books and gallery catalogues dealing with Native art, and the jewellery itself. Robert Reid, Adelaide de Menil, and Geoffrey Andrew spoke in Reid's defence. Sherry Grauer was also in the witness box.

The prosecution presented its case. Reid, it claimed, should have filled out a customs declaration form before entering the United States. Then Reid took the stand. There is no record of what Bill told the jury or what his supporters said in his defence before the jury retired. But the case could not have been clear-cut because the jury deliberated for two hours. When they returned, the foreman gave the court their verdict. William R. Reid was found not guilty of smuggling jewellery into the United States on the grounds that there was "no proof that the merchandise . . . should have been invoiced pursuant to the laws of the United States." Since there were no grounds for a legal charge, Judge MacMohan dismissed the case and returned the $4,000 bail bond to Reid. He chose, however, to keep the confiscated jewellery.[25]

Reid was obviously relieved by the jury's verdict, but he was puzzled as to why the court insisted on retaining the confiscated jewellery. Back in Montreal, he was depressed and unable to work. Grauer found his frequent and intense bouts of depression difficult to cope with. The relationship went off the boil — on her part at least. She fell in love with someone else and in early March she left Montreal and moved to Regina with her new beau.[26]

Reid assured Grauer that she did not have to feel guilty about leaving him. This did not, however, stop him from missing her, needing her support, and trying to convince her that she needed him too. Playing for time, he asked Grauer not to marry anyone else for a year. He reminded her that, when the outcome of the trial had been hanging over his head, he had been in no position to discuss their future. He humbled himself by claiming to be old and fat, flabby and broke, neurotic and lazy. But he took pains to remind her that he was a good workman, "reasonably good in bed," and "something of a man."

Lonely in Montreal without Grauer, Reid badly needed a change of scene. This is what he got in March when he moved to New York. Shortly after arriving, he wrote Grauer a rambling, almost stream-of-consciousness letter from his dingy hotel room on Madison Avenue. "It's tough here," he told Grauer, "but that is the kind of abrasive you need to sharpen you." And even though he found the city "a filthy, disgusting, violent, expensive, inconvenient hole," it was a place where one could feel alive. It was, Reid insisted, the sort of place that "perhaps everybody should come to for a while to try out his strength against obstacles worth pushing against."[27]

No matter how hard he tried, Reid could not entice Grauer to join him in New York. He was equally unsuccessful in his attempts to write the essay for de Menil's book. Moreover, he did not like the new vogue for computer-generated art, austere hard-edge colour abstractions, and minimalist sculpture. New

York's latest styles only made his Native design–based jewellery appear more anachronistic than he often felt it was. Within weeks of arriving in the city, Reid fell into another deep depression. This made him consider the worst that could happen. "I may have to come crawling home and apply for welfare," he told Grauer, "if I can't beat off the depression enough to do this damn book."[28]

Reid's fears were realized when the depression that had made his friends concerned about his mental health during his early days in Vancouver and that had become chronic since his arrest in September 1969 made him confess to Sherry that he had come "pretty close to cracking up completely."[29]

Reid moved back to Canada. He landed on the doorstep of friends who lived in a suburb of Toronto. Within a few days of settling in Willowdale, he was on a course of tranquillizers and had become an outpatient at the Clarke Institute of Psychiatry in downtown Toronto. This may have been the first time that Reid had been diagnosed as suffering from manic depression, or bipolar illness. He responded well to a strict regime of lithium and within weeks could joke about his illness. "Although I'm pretty sick," he told Grauer in April, "I probably won't die."[30]

Though still depressed in the early summer of 1970, Reid was on a less extreme emotional seesaw. He moved back to Montreal, where he found an apartment on Sherbrooke Street, across from McGill University. It had large rooms — the living room was some twenty-five by thirty feet. The ceilings were eleven feet high. And there was a wall of windows. Shortly after moving in, Reid built what he considered to be the "essentials": a combination bar — fourteen feet long — and a six-by-seven-foot bed. He decorated the unit with purple upholstery and painted it in burgundy and gold.

Reid was obviously trying to build a new life for himself. He entertained his friend Robert Reid in his new apartment and became a regular dinner guest at his home. He went to concerts — Leonard Cohen was a favourite — with an old girlfriend. He picked up with Alanis Obomsawin, whose songs and stories had made her one of the most exciting performers in Canada. (In the summer of 1970, Reid joined Obomsawin and a group of Native craftsmen at the Mariposa Festival on Toronto Island.) And he became associated with Montreal's second exposition in four years, *Man and His World*.

Sensing that Reid was depressed, the west coast designer Rudy Kovach asked him to help re-design ten pavilions left over from Expo 67. "I don't know exactly what I did there for six weeks," Reid told Grauer, "except walk miles and miles between jobs making a lot of drawings that never got off the drawing board."[31] When *Man and His World* opened in the summer of 1970, Reid was offered another job. He would be paid ten dollars an hour to demonstrate carving from 2:00 to 6:00 P.M., two days a week at an exhibition, *People of the Potlatch,* that had been organized by the University of British Columbia.

After the arrival of various sized chisels and adzes from British Columbia in the middle of July, Reid produced two carvings. The first was the exquisite *Wolf Feast Dish,* whose elegant lines and subtle rhythms echoed the designs on his silver and gold bracelets. And the second was a female mask that explored the interplay between face-modelling and face-painting that Reid had admired on the masks he had photographed at the British Museum.[32]

Reid had been hired to demonstrate carving in order to spell off his former pupil, Robert Davidson. Though only twenty-four years old, Robert Davidson had already carved and raised a totem pole on the Queen Charlotte Islands. He had become an accomplished print-maker and jeweller. He had represented Canada at the World Council of Craftsmen in Dublin, Ireland. And, after founding the Rainbow Creek Dancers, he had become noted for

Wolf Feast Dish

Mask, woman

reviving traditional Haida songs and dances. During Reid's two-year-long absence from Vancouver, Davidson had taken his former teacher's place as the province's premier Native artist.

Towards the end of *Man and His World,* Davidson staged a potlatch. He wanted to honour Mayor Jean Drapeau and the many other people who had contributed to the exposition, as well as to celebrate the completion of a ten-foot totem pole. Davidson's wife, Susan, imported salmonberries from British Columbia and the guests ate the whipped dessert she made with soapberry spoons that Reid and Davidson had carved for the occasion. A local photographer captured Reid and Davidson dressed in Chilkat blankets and headdresses. Davidson took great pleasure in guiding his former teacher through the rituals associated with the potlatch. Davidson later recalled, "It seemed like he relied on me to show him how to get in touch."[33]

Bill Reid, Robert Davidson and
Mayor Jean Drapeau, 1970

ᏩᎤᏓ

What Reid called his "depression and despair of the previous months" began to lift during his employment at *Man and His World*. As he told Grauer, he "drank too much & stayed up too late"; he had also met some wonderful people. Moreover, wearing ceremonial Native dress at the potlatch had made him into the "Haida prince" that he often told Grauer, in jest, that he was.

By early November 1970, Reid was feeling so good that he paid a short visit to Grauer, who was still living in Regina. The visit revitalized him. Back in Montreal, he threw himself into his work. (When he was manic, he could spend ten hours a day at his jewellery bench.) As a result, he began producing "better stuff" than ever before.[34] Sales were also good. He had enough money to lend his friend Robert Reid $2,000. And he was in a position to contemplate paying off the many debts he had accumulated during the trial.

With renewed vigour, Reid was finally able to write the essay for de Menil's book, *Out of the Silence*. Largely cribbed from the essay he had written for the *Arts of the Raven* catalogue, Reid's text reinforced the message that de Menil was conveying in her photographs: Northwest Coast art was dead, Native culture was a thing of the past.

It was also in the early autumn of 1970 that Peter Page arrived on Reid's doorstep. The two men had met briefly in 1969 before Reid had left England.

Examples of Peter Page's jewellery, circa 1970

Reid's junior by more than twenty years, not only was Page knowledgeable about industrial design, he was a first-class jeweller. Reid envied Page's lengthy schooling and his early start as a jeweller. He admired his technical expertise. He empathized with his wish to make jewellery for the arms, ears, necks, and fingers of beautiful women. Always happy to have a much younger co-worker around, Reid invited Page to share his workbench and living space. Page easily fell into Reid's daily routine. When Reid stopped at 11:30 every morning to do the Royal Canadian Air Force exercises, Page joined him. When Reid turned on the television to watch *Coronation Street,* Page viewed the daily program too. Page also listened to the CBC and to Reid's running commentaries on the announcers he had known during his employment there in the 1940s and 1950s.

Sharing living quarters with Reid did not always run so smoothly. There were Reid's silences when he was depressed and his lengthy monologues when he was manic. Whenever Page invited his girlfriends to the apartment, "Bill chased them around." And when things went wrong, Page was treated to a barrage of abuse. On one occasion, Bill was "terribly angry" when Page had mistakenly deposited one of Bill's cheques into the wrong account. "I said to him," Page recalled, "'You can sod this workshop' and we had a tremendous row." Page threatened to leave. Reid, who was dependent on the young jeweller, quickly apologized. "From that moment on," Page concluded, "we never looked back."[35]

Reid needed Page's help at the bench. An English client named Stephen Hodgkin had commissioned Reid to make him a signet ring. "I did the job," Page recalled, "because Bill didn't want to do the sort of ordinary, as it were, 'European' type of job. So I designed it and he sold it under his own name."[36] On another occasion Reid was about to set abalone shell into his eagle brooch. He hesitated, fearing that he might crack the fragile shell. So "Bill chased the gold," Page said, "and I did the inlay."[37] Early in 1971, Victoria's Provincial Museum asked Reid to contribute a work to its forthcoming exhibition of contemporary British Columbia Indian artists. The result was a stunning 22-carat gold box with a killer whale soldered to the lid by the tips of its flukes. Page helped Reid with that job too.[38]

There is nothing unusual about jewellers sharing tasks at the bench. They are less concerned about copyright and sharing their ideas than artists or writers are. And Peter Page is eager to make the point that, on a few occasions, Reid helped him design and make his jewellery in the same way.

Towards Christmas 1970, Reid made a final attempt to patch up his relationship with Sherry Grauer. He told her that he wanted "so much for the next few years to have some kind of settled life to match the professionalism I seem to be able to bring to my work."[39] It was not as though Reid had been pining for Grauer since she had left him earlier that year. In addition to flirting with the women whom Peter Page brought to the apartment, there were, he told Grauer, "a couple of birds of passage, or sisters of mercy" who had "fluttered in & fluttered out again with no ruffled feathers on anybody's part." There was also another "little wriggler" who had not yet left Reid's metaphorical nest.

The woman in question was a young student from the University of British Columbia who had been associated with the *People of the Potlatch* exhibition in Montreal earlier that year. Reid had no idea whether there was any future in the relationship but, with Peter Page planning to leave in the new year, he did not like the idea of living on his own. However enamoured Bill might have been with the young student, he continued to woo Grauer. In fact, he planned to visit Grauer as well as the young student during his Christmas trip to Vancouver. If things went well with his former lover, the young student would not mind. "She knows about you," Reid told Grauer, "& would understand."[40]

Reid duly travelled to British Columbia for Christmas in December in order to explore both relationships. But he put off calling Grauer until the end of his trip, only to discover that since he had last heard from her, she had become engaged. Once back in Montreal, Reid attempted to settle his financial debt. He owed Grauer $4,500 — a large sum when his earnings were so precarious. In lieu of payment, he sent her the sterling silver and white gold necklace he had made after returning from England. Grauer thus became the owner of Reid's second necklace designed in the modern idiom and nicknamed the *Horse Barnicle Necklace*.[41]

Before travelling to Vancouver at Christmas 1970, Reid had told Grauer that his relationship with the university student was "the most illogical, irrational thing I've ever been involved in in my illogical irrational life."[42] However well things had gone with the young woman during his visit to Vancouver, his fear that the relationship might result in nothing but another great load of grief was borne out in the new year. Once again Reid was jilted.

PART III

BITTER HARVEST

CHAPTER II

Becoming an Indian

Bill Reid had mixed feelings about his short visit to British Columbia in 1970. He had lost a potential partner, perhaps, by having failed to contact Sherry Grauer upon his arrival. His aunt, his mother's favourite sister, Ella Gladstone, had died during his visit. And while he was looking forward to becoming a grandfather, he was troubled by the decision of his recently married daughter, Amanda, to make her new life in the remote village of Skidegate. There was, on the other hand, a positive side to Reid's visit. He had enjoyed a happy reunion with his "son," Raymond Stevens, whom he persuaded to return with him to Montreal. And although he had travelled to Vancouver with the idea that no one else apart from himself and Robert Davidson were producing contemporary Native art, once he got there he realized that nothing could have been further from the truth.

A lot had happened since Reid left Vancouver in 1968. The non-Native contemporary art scene was even more vibrant than it had been in the 1960s.[1] (A younger generation of artists, including Toni Onley, Gathie Falk, and Roy Kyooka, had joined Gordon Smith, John Koerner, and Jack Shadbolt.) A new generation of largely city-based Native artists had emerged too. Mungo Martin's grandson, Tony Hunt, was well established as an artist in Victoria. Robert Davidson, now permanently based in Vancouver, was, according to the art critics, the most accomplished living Haida artist. Another carver and goldsmith hailing from Old Masset, Pat Dixon, would soon be touted as the new master of Haida art. And the Skidegate artist Pat McGuire, who was re-inventing forms rather than just building on the work of the past, was, Reid discovered, the most innovative artist of the lot. Although Reid criticized McGuire for sometimes operating too far from the margins of traditional Haida art, he credited him with giving argillite carving something it had lacked for many years: the realization of precise work and fine finish.[2] Tragically, just after Reid had left Montreal for Vancouver, McGuire died from a heroin overdose.

A few months before arriving in Vancouver, Bill Reid had told the budding Haida artist Gerry Marks that he would not find anybody either in Prince Rupert or on the Queen Charlotte Islands who could teach him how to carve because "no one knows how to carve up there."[3] But there was a place, the Native-run Gitanmaax School of Northwest Coast Indian Art at 'Ksan, where large numbers of Native artists were improving their carving techniques and engraving skills. The school had been established on the bank of the Skeena River near Hazelton in 1966, and its students blended the stylistic traditions of the northern tribal groups with those of their non-Native American instruc-tors, of whom Duane Pasco was the most influential. Reid was familiar with the distinctive 'Ksan style, which focused on single figures and introduced perspective into print-making and naturalism into carving. Committed to an individualistic and tribal-based view of Native art, Reid was unsympathetic to the way in which 'Ksan's artists amalgamated a number of styles in their work. He felt that the centre and its school were "an ill conceived, impractical waste of time and money on everybody's part, and," he told the Provincial Museum curator, Donald Abbott, "I don't see why I should throw any of my time away on it."[4] It is not surprising that when Reid was invited to teach there in 1966, he had refused.

Reid was not alone in criticizing the Gitanmaax School of Northwest Coast Indian Art. The Carrier Nation artist Larry Rosso was "kind of glad" that he had not remained at 'Ksan because he felt that most of the pupils emerged with no individuality.[5] Even so, the Gitanmaax School did produce artists of the calibre of Gerry Marks, Walter Harris, Freda Diesing, Vernon Stephens, and Dempsey Bob. But this did not sway Reid's view that anyone who went through 'Ksan would produce "nothing but a pile of junk."[6] Even after the school had become famous, Reid wondered whether its teachers had "unleashed a monster" on the world.[7] By the mid-1970s, however, the "monster" — innovation, which was not new to the history of Native art — had inflicted itself on almost every Native artist on the coast. Even Reid's own work would change: moving towards naturalism and borrowing ideas from contemporary non-Native western artists. This, along with his increasing use of western technology, would make him as eclectic as any artist who emerged from 'Ksan.

Davidson, McGuire, and the artists at 'Ksan, along with many other carvers, print-makers, and jewellers, were different from the generation before them. They considered themselves to be artists, not craftsmen. They did not produce work primarily for the tourist trade, but fed the appetites of the new and discriminating group of non-Native collectors and gallery curators. Moreover, mindful of the legalization in 1951 of the potlatch, they also produced ceremonial work for their own people. Some artists like Ron Hamilton (Ki-Ke-In) made work exclusively for their own people.

Reid found more artists, more styles, and more commercial outlets devoted to Native art on his short visit to Vancouver in the winter of 1970, and he also discovered that the University of British Columbia's anthropology museum, confined to the basement of the library since 1949, was about to get a new home. The museum's long-time patron, Walter Koerner, had persuaded the federal government to contribute $2.5 million towards the construction of a new building, and the province's leading architect, Arthur Erickson, had agreed to design it. Reid was offered a part-time job planning the building. And the museum invited him to join the staff once the building was completed. This was an attractive proposition. He wrote to Grauer, "I could relax for a couple of days a week, within the comfort of the academic community & the faculty club."[8]

Reid also learned, on the same trip to Vancouver, that things were happening at the Provincial Museum in Victoria. Northwest Coast Native artifacts were becoming more difficult for museums to acquire. Many anthropologists were questioning the validity of taking them from the indigenous people to whom they belonged. In fact, some public institutions were preparing to repatriate a small number of their artifacts to a handful of museums that were being built in remote Native villages. By the early 1970s, salvage anthropology and the replication of nineteenth-century artifacts were becoming questionable museum practices. (These were, of course, activities in which Reid had actively and recently participated.) Indeed, the word "decline," which Reid, Duff, and others had used to describe contemporary Native art, had suddenly become inaccurate. "Renaissance," "revival," and "re-birth" was how anthropologists now chose to describe contemporary Native art and culture. (A more appropriate, if less dramatic term would have been continuation.) The spirit of the renaissance that was in the air at this time mainly represented a change in white attitudes. Native artists had never stopped doing what they had always done: making art.

Sensitive to these new ways of thinking about Native culture, the Provincial Museum's curator, Peter Macnair, began organizing an exhibition devoted solely to the work of living artists.[9] When Reid returned to Montreal following his visit to Vancouver, Macnair invited him to participate in the museum's forthcoming *The Legacy* exhibition. Reid was pleased to be asked and submitted the magnificent killer-whale gold box that Peter Page had helped him to make.[10] The box, for which the museum paid Reid three thousand dollars, was one of ninety works commissioned for the exhibition. It was to become the core of the museum's permanent collection of contemporary Native art.

Now back in Montreal, Reid had time to reflect on his visit to Vancouver. He wrote enthusiastically to Grauer about the "thriving, aggressive, vital Indian community" that was "too startling to be ignored."[11] What Reid had observed was a result of more than the institutional support that Native artists were being given by anthropologists, various levels of government, and museum curators. Native peoples themselves were beginning to take their future into their own hands. They lobbied the government for more control over their lives by founding national organizations such as the Native Indian Brotherhood and local societies such as the BC Association of Non-Status Indians and the Union of BC Indian Chiefs. When the Liberal government of Pierre Elliott Trudeau took a final stab at trying to assimilate Native peoples into white society by proposing in 1969 to abolish their special status and Indian reserves, Natives across the country were angry — as Harold Cardinal made clear in his book, *Unjust Society: The Tragedy of Canada's Indians*: "We will not trust the government with our futures any longer. Now they must listen to and learn from us."[12] Far from appeasing Native peoples, the federal government's white Paper had paradoxically "stimulated Indian nativism as no claims commission or treaty settlement had ever done."[13] The Liberal government had not only misjudged the feelings of status Natives but underestimated the extent to which non-status Natives wanted to reaffirm their ancestry. When status Natives let their feelings be known, the government backed off.

Bill Reid clearly saw the advantages that would come his way from the sponsorship of contemporary Native art by non-Native institutions, by all levels of government, and by the Native peoples themselves. He also knew that the imminent recognition of non-status Natives would legitimize his identity as a Native, making funds from such government departments as the Indian Affairs Branch in the Department of Citizenship and Immigration available to him. This, along with the new museum at the University of British Columbia and the forthcoming exhibition of contemporary Native art at the Provincial Museum in Victoria, would likewise provide greater exposure for, and recognition of, Reid's work.

∽✺∾

It is not surprising that, after returning to Montreal in January 1971, Bill Reid told Sherry Grauer that it seemed like a stupid place for him to be. This was not the first time Reid had questioned his residence on the east side of the North American continent. The year before he had visited Jones Beach near New York City and noted, nostalgically, how the sand had been "littered with shells: moon snails and clams, like the west coast, and dull black scallops, beautiful and ominous."[14] Back in Montreal a few months later, he experienced the bombings and robberies of a terrorist campaign that culminated in murder by the FLQ (Front de Libération du Québec) of the province's minister of labour and immigration, Pierre Laporte, and the kidnapping of Britain's trade commissioner, James Cross. The October Crisis, which saw the Liberal government invoke the War Measures Act for the first time, made Reid uncomfortable. This was not because he was antipathetic to the FLQ's demands or to their illegal tactics — "It's always bad when innocent people suffer," he noted after the death of Pierre Laporte, "but then many do all the time." Reid felt uncomfortable in Montreal because he was "very aware now how much a stranger I am."[15]

Yet Reid remained in the city for another year and a half. Why? He told Sherry Grauer that inertia kept him there. His proximity to New York, where he still hoped to make his name as a jeweller working in the modern idiom, had something to do with it. He also liked being close to Toronto. (After retrieving his gold and diamond necklace from the American customs early in 1971, thanks to the intervention of officials at the Canada Council, he exhibited it at the Art Gallery of Ontario's *Jewellery '71: An Exhibition of Contemporary Jewellery*.) Certainly, Grauer's marriage to a Vancouver architect in 1971 was another reason Reid chose to remain in Montreal. Then there was the arrival of Raymond Stevens. Reid hoped to spend a little more with his "son" before he reached adulthood. And Reid must have felt that Montreal was the place to do it.

Now in his late teens, Raymond took the place of Peter Page — who had returned to England — at Reid's bench. Despite Reid's efforts to teach the young man how to make jewellery, he showed little talent. Nor was he particularly interested to learn. Even so, Raymond was good company for a lonely man who now had a rare opportunity to fulfil the role of father.

Even before Raymond arrived in Montreal, Reid was on a psychological high. Working at full capacity, he completed orders for old patrons in Vancouver and New York, as well as for a new patron in Hamilton, Ontario. He sold jewellery through Montreal's Lippel Gallery of Tribal Arts. And he provided several museums in British Columbia with examples of his work. Despite spending up to ten hours a day at the bench, he still took time out to do his Royal Canadian Air Force exercises in the morning and to walk in the grounds of McGill University, which lay across the road from his apartment, in the afternoon.

Reid's manic pace was rewarded with praise. When Peter Macnair received the gold killer-whale box for *The Legacy* exhibition, he exclaimed, "Your masterpiece has arrived; you have arrived; the focal point of the show has arrived."[16] This spurred Reid on to make more gold boxes. Taking his inspiration from Charles Edenshaw's argillite chest, *Discovering Mankind*, Reid created *Bear Mother*, which was purchased by the National Museum of Man in Ottawa.[17] He made another gold box, featuring his wolf crest and two figures, a bear and a human being, for his patron Adelaide de Menil.[18]

Discovering Mankind, *argillite chest, Charles Edenshaw*

Throughout his years in Montreal, Bill Reid continued to draw on the work of his great-great uncle and his Haida contemporary, Art Price. He also returned for inspiration to the drawings of tattoos featured in Alice Ravenhill's *A Corner Stone of Canadian Culture: An Outline of the Arts and Crafts of the Indian Tribes of British Columbia*. And he made new versions of his own jewellery. It was also during these years that he became a technical virtuoso. Repoussé, casting, and soldering gave the figures and designs on the boxes, bracelets, and other objects that he fashioned out of gold and silver greater depth and more volume. Exaggerating the features of his animal and mythical figures made them look more naturalistic. This resulted in his figures appearing flabby or ugly or sometimes even grotesque. By focusing on volume rather than on line, Reid was losing the sense of tension, restraint, and compactness that he had so admired in the work of Edenshaw and his contemporaries. What might be called Reid's baroque approach to jewellery-making during the 1970s owed less to the work of Edenshaw than to Reid's knowledge of the repousséd gold pendants of pre-Columbian goldsmiths. It was even more in tune with the funky art of the Ontario artist, David Gilhooly, whom Reid admired at the time.

Nevertheless Reid could sell everything he made, providing, of course, he stuck to Native themes. He had learned years ago that he could not charge the same amount for his modernist jewellery as he could for a work designed in the Native idiom. Peter Page, who had become a first-class jeweller since returning to England, was lucky if he got $500 for a piece of contemporary jewellery. Reid, on the other hand, could charge $1,500 for a work of his own design and as much as $850 for a reproduction of a brooch — as long as they were rendered in the Haida style. No one else in Canada, according to Vancouver jeweller Toni Cavelti, could have commanded such high prices for their jewellery.[19]

❧

While Reid had been living with Sherry Grauer, he had discovered a new material. "God decided the world needed a good carving material," he told an interviewer in 1982, "and provided us with boxwood."[20] Boxwood possesses a beautiful finish and can be carved in detail. From a small piece of this unique wood, Reid created *Raven Discovering Mankind in a Clamshell*.

Raven Discovering Mankind in a Clamshell, *1970*

More naturalistic and organic than any work Reid had previously made, the small boxwood carving signalled a departure from his strict adherence to classical Northwest Coast art forms.

There was nothing strikingly unusual about the choice of motif for *Raven Discovering Mankind in a Clamshell.*[21] In the mid-1950s, Reid had chosen the creation myth as a theme for his silver bracelet *The Raven and the First Men.*[22] Years later, while visiting the Metropolitan Museum of Art, Reid had admired a sixteenth-century Flemish rosary bead depicting the birth and death of Christ. It, too, had been carved in boxwood.[23]

The version of the creation myth that Reid chose to render in his boxwood carving had been told to Franz Boas by Charles Edenshaw in 1897. The story takes place in myth-time, just after the great flood. It recounts the Raven's discovery, and subsequent release, of five male creatures from a clamshell. Charles Edenshaw had depicted this version of the creation myth at least twice: on an argillite dish and as the central motif for an argillite chest.[24] Two non-Native artists had produced graphic versions of the myth in Ronald Campbell's *The Story of the Totem* (1924) and in Marius Barbeau and Grace Melvin's *The Indian Speaks* (1947). A few years later the Haida artist

Claude Davidson — the father of Robert — gave Edenshaw's version of the myth its most realistic rendering. Davidson poised a spread-winged raven on a dais above the heads of five humans who are about to enter the world.[25]

Reid had access to these renderings of the Haida creation myth and was also in tune with the contemporary artists in his midst. Sherry Grauer's mesh wire sculptures, George Norris's twenty-foot-high stainless steel crab — it was installed in front of Vancouver's Centennial Museum in 1967 — and David Gilhooly's grotesque ceramic sculptures all informed the way in which Reid would represent the creation myth in his own work. In this sense, Reid made what was to become one of his most popular works by looking back to traditional Native art as well as forward to his Native and non-Native contemporaries.

Reid introduced a great deal of variety into the people in *The Raven Discovering Mankind in a Clamshell.* Some of his six figures are emerging from the shell enthusiastically; others are not sure whether they want to enter the world at all. Like the boxwood rosary bead, Reid's work possessed, on its own scale, a gravitas and a monumentality that was characteristic of the totem poles that he and Cranmer had carved for the university a decade earlier. Reid did not carve *Raven Discovering Mankind in a Clamshell* with a larger work in mind, though it is now incorrectly referred to as a maquette. He had no idea that this diminutive carving would be transformed, a decade later, into his signature work when a much larger version of it, *Raven and the First Men,* gave the new museum at the University of British Columbia what one person aptly called its beating heart.

No matter how pleased Reid was with his boxwood carving, he confessed in 1971 that he was still uncertain "about working in what might be termed a decorative art rather than a major art form." He was uncomfortable peddling the bones of his ancestors and being a white "artifaker." "Look," he told a reporter in 1974, "I have a hard job assessing what I do."[26] Although Reid liked others to treat him as a fine artist, he often thought of himself as a craftsman. Indeed, in May 1970, he advertised his "company" in the short-lived arts magazine *The Atlantic Reporter* as "Artifakes Inc. Better than Originals: London, Paris, Rome, Montreal, Halifax, Bill Reid, director."[27] Though clearly a spoof, Reid's description of his bogus company showed that, however capable he was of making a beautifully crafted gold box, a silver bracelet, or a miniature boxwood carving, he was still determined "to expand his talents in the larger context of North America and Europe."[28]

Even so, he was not entirely happy about making what he called baubles for the pretty people. "Those of us involved in this peculiar business," he observed in 1974, "tend to have a lot of trouble justifying ourselves to ourselves sometimes, and so assume a kind of cynical attitude about the whole thing."[29]

∽ↄ◡◠

Robert Reid insists that Bill decided to go "all Native" while he was living in Montreal.[30] Sherry Grauer agrees. Bill told her, "I used to be an assimilationist, but I now see that the way to go is to keep this [Native art] alive." As a result, Grauer concluded, "he became an Indian before my eyes."[31]

The Ottawa-based artist Art Price, who made jewellery and carved sculptures in both the Native and contemporary idiom, appreciated how difficult it was for Reid to decide whether "to go all Indian — in his art — or all western."[32] Knowing that Price had an intimate knowledge of and respect for traditional Native art, Reid invited him to Montreal in order to ask him for his advice. The two men met in February 1972 for lunch; they visited the Lippel Gallery of Tribal Arts; then they took a taxi to Reid's Sherbrooke Street apartment. There, Reid told Price about his frustration over not being able to decide whether he should continue to work in the Native idiom. Though Price appreciated that Reid was at a critical juncture in his career, he was unable to give his friend advice.

Six months later, Reid had made his decision. During Reid's month-long visit to Vancouver in the late summer of 1972, Walter Koerner commissioned him to produce a large wood carving for the new museum at the University of British Columbia. It was at this point that Reid decided to use his small boxwood carving of the raven as a maquette. Pursuing the idea of producing a work some seven or eight feet high, Reid asked Sherry Grauer, to whom he had given the original carving, for her permission to use the design. She complied and Reid exclaimed, joyfully, to Harry Hawthorn, "It seems I'm going to be working for you in an indirect way again."[33]

Audrey Hawthorn, who had admired the small boxwood carving in the summer of 1970 in Montreal, insisted that it was Walter Koerner who suggested that it could form the basis for a major work. "Koerner had a very keen eye, was very sophisticated about art," she recalled, "and he looked at this and turned to his wife and said, 'This tiny carving would be a monumental carving on a large scale, Bill. I will support you while you get such a carving made.'"[34]

The timing couldn't have been better. The commission came to Reid when there was nothing to keep him in the east, for as he told Hawthorn, "inflation had hit the artifake market pretty hard."[35] With the prospect of a large commission in Vancouver, Reid left Montreal in May 1973. He made the long journey to the west coast by car, accompanied by Raymond and a thirty-year-old graduate student in Renaissance literature, who, according to Reid, fetchingly looked like a go-go dancer. The trio took the southern route across North America because, as Reid told Grauer, he wanted to drive through "Indian country."

∾ᴐᴄ᷍ᴀ

In 1973 Reid was considerably thinner — he had lost fifteen pounds — than when he had left British Columbia in 1968. His once thick black hair was straggly — he wore it long in keeping with 1970s hairstyles — and it had turned a dull grey. He now had a stoop and moved slowly. He had warned Sherry Grauer three years earlier that his physical appearance had altered, "not altogether for the best." But it was not just the inevitable effects of aging — he was now fifty-three — or the lingering effects of the nervous breakdown that had landed him in the Clarke Institute that prompted Reid to describe himself to his former lover as "a little old man." Something had happened that made "any remnants of any prince-like demeanour, no matter how imaginary," disappear. What was wrong? Why did Reid guardedly tell Grauer that he hoped the physical ailment dogging him might be reversible?[36]

Bill Reid had confided in Walter Koerner and his friends, Audrey and Harry Hawthorn, what was wrong on his visit to Vancouver in the late summer of 1972.[37] He had been diagnosed with Parkinson's disease. If the description of his physical condition to Sherry Grauer is anything to go by, he might very well have unknowingly had the disease two years earlier when his depression — an early symptom of Parkinson's — had grown worse. Having taken large doses of lithium since the spring of 1970 might, as some researchers now believe, have diminished the symptoms of Reid's disease. Dates were never Reid's strong point, but in 1985 he told a reporter about his sixteen-year-long struggle with Parkinson's.[38] This would put the onset of the disease in 1969 or 1970, around the time he was complaining to Sherry Grauer about his physical ailment. Elsewhere, however, he recalled that it was in September 1973 that he had found himself carrying his right hand in a funny position.[39] Subsequent to this, he had a pain in his left shoulder. Then he had difficulty turning his head. After that, the tremors began.

Named after James Parkinson in 1817, Parkinson's disease, or the shaking palsy as it was more crudely known, is a chronic neurodegenerative condition affecting a small group of neurons clustered in the upper brain stem, which controls and coordinates movement. The disease occurs when the brain is unable to produce sufficient amounts of neurotransmitters, or dopamine. No one has discovered the link between the chemical changes that occur in the brain and the changes in motor function. And, notwithstanding various genetic, viral, and environmental factors, no one has discovered the cause of the disease.

The prognosis for anyone suffering from Parkinson's disease was not good in the early 1970s. Patients who generally contracted the disease in late middle age were given a life expectancy of not more than ten years. Radical treatments ranged from nigral brain cell transplants to stereotactic surgery. But most doctors preferred to medicate their patients in order to prevent the breakdown of dopamine; this had the effect of keeping dopamine in the brain for longer periods and thus stabilized the condition. But they also had other effects. Some of the drugs caused the patient to hallucinate. They boosted sexual drive. And they usually resulted in constipation, bloating, and dramatic mood swings. None of the medications and treatments available to Reid and used by him halted the progress of the disease; they simply masked it by mimicking or replacing dopamine for limited periods of time.

Parkinson's is a cruel ailment. As with multiple sclerosis, it immobilizes the patient slowly. Resting tremors cause the limbs to shake when the patient is in repose. Speech becomes slurred until it is reduced to an inaudible whisper. Balance is impaired, and the patient has difficulty initiating movement. The so-called restless leg syndrome, which gives patients the feeling that mice are crawling up and down their arms and legs, makes sleep impossible. For Reid, the tremor was not the worst aspect of his illness, though: "It is the rigidity, the muscles just keep tightening up."[40] While the mental capacity of most sufferers is mercifully left intact, the horror of being trapped in a pain-racked body that reduces the patient to a shuffling gait and makes swallowing difficult to the point of suffocation has many psychological effects. Clinical physicians associate introversion and depression; motor, mental, and emotional rigidity; and, ironically, increased ambition with patients suffering from Parkinson's disease.[41]

For someone so dependent on the intricate movement of his fingers, this was a devastating affliction. Yet, during the early 1970s, Reid found that, by taking a cocktail of drugs, his tremors could, on good days, be kept under control. He told a reporter for *The Native Voice* in 1974, "I'm controlling it now with drugs. Actually, my case is fairly mild. I have what is called a resting tremor — that is, when my arm is at rest it shakes. But not when I'm working. It's all right then."[42] According to Professor Johannes Lakke's research into artists with Parkinson's disease, creativity does not diminish. If anything, the patient becomes extraordinarily focused, increasing productivity.[43] When Reid's medication kicked in, he put his heightened — though hardly new — single-mindedness into his work.

Executing large-scale commissions like *Raven and the First Men* was, however, another matter. When Reid told Walter Koerner that he might not have the physical ability to complete the job, his patron remained undeterred. "If you can direct it," Koerner told him, "I will help support the staff whom you select to carve it."[44] Reid was used to having the help of assistants. They had helped him construct both the Haida village and the Haida screen. He had watched artists at the Central School of Art and Design transform intricate pieces of jewellery into large sculptural works with the help of artist-technicians. So Koerner's offer to help him scale up his small boxwood carving into a monumental work by using other people's hands — providing the design and the conception of the work were his own — was little different from how he had previously worked.

∾∾

When Reid moved back to British Columbia in the spring of 1973, he accepted Robert Davidson's offer to put him up in his cedar-beam house in Whonnock, forty miles from Vancouver. In return for his hospitality, Bill offered to help Robert with his jewellery. Since studying with Reid, Davidson had put his teacher's advice to good use. In 1969 he had adapted his superb sense of design to the print medium. In 1971 he had exhibited masks, argillite carvings, metalwork, and prints in his first solo exhibition at Vancouver's Centennial Museum. Now, thanks to the support of the Leon and Thea Koerner Foundation, Davidson had a regular job demonstrating carving at the University of British Columbia's museum. This gave the artist enough time to produce a series of silkscreen prints for an exhibition at the Images for a Canadian Heritage Gallery in Vancouver.

There was nothing unusual about transferring Native designs onto paper. In the late nineteenth century, anthropologists had persuaded Charles Edenshaw and Tom Price to draw their own crests and those belonging to other Natives onto paper. Fifty years later, Mungo Martin had worked on paper too, and Ellen Neel had transferred Native motifs onto notepaper, silk scarves, and ties. In the mid-1950s Bill and his friend Robert Reid had made engravings for *People of the Potlatch*. And in 1970 he and Davidson had made a print for the organizers of *Man and His World*. But it was the Victoria-based artist Tony Hunt who began the craze for buying Native prints in 1960.

Bill Reid was aware of the extent to which Robert Davidson and so many others were earning a bread-and-butter income by making prints. While still in Montreal, he had produced four silkscreen prints depicting the raven, grizzly bear, dogfish, and killer whale. These graphic adaptations based on motifs from his jewellery had sold for twenty dollars each. They were good enough for Harry Hawthorn to call "terrific."[45] This was the work that Reid exhibited alongside Davidson in the spring of 1974.

Seeing Reid's and Davidson's work together at the Images for a Canadian Heritage Gallery showed the degree to which teacher and student had parted company. The motifs on Davidson's prints were abstract adaptations of Northwest Coast designs. Reid's bold designs were, by contrast, more literal and less innovative than Davidson's. According to one critic who reviewed the show, Reid's less imaginative forms allowed him to ride "the undercurrent of the avant-garde art of today."[46] As contemporary art movements passed from Pop to Op and from Minimal to Conceptual, Reid was looking more and more like the traditional non-modernist artist that he did not want to be.

By the time the exhibition was over, Reid had left Whonnock and was living in the architect-designed cedar and glass home owned by his old friend, the sculptor Frank Parry. It was from here that he renewed his contacts with the Vancouver Art Gallery; contributed work to the World's Fair in Spokane, Washington; designed and executed a gold medal for the National Film Board of Canada in memory of the documentary filmmaker John Grierson; and produced more jewellery. Within a year of returning to British Columbia, Reid was so active in promoting his work that he had stolen the limelight from Robert Davidson. His prints were now dominating the Native art market. "I can take one of these prints to Denver or New York," Bill Ellis of Canadian Native Prints Limited exclaimed, "and they'll say — 'Oh. Bill Reid.' But if I try to show them a Pellan, Snow, or Shadbolt print, they don't know who I'm talking about."[47]

Reid's jewellery was selling equally well. At $4,000 for a gold bracelet, his work was priced "out of everything but the millionaire's market."[48] And his prices were about to climb even higher because he was going to have a solo exhibition in the province's leading public art gallery.

Bill Reid: A Retrospective Exhibition ran from November 6 until December 8 in 1974. It was different from previous exhibitions of Native art because it was devoted to the work of one artist. It encompassed film and ranged from small pieces of exquisitely crafted jewellery to bold monumental carvings. And most important of all, because the artist was living, the well-worn theme of decline and decay, which dominated most exhibitions of Native art, was absent. As Edmund Carpenter wrote in the catalogue accompanying the show, "The spirit of Haida art, once the life blood of an entire people, now survives within him, at a depth, and with an intensity, unrelated to any 'revival' or 'preservation.'" Harry Hawthorn added to Carpenter's generous tribute by claiming that "Bill Reid was alone when he began the creative regrowth of Northwest Coast art in jewelry, and was one of only three or four when he carried on the renewal of the traditional large scale carving." Claude Lévi-Strauss, professor of social anthropology at the Collège de France in

Paris, went to greater heights in his praise: "Our debt to Bill Reid, an incomparable artist, is that he has tended and revived a flame that was close to dying out."[49]

Reid had met Lévi-Strauss at Harry and Audrey Hawthorn's home in 1973. This leading exponent of structuralism, who had predicted in 1943 that Native art would soon take its place in museums of fine art, commissioned Reid to make a bracelet and a medallion. The following year Lévi-Strauss returned to Vancouver and this time he asked Reid to make him a ring. The two men got on well. They were both convinced that Northwest Coast art was comparable to ancient Egyptian and classical Greek art. (This made Native artists of previous generations the intellectual equals of their western counterparts.) They both made generalizations about Native culture: Lévi-Strauss from a linguistic base and Reid from an aesthetic or visual one. They both built their reputations on providing new ways of interpreting familiar facts and of looking at familiar objects. Meeting Reid led Lévi-Strauss to make the influential claim that the artist's "primary inspiration, that of the Haida tradition, unites with primary sources of the Kwakiutl freedom of invention, the deeply human sensibility of the Tsimshian and, perhaps above all, with the dreaming lyricism of the Tlinget."[50] With little knowledge of other contemporary Native artists, Lévi-Strauss had all too easily made Reid the linchpin between the old and the new.

Of all the contributors to the catalogue, only Wilson Duff grappled with a problem that had preoccupied Reid since he had become involved in Native culture: how the artist can create work that combines classical Haida and western art traditions. Though Reid's eye could look in both directions at once, Duff wondered why he could not stop talking about "artifakery." "What is the unfinished business?" he asked. "Where is the haunting doubt in this birth of a new art form from an old style, this birth of new melodies from old rhythms?"[51] In Duff's view, Reid had gone some way towards answering this question by recognizing that Native art was as much a system of visual logic as a method of pictorial representation. As Reid had discovered when making the Haida screen, meaning was to be found in the way that one figure related to another rather than in what the figure signified in its own right.

Most of the commentators who wrote about Reid's solo exhibition were not so reflective. For the art critic Joan Lowndes, "the dazzling complexity and virtuosity" of the 203 objects on display showed that "like the Haidas of the great days, he can work at any scale and in a variety of materials from wood, slate and ivory to silver and gold."[52] Though Lowndes was familiar with the work of other Native artists, she made no reference to their work. Nor did the city's leading art critic consider Reid's work in relation to that of his mentor, Bill Holm, or compare it to that of any other non-Native artist. Positioning Reid's work well above that of other artists did more than diminish their efforts, it ignored the achievements of those carvers, engravers, and basket makers who had kept Native art alive throughout the twentieth century.

But *Bill Reid: A Retrospective Exhibition* was inevitably a white affair. The lenders of the dazzling gold and silver jewellery and the exquisitely carved spoons and boxes and totem poles were, with the exception of a small number of Reid's relatives, his white patrons. The 750-strong crowd who gathered at the opening to hear the director of the National Museum of Man declare that "no single person in this century has been so effective as Bill Reid in gathering those threads together to restore strength and continuity to Canada's greatest artistic inheritance" were overwhelmingly white, as at any fashionable opening.[53] The exhibition's organizers were all pillars of the Vancouver establishment: the Vancouver Art Gallery and its patrons, the Vancouver Foundation, contributed to the cost of mounting the show. The photographs of abandoned villages, with their decaying weather-silvered totem poles, that formed a backdrop to Reid's work had not been taken by a Haida photographer but by Adelaide de Menil. The film — *Totems* (1958) — and the video — *Profile: Bill Reid* (1974) — which ran during the course of the exhibition had likewise — and not surprisingly — been made by white film crews. And the mortuary pole, which bore witness to the Haida's past accomplishments at the entrance of the gallery, was inescapably a product of white initiative and white funding. It was so obvious that it escaped comment at the time that the commentators and critics who evaluated the merits of the exhibition were white too.

Reid's autobiographical essay, charting how he had come to produce Native art, gave everyone who viewed the exhibition an irresistible storyline. The essay, which appeared at the heart of the catalogue, was one of revelation and discovery. It proclaimed that Reid's mother had concealed her ethnicity from her children; her eldest son had discovered his Native ancestry only when he was in his early teens: "My interest in my maternal ancestors began quite late in life and was reflected only occasionally, and then from the non Indian viewpoint during my broadcasting career." Reid also insisted that his only contact with Skidegate had been when, as an adult, he had visited his grandfather Charles Gladstone — "the last in the direct line of Haida silversmiths" — who had learned from Charles Edenshaw, "the greatest of them all." It was only then, Reid claimed, that he had decided to try to emulate his grandfather and the other Haida silversmiths and goldsmiths by learning the jewellery-making trade; only then that he began to take an interest in learning about Haida culture.

Reid's "late" discovery of his ancestral link to the Haida, as charted in his autobiographical statement, gave the white community two perspectives on his struggle story. They could congratulate themselves that the cultivation, support, and promotion of Bill Reid's knowledge of Native culture had come through their institutions — the University of British Columbia, the Canada Council, the Canadian Broadcasting Corporation, the Vancouver Art Gallery, and the Provincial Museum — and through white technology — the Ryerson Institute in Toronto and the Central School of Art and Design in London. Equally, they could associate Reid with Charles Edenshaw, the last of the great carvers, whom they wrongly believed to have lived at a time when Native peoples had been free of the economic and social woes for which non-Native society was largely responsible.

Reid used one word to sum up the public's response to his exhibition: "smashing." He told Peter Page and his wife, Sandi, about the "rave reviews," about being elected the artist of the year by a "bleeding local critic" — Joan Lowndes — and about receiving "lots of orders for LOTS of money, about 4 times as much as before." Best of all, Reid had received "accolades" from the Native community, including Sophie Reid, whom he had taken around the exhibition.[54]

What accounted for the overwhelming success of Reid's solo exhibition? Was it Vancouver's own version of the first multimedia blockbuster: London's Tutankhamen exhibition? Could any other contemporary Native artist, such as Robert Davidson, have received the degree of attention that Reid had been shown? And why was it that, only a few years after Reid had felt that nobody was interested in Native art, suddenly they now were?

The growth of institutional support was one reason for the overwhelmingly favourable response to Reid's retrospective exhibition. Reid's ability to make the most out of his connections with the museum and gallery establishment was another. High doses of lithium and fewer bouts of depression had enabled his communication skills to flourish. The wide-ranging body of work that he had produced during and since his years in Montreal was more than technically proficient — it also met western standards of taste. Most importantly, Reid was an acceptable Native to the white community. He did not carry the cultural baggage of Tony Hunt, who had been in prison; of Pat McGuire, who had been a drug abuser; or even of Robert Davidson, who made some people feel uneasy because he had been born and raised on a reserve. Reid, above all, did not look Native.

Bill Reid was a white man's Indian. He was not a social commentator on or a crusader for Native rights, like Harold Cardinal. Viewers at the exhibition were thus allowed to revel in the beauty of Reid's jewellery and carvings without confronting the issue of land claims or the social and economic disparity and political injustice that most Natives experienced on the reserves and in the less salubrious areas of the cities. Reid gave the white community, of which he was very much a part, a sanitized image of Native society.

Reid's knowledge of Native art and culture had not been fostered on the reserve or through his association with British Columbia's landscape. He had not been raised with a sense of being different from, or inferior to, the average Canadian. He had acquired his technical skills as a jeweller and his knowledge of Native art through white salvage operations, through his association with curators in white museums, by reading books written by white ethnologists, and by his training at white art and design schools. So great was Reid's belief that all this had allowed him to take the art form a stage further, he told a reporter, that if a jeweller had arrived in the Queen Charlotte Islands about the turn of the century "there would have been an amazing outpouring of silver work comparable to the magnificent slate carvings which were then produced."[55] But this had not, of course, happened. The Haida had been made to wait (so the messianic assumption went) for someone of Bill Reid's sophistication to take the art to another level.

Reid's art, as one commentator had observed in 1959, assuaged "the white man's burden of guilt" and created "a living memory to the arts of the once great nation."[56] Reid thus made it easier for non-Native Canadians to relate to Native art because he was an individual and not the product of a social experience that most Canadians preferred to ignore. At the same time, he allowed Natives to take pride in what he had accomplished, first as a radio announcer, then as an artist, and now as a spokesperson and entrepreneur who knew how to bridge the chasm separating the Native from the non-Native world. The remoteness of Haida Gwaii from Victoria and Vancouver, and the privileged position that the non-Native world had always given to the Haida Nation, also worked in Reid's favour.

And then there was Reid's illness. Headlines such as "Haida artist fights Parkinson's disease" brought him more than sympathy; it tolled the bell on the future production of his art. Reid's work, like the residue of Native culture on display in the country's museums, was not in slow decline; it was in danger of coming to a sudden end. This gave Reid's exhibition a frisson that it might not otherwise have had.

Far from Bill Reid's artistic career ending, however, it had only just begun. With substantial backing from private and public institutions across Canada, after his solo exhibition in 1974 he went on to produce his most monumental work even though it meant using other people's hands — and sometimes other people's ideas — to bring it to fruition.

CHAPTER 12

The Best and Worst of Times

Reid carving pole on Queen Charlotte Islands

In 1962 Bill Reid told a reporter that he was "becoming almost a human monument."[1] Though this was hardly true at the time, by 1974 Reid had become just that. He had eclipsed his former student, Robert Davidson, in popularity. Local critics were taking a serious and respectful interest in his work. Academics, such as the art historian Joan Vastokas, had elevated him to the same pedestal as the master Renaissance jeweller Benvenuto Cellini.[2] And even though his prices had quadrupled in less than a year, Reid had no difficulty finding a buyer for every piece of jewellery that left his bench and for every edition of prints that Canadian Native Prints produced for him on an annual basis.

Things had never looked better for Reid than in the winter of 1974–75. And yet, just as he had wanted to leave the province following the completion of the Haida village and after it of the Haida screen, he told everyone who interviewed him that he was headed for New York. Why did he want to leave Canada? For one thing, he was bored with making Native art; one way to escape boredom was to turn himself into a fine-art jeweller in the Big Apple. For another, he had to leave town soon because, as he told Peter Page and his wife, Sandi, he was having "a great love affair" with a beautiful, charming, intelligent, and splendidly youthful forty-year-old woman. He loved the Vancouver-based woman "dearly." She loved him "dearly." There was only one problem: they both loved her husband "dearly."[3]

Reid did not leave Vancouver, however. He had to sort out "lousy castings" of his work. His old malady, built-in inertia and laziness, also kept him from moving. His lover was reluctant to leave her husband and take her chances with Reid in New York. Above all, he did not want to forfeit the large sums of money that anything he made was now able to command.

The 1970s were good years to be a Native artist in British Columbia. The economy was booming. The old patterns of frugality that had kept the hands of middle-class Canadians in their pockets were eroding. Every level of government seemed willing to offer financial support to any group or individual interested in promoting Native culture. The number of commercial art galleries had grown exponentially — in 1970 there were twenty-five in Vancouver alone. Foreign collectors, who had been robbing the northwest coast of its material culture since the late eighteenth century, turned their attention to this new generation of Native artists when the federal government passed a law — Bill C-33 — in 1977 to stop the export of historic Native artifacts. With the bill in place, the province's 2,500 Native artists suddenly had a market for their work beyond Canada's borders. Finally, having "discovered" artists among curio-making Native craftsmen and -women, public art galleries and museums had begun to mount exhibitions of their work.

Not every project associated with the sale and exhibition of contemporary Native art came to fruition. In 1975 Bill Reid's old friend from Montreal, the designer Robert Reid, embarked on the production of a book that would bring glossy illustrations of Bill's work together with his account of the myths and legends that adorned his jewellery and carvings. It was an ambitious project that promised to offer a collector's edition: bound in leather, preserved in a gold-tooled slipcase, and packed in an argillite box. Perhaps the undertaking was too ambitious because Robert Reid never got it off the ground.

Three years later, several members of the artistic community had equally bad luck when they attempted to save a thirty-metre-long mural, designed by Bill Reid for the Conference on Human Settlements in 1976. Commercial artists had painted the halibut design onto a wall of the Planetary Hall. When it was learned that the Vancouver Parks Board was preparing to demolish the building, Jack Shadbolt and a few other Reid supporters mounted a campaign to save the mural. Their efforts were in vain — a year after the conference, bulldozers demolished Hangar No.3 — although not forgotten. Two years later, a distraught non-Native resident of the Queen Charlotte Islands, Bill Ellis, was still lamenting the destruction of the mural at Jericho Beach. "At the very least the Parks Board could have invited Bill Reid to drive the bulldozer, as in Joyce Cary's *The Horse's Mouth*, where Gully Jimson destroys his masterpiece," Ellis told a Vancouver newspaper.[4]

Other initiatives celebrated Reid's ascending star. During the decade following his *annus mirabilis* exhibition at the Vancouver Art Gallery, no fewer than seven universities gave Reid an honorary degree.[5] In 1979 Reid joined the pianist Glenn Gould and the founder of the Grand Ballet Canadien, Ludmilla Chiriaeff, in receiving the Diplôme d'Honneur from the Canadian Conference of the Arts. In 1977 he banked $20,000 by winning the Molson Prize. A decade later he was receiving even more lucrative awards, including the Royal Bank $100,000 prize in 1990.

The citations accompanying the degrees and awards that Reid received throughout these years were similar. Reid was a renaissance man. Reid promoted Native culture through his writings, radio programs, films, and works of art ranging from intricate gold boxes to monumental totem poles. Doing all these things had allowed Reid to single-handedly save Haida culture from its certain demise. And why had Bill Reid been able to do this? The implied answer was clear. He possessed white know-how, white technical skills, and white industriousness — qualities supposedly lacking among Native peoples.

It was easy for the white establishment to relate to the Haida people through Reid. As the anthropologist Michael Ames rightly observed, "He was sort of adopted as a representative of that strange exotic world that is on the fringe of our imagination and we don't know quite how to relate to when we see all of the drunks on the street. Here was a contrast so he received much more notice than a lot of other artists."[6]

The belief that Bill Reid inhabited both the Native and non-Native worlds was, however, misconceived. His jewellery was made for the wrists and necks, the lapels and cuffs, of wealthy Canadians. The audience to whom he read his text from *Out of the Silence* at the Queen Elizabeth Theatre during Heritage Week in 1976 was — with the exception of Sophie Reid, who attended the performance — mainly white. And the ideas embodied in the catalogue *Form and Freedom: A Dialogue on Northwest Coast Art,* which Reid produced with Bill Holm in 1975, were derived from Western writers on aesthetics, such as Roger Fry.[7] What Reid did in all his writing on Native art and culture was to transfer the sense of hierarchy and status that Natives had long associated with the ownership of artifacts, myths, and stories to the white world.

☙∿❧

Form and Freedom was a handsome volume illustrating some one hundred works that had been collected by Adelaide de Menil and her husband, John. The de Menil collection was about to be exhibited in New York and Toronto, and Bill Reid and Bill Holm provided a catalogue to accompany the exhibition. In it, the anthropologist Edmund Carpenter wrote a short but scholarly introduction. Using the more formal William for his Christian name, Reid wrote a prologue. Most of the catalogue's text, however, was given over to what the Vancouver anthropologist Marjorie Halpin called an informative and entertaining dialogue "between two likeable, knowledgeable and articulate friends."[8]

Reid and Holm did not take the imaginative leap, evident in Wilson Duff's seminal publication, *Images: Stone, BC,* which had accompanied an exhibition of pre-historic Northwest Coast sculpture at the Art Gallery of

Greater Victoria earlier that year. Compared to Duff, they were more interested in aesthetics than in symbolism; in the form or the look of an object than in its meaning. They subjected every work in the collection to the same sort of analysis that an art historian or art critic would have given to a painting or a sculpture. For example, a carving was good when it conformed to western standards of symmetry, elegance, harmony, and fine craftsmanship. When it did not conform to the standards governing western aesthetics, it was, in Reid's view, not art.

By making the objects conform to critical standards that were in line with western aesthetics, with western concepts of humanity, and with western ideas of universality, Holm and Reid were acting as the gatekeepers of Native art's admission to the canon. That they were basing their judgments on their personal tastes as much as on their knowledge of Native art did not pass Holm by. As he told Reid during the course of their dialogue: their comments said more about themselves than about the objects they were discussing.

Reid was not as reflective or as subtle in his comments as Holm. According to him, Coast Salish artists carved "funny-looking houseposts." They were incapable of producing anything except blankets. And, he gratuitously added, they were "nuts."[9]

Reid had long felt that traditional Haida art possessed an intrinsic value or universality that made it as good, and as accessible, as other great works of art. However when it came to contemporary Native art Reid was, as he told a group of students at the University of British Columbia in 1976, "a little bit worried about some of the stuff." Avoiding any reference to his own work, he suggested that many contemporary artists seemed to be "feeding on themselves." As a result, they were losing touch "with the old forms."[10] Like Ellen Neel almost thirty years earlier, Reid put the blame at the feet of the art critics. Their indiscriminate and gushy praise had done more harm than good. Indeed, it was insulting when they pronounced everything good.[11]

Some Native artists were uneasily conscious that what they were marketing was not their art but their ethnicity. Robert Davidson sometimes wondered if his prints and carvings were popular only because he had black hair and brown eyes. Norman Tait was amused that he could work in any style and still command a reasonable price for his work. And Don Yeomans claimed that it was "bad enough having your art on the line, but your personality, your appearance to be evaluated by the person who's buying your Indianness, it just doesn't interest me."[12]

Reid wanted to do more than remind collectors, critics, and the public in general that, by supporting the best Native artists, they were buying art, not ethnicity. He wanted Native artists themselves to realize that their success required that their work be shown in a proper venue and reviewed by an intelligent art critic. This could only happen, in Reid's view, if Native artists did two things. Develop "a knowledge of Europe's best forms" in order to make their work comply with western standards of aesthetics.[13] And produce "an acceptable piece of merchandise" that would speak to both "the white and Native communities."[14]

∽∘c∘∾

In the summer of 1977 Reid put some of these ideas into practice. Vancouver's Centennial Museum was in the process of organizing an exhibition to celebrate Queen Elizabeth II's silver jubilee. Hearing of the museum's *Treasures of London* exhibition, Reid contacted the director. He suggested that a workshop, devoted to helping Native artists perfect their technical and design skills, be run in conjunction with the exhibition. Reid was convinced that, as with the Navajo craft industry, Native jewellery could provide a good economic underpinning for the production of *all* kinds of Native work. The Haida artist Reg Davidson agreed: "Rich people will always want jewellery."[15]

Reid did not want to teach the six-week-long workshop himself, so he invited his old friend Peter Page to run it. He did, however, have a hand in setting up the workshop prior to Page's arrival in Vancouver. Reid told the museum what kind of equipment to purchase — flexible shaft drills, draw plates, a polishing machine, and torches. He designed the artists' workbenches. And, in consultation with his old friend Doug Cranmer, he suggested which artists they should invite to participate in the program.[16]

The first thing that Page discovered upon meeting his eight students who came from Skidegate, Village Island, and Galiano Island, among other places, was that some were considerably more technically skilled than others. He also observed that being an expert wood carver was no guarantee that they would be good at soldering and working with precious metals. By the end of six weeks, however, Page had taught his pupils how to make hinges, fastenings, and clasps. He had shown them how to transform a flat design into a more sculptural form by chasing or repoussé. Skills and techniques that had previously been a mystery to the students suddenly became possible to master.[17]

The non-Natives who visited the workshop, which ran in tandem with the *Treasures of London* exhibition, were puzzled when they saw Peter Page. "How can an Englishman presume to teach Native craftsmen?" they frequently asked. Page insisted that he had "no desire to interfere with traditional and established methods of working or the form and shape of traditional design."[18] Yet whether he intended it or not, showing his students how to make clasps and hinges and how to chase a piece of metal did make their work more attractive, as Reid hoped it would, to the white sector of the market. It also gave the next generation of artists the tools, literally, to match and even surpass the achievements of Bill Reid himself.

∽∾∾

The summer before asking Page to head the workshop, Reid had travelled to Skidegate. Not only had he looked forward to living there for the first time in his life, he had hoped to carve a totem pole. As with the making of the Haida village at the University of British Columbia, Reid wanted to honour his ancestors and to give something back to the people from whose tradition he was now earning a handsome income.

In 1878 the geographer George M. Dawson had counted more than fifty totem poles skirting the village in Skidegate Inlet. When Reid was there in 1932, only three poles remained standing. When he returned in the 1950s, only one pole — the beaver pole — stood above the pebbly beach where his grandfather, Charles Gladstone, had worked in his carving shed. By 1976 that solitary pole was in danger of toppling to the ground.

It became part of the Bill Reid myth that he was the first, in modern times, to raise a pole on Haida Gwaii. Yet while Haida carvers had not erected as many poles as the Kwakwaka'wakw since the enforcement of the potlatch law at the beginning of the twentieth century, they had not been idle. Robert Ridley had carved a pole in Old Masset in 1925 and, a little over thirty years later, Pat Dixon and John Cross had raised one in Skidegate. But just like the totem poles that Reid had helped move from Skedans, Tanu, and Ninstints to museums in the 1950s, Ridley's pole was "salvaged" for Victoria and Dixon and Cross's pole was "salvaged" for white tourists in Vancouver. Many other carvers — including Robert Davidson, Walter Harris, Norman and Josiah Tait, Joe David, Henry and Tony Hunt, and Freda Diesing — had also carved poles in their own villages up and down the coast long before Reid decided to do the same.

Reid's daughter, Amanda Reid-Stevens, now settled in Skidegate, suggested that the band erect a totem pole in front of its new Skidegate Band Council administration building — and hire her father, Reid, to carve it. Unlike other artists Reid was disqualified from government funding because he was a non-status Native — Davidson had been funded by the British Columbia Cultural Fund and Tony Hunt by the Provincial Museum. This meant that money for materials and hands to help him carve the pole had to come from private initiatives.

By the time Reid arrived in Skidegate in 1976, a group of Swedish-Canadian contractors was in the process of constructing the administration building, which had been designed by Reid's friend Rudy Kovach. Reid's frontal pole would stand at the rear of the building and look out to Skidegate Inlet. The community would provide Reid with living space — a three-bedroom trailer on Second Beach — and help him find a log — it would need to measure over sixty feet. Reid would have to construct a carving shed — a wood frame struc-ture covered in plastic — and choose the motifs for the pole.

The traditional function of totem poles had been to display, through a series of crests, the owner's family history, his identity, his accomplishments, and his wealth. Unlike post-Renaissance western art, it was the patron's name, and not the artist's, that became part of the discourse and ceremony sur-rounding the pole. Thus Native carvers made their reputations by creating works that sang the praises of the chiefs rather than celebrated their own skills. Traditionally, it was the person in whose honour the totem pole was being carved who chose the motifs.

In the recent past, however, things had changed. It was now the carver who decided which crests would appear on the pole. Sometimes, as in the case of the Nisga'a carvers Dempsey Bob and Norman Tait, relatives or village elders would suggest the motifs. Or, as for Robert Davidson, the pole was a symbol of Haida identity in general demonstrating the continuing importance of Haida culture. A generation earlier, before these changes, Davidson's father, Claude, would never have depicted crests he was not entitled to carve.

Before he proceeded to carve, Reid asked several elders in Skidegate which crests they wanted to appear on his pole. But he claimed to have received little help. "Nobody knew exactly whether they were ravens or eagles," he said. The village did not want the building to be architect-designed and, according to Reid, did not want a totem pole. As Reid told a number of reporters, what they wanted "was two mobile homes shoved together — an instant office" or, even worse, a "skating rink."[19]

It is highly unlikely that anyone in Skidegate had, as Reid suggested, forgotten whether they were an eagle or a raven. It is more likely, as he observed elsewhere, that during the carving of his pole "this symbol of the past began to intrude on that relatively unruffled surface" of the lives of the people in the village. When he started the project, he said, "there was no interest, nobody, it was a subject of curiosity, it wasn't a village activity."[20]

Although none of the villagers questioned Reid's respect and admiration for the artistic tradition of the Haida, he continued to be known to them as Charlie Gladstone's grandson and as Sophie Gladstone's eldest boy. They admired him more for his notoriety as a former radio announcer on the CBC than for his recent success as a jeweller and carver. As the Native artist Don Yeomans observed, Reid was "an enigma for the people in the village."[21] This became apparent when he tried, around the same time, to lease land on the Skidegate Reserve in order to build a summer home. The village refused him a plot, fearing that it might set a precedent for leasing to "outsiders."

Finding hands to help him carve the pole was as difficult as being accepted by the residents of Skidegate. Virtually every carver of a totem pole requires assistants. Although Reid was controlling his Parkinson's disease with drugs, he had many bad days. Knowing full well that he might not have the physical stamina to see the project through, it was vital that he had help. If hands were not initially forthcoming, it was, Reid suggested, because the people were "too shy to volunteer to help me."[22] It may also have been because he made no secret of the fact that he was disappointed with the younger generation of

Natives. "These goddamn Indians won't come to work and if you say anything to them," he told Tak Tanabe during his visit to Skidegate, "they just bugger off."[23] Nor could Reid have won confidence among the residents of Skidegate by the cynical, flippant, and irreverent way in which he talked about his work. "He will call himself a 'monument builder' in one sentence," a reporter noted during an interview with Reid, then talk about himself as "a maker of 'arti-fakes' in the next."[24]

Reid worked alone on his totem pole for the first few weeks. Then he sought help from the Nisga'a artist Norman Tait, who had already carved two poles, and from the Nuu-chah-nulth artist Joe David, whom he had met at the World's Fair in Spokane in 1974. Reid also got in touch with George Rammell, a non-Native sculptor and technician at Capilano College in Vancouver. "Just bring a sleeping bag," Reid told him.[25]

Of these three men, only Joe David took up Reid's invitation. Though David was not of Haida ancestry, Reid must have thought he was a good choice. Born in Opitsaht, off a remote island in Tofino Inlet on the west coast of Vancouver Island, David had studied with the non-Native American artists Bill Holm and Duane Pasco and at an art school in Texas. In 1976 his silkscreen prints were commanding the attention of influential critics like Joan Lowndes.

Several Natives of Haida ancestry joined the project too. Gerry Marks, whom Reid had met in Montreal and who had gone on to study with the Haida carver Freda Diesing in Prince Rupert, welcomed the opportunity to become Reid's assistant. Robert Davidson, who was carving and painting a cedar-plank house in honour of his great-grandfather, Charles Edenshaw, in Old Masset joined Reid for about ten days. "You are the better one, the better designer," Reid told Davidson, who designed "the wings, the pectoral fins, the tail and things like that."[26] Two other young Haida, Gary Edenshaw — no relation to Charles Edenshaw — and Clayton Gladstone, joined the project at a later stage. Though Edenshaw was unskilled, he supplied the muscle lacking in Reid's arms and back.

By the time Joe David arrived in Skidegate, Reid had roughed out the fig-ures on the pole with the help of Robert Davidson. Reid asked David to con-centrate on the detail. "I completely understood that I should be very careful,"

David recalled, "and very certain that the work that I was doing was exactly what he wanted. Luckily for me, we were very compatible, we were very quiet in our work. Our spaces were respected."[27]

Reid and his fellow workers had begun by stripping the bark off the log and removing the bumps and the knots — all with the help of power tools. After plugging the holes, they split the log, removed the heartwood — the first part of a log to rot — then rounded or smoothed the log into a symmetrical, evenly tapered column. Using a lumber crayon, Reid drew a line down the middle and traced his design onto one half of the pole. (Unlike Mungo Martin and Douglas Cranmer, who could hold the entire design of a totem pole in their heads, Reid had to rely on a sketch, scaled at half an inch to one foot.) He transferred the paper to the other side of the pole and traced the other half of the design. Reid and his helpers then roughed out the segments of the design with a power saw in preparation for the fine carving.

Like most carvers, Reid and his assistants started carving the lowest segment of the pole. They began with the grizzly bear, then worked their way up to the raven and the frog, the killer whale, the dog fish, and, finally, to the

Skidegate pole

three watchmen crowning the pole. These, along with less prominent crests, were on the totem poles that had stood in Skidegate at the end of the nineteenth century. Reid had also used these crests in his own work and had seen them represented in the work of other artists. The grizzly bear and the watchmen, for example, were in the same position as the figures on the Haida pole that Reid had admired at the Royal Ontario Museum more than twenty-five years earlier. Many of the other figures had been featured on his bracelets, earrings, cufflinks, and pendants or had been attached to the top of his exquisite gold and silver boxes. The pole, which rose more than fifty-five feet into the air, gave these figures an imposing monumentality that certainly represented Reid's most accomplished large-scale carving to date.

Reid did not complete the totem pole in six months as he had hoped to do at the outset. His diminishing stamina kept the project behind schedule. "When we were working on the pole," Gary Edenshaw recalled, "he was always getting the Parkinson's."[28] There were other projects to be completed as well, such as the commission from Governor-General Jules Léger to produce a gift for Queen Elizabeth's silver jubilee. And there was the difficulty of hiring assistants and of instructing them. "I almost had to tell the natives which end of the hammer to hold," Reid complained to a newspaper reporter.[29]

Reid's seemingly contradictory lack of confidence in and respect for the Haida, coupled with his ambivalence towards the project, was the cause of much conflict. Noting how Reid did not like the way Natives left decisions until the last minute made Skidegate resident Diane Brown conclude that he seemed to have more faith in someone who had been to school and written books. "He didn't question that." Moreover, Brown continued, "we accepted who he was," whereas Reid gave her and the other villagers the impression that they were "pitiful remnants of what our ancestors were."[30]

Everyone who visited Reid during the summers of 1976 and 1977 told the same story: "Bill had a difficult time there winning approval and acceptance of the Native community"; "People in Skidegate didn't like him . . . Bill has different values, different ideas"; "Bill had a hell of a time being accepted in the community."[31] Coming back to a place not visited for a long time can cause all kinds of conflicting feelings. For example, when Gerry Marks returned to Old Masset after a long absence, he recalled, "It was very depressing for me to see

how people lived." This was partly because he had "created all kinds of illusions and dreams that [he] had about Northwest Coast people."[32] Unlike
Marks, however, Reid had no illusions. He said things and behaved in a manner that made his assistants and the villagers often regret his presence. He
made no attempt to hide his feelings.

Despite all these difficulties, by the late autumn of 1977, the totem pole
was virtually finished. When Reid returned to Skidegate for its installation
over six months later, sufficient time had passed to alter the colour of the pole
and to change the villagers' attitude towards it.

Robert Davidson recalled that during the process of carving his pole in
Old Masset in 1969, the people there "didn't react, nothing." After he had
completed the carving, however, his "Tribute to the Living Haida" brought the
whole village together.

Reid's experience was just the same. On June 9, twelve hereditary chiefs
from Skidegate and Old Masset, all wearing ceremonial headdresses and
button blankets, gathered in front of the new administration building. Several
men and women lifted the pole. Then, as they carried it out of the carving
shed, Ernie Wilson encouraged them, to "Think strong. Be strong."[33] When
they placed the pole in front of the new building, Gary Edenshaw performed
a traditional dance. Then, following Reid's instructions, the pole was raised
above the heads of the cheering crowd.

As with any Native ceremony or "doings," to use the Haida expression,
there were many speeches. Reid told the crowd of 1,500 people that it had
been his lifelong dream to carve a pole to celebrate the memory of the great
carvers and of the people who had supported them. During the process of
carving his pole, Reid said, he had not only honoured the dead, but had
shown the living that "a new breed of offshore people is coming to be, from
the people of all the races from all over the world who have assembled on
these islands together with the original inhabitants, the Haidas."[34]

Speaking the day after the doings, Reid's uncle, Percy Gladstone, echoed
his nephew's sentiment. "Now we see the mixing of two cultures. We Haidas
have adapted both," he continued, "and we live very comfortably here in the
village of Skidegate." But it was the cultural aspect of the pole-raising that had
brought "a great big lump" to Percy's throat. "I have never seen before all our

chiefs together, and I know that many of you experienced the same feeling. What have we been doing for the last hundred years?" he asked. "We have been drifting away from our culture, our beautiful culture."[35]

The Old Masset artist George Yeltatzie had predicted a few years earlier that if and when the carvings "come alive again," the people will all begin to remember.[36] Robert Davidson certainly experienced "a big turning point in terms of starting to accept my Haidaness" when he raised his pole in 1969. Equally, the doings associated with Bill Reid's totem pole boosted the Skidegate residents' awareness of and pride in their cultural heritage too. Many of them, beginning with Reid's now-deceased grandparents, Josephine Ellsworth and Charles Gladstone, had lost confidence and hence interest in their culture. While other Haida people had never ceased to carve, the banning of the potlatch and the introduction of religion had forced them to make their art in limbo. Clive Cooking continued this line of thought in *The Native Voice*, writing that previously Natives had produced art "without the reasons for doing so."[37]

The carving of totem poles, and the making of masks and screens and all the other paraphernalia associated with the doings, did help put cultural ceremonies back at the centre of Native life. Whether Reid fully grasped this at this time is unclear. In keeping with his view that he belonged to the new generation of "offshore Haida," he had not danced, and he had not worn a button blanket or a headdress. (He had donned a black ten-gallon Stetson hat for the occasion.) Nevertheless, according to one participant, the Haida had felt "a huge sense of pride," because, Diane Brown maintained, "he made us research and do more than if he wasn't there."[38]

Before Reid left Haida Gwaii after the pole-raising ceremony in Skidegate, he travelled to Old Masset to attend the doings associated with the inauguration of Robert Davidson's house honouring his great-grandfather, Charles Edenshaw. But Reid was not entirely comfortable. As Davidson recalled, "He put us down for singing our songs, shuffling our feet, beating the drum." And, he continued, Reid was "very sarcastic about us reclaiming that part of ourselves. He didn't understand it and he didn't want to understand it; he was very impatient about it."[39] As Reid told a friend, these sorts of events were best suited to church basements.[40]

Bill Reid's life and his work were not centred in the remote village of Skidegate. His markets, his patrons, his museums, and his friends were in the metropolitan centres in the south. He did not seek to create a cultural context for his work by re-kindling the ceremonial traditions of the Haida people, like Robert Davidson did. In carving the pole in Skidegate, he had created a work to honour his ancestors in a retrospective and commemorative way. Moreover, living in Skidegate had not made him feel more Native or more optimistic about the possibility of reviving the culture there. If anything, his experience had made him even more of the middle-class WASP he often claimed he was. Reid must have realized that his work, like the ceremonies and the songs that the Haida performed at the pole-raising ceremony, was not only a compilation of the past and the present but also, in important respects, of his own creation.

CHAPTER 13

Big Is Beautiful

Bill and Martine Reid, Granville Island

In the summer of 1976 Wilson Duff committed suicide. British Columbia lost a brilliant scholar of Northwest Coast peoples. Reid, who was anticipating a visit from Duff on the Queen Charlotte Islands that summer, was devastated. Reflecting on their friendship in an essay for the art magazine *Vanguard,* he recalled how he and Duff had met to drink a little and exchange long periods of uncomfortable silence — especially when they were talking about something other than Native art.[1]

Reid owed Duff an enormous debt. The anthropologist had helped him through bouts of depression. He had given Reid his first opportunity to carve on a large scale by arranging his ten-day-long "apprenticeship" with Mungo Martin in 1956. And he had made Reid's year in England possible by supporting his application for a Canada Council fellowship. Reid had shown his appreciation by producing a silver medallion, ironically inscribed with the words "survivor, first class," to celebrate Duff's fiftieth birthday. On the day that Wilson Duff was found dead in his office at the university, he was wearing the medallion around his neck.

A few months before Duff ended his life, he had written to Peter Macnair, who had taken his place at the Provincial Museum in Victoria. Duff wanted help with one of his Ph.D. students whom he described as capable, sensitive, and responsible.[2] The attractive young student from Paris had arrived at the university the previous September on a three-year Canada Council exchange fellowship to study the language, myth, art, and ritual of the Kwakwaka'wakw people. No novice to the discipline of anthropology, Martine Widerspach-Thor had studied at the prestigious Ecole Practique des Hautes Etudes in Paris where she had attended the seminars of the world-famous anthropologist Claude Lévi-Strauss. In the spring of 1976, she was completing the first year of her course work towards a Ph.D. In preparation for her fieldwork, Duff asked Macnair for help and introduced her to the province's most well-known contemporary Native artist, Bill Reid.

Although Widerspach-Thor's fieldwork among the Kwakwaka'wakw had been based in southern British Columbia, following Duff's death she travelled to the Queen Charlotte Islands. There, the student and her two travelling companions visited Reid, who was in the process of carving his totem pole for the new administration building in Skidegate. Always hospitable — especially to a young attractive woman — Reid put the party up in his three-bedroom trailer on Second Beach. After a few days, Widerspach-Thor's two friends left, but she elected to stay behind. When Tak Tanabe visited Reid in Skidegate shortly after Widerspach-Thor's departure, Reid was ecstatic about the wonderful anthropology student.[3]

Everyone knew that Bill Reid had a great need for the love and admiration of women. But until Martine Widerspach-Thor came onto the scene, few people realized the extent to which he also needed someone to organize his life.

Reid obviously liked the French connection. Shortly after meeting his future wife, he told a reporter that he was now making his home in Toronto, Montreal, and Paris.[4] Reid admired Martine's ability to transform a potentially boring occasion into a lively one. He also liked her sense of drama, from the way she entered a room to how she wore her clothing. Martine could upstage every woman at a party or celebration by dressing slightly above what the occasion called for — and get away with it. When Peggy Kennedy asked her mother what she thought about her future daughter-in-law's appearance, Sophie Reid, who was now living in a nursing home, replied, "It's not so much dressing, it's more like putting on a costume for Martine."[5]

To Audrey Hawthorn, the union between the fifty-six-year-old artist and the twenty-five-year-younger woman "was a wonderful thing because Martine made his life much more easy and comfortable."[6] When the couple met, Martine recalled that all Bill could talk about was dying: "He was a very suicidal man."[7] The young student helped Reid come to terms with his debilitating disease, which had put him on a suicidal course. She also strengthened his European orientation by creating a cultivated Euro-Canadian living space. Visiting their home in the Vancouver area of Kitsilano in 1983, the journalist Lloyd Dykk encountered what he called "brilliant litter." Glass bowls were filled with crushed dried flowers. Pottery by two of British Columbia's leading potters, Wayne Ngan and Tam Irving, was on display. Hanging on the walls of the palatial apartment were paintings by Bill's old friends, Tak Tanabe and Joe Plaskett. And, along with an African mask, many examples of Bill's own work were on show. "He makes no bones about himself as being, culturally, an Anglo-Saxon," Dykk concluded at the end of the interview.[8]

Not everyone took a charitable view of the relationship. Reflecting on Reid's attraction to "flashy women," Art Price felt that women like Martine were a great boon to Bill's ego.[9] Tak Tanabe saw the blond and handsome Martine as "a trophy wife."[10] It is indisputable that Martine Reid, as she became in 1981, was a stunning model for Reid's jewellery. "I love to wear Bill's jewellery — especially his family crest," she recalled.[11] As with Sherry

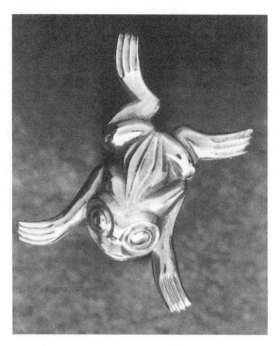

Gold brooch, frog, 1971

Grauer before her, Martine inspired Bill to create some of his most stunning pieces of jewellery. Working in the Native style, he transformed his diminutive frog brooch into a pair of earrings for Martine. Returning to the medium of boxwood that had inspired *Raven,* he created *Transformation Pendant with Detachable Mask* based on the dogfish motif.[12] And the modernist sterling silver and white gold necklace that Reid borrowed from Sherry Grauer for an exhibition in the early 1970s eventual found its way to Martine's neck.[13]

There was plainly more to the marriage, which lasted until Reid's death, than sexual attraction and artistic inspiration. Martine possessed not only striking good looks and a sophisticated aloofness but a clear vision of the direction in which Reid and his work should be moving. Harnessing Bill's uninhibited and naive wish to show his work and to read his writings on Haida culture at every possible opportunity, Martine helped turn what he had jokingly called "Artifakes Inc." into a serious proposition. When she became a sessional lecturer on Native art at the University of British Columbia, Bill spoke to her class. Whenever she helped a gallery or a museum mount an exhibition of Northwest Coast art, Bill's work was prominently featured. And when the media interviewed Martine, she championed Reid's "deep carving," she noted his ancestral link to Charles Edenshaw, and she insisted that her husband was a born maker who could effortlessly slip into the Native past.[14] During the last decade of Reid's life, Martine ensured that her husband's reputation would live beyond his grave by buying back many of his works. (In January 1999 she helped found the Bill Reid Foundation, an organization that aimed to preserve his art and legacy.)

Martine was a major entrepreneurial force behind her husband's work during the last two decades of his life, and with her sophisticated and probing understanding of Northwest Coast culture, she also influenced his work in a number of ways. For example, she brought back from France two sticks of boxwood, which Reid used to produce the maquette that inspired his imposing eighteen-foot-high sculpture, *Killer Whale.* (From 1985 the sculpture dominated the entrance to the Vancouver Public Aquarium.) Reid was the first to admit that he was "pretty shaky on who did what to whom in what myth."[15] After meeting Martine, however, he became more conscious of the myths associated with the creatures he was depicting in his art.

❧

When Reid raised his pole in Skidegate in 1978, most people thought it would be his last monumental work, and rightly so. He had been suffering from Parkinson's disease for at least seven years and his condition was getting progressively worse. The cocktail of drugs that structured his day was becoming less effective. What he called the "wild fluctuations between complete incapacity and complete normality" meant that he could work only three or four hours a day. This was frustrating because Bill needed his art, his writing, and his storytelling to keep his mind off his disease. Being active was his best therapy. "If you didn't work," he told a reporter, "you would just go crazy."[16]

And there was much to do. Most pressing was the long overdue sculpture for the new museum at the University of British Columbia. Reid and Walter Koerner, who commissioned the carving in 1972 for $125,000, had already decided on the motif. Reid would produce a larger version of the small boxwood carving *Raven Discovering Mankind in a Clamshell,* which he had carved in Montreal. In 1976 Reid had attended the opening ceremony for the new museum. He had seen the area below the rotunda that Arthur Erickson had designed for his proposed sculpture. As if heralding the completion of the work, in 1977 Reid issued a limited edition of a print based on his boxwood carving entitled *Raven and the First Men*. And, in preparation for the scaled-up version of the original carving, he made some alterations to his initial rendering of the myth.

When Reid had carved *Raven Discovering Mankind in a Clamshell*, he had depicted a woman emerging from the shell. According to Haida mythology, however, the first Haida men *and* women were created only after the raven had flung chitons, or mollusks, at the groins of the male-like beings who emerged from the shell first. Recognizing his error, Reid asked Sherry Grauer, who owned *Raven Discovering Mankind in a Clamshell*, if he could delete the female from the diminutive carving. Grauer refused. Though Reid could not correct his earlier mistake, he made sure that no female was included in the work for the museum.

That carving required a large block of wood, exceeding the dimensions of most trees. At the beginning of 1976, the museum took delivery of 106 yellow cedar beams that had been selected and matched for Reid by the well-known Vancouver sculptor George Norris. The beams were left to dry, first in the university's carving shed, then in a kiln at Western Forest Products. In December 1977 the wood was transported to Koppers International Canada Limited in the Vancouver suburb of Burnaby. There, under the supervision of the chief engineer, Jan Wynam, the planks were planed, then bonded into a four-and-a-half-tonne laminated block. Early in 1978 the laminated block, now 2.1 metres square, was moved to the carving shed at the university. By this time George Norris had made a full-scale plaster model of the proposed carving in his garage. Using this as a guide, Norris then began to rough out the laminated block of wood with a power saw. In the autumn of 1978, Gary Edenshaw and Reid himself joined Norris. By November, Norris had quit the project, leaving Reid and Edenshaw to begin the fine carving.

Work progressed slowly until, early the following year, Bill and Martine paid a visit to the studio of George Rammell. A graduate of the Vancouver School of Art, Rammell was an active sculptor — in 1977 the Burnaby Art

Gallery had given him a solo exhibition that displayed his superb knowledge of human anatomy. When Reid met him, Rammell was transforming a four-tonne block of marble into a sculpture, *Pyrolith*, which dealt with the theme of creation. Recently laid off work as a technician at Capilano College, he was elated when Reid invited him to become his assistant.

Rammell was under no illusions about what Reid wanted: "He hired you with the understanding that you were going to contribute your artistic abilities, not just your technical process but your actual vision." Reid told Rammell not to look at Norris's plaster model of the raven but to "make it feel like a clamshell and oh — by the way — if the balls are in the wrong place feel free to change them." Reid gave Rammell lots of creative space. He would disappear, provoking Rammell to contemplate how Canada would treat him if he destroyed something. Then, looking like a movie star in his dark sunglasses, Reid would arrive at the carving shed in a friend's Rolls-Royce, full of complaints about his social obligations. Reid must have been happy with what he saw on these fleeting visits to his studio because he left Rammell in charge of the project.[17]

And challenging work it was for Rammell and Reid's other assistants. The sculpture was composed of intersecting circles, which were asymmetrical. "He was throwing the French curve into everything at that point," Rammell recalled, "and it was really tricky because that wood, you can't add on, the way you can with plaster." Rammell found it difficult to avoid working in his own style: "The figures in the shell were like little Haida people and had to feel like Haida people." Things were not made any easier when the usually articulate Reid, who would evoke Charles Edenshaw's name during his visits to the studio, seemed to have difficulty explaining himself. He would grunt in response to Rammell's questions — "and you were supposed to interpret that grunt."[18]

It was not just the lack of direction that made working for Reid frustrating. Rammell was not himself Native and Gary Edenshaw, who was, did not approve of his involvement in the project. Wanting a greater role for himself, Edenshaw moved into Rammell's territory: the figures emerging from the clamshell. When Reid discovered what was happening, "there was a major blow-up" and, Rammell recalled, "Gary suddenly was off the job." Although Gary Edenshaw later rejoined the project, Rammell remained confident that he knew what the piece was about, knew what Native society was about, and could get the job done according to Reid's wishes.[19]

Two other carvers who were both descendants of Charles Edenshaw, Reg Davidson, the brother of Robert, and Jim Hart, joined Rammell in January 1980. "It was too far gone by the time I got on to it," Reg Davidson recalled, "so I didn't learn anything from it. All that I was doing was just cleaning up."[20] Feeling that Rammell had largely resolved the piece, Davidson quit. Jim Hart remained on the job until the fine carving was finished.

When Reid hired him, Hart had been working with Robert Davidson in Whonnock and before that he had helped him on the Edenshaw Memorial House in Old Masset. Although an experienced carver, Hart soon discovered how difficult it was to cut through the end grain of a beam and the glue line — an activity that literally peeled off the edge of his tool. Getting Reid to talk during his rare visits to the studio was equally difficult. "I used to have a hard time to sit down and talk to him," Hart explained. "He always wanted to keep himself on an elevated plane." This attitude seemed wrong, the young artist believed, because it had been he and Rammell who had done the lion's share of the work. Most of what Hart got from Reid — "It's got to have depth; it can't be a surface piece" — came through Rammell. "He would tell Rammell things and Rammell would spout it out . . . and talk about what they used to talk about." Hart hung on to Rammell's every word because he wanted to hear what Reid had to say about the carving.[21]

Coming to grips with Reid's moodiness and, during his bouts of depression, with his silence was especially difficult for the Native artists who wanted his approval and advice. Gerry Marks, who had worked with Reid on the pole in Skidegate, felt that "there was little energy flow between us."[22] Norman Tait, who had asked Reid a lot of questions about Native art during his visits to his Vancouver apartment in the 1970s, was told, "Think about it. He thought that if I thought about it I would dig it out for myself."[23] Don Yeomans, who assisted Reid a decade later, had a less encouraging experience. The young Haida, who had been trained by Freda Diesing in Prince Rupert, was articulate and bold. When he told Reid which direction the piece he was working on should take, an exasperated Reid replied, "It's my piece — who's paying you?" Yeomans commented later, "And that was how it was always settled."[24]

Defending Reid's tendency to ride roughshod over the feelings of his helpers, the artist Joe Plaskett has noted that "there has to be a ruthlessness" in organizing so many assistants.[25] Reid expected his assistants to "deliver on every level at once." Rammell acknowledged, "It was still his work, he was paying the bill, it was his signature."[26] Even so, Reid's helpers sometimes felt that they did not always get the credit they deserved. For example, the names of the assistants who had worked on *Raven* were not included on the plaque that hung on the wall beside the sculpture. Reid himself had approved the text, and, as Michael Ames, the head of the museum at the time, noted, "I guess we weren't smart enough to ask . . . it happens all the time in the museum where a lot of stuff is anonymous."[27] Similarly, Jim Hart felt that Reid had deliberately left him out of a documentary film that charted the making of *Raven*. The young carver harboured a grudge until he received a photograph of himself working on *Raven* from an official, Stephen Inglis, at the Canadian Museum of Civilization. "I have no real proof I did it except the copy of the photo you sent me," a grateful Hart told Inglis.[28]

Reid's invaluable assistants were not, as Don Yeomans told everyone at the memorial service at the University of British Columbia in 1998, "the worst kept secrets in this business."[29] During the carving of *Raven*, the University of British Columbia's faculty newspaper printed a photograph of Gary Edenshaw working on the sculpture in January 1979.[30] A year later, the *Vancouver Sun* reported that George Norris, George Rammell, and Jim Hart were helping Reid give the sculpture "the final surface tool finishing."[31] Moreover, in virtually every newspaper interview, Reid gave credit to his co-workers.[32] Finally, at the unveiling of *Raven*, he publicly thanked Norris, Edenshaw, Rammell, Hart, and Davidson for their help.[33]

While Reid was sometimes slow or negligent to acknowledge the contribution of his assistants, everyone who worked on *Raven* learned something. Reg Davidson learned patience. George Rammell learned how to make and repair Native tools. Although Jim Hart later called Reid "a real S.O.B." for not giving him sufficient acknowledgement, he admitted learning a lot from "the old man." Reid had taught Hart how to handle tools. He had made him feel comfortable working on a large carving. He had introduced him to non-Native art: "For a lot of years of my life I thought that Haida was the only art in the world."[34]

Above all, as with Robert Davidson before him, Reid had taught Hart how to survive in the city. This was vital because Hart felt that some members of the museum staff did not trust him. "They figured I was drinking and all. But they did not know me, I guess." There was one person at the museum who was particularly unfriendly. "She was a German woman and she had that strong edge and after a while I didn't want to talk to her or to see her," Hart admitted. The situation did not improve until the day the carving was installed in the museum. Wearing a suit for the occasion, Hart found that

Raven and the First Men

some members of the museum staff began to treat him differently: "It was like, 'I guess he did have some potential,' and I didn't like that."[35]

On April 1, 1980, no less a figure of the white establishment than Prince Charles, who was in British Columbia to attend the annual meeting at Lester B. Pearson College near Victoria, unveiled *Raven and the First Men*. During the opening ceremonies, the music of Handel, sung by a choir accompanied by an organist and trumpeter, flooded the museum. The chancellor of the university, J.V. Clyne, set the tone for the proceedings when he told the gathering, "This university and its people have for a long time played an important role in the preservation of Indian artifacts and a culture that was at one time in danger of being lost."[36] For those who required an explanation of the myth behind the carving, Reid had prepared a text. After giving an account of the creation myth, he returned to a familiar theme: "Most of the villages are abandoned and in ruins and the people have changed."[37]

There were notable absentees from the ceremony: virtually no Native people were present. Two months later, however, the museum made amends for this lacuna by inviting one hundred Natives from Skidegate and Old Masset to Vancouver for a second unveiling ceremony on June 5. The museum's curator, Marjorie Halpin, hoped that the celebration would mark "a new stage in the relationship between Native people and whites. It's always been a we-they situation. Both sides have been asserting their differences for so long; maybe the celebration will transcend that." [38] Halpin's hopes for the June celebration were largely fulfilled. Not only were the Natives on show, they were in charge. The event accommodated artists such as Robert Davidson, who wanted to give Native art a ceremonial function.

At the second unveiling ceremony, Reid exchanged his suit for a button blanket. The Natives danced and sang or helped prepare the feast of smoked salmon, herring roe on seaweed, and razor clams. But, just as Reid had shown his Native assistants that they could carve to the music of Mozart, he also invited the non-Native Leon Bibb to sing and the Paula Ross Dance Company to perform.

While the second inaugural celebration of *Raven* did little to boost Reid's reputation among non-Natives, it did raise his profile among the Haida people. Tribal loyalty had been growing in British Columbia since the collapse, in 1975, of both the BC Association of Non-Status Indians and the Union of BC Indian Chiefs. This second celebration at the Museum of Anthropology gave the Haida a focal point. It reinforced the on-going process of making the Haida Nation the fundamental unit of their identity. A major component of that new identity was self-reliance. This manifested itself in the rejection of the forms and values associated with large, centralized, and bureaucratic entities whether government, business, or Native. It also heralded the erosion of the distinction between status and non-status Natives. Thus, the birth of the male-like beings, so well depicted in Reid's *Raven*, became synonymous with the rebirth of the Haida Nation.

It is difficult to know whether Bill Reid felt comfortable at the second ceremony inaugurating *Raven and the First Men*. As was the case with the celebration surrounding the raising of the totem pole in Skidegate, Reid's work provided a ceremonial context for Native art and culture. Yet his not-so-happy experience of carving the pole in Skidegate was still very much on his mind. Moreover, his future patrons were not the Haida but private patrons such as Isabelle Graham, who would finance the cost of Reid's carving at the Vancouver Aquarium, or the committee at Expo 86, or the executive officers of Teleglobe Canada. The university's Haida House, the cedar-plank house carved by Reid and Cranmer in the early 1960s, would be used less as a venue for Native feasts than as a place for Reid to host dinners prepared by the popular restaurateur John Bishop, and black-tie concerts of popular and classical music. In the 1990s, when Reid did occasionally potlatch, it was largely to give Native names to the white patrons, who had made his large public commissions possible.

Unlike Robert Davidson, Reid remained obsessed by the form, not the function, of Native art. Moreover, it was not simply the gratification that he got from producing a well-made object. Reading from his text for *Out of the Silence* at the Queen Elizabeth Theatre, taking a boatload of people to the deserted Native villages on the Queen Charlotte Islands, or giving a friend a late-night tour of the Museum of Anthropology — to which he had his own key — enabled Reid to continue his role as publicist and impresario of Native art.

Reid had long insisted that his social circumstances demanded that he work in an eclectic sort of way. This is why he told a reporter in 1980 that *Raven* was the product of "European technology applied to old forms. Without the knowledge of anatomy I gained from classes it would have been difficult. It's hard to learn, and Indians aren't interested. They want to carve masks and poles."[39] This was, of course, how Reid set himself apart from contemporary Native artists, a task made all the easier with the urbane and sophisticated Martine Reid at his side.

But was the *Raven* still Haida? Or had it become something else? To Norman Tait, the carving had a touch of Haida but was not Haida. Tait has suggested that Reid "started breaking the rules then developed his own style, which is quite unique and very different from the standard designs that we do and Bill Holm does and Bob Davidson does and Tony Hunt and so on."[40] Many critics debated *Raven*'s merits as fine art. Some felt that it did not conform strictly enough to the old styles. Judging the work on aesthetic grounds alone, Robert Davidson noted that the bird had awkward stubby legs. He felt that the raven's eye sockets should have been carved deeper in order to give it more strength. "Above all," Davidson continued, "the head was out of proportion with the rest of the body."[41]

Few critics took time to note that other Native artists, like the thirty-year-old Tsimshian Roy Henry Vickers, were not adhering to the rules of traditional Native art either. Few acknowledged, as the art critic Eve Johnson would do six years later, the debt that Reid's work owed to the funky ceramic sculptor David Gilhooly.[42] And, finally, few appreciated the extent to which *Raven*'s success rested on the way it merged traditional Haida art with western aesthetics.

Reid's jewellery had been popular among the white community because it combined western naturalism with traditional Haida design. So, too, with *Raven*. Like the jewellery and the Haida screen that Reid had produced for the Provincial Museum in the late 1960s, *Raven* was not made for ceremonial use but for display in a museum. On the other hand, unlike so many objects exhibited in museums across the country, *Raven* had nothing to do with salvage anthropology. It had not been appropriated, stolen, or bought for a token fee. It was free of any associations with white liberal guilt. Thus non-Natives could view the monumental carving as a work of art that combined Haida iconography and, thanks to George Rammell's superb rendering of the human forms, western naturalism. If the concept of post-modernism had been in vogue at the time, Reid's *Raven* would have fitted the bill. It was anti-modernist and nostalgic. And it fused classical human anatomy with traditional Native design in a new way.

Raven was a hybrid. It was neither Native nor western but bridged two traditions. This ambiguity worked in Reid's favour. *Raven* was suitable for exhibition either in an art gallery or in an ethnographic museum. Indeed, Reid's ability "to be quite sincerely, two things at once" was, as one critic rightly pointed out, "the key to his pre-eminent position in the art world. He sees himself as an artisan and as a propagandist for the northwest coast."[43]

Raven was also excitingly innovative within the context of Native art. The hunched-wing bird looked down on the viewer. Like the cast of figures crowning Reid's gold and silver boxes, *Raven* had been abstracted from two-dimensional space and fashioned in the round. Even the formal elements of Native design underwent a change in Reid's hands. The face on the *Raven*'s tail was an elaboration of the joint mark; this made the ovoids all but disappear.

Raven's myth, or story, was easy for Reid's non-Native viewers to comprehend. It told how humankind had come into being through the transforming abilities of a mythical bird. This appealed to a society that was constantly on the lookout for unconventional answers to large questions. It was also in line with the anthropology and museum community's fascination throughout the 1970s and 1980s with myths and shamanic beliefs. Reid had insisted in the preface of *Form and Freedom* that there was evidence to support the veracity of the Haida creation myth. Here, then, was the proof.

Also at work in the favourable public reception of *Raven* was the fact that it had been made by a person well known to the community, first in radio, then as a proponent of Native art. His celebrity status was not the only thing that took the anonymity out of *Raven*. Reid asked his viewers to take an imaginative leap by suggesting that he and the raven — trickster, transformer, tease, and troublemaker — were one and the same being. The anti-heroic, paradoxical, and chameleon-like behaviour of the raven was in line with Reid's own attitude towards the world and its people. The carving thus had a cachet that it might not otherwise have had.

∽∾∾

Raven and the First Men changed the visual landscape of Vancouver. Public sculpture would no longer be divided into two general categories: Native art — usually represented by totem poles — and controversial modernist sculpture, like George Norris's *Crab* at Vancouver's Centennial Museum. By showing that *Raven* was suitable for exhibition in an art gallery as well as an ethnographic museum, Reid had brought Native carving into the public sphere as fine art. By so doing he gave the city an art form that was both modern and indigenous; that spoke to the white and to the Native communities. Reid was therefore right when he called *Raven* the culminating piece of his career because it represented a fusion of his interest in European and Northwest Coast artistic conventions. With the possible exception of *The Spirit of Haida Gwaii,* none of Reid's future projects would be as beloved by the people of Vancouver as *Raven.*

Chief of the Undersea World, *1984*

∽∾⌒∾

By the time Reid unveiled *Raven* he was working at a slow pace. Moreover, since 1978, he had been getting by on recycling old ideas but, as he told a friend, "that can't last too long."[44] Much of what Reid now produced was based on his earlier work or on the work of other Native artists. For example, the killer whale that Reid fashioned out of boxwood in 1983 had two sources: first, the killer whale that crowned the magnificent gold box that he made for the Provincial Museum in 1971; and second, an argillite carving of a vaulting whale produced in 1977 by the Haida carver Walter Russ.[45] Reid submitted a larger version of his diminutive boxwood carving to the Vancouver Public Aquarium's jury for consideration. The jury liked it and, with the help of Jim Hart, Jack Carson, and several other assistants, the killer whale was scaled up into the eighteen-foot-high bronze sculpture. In 1984 the five-metre-high *Killer Whale* or *Chief of the Undersea World,* as it has also been called, was installed outside the entrance to the aquarium. Robert Davidson was just as critical of the *Killer Whale* as he had been of *Raven.* The finished work was, Davidson claimed, well below the standard of the boxwood maquette on which it was based. In his view, its overall shape looked more like a jellybean than an ovoid.[46]

A year later, a silver brooch that Reid had produced as long ago as 1957 and an argillite pipe that he had seen in the British Museum ten years later gave him the motif for the 8.5-metre-long low-relief bronze *Mythic Messengers.*[47] Commissioned by the telephone and telex company Teleglobe Canada for its international centre in Burnaby near Vancouver, Reid's mural relief took a novel approach to the theme of communication. The gracefully arching tongues linking the human, animal, and mythical creatures give the work a wonderful rhythm and a wonderful realization of the theme. The mural, which was donated to the Bill Reid Foundation in April 2001, is undoubtedly one of Reid's most successful works.[48]

The production of imposing sculptures such as *Raven, Mythic Messengers,* and *Killer Whale* gave the general public the impression that Bill Reid was not only

Mythic Messengers, *bronze relief*

creating new pieces and formulating new ideas, but doing most of the physical work himself. This reinforced the view that Reid was the heroic singular artist. It is true that he was producing larger work and getting paid higher fees than ever before. But, unknown to most of the public, his debilitating condition demanded that he do less carving and modelling himself.

Reid's achievement was to turn his disability to positive effect. He never allowed his poor health to truncate his career, and his friend Robert Reid was right when he observed that Bill's illness "gave him a sense of purpose and drive."[49] Bill's realization that scaled-up versions of old work could have a large impact now spurred him on to produce some of his most memorable work.

CHAPTER 14

BILL REID™

Reid at home

In 1986 Bill Reid was the mystery guest on the popular television program *Front Page Challenge*. One of the panelists, Allan Fotheringham, asked him if he had ever made any money from his work. Without missing a beat, Reid told the newspaper columnist that he had not earned very much, but enough.[1]

Here was the ironic Bill Reid at his best, because he was often actually shocked by the amount of money that people were willing to pay for his work. After he had quoted a price, his heart would leap if the client were still standing. This meant, of course, that he could have asked for more.

Reid had no qualms about charging high prices for his work. "I like making things," he told a reporter for the *Toronto Star* in 1993, "and people indulge me in my pursuits."[2] To Gitxsan artist Earl Muldoe, Reid's attitude seemed greedy. "I'll tell you what," Reid replied in response to Muldoe's observation, "I've worked so long at this on starvation wages, I think before I die I can get top money for most of my work."[3]

❧

According to Robert Davidson there were two kinds of Native artists: those who sold their work and those who sold themselves.[4] Like most financially successful artists, Bill Reid was both. He produced stunning work that appealed to a non-Native public and he practised the tricks of the self-marketing trade. He gracefully accepted being the focus of attention, then entertained his clients with clever but casual conversation. He possessed a gift for ironic self-mockery. He got a gleeful thrill out of knocking established conventions — and getting away with it. He had a talent for thinking on his feet and for making the distinction between what the advertising world calls "creatives" and others. Finally, like all successful self-promoters, Reid knew how to jump from imaginative to more rational modes of discourse.

Throughout the 1980s and the early 1990s, Reid did several things to promote his writings and his art. He appeared at schools, charity events, banner signings, exhibition openings, concerts, dinners, and book launches. He gave his name to the University of Northern British Columbia's newly created Bill Reid Endowment Fund devoted to excellence in the verbal and visual arts. All these activities gave Reid many photo opportunities to publicize his achievements, charitable acts, awards, and supervision of his various projects.

And there was much to photograph: Reid at the book-signing of his old friend, Doris Shadbolt, whose lavishly illustrated monograph, *Bill Reid*, appeared in 1986. Reid at the opening of his second solo exhibition, *Bill Reid: Beyond the Essential Form*, at the University of British Columbia's Museum of

Reid with Barbara Shelly

Anthropology the same year. Reid accepting the Bronfman Award for Excellence in Crafts (1986), Vancouver's Lifetime Achievement Award (1988), and the National Aboriginal Achievement Award for Lifetime Achievement (1994). (During a reception at the latter event, a photographer caught the prime minister, Jean Chrétien, pushing Bill in a wheelchair.) Reid added yet another laurel to his wreath when he joined thirty Nobel Prize winners by becoming a member of the Academy of European Arts and Sciences.

By the early 1990s, Bill Reid was big news beyond British Columbia. His reputation had spread to central Canada. Guests attending the opening of his first solo exhibition at Miriam Shiell's prestigious gallery in Toronto clamoured to touch the artist. Reid put a lot of energy into the trip to Toronto in 1993. According to Shiell, it paid off by creating the view, long held in British Columbia, that Bill Reid was a national treasure.[5]

Reid contributed to the pictorial and written archive of himself and his work in many ways. When he completed a new carving or a piece of jewellery, he asked the Vancouver-based photographer Ulli Steltzer to photograph it: "That's how I photographed the clamshell in his hands."[6] Though his illness prevented him from sitting still for more than a few seconds, Reid agreed to pose for the Museum of Anthropology's photographer, Bill McLennan. "I was down on the floor changing a roll and I turned around," McLennan recalled of his photo session with Reid in front of *Raven and the First Men*, "and he had climbed up on the *Raven*; and I thought, 'Oh my God, he is sitting on the artifact.'"[7] Taking advantage of this bizarre situation, McLennan climbed to the top of his ladder and got three shots in quick succession. Two of them were out of focus because Reid's leg was shaking. The third take was perfect because he had remained perfectly still.

Reid also sought to ensure that his personal papers would be preserved for posterity. Housing the largest collection of his work, the Museum of Anthropology seemed the logical venue for his papers. The museum secured a grant from the Leon and Thea Koerner Foundation in order to establish an archive in Reid's name. Then they proudly issued a flyer announcing that Reid's papers and photographs were soon to be made available to students and scholars alike.[8] But few researchers had an opportunity to view the Bill Reid Archive. The collection was withdrawn from the museum before the archivist had completed cataloguing it.

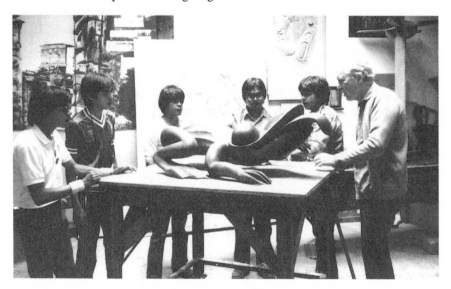

Reid with students in Granville Island studio

Reid, with the help of Martine, preferred to put his energy into securing a niche for his work in the fine art world. In 1986 he went some distance towards doing so when he sold his magnificent carving, *Phyllidula, the Shape of Frogs to Come,* to the Vancouver Art Gallery.[9] (Reid received $50,000; this represented the biggest sum the Vancouver Art Gallery had paid for a work of art.) Throughout the 1980s and early 1990s, Reid sold prints and drawings, carvings, and miniature bronze and gold replicas of his monumental work through two Vancouver galleries — the Equinox Gallery, then the Buschlen Mowatt Gallery — and in Toronto through the Miriam Shiell Gallery. When the Museum of Anthropology received funding in the spring of 1994 from the Royal Bank of Canada to build display cases for its collection of Reid's work, he told them to make "Fifth Avenue" display cases. "He didn't want people to look down on the work," Bill McLennan recalled, but to view it at eye level.[10]

Reid knew not only where and how to sell and to display his work but also the value of pairing the visual image with the written word. During the last two decades of his life, every exhibition or unveiling of a major work was accompanied by his writings. Even when he shared exhibition space with other artists — the Glenbow Museum's Olympic Arts Festival exhibition, *The Spirit Sings: Artistic Traditions of Canada's First Peoples* in 1987, is one example — Reid's own words appeared in the catalogue. He rarely wrote anything new for these occasions but recycled the text of a lecture, an earlier piece of writing, or a radio talk.

Bill Reid had consistently written or spoken about his own and other people's work since the 1950s. Thus it was not surprising that, in 1980, he wrote a short essay to accompany the unveiling of *Raven and the First Men.*[11] Nor was it out of character when, three years later, he produced a foreword and ten decorative chapter headings for George MacDonald's impressive book *Haida Monumental Art: Villages of the Queen Charlotte Islands.* Not one to waste an image, Reid made larger versions of these drawings. He eliminated the cartouches that had given the images depth on the page and wrote a text recounting the myths they represented. In the winter of 1983, he exhibited both the drawings and the text at Elizabeth Nichol's Equinox Gallery.[12] The gallery produced a collector's edition of the work on show — it came with a personal message from and a tipped-in photograph of the artist. A year following the Equinox Gallery exhibition, the drawings were used to illustrate the Haida myths that Reid wrote in collaboration with the poet Robert Bringhurst. *The Raven Steals the Light* was published in 1984.

Most critics in British Columbia liked the way that Reid's drawings of the myths combined European naturalism and shading techniques with traditional Native designs. Writing in the popular American publication *Northwest Arts,* art critic Barry Herem had a different view. Though he acknowledged the critical and financial success of the work, he found Reid's designs flaccid, his lines wobbly, and his markings murky.[13] To Nuu-chah-nulth artist Joe David, Reid's drawings were also "really awful."[14] But unlike Herem, David kept his thoughts to himself until after Reid's death.

Johannes Lakke's research on artists with Parkinson's disease offers a clue as to why Reid's ability to draw had suddenly deteriorated. After all, wobbly lines and flaccid designs had never previously marred his work. But irregular or awkward perpendicular strokes, an unusual manner of hatching along with compositional imbalances, and changes in format and style do characterize the graphic work of artists with Parkinson's disease. These were the very flaws that Herem noted in Reid's work. But the art critic was wrong on one important point. The faults in Reid's drawings were not due to his lack of skill but to the effects of Parkinson's disease.[15]

Reid himself ensured that his disability was public knowledge. He helped publicize Dr. Donald Calne's groundbreaking research on Parkinson's disease by subjecting himself to positron emission topography (PET) — a brain scan. In August 1984 he allowed filmmakers into his Marine Drive apartment and his workshop on Granville Island for the purpose of making the film *An Artist with Parkinson's Disease: A Portrait of Bill Reid.*[16] Directed by Nina Wasnicki, the film was not an exercise in self-promotion on Reid's part. Viewers watched him struggling with easy tasks. They saw him shaking, rocking back and forth, and, during a crowd-filled evening celebration at his studio-workshop, escaping from well-wishers. They also heard his voice, now reduced to a rasping whisper, admit that he sometimes lost his judgment, fluttered around the studio like a butterfly, and took longer to do things than before. Reid later regretted talking so candidly about the pain, the mental anguish, and, above all, the debilitating effect that Parkinson's had on his ability to work. But allowing the public to witness the cruel effects of Parkinson's disease was a heroic act.

∝∾ᴄᴈ

Showing himself at his worst was the price that Bill Reid sometimes had to pay for publicity. In most cases, it was a chance worth taking because it usually worked in his favour. No other Bill Reid project, for example, caught the imagination of the media and consequently the public throughout the 1980s as the making, paddling, financing, and political discourse associated with the canoe, *Loo Taas* (also *Luutaas* and *Loo-Taa*).

The first carvings that Reid ever made were of a Viking ship and Arab dhow. At the age of thirteen, after moving to Victoria, his fascination with boats mounted when he saw canoes displayed in the Provincial Museum and paddled in Victoria's Inner Harbour during the annual midsummer Indian canoe races. Years later, when Reid made his radio program on the Skeena River for the CBC, he included eyewitness accounts of the sixty-foot-long Haida war canoes that had travelled up the river at the turn of the century. By the early 1960s, Reid had paddled in a twenty-foot-long dugout canoe that had been made with traditional tools by his friend Bill Holm.

Canoe-making was not a dead art when Bill Reid decided to construct one in the early 1980s. Nuxalk carvers in Bella Coola (Komkotes), Nuu-chah-nulth carvers at the mouth of the Nitinat River at Clo-oose, Kwakwaka'wakw carvers at Alert Bay, and the Coast Salish at Musqueam had, along with many others, had kept the art of carving and painting canoes alive. On the Queen Charlotte Islands alone, Robert Davidson Sr. had carved a canoe in 1906 and, helped by his wife, Florence, and his brother, Albert, made another canoe thirty years later. (Initially produced for an American collector, the canoe eventually found its way to the National Museum in Ottawa.) Finally, as recently as 1969, another Haida artist, Victor Adams, had also carved a canoe in Haida Gwaii.

Reid was aware of this activity; he had watched Henry Hunt carving a Haida canoe at Thunderbird Park under the supervision of Mungo Martin during his short apprenticeship in 1956. He had hosted a benefit concert in the Haida House at the Museum of Anthropology in 1981 in an effort to raise funds for the purpose of repatriating Davidson's seventeen-metre canoe from Ottawa.[17] (The Davidson canoe was not returned to British Columbia until 1986 and then only on temporary loan to Expo 86.) He had also read about canoe-making in Wilson Duff's essay, "Thoughts on the Nootka Canoe" (1965), and in Franz Boas's seminal work, *The Kwakiutl of Vancouver Island* (1909). And above all, he owned a copy of a film that documented the carving of Bill Holm's canoe in the early 1960s.

Reid's own involvement with canoes began in 1967. That year he repainted the design on a canoe that had been carved in the 1930s by the Nuu-chah-nulth artist David Shaw, for the Museum of Anthropology.[18] More than fifteen years passed, however, before he made a canoe of his own. The impetus came in 1982 when the Museum of Anthropology and the organizers of Vancouver's international fair, Expo 86, commissioned Reid to produce three canoes. "I knew the theme was transportation," Reid told a reporter, ". . . It seemed to me absolutely necessary to have a representative craft from the Native people who were dependent on the water as their means of getting around."[19]

Reid began his career as a canoe maker by producing a half-scale replica of a 5.7-metre canoe on loan from the National Museum of Man. A year later,

Launch of Loo Taas *at Expo 86*

in 1985, he supervised Gary Edenshaw and Simon Dick's construction of a 7.5-metre canoe. It was this canoe, made possible by the donation of a log from Western Forest Products, that Reid launched during Vancouver's Asia-Pacific Festival. One of these canoes became the property of the University of British Columbia; the other was sold to a private collector.

By the time the National Museum in Ottawa had sent Robert Davidson Sr's canoe to Vancouver for display at Expo 86, Reid had commenced work on a much larger canoe. Known as *Loo Taas,* or wave-eater, the impressive red cedar boat was fifteen metres long.

For the local and national press, every stage of the *Loo Taas*'s making was a newsworthy item. First there was the drama of finding an appropriate log. Reid rejected the first log because it was cracked and too knotted. He eventually settled on a 750-year-old eight-foot-wide red cedar tree from the Queen Charlotte Islands. The 200-foot-long tree was cut down to 80 feet then hauled some forty kilometres in MacMillan Bloedel's logging truck to the carving shed in Skidegate. Next, there was the difficulty of financing the project. Expo 86 officials pulled out of their original commitment and the Bank of British Columbia (later the Hong Kong Bank of Canada) stepped in. Reid was photographed making the first cut of the log at Skidegate with the bank's president, Edgar F. Kaiser, at his side. After work commenced, there was trouble with Reid's assistant, Gary Edenshaw. He was unhappy, as he had been during the carving of *Raven,* because Reid was employing non-Natives to help him carve the canoe. Edenshaw also wanted to carve intuitively, in the traditional Haida manner, rather than follow Reid's carefully worked-out calculations. Unable to carve in this way, Edenshaw left the project in a huff. Reid found himself in the news once again.

The final stages of making the canoe — the steaming of the log — fascinated everyone. This procedure entailed placing red-hot stones in the carved-out centre of the log, then filling it with water. The process took two hours. Much to Reid's relief, the canoe expanded twenty-two inches to its intended shape. The press captured this event, along with the towing of the finished canoe from Skidegate to Vancouver and, finally, *Loo Taas*'s positioning in front of the royal yacht in False Creek during the opening ceremony of Expo 86.

Reid clearly enjoyed the attention he was getting because of the press's interest in *Loo Taas*. He also recalled getting "more satisfaction out of building that boat than out of anything I've ever done."[20] In his earlier writings, Reid had insisted that the formline was the dominant, and most fundamental, element in Northwest Coast art. After witnessing the making of *Loo Taas,* he changed his mind. It was the ovoid, which he felt was derived from the canoe, that had the premier place among the design elements of Northwest Coast art.[21] He often demonstrated his theory to his friends by sketching two canoes, one gunnel inverted on the other, to show how they formed a perfect ovoid.

A year after *Loo Taas* was launched, it was in the news again. Some members of the press were concerned about the extent to which Reid had been involved in all aspects of the project. A journalist for the *Vancouver Courier* was unhappy to learn that the Haida artist Sharon Hitchcock had not only painted the killer whale on the bow of *Loo Taas,* but had also conceived the design. "Why Reid chose to take credit for work he did not do is unclear," the journalist commented.[22] Reid received more attention when it became clear that the canoe needed overhauling and money had to be raised to pay for its restoration. Reid was photographed signing 230 killer-whale banners that he had designed during Expo 86. At $50 to $100 each the canvas street banners were a bargain. When sufficient funds were accumulated, two carpenters — Jack Carson and Paul Dupre — were hired to give *Loo Taas* oak ribs, steel shafts, and a steel plate. Once this work was done, the Hong Kong Bank of Canada donated the much-restored canoe to the recently established Native museum in Skidegate, and twenty people volunteered to paddle *Loo Taas* nine hundred kilometres from Vancouver to Haida Gwaii.

Reid did little to palliate the controversial reporting that surrounded the making, the financing, and the restoring of *Loo Taas*. If anything, he exacerbated it. In an interview with Stephen Godfrey of Toronto's *Globe and Mail,* Reid complained about his assistants — "Haida time is nobody giving a damn about anything." And he criticized the Haida people in general. In his view, the adults were brash, they gambled and drank too much and raised their children, who smoked marijuana, without any discipline.[23]

Reid had made these sorts of condescending remarks ten years earlier during the carving of his totem pole. That he chose to make them again was due less to what he saw in Skidegate than to his disappointment over the death, at the age of twenty-eight, of his "son," Raymond Stevens. Raymond's drug-taking had led to his death when he "fell" from a bridge in Toronto in 1981.[24] However, it was left to Reid's Toronto-based brother, Robert, to make arrangements for Raymond's burial just as it had been left to Binkie, after the divorce, to raise the child.

∽∽

Following his marriage to Martine in 1981, Bill had begun making regular visits to Paris. Attempting to break into the European art market, he had a modest exhibition in the mid-1980s at the Galerie Mansart. The show, which was an overwhelming critical success, coincided with the Musée de l'Homme's preparations for the celebration of Claude Lévi-Strauss's eightieth birthday. The museum planned to mount an exhibition, *The Art of American Indians*, in which Reid's work would be featured. What better way to celebrate the anthropologist's birthday, Reid thought, than to paddle *Loo Taas* under Paris's oldest bridge, the Pont Neuf. So in the autumn of 1989, *Loo Taas* was flown, along with Reid, fifteen paddlers, and a contingent of dancers and spokespersons, to northern France.

As with almost every project that Bill Reid proposed to undertake during the last two decades of his life, the federal and provincial governments helped bring it to fruition. Ottawa gave Reid $12,000 towards the project and British Columbia chipped in $5,000. And, also like every other event associated with Reid, the voyage from Rouen to Paris became a print and photo opportunity for the press.

Canadians got a day-by-day account of the six-day voyage. They read about how the fifteen paddlers and the contingent of Haida dancers and singers were warmly greeted along the route by large groups of photograph-taking onlookers and how they were applauded when they stopped to dance and sing Native songs. The attention made one Haida feel like a rock star. "It's wild," Reg Davidson told a reporter, "people coming up to you and pawing you. And the kids here whooping like Hollywood Indians."[25] The hereditary chief of Reid's Raven moiety, Miles Richardson III, had no doubt about the significance of the voyage for his people. It showed the world "that we are the

Haida" and, he continued, that "we're the living generation of an ancient and proud nation."[26]

Reporters also gave Canadians a less romantic story of the voyage: the problem of uncrating and launching the canoe on the docks at Rouen, the loss of the canoe paddles in transit, and the scramble to find suitable replacements. Then there was the press's disclosure of how some of the paddlers were hungover, how most of them vomited and gasped for breath from the pollution they encountered while paddling on the Seine, how they appeared to be naively impressed when French villagers reached out to touch a "real Indian." Moreover, their physical exhaustion resulted in the canoe being towed for almost half its journey — "Maybe we could have done it a hundred years ago," one of the Haida paddlers, Colin Richardson, told a reporter, "but not now."[27] Admittedly, the paddlers missed the reception platform on the outskirts of Paris — a French police boat had to direct them to the dock at Ville de Boulogne Billancourt. Even so, they arrived at the Hôtel de Ville two hours ahead of schedule.

When the paddlers looked for a McDonald's as soon as they arrived in Paris, they were acting no differently than any other young Canadians on their first trip to Europe. And if the journalists who accompanied Loo Taas filed stories of hangovers among the crew, these no doubt derived from the journalists' own first-hand experience of the causes. The churlish tone of much of the reporting began when the Haida contingent refused to use Canadian passports. It became even more negative when a photographer captured Reid removing a Canadian flag from one of the barges accompanying Loo Taas.[28] Miles Richardson proudly told a reporter, "We have our own flag, our own identity, our own constitution, and our own passports" — the flag and passports having been made specially for the occasion.[29]

The public's reaction to Reid's insistence that the flotilla fly a Haida rather than a Canadian flag was mixed. Some Canadians criticized him and the Haida for using government funds to insult the country — "How dare they expose Canada's dirty laundry in Europe?"[30] Others were stunned by Reid's behaviour. Did he not know that many people considered his art to be a "national" treasure?[31] But Lon Demerais of the Union of BC Indian Chiefs saw things differently. He told a reporter that Reid's actions were justified: "At no time in the history of Canada were the original peoples ever asked if they

Reid pulling down Canadian flag in Paris, 1989

wanted to be citizens."[32] Stephen Hume, a reporter for the *Vancouver Sun*, agreed. "The Haida paddling up the Seine flew their own flag instead of the Maple Leaf of self-righteous lies and self-deception. Who can blame them?"[33]

Reporters in France and Canada did more than cover *Loo Taas*'s journey from Rouen to Paris. They also told how Jacques Chirac, then mayor of Paris, had congratulated Reid for bringing Haida art to the world stage.[34] Reid's old friend Peter Page travelled from London in order to attend the celebration at the Hotel de Ville. He noted Martine Reid's absence then sudden appearance and recalled how striking she looked wearing a Haida button blanket.[35] (Despite his illness and marriage, Reid had remained a ladies' man. It was common knowledge in the Vancouver art world that his involvement with others put a strain on his relationship with Martine. This was one of the occasions in which she displayed notable patience and tenacity in holding the marriage together.)

Reid was no stranger to the French press. He had received stunning reviews of his Paris exhibition in the mid-1980s and, since then, had been featured in the Parisian newspaper *Le Monde*. Now his domination of the exhibition held in Lévi-Strauss's honour put him in the news again. The inclusion of Reid's large cedar carving, *Sea Bear,* along with a small collection of his jewellery and masks enabled the Musée de l'Homme to demonstrate that it was concerned not only with prehistoric art but with the art of living peoples. The paddler Colin Richardson echoed these sentiments when he told a reporter that the exhibition showed that "the Haida people still exist. We use the canoe in our real life. We're not a dead culture."[36] Reid endorsed this view: "Native art is right out there where you can see it," he told a reporter. "It's living and breathing and doing things."[37]

ᘯᘓᘖᘮᘯ

The extent to which contemporary Native art had become news was made clear when Reid supervised the making of his last monumental project. Known variously as *The Spirit Canoe, The Spirit of Haida Gwaii,* and *The Black Canoe,* the sculpture weighed over six tons and was almost four metres high. Originally commissioned for the Canadian Embassy in Washington, D.C., by the firm of R.J. Reynolds at the request of the building's architect, Arthur Erickson, more people would view *The Spirit of Haida Gwaii,* and two later versions of the work, than any other Bill Reid sculpture.

Communication, exemplified more than anything else by the canoe, was not a new theme for Northwest Coast artists. The Haida had long made canoe-shaped panel pipes into which they crammed human, animal, and mythical figures. Reid was aware of these imaginative argillite carvings. He had seen several of them illustrated in books by Marius Barbeau, Leslie Drew, and Douglas Wilson. He had included a number of argillite "canoe" carvings in the *Arts of the Raven* exhibition at the Vancouver Art Gallery in 1967. And he had viewed two panel pipes of particular significance for his future sculpture — *Canoe with Figures* and *Canoe with People* — at Vancouver's Centennial Museum.[38] Indeed, as Reid told a writer for *Canadian Art, The Spirit of Haida Gwaii* was "based on a series of old carvings dating from the 1840s — as 'mystical creatures' paddling canoes, fighting and having 'a furious time.'"[39]

The Spirit of Haida Gwaii

While communication remained the main theme of the work, Reid got the idea for *The Spirit of Haida Gwaii* one Sunday afternoon while observing a rambunctious family on a canoe outing to Lost Lagoon in Vancouver's Stanley Park. He said, "I imagined it as taking the kids for a ride in the family station wagon, and they are behaving in the usual manner of kids — chewing each other up and scratching and hollering."[40] Not surprisingly, Reid's working title for the sculpture was "Sunday Afternoon on Lost Lagoon." And this is why an early clay model of the work featured a paddler wearing western clothing.[41]

Reid not only learned how to give the interlocking figures in *The Spirit of Haida Gwaii* a sense of crowding and dynamic movement by studying the work of largely anonymous artists from an earlier era. He also got the story behind the mythical figures he was depicting by reading the myths collected by John Swanton, Franz Boas, and other early visitors to the Northwest Coast.

Reid's assistants working on The Spirit of Haida Gwaii

Reid began the first of a series of clay model sketches in 1986. Then, over the course of the next six years, he oversaw the construction of a full-sized plaster mould consisting of an armature of welded steel and wire mesh. After his assistants had sawn the mould into nearly one hundred interlocking units, they were shipped, much to the disappointment of the local foundry owner, Jack Harman, who had cast all of Reid's work to date, to the Tallix Foundry in New York State. There, the pieces were cast, welded together, chased, then covered with a layer of black shoe polish to make the finished work resemble an immense argillite carving. Reid's canoe-load of mythical, animal, and human figures was delivered to Washington, D.C., in 1991.

In perhaps his most ironic piece of writing, Reid attempted to give meaning to some of the passengers on board *The Spirit of Haida Gwaii*. The broad-back bear occupying the bow of the canoe looked to the past while his counterpart, the bear mother, looked to the future. Then there was the hooked-nose dog-fish woman — the most desirable and fascinating woman from myth-time — and the more mysterious mouse woman whom no one had ever seen in the flesh. The amphibious frog was placed partly in and partly out of the canoe. The unimaginative but industrious beaver was included in order to give the work Canadian content. The wolf — one of Reid's own crests — which he described as troublesome, volatile, and ferociously playful, was portrayed chewing the eagle's wing. Reid included two human figures — a Haida paddler, whom he called "the ancient reluctant conscript" after Carl Sandberg's poem, "Old Timers," and a Haida chief, Kilstlaai — but did not allow them to engage with the other creatures in the boat. Indeed Kilstlaai appears to be paddling the canoe, to know where he is going, and to have some vision of what is to come. Yet it is the raven that is steering the canoe with his wings and tail.

Reid was reluctant to give the voyage of his ship of fools a destination. All he could say was that although the canoe appeared to be moving, it remained anchored, forever, in the same place.[42]

Just like traditional works of Native art, *The Spirit of Haida Gwaii* would be given many meanings. But, unlike them, the process would not be achieved by celebrating the rights and feats of the owner of the work and his family at traditional ceremonies. Moreover, unlike *Raven and the First Men,* which represented a specific Haida myth, *The Spirit of Haida Gwaii* had no mythological or tangible historical base. This allowed it to be anything to anybody, to speak both to the Native and non-Native worlds.

After *The Spirit of Haida Gwaii* was installed in Washington, Reid gave a new dimension to the meaning of the work when he said that it represented "the kernel of the founding nations."[43] This was a large claim to make for a work that had its genesis in his observation of a fractious family on a Sunday afternoon during their outing to Lost Lagoon. However, Reid's interpretation appealed to the academic and museum community, the art critics, the general public, and other Native artists, all of whom added new meaning to the work. For students of architecture, Reid's merging of traditional Haida art forms with western naturalism could be seen as complementing Erickson's post-modern building that brought colossal, free-standing columns together with a giant rotunda. For the Canadian political scientist James Tully, *The Spirit of Haida Gwaii* was a metaphor for the constitutional debate that was dominating politics in Canada. While the canoe-load of disparate creatures might appear to be squabbling, according to Tully, they respected one another's cultural differences through mutual recognition, continuity, and consent.[44] Robert Davidson was also thinking of *The Spirit of Haida Gwaii* when he said of the Haida: "We're all in the same boat; we all come from that holocaust. We are the survivors of it and it does take a while for trust to happen after being let down so many times."[45]

Once again, Reid knew how to make the most out of a good thing. Four years after the installation in Washington, he oversaw the casting of another version of the work for Vancouver International Airport. Due to its green patina, it was known as *The Jade Canoe;* it fetched Reid a record-breaking commission of $3 million. Reid also managed to sell the plaster pattern that had served as a model for the bronze. In 1996 it was bought by the new Canadian Museum of Civilization in Ottawa and installed in the Grand Hall. Reid had produced a statement on the work for the unveiling in Washington, and over the next few years his short essay appeared in various publications.[46] It even inspired the composer Bruce Ruddle to write an opera. (Sung by the Vancouver Bach Choir, *The Spirit of Haida Gwaii* was premiered at Vancouver's Orpheum Theatre in 1998.) Surely no artist could have dreamed of having so many versions of his work reproduced and interpreted in so many ways. Yet none of these manifestations of the original work was accidental. They were masterminded by Bill Reid and publicized by the press, who were always eager for copy on Canada's most celebrated Native artist.

CHAPTER 15

Things Fall Apart

Bill and Martine, 1997

By 1990 it was unusual for any Native artist to be carving or making prints on the kitchen table. Most had studios. Most worked in the city, not in the villages of their birth. And most had gallery dealers to represent them. In 1993 when the *Financial Times* made money and Native art the subject of an issue, Bill Reid topped the list of earners. His miniature gold replicas of

Raven and the First Men were selling for $125,000 each — the amount of the original commission for the full-scale carving of *Raven*. Even the less well-heeled Reid enthusiast had to pay $500 for a limited edition of a thumbnail-sized silver frog pin. *Financial Times* writer Alan Bayless was right when he claimed that Reid had become big business.[1] And this was three years before the Vancouver International Airport Authority had made Bill Reid the highest-paid artist in history of Canadian art by purchasing *The Jade Canoe* for $3 million.

There were several reasons why Native art was the artistic flavour of the 1980s and early 1990s. Non-Natives were better disposed towards Native peoples than they had been at any point in the century. A culture that some claimed had died out was undergoing a rebirth of which the non-Native community could claim to be the midwives. Native artists were producing work that bridged Native and western aesthetics, making it accessible to white patrons who were proud to display it in their homes.

Bill Reid's own popularity grew exponentially during this period. The *Financial Times* reporter attributed the enormous demand for his work to his illness — he "may be nearing the end of his productive career."[2] But healthy artists were not doing badly either. In 1993 Robert Davidson could command $3,000 for a print that he had sold for $500 in 1986. And the manufacturers of ties, T-shirts, scarves and chocolates, all bearing Native designs and usually manufactured in the United States, were making a healthy profit from Native "art" too.

Not everyone was gripped by what came to be called "Reid-o-mania" in the early 1980s. Some writers wondered whether Reid's promoters, such as Canadian Native Prints, who issued a new Bill Reid print every year, were trying to create a superstar out of a man whose real claim was as a craftsman. Others felt that Reid's place at the top of the Native art world had put him in a vulnerable position. "As soon as you've been there for too long," Don Yeomans shrewdly observed, "they will kick the blocks from under you."[3]

Because Reid lived in the middle of his work, he was frequently oblivious to those around him. Anyone who got close to him became immersed in his work and his ideas. He did pay tribute to his assistants during the ceremony commemorating *Raven* in April 1986. But when *The Spirit of Haida Gwaii* was unveiled in Washington, D.C., George Rammell was not invited to the ceremony; he complained, "I did most of the work on that and I didn't even get an invitation."[4] It was the great artists of the Haida past who always got the lion's share of Reid's praise. Though he never forgot the debt that he owed to Charles Edenshaw, he announced to the world in the early 1980s that he was his great-great-uncle's equal. What Reid did was to "restore" a badly worn silver bracelet that had been made by his most respected mentor.[5]

Reid never swayed from his belief that art, and Native art in particular, was a kind of magic, and that the art gallery and the museum was the best place to view it. This line of thinking made him enemies among Native artists such as Ron Hamilton who felt that "the glass and concrete castles that we call museums" turned the artifacts they contain into "alienated things."[6]

Reid first collided with the younger generation of Native artists and writers in 1982. That year, the Native writer Marnie Fleming accused the Provincial Museum of failing "to reflect on the history and socio-cultural circumstances of Indian art objects and the people who made them" when they mounted the exhibition *The Legacy: Continuing Traditions of Canadian Northwest Coast Indian Art*. Annoyed by Fleming's review of the exhibition, Reid wrote a letter to the art magazine *Vanguard,* where the review had appeared. He began his lengthy peroration by noting how Fleming had failed to realize that the exhibition was an exhibition of art and that the work on display should be treated as such. He considered any attempts to use Native art, past or present, to air grievances as "aggressive propaganda." Moreover, he was certain that Fleming's view represented only "the most obsessed militants in the Native communities."[7]

Not only did Reid find himself at odds with some members of the Native community; sometimes he crossed swords with the white establishment. He disappointed his most consistent patron, Walter Koerner, by failing to acknowledge his support. When he was a member of the committee formed to consider the establishment of a First Nations House of Learning at the University of British Columbia, he would miss a meeting, then turn up and make the same speech he'd given before. Above all, as the committee's chair, Tom Berger, recalled, "he wasn't altogether certain that Native people had to produce more lawyers and doctors and teachers; he thought that they should learn to repair small motors on the reserve."[8] This was not, however, the mandate of the committee, which left Reid as the odd man out.

Reid's remarks and actions highlighted his relationship with a new generation of Natives and some of their non-Native supporters. But all was not peaceful on other fronts, either. The anti-white, anti-liberal, and "anti-everything" comments he made in the company of Natives in Haida Gwaii, and his remarks to the Natives about the "purple-haired ladies of Shaughnessy or the lawyers," prompted George Rammell to ask out of frustration, "Bill, what hat are you wearing today?"[9] Bill's trouble, according to the anthropologist Marjorie Halpin, was that "he's never been too sure who he is."[10]

Bill Reid had an opportunity to become an Indian in the eyes of the law in 1985. That year the Canadian government amended the Indian Act to allow non-status Natives to become legal members of the First Nations people. Reid applied for status as a Native. Sophie Reid was probably unaware that her son had reclaimed the Native ancestry that she had given up when she married William Reid. Her death in 1985 also meant that she would never visit Bill and Martine on the Musqueam Indian Reserve in South Vancouver where they moved several years later, or on Thetis Island, where they had a summer cottage. In any case, Sophie Reid had drifted into the background of Bill's life. According to her daughter, Peggy, Bill seldom visited his mother during the last years of her life. "He didn't like her being so out of it," she claimed, so he stayed away from the nursing home.[11]

Though art dealers like Bud Mintz, who ran Potlatch Arts in Vancouver, liked to boast that they sold art, not Native blood, Reid was "not Haida enough for some and too Haida for others."[12] "To the white world," one journalist observed, "he is Haida but to the Haida, he is white." When Gary Edenshaw left the *Loo Taas* project when Reid brought a white carver on to the job, the same journalist asked, "Is Bill Reid's half-Haida heritage sufficient?" Edenshaw replied: "Every little bit counts."[13]

∽∾∽

Most people were unaware of the distance that, by the early 1980s, lay between Reid's conception of an idea for a work and its execution. For example, many Reid admirers purchased limited editions of silver, gold, or bronze replicas of *Raven and the First Men* and *Killer Whale,* and castings of individual figures from *The Spirit of Haida Gwaii,* believing that Reid had been

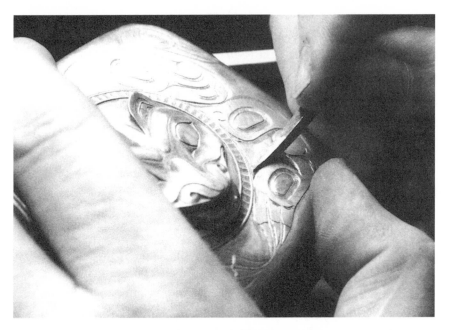

Reid carving top of box, 1985

involved in their production.[14] Increasingly, however, questions were being raised about the extent to which he was involved in the production of his work. After Reid's death, his assistant George Rammell thought it was "a bit of an embarrassment, as far as the value of the work to collectors, because people want to know that the artist did it himself." He continued, "They're buying the myth of the individual hero, as opposed to a person that directs."[15]

It was not uncommon, indeed it was essential, that Native artists had help with their large projects. Robert Davidson and Tony Hunt had long benefited from the contribution of assistants. Jim Hart and Norman Tait would employ assistants to help them complete their projects, too. Rammell often referred to Reid as the conductor of an orchestra and himself as a musician — in this case, he was surely the concertmaster.

Speaking after Reid's death, Don Yeomans recalled how Bill had asked him to carve the speaker's staff for *The Spirit of Haida Gwaii*. Short of time, Yeomans had given the job to the non-Native artist Phil Janzé. The issue of authenticity had previously arisen in the mid-1980s when a patron, who had commissioned Reid to produce a totem pole, unexpectedly arrived in Skidegate where the pole

was being carved. The Ontario collector expected to find Reid, not six apprentices. "He was really upset," Don Yeomans recalled, because "he was paying Bill
Reid prices for something Bill hadn't touched."[16]

There were often up to nine assistants on Reid's larger projects, and
according to Rammell, the studio assistants had a profound effect on the
overall composition of Reid's work.[17] Sometimes their ideas would develop
during Reid's supervision. At other times George Rammell, Rosa Quintana,
Nancy Brignall, John Nutter, Jeff Miller, and Chang Sun, among many others,
would develop a particular work according to how they thought Reid wanted
it — after all, most buyers were buying work by Reid and it was his signature
that counted.

George Rammell was a master at translating Reid's moods and his growls.
In spite of limited instruction, he knew how to direct the dedicated crew to be
as effective as possible. But while Reid enjoyed a genuine collaboration with
his assistants on *The Spirit of Haida Gwaii*, to name just one project, it was
never, according to Rammell, a co-authorship. What Rammell called Reid's
curvilinear and animated style, along with his contextual shift from Native to
high art conventions, were entirely his own.[18] Every work was based on Reid's
idea and Reid's vision. Sometimes a work was resolved in a carved or modelled maquette at the bench; at other times it was conceived on the floor of
the workshop or in the foundry. But in the end it was Reid's conception and
Reid's idea that shaped every work — be it a piece of jewellery or a totem pole
— that left his studio.

In this sense, Reid might be compared to the Maestro di designo or
Capomaestro who, during the Renaissance, saw to it that his assistants transformed his designs into finished works of art. Walter Koerner, who ended up
paying over $125,000 for the *Raven*, can be compared to the Renaissance
patron Lorenzo de' Medici. The octogenarian businessman possessed an eye
for quality, had a flair for monumental display, and the money and the deter-
mination to bring any project he commissioned to fruition. Nor was Reid
himself unlike the Flemish artist Peter Paul Rubens, who created centres of
art production that can almost be called factories, in which "all the drudgery,
the work in between, was done by others — and yet the finished work bore the
unmistakable stamp of the master."[19]

In temperament, Reid was not dissimilar to Renaissance artist Michelangelo. Like him, Reid was incapable of conveying his ideas to his assistants. He was also irritable, impatient, and frequently dissatisfied with the realization of his ideas. Indeed, two days before the unveiling of *Raven*, Reid was unhappy with how his assistants had rendered one of the figure's arms. So he took a saw and cut it off. Michael Ames, who witnessed the event, was shocked. Under Reid's instructions, one of his assistants re-carved the dismembered arm. This demonstrated to Ames that while Reid's hands might not have carved the work, his eye was always there.[20]

It is true that Bill Reid had less involvement once the clay model or diminutive carving left his hands. Yet Auguste Rodin never made a bronze sculpture, though he did oversee the making of plaster casts based on his clay models. It was equally common for Reid's contemporaries — Barbara Hepworth and Henry Moore, to name just two sculptors — to authorize the production of miniature bronze replicas of their major works. And while photographs of Henry Moore showed him working on his large plaster sculptures, "for the last thirty years of his life, virtually all of Moore's plasters were enlarged by assistants from palm-sized maquettes, and then shipped off to bronze foundries."[21]

Bill Reid was acting no differently than other twentieth-century sculptors. Although he had produced the four-inch maquette of *Killer Whale*, it was his Haida assistant, Jim Hart, who carved the four-foot model. George Rammell used this as a maquette for the eighteen-foot-high clay plaster cast from which the bronze was made at the Tallix Foundry in Beacon, New York. Even if Reid's hands left the work after he had carved the maquette, his critical eye scrutinized every stage of the project. Following a visit in the mid-1980s to the Tallix Foundry, where two four-foot copies of *Killer Whale* were being cast, Reid told his old friend Robert Reid, "I sent Mr. Claudio [the foundry manager] a list of requirements I thought necessary and a number of suggestions as to how this may be achieved." When Bill arrived in New York, he found that one whale was not up to standard. He corrected the mistake before he and the whales made their way back to Vancouver. During the final stage of preparing *The Spirit of Haida Gwaii* for casting it was the same. Reid "pulled out his pencil and began editing the mouse woman's teeth" in the Tallix Foundry.[22]

As Joe Plaskett rightly put it, Reid was "the leader and the creative intelligence" behind every major project that left his workshop.[23] And Reid remained the leader whether it was in Skidegate, or at the university's carving shed, or at the Tallix Foundry, or, from the early 1980s, in the studio on Vancouver's trendy Granville Island — a space he is alleged to have ruthlessly taken over from George Rammell.

∾ᴐᴄᴑ

In 1986 Reid's second solo exhibition, mounted by the Museum of Anthropology, *Bill Reid: Beyond the Essential Form*, saw the first large-scale critical assessment of his work. Karen Duffek, who wrote the essay for the catalogue, attempted to set the tone by praising the way in which Reid had blended Haida iconography with western naturalism. The Seattle artist and art critic Barry Herem had a different take on the work on display. Although he was thankful that the curators had not included Reid's drawings in the exhibition — "a smart move" — he adjudged that Reid was "remiss in allowing the museum to imply that he is solely responsible for the art's rebirth in recent times."[24] Robert Davidson was unhappy with the exhibition for other reasons: it was time that Reid put his work into a ceremonial context. Reid, who had little interest in invented or reinvented ceremonies, replied to Davidson's remark: "Robert's main criticism seems to be that I don't whoop and holler."[25]

Other critical voices joined the chorus. The Bentbox Gallery owner, David Young, told the *Vancouver Sun* reporter Eve Johnson that while Reid "should get credit for what he's done," there had "been an overstatement of the merit of his artwork." The Provincial Museum ethnologist Peter Macnair agreed. Reid was "not the brilliant innovator that some of his successors are today." He was a copyist and, Macnair continued, "if you read Bill Reid on Bill Reid, he'll admit to this."[26] Others were willing to give Reid credit for the work that he had produced prior to the early 1980s. According to Toronto gallery dealer Miriam Shiell, the cut-off date for the work solely made by Reid was 1982. After that she felt that only "studio pieces were made with his approval."[27]

Reid was very much aware of the criticism and the competition from other brilliant Native artists such as Art Thompson, Ron Hamilton, Tony and

Richard Hunt, Dempsey Bob, and Robert Davidson. "I sure am the Grand Old Man, as far as the little cousins are concerned," Reid told Eve Johnson in 1986. "Their new pastime is thinking up slighting things to say about poor old Bill who never did them any harm. 'Saw your frog, Bill. Liked the front part okay, but not the back. Gee Bill, don't you think that whale is a bit unbalanced? If I'd been doing it, I wouldn't have done it that way.'"[28] Times had certainly changed since Doug Cranmer told an interviewer on CBC Radio in 1965 that Native art was immune from criticism.

By the middle of the 1980s it had also become big business. It was funding scholars who, influenced by deconstructionist thinking and by the writings and lectures of anthropologists such as Marjorie Halpin, Michael Ames, James Clifford, Karen Duffek, and Aldona Jonaitis, were taking the work of contemporary Native artists seriously. Anthropologists were also re-evaluating their own role as the arbiters of what was good and bad in Native art and recognizing the extent to which the unchanging image of the "other" had been a fictional construct that formed the identity of non-Natives.

The vogue for acquiring and displaying Native art gave museum directors new or larger buildings (the Canadian Museum of Civilization opened in 1989). It also gave them larger acquisition budgets — providing, of course, they were willing to challenge non-Native notions of authority and representation, consider repatriating some of the Native artifacts in their collection to the Natives from whom they had been bought or stolen, hire Native curators, and, above all, invite Native artists to help them mount exhibitions of their work. The recognition that Indian handicrafts were fine art and not museum artifacts prompted public art galleries to broaden their collection policies, too. The National Gallery of Canada set an example when it revised its collection policy in 1985. From that year on, Native art was added to the gallery's permanent collection.

The Native community also got a share of the funding that provincial and federal governments were allocating for the promotion, exhibition, and preservation of Native art and culture. Programs were devoted to studying Native art and language in public schools and universities and to repatriating a small number of artifacts from the National Museum in Ottawa to newly built museums in Alert Bay, Cape Mudge, Skidegate, and other villages. The federal government's support of conferences such as the National Native Indian Artists Symposiums was also evidence that assimilationist policies were being reversed. Native peoples were thus allowed to celebrate their art and culture rather than forced to forget it.[29]

What was happening had more than an artistic dimension. It was one aspect of the increasing political assertiveness of First Nations people. In 1981–82 they had forced reluctant provincial and federal governments to include Section 35, guaranteeing the existing aboriginal and treaty rights of all Aboriginal peoples, in the Canadian Constitution. In 1984, at the first in a series of First Ministers' conferences on Aboriginal rights, they lobbied for the inclusion of self-government as a Native right protected by Section 35. It was over the issue of land claims that the Haida set up roadblocks, defied court injunctions, and encircled trees — all in an effort to stop the continuation of logging on their land. The protest, which began in 1985, reinforced Margaret Atwood's claim, two decades earlier, that "the Indian emerges in Canadian literature as the ultimate victim of social oppression and deprivation."[30]

Reid was a loner, not a joiner. He had made it clear, on more than one occasion, that art and politics were two separate things. Moreover, he never identified with national Native movements but rather with the Haida — particularly those who had inhabited Haida Gwaii before the twentieth century. In 1983, during his acceptance speech for an honorary degree from the University of Western Ontario, he insisted that the "flowering" or "renaissance" of Native art did not reflect the conditions on the reserve, where poverty was rife. Indeed, many artists had left the reserve behind them in aspiring to live the same sort of westernized lives as their patrons. And Reid often described himself as "just a European middle-class member of Vancouver WASP society."[31] On the other hand, he had not always stood on the sidelines of the political playing field. In the 1950s he had accused a Vancouver columnist of making denigrating remarks about totem poles and urged the government to treat the Natives as equals.[32] And almost thirty years later he shifted his focus to the land.

In 1980 Bill Reid made a trip to Windy Bay on Lyell Island. Never before had he felt the full impact of the magic of the Islands, and on no previous visit to Haida Gwaii had he been so disturbed by the logging. He noted "the huge swath, miles long and nearly a hillside wide, that marked the rapid advance of the loggers." It would, he feared, proceed "over the hilltop and move down the river valley to the sea." In 1980, he insisted, "I'm not opposed to logging, loggers, or the lumber industry, but for heaven's sake, can't we, while we still have a little bit of a last chance, institute true multi-use of the forest, with due regard for its own regeneration, the wildlife it nurtures, and most important and most neglected, its esthetic values?"[33]

Linking the land question with the preservation of the wilderness and with the protection of the environment gained strong support among the non-Native community. This was a critical new political development. And it was one that appealed to Reid for two reasons. First, he believed that it was the land and not the contemporary Native peoples that needed saving. And, second, he needed to maintain his links with the Native community in order to preserve his status as a Native among the white community.

In 1984 Reid contributed an essay to the Island Protection Society's fund-raising publication, *Islands at the Edge: Preserving the Queen Charlotte Islands Wilderness.*[34] Two years later, he joined wildlife artist Robert Bateman and environmentalist David Suzuki in welcoming the Save South Moresby Caravan to the CN Rail station in Vancouver. And when the provincial government set up the Wilderness Advisory Committee in 1985, Reid delivered a statement to its final public hearing on February 1, 1986. Claiming that "a large overburden" had come through his involvement with Native art forms, Reid told the committee that he had "become more and more involved with the Haida people and the people of the West Coast generally." All this committed him to preserving South Moresby, a place where he felt the past was intact and unchanged.[35]

Reid had told a reporter in 1985 that logging Lyell Island would "destroy one of the world's last primeval forests, destroy a people and rob the world of something precious."[36] It was the land that was worth preserving, not the songs, the dances, the stories, or even the language, which had, Reid insisted, already been wrecked, to use his word. "If they're going to find their way back to the world of cultured men, then they have to begin at the beginning. They have to be able to walk through a stretch of the bush and say, "This is what it was, this is exactly what it was.""[37]

Reid did not join the roadblocks that the Haida set up in 1985 in order to halt the logging on the south slope of Lyell Island. He did, however, make a print of a killer whale to help raise money for the battle against the logging. But when the government allowed Western Forest Products to log sixty-five acres on Lyell Island in the autumn of 1985, Reid told a reporter, "I'll go when I'm recruited."[38]

Towards the end of the following October, the Haida spokesperson, Miles Richardson, made it clear that he wanted Reid to take a stand. He had to do more than talk on the steps of the CN station, or at the Robson Media Centre, where he had celebrated the beauties of all the areas — South Moresby, the Stein River Valley, Meares Island — that were under the threat of the lumberman's chainsaw. Don Yeomans was in the Granville Island studio when Reid received the telephone call from Miles Richardson in October 1986. "I told him," Yeomans recalled, "you don't want any part of this, you told me yourself." Reid replied that he did not have any choice: "They told me that if I'm not on the road in two days, I'm not allowed to come back."[39]

A few days later, Reid flew from Vancouver to Skidegate. From there he travelled by helicopter to Lyell Island. Shortly after 7:00 A.M. on a Monday morning in late October, he joined the group of Haida men and women who were violating the trespass law by setting up a blockade. Their demands were simple: stop the logging and put the area and the rest of Haida Gwaii under Aboriginal title. Reporters were on hand to hear Reid call for "tourism, not logging."[40] A television crew captured the moment when a foreman for Western Forest Products' subcontractor, Frank Beban Logging, approached Reid:

"Good morning, Mr. Reid, what are you doing?"

"Just whittling."

Sitting next to a small fire for warmth, Reid's hunched figure was illuminated by the glare of headlights from logging trucks. He was wearing a plastic rain cape and a Cowichan hat. And he was carving. For the entire morning Reid kept sixty loggers idle. "When he saw the effect," Don Yeomans recalled, "he was pleased."[41]

Reid did not succeed in stopping the logging permanently. When the provincial government, under the premiership of Bill Vander Zalm, refused to settle Haida land claims at a conference that included nine premiers and

Aboriginal leaders from across the country in Ottawa in March of the following year, Reid protested with the only weapon he possessed. Two days after the talks broke down, Reid stopped work on the large plaster model that he and his assistants were constructing in preparation for the bronze at the Canadian Embassy in Washington, D.C. Reid told a reporter that "he was not comfortable selling symbols of the Haida people to a Government that refuses to deal with Haida land claims and act to prevent logging on Lyell Island." "I don't treat this decision lightly," he confided to another interviewer. "I know I'm walking away from the most prestigious commission available today."[42]

This time Reid, along with all the other protesters, had more to celebrate. Under pressure, Premier Vander Zalm reluctantly negotiated with the federal government, with the result that the South Moresby archipelago became the Gwaii Haanas National Park under the joint administration of the Council of the Haida Nation and the federal government. Although this did not solve the Haida's land claims, it did force British Columbia's government to transfer its interests in the future parklands to the federal Crown. Reid withdrew his protest and the newspaper cartoonists, who had had a field day, turned to other issues.[43] Work on *The Spirit of Haida Gwaii* resumed.

Joining the South Moresby blockade had drawn Reid into the centre of Native politics. While he would still refer to the Natives as "them," his whole life, as Tom Berger rightly observed, now gained meaning from his own Native ancestry.[44] Although many Haida felt that "he didn't go far enough to realize we are our ancestors," as Skidegate-based educator Diane Brown put it, "in the end he got there."[45]

At the moment when critical evaluations of Reid's work and his commitment to the Haida were threatening to raise difficult questions, the publicity associated with the Haida cause on South Moresby took priority. Don Yeomans summed up the situation: "There is nothing more cohesive than mutual need."[46]

Reid's involvement in saving Lyell Island from logging was not simply to do with land claims or with Aboriginal rights or with his own Native heritage. It is true that since first travelling to Haida Gwaii with Wilson Duff, Reid had shaped his Haida identity partly by retrospective association with the men who had carved totem poles in the nineteenth century, just as he rekindled memories of his grandmother Josephine and of his grandfather, Charles

Protesting against logging of Lyell Island, 1987

Gladstone. But his Native identity was also formed by his association with something that had not changed like the rotting totem poles that he and Duff had found above the beaches of Tanu and Skedans: the land.

When Reid called for the preservation of South Moresby on the steps of the courthouse and at the CN station, he was sincere. When he tore down the Canadian flag from the barge accompanying the *Loo Taas,* he was making a personal political statement. And when he told a reporter in Paris that all his strength and carving ability came "from the Haida past and ancestry . . . and from the support of their descendants, many of whom are here today," he was not just caught up in his own rhetoric but meant what he said.[47] When he looked backward, he thought of the people; when he looked forward, he thought of the land. Traditional Native dancing, singing, and dramatic re-enactment were gone; what were worth preserving, in Reid's view, were the pristine forest and shore.

⨯⨯⨯

During the last few years of his life, Bill Reid became the ancient reluctant conscript, the lowly paddler whom George Rammell had modelled — some felt in Reid's own image — near the stern of *The Spirit of Haida Gwaii*. Reid could never refuse an invitation — especially if it was from abroad. Accompanied by Martine Reid, a small group of around-the-clock nurses, and sometimes his daughter, Amanda, he was wheeled into openings in Japan, Sweden, and Hungary.[48] He watched the crane lower *The Spirit of Haida Gwaii* into place on the pool that Arthur Erickson had designed for it outside the Canadian Embassy in Washington. Closer to home, he relished the attention he received at his large-scale commercial exhibition, *Bill Reid: All the Gallant Beasts and Monsters* in 1991, marking the publication of a glossy coffee-table book by his gallery, Buschlen Mowatt.

In August 1994, he made what was to become his last visit to Haida Gwaii. He was very happy on this trip to Windy Bay. The party of twenty included his doctor, Stanley Lubin; Martine; a host of care-workers; friends; and Bill's sister-in-law, Barbara Reid. (Robert Reid, who had recently retired to Vancouver, only to die before Bill, chose to stay at home.) The party was joined in Windy Bay by Chief Chee-Xial, who flew in by helicopter. Everyone had a good deal of fun. During the evening Gary Edenshaw, who now used his Native name Guujaaw, led everyone in song around the campfire. And during the day Bill fished from the back of the powerboat, was paddled around the bay in the *Loo Plex* (the fibreglass version of *Loo Taas*), and got to see Windy Bay from the air when he rode in the helicopter. After the party returned to Skidegate, the *Loo Taas* was pulled out of the boathouse that stood near the new Qay'llnagaay Heritage Centre and Reid was taken for his last ride.[49]

In spite of this happy interlude, chaos increasingly seemed to surround the last years of Reid's life. There was his unsuccessful attempt to get funds allegedly owed to his company, William Reid Ltd., by Buschlen Mowatt Fine Arts Ltd. There was his all-too-public inability to get sufficient financial support for an exhibition at the Smithsonian Institution in 1989. There was the absence of a government contract for *The Spirit of Haida Gwaii*, which took the wind out of Reid's sails when he stopped working because of logging in South Moresby. Embarrassingly, his masterpiece became a hostage at the Tallix Foundry in Beacon, New York, until Nabisco Brands Inc., which had originally financed it, came up with a further $250,000 for casting. Later came the complaints, from some areas of the public sector, when the Vancouver International Airport Authority not only paid Reid the enormous sum of $3 million for *The Spirit of Haida Gwaii* — also known as *The Jade Canoe* — but removed Robert Murray's large conceptual steel sculpture, *Cumbria*, which had dominated the approach to the airport.[50] There was, too, the withdrawal by Old Masset elder Florence Davidson (jaaarahl q'iigangaa), daughter of Charles Edenshaw, of the name that she had bestowed on Reid, Kihlguuline, "the one who speaks well." While Reid was reportedly "cut to the quick," he, and others, including Robert Davidson, continued to use the name.[51]

Above all, Reid's declining health coloured these years. In the early 1980s he could impress a reporter by sketching *Raven and the First Men*, perfectly, upside down. Parkinson's disease, he told a reporter, was just "a pain in the butt."[52] Increasingly, however, his shaking hands made it difficult for him to draw with his mechanical pencil or to carve, or to engrave, or to model in clay. According to Don Yeomans, up to 1991 "if you brought him anything he would grab it and try to make the changes, but beyond that year I noticed that he wouldn't take his stuff any more because he knew that he would only destroy it." There was the slow, sad frustration of his declining years. "The last thing to go in this business isn't your dexterity, isn't your eyes," Yeomans said; "the last thing to go is your ego."[53]

Yet many people still believed that Reid was active. The Native art gallery dealer Derek Norton remembered, "There were an awful lot of Bill Reids around way after the time that he could possibly do the work."[54] Yet anyone who visited Granville Island could see — and hear — Bill pushing his walker, with its mountain-bike handlebars and its wire carriage, on the uneven pavement between the yachts in the dry-docks, the woodworking and glass-blowing studios, the architects' offices, and the fish and vegetable market. Some even peered into the studio where they might have seen him suspended in mid-air on the "chair" that George Rammell had rigged up so that Bill could see the top of *The Spirit of Haida Gwaii*. The public was, however, usually prevented from entering the studio. "I kept pushing the door closed so that we could concentrate, but people would climb under and Bill would open the door because he loved having fans watch." As Rammell recalled, it was like working in Grand Central Station.[55]

Reid's friend Robert Bringhurst has written that Reid was "a strong, proud, capable man who, when allowed by his disease, could do absolutely everything and anything for himself."[56] Yet Audrey Hawthorn later noted with sadness that in his last years Reid just could not do the beautiful work he had done.[57] While he might have lost his confidence in the early 1990s as Yeomans suggests, he certainly never lost his will to produce. And while the drawings he made in the 1980s are poorly composed and executed, he did manage to do them. But the most troubling difficulty, as Reid candidly admitted, was that he had lost his judgment. He found himself doing ill-judged things during his infrequent visits to the studio on Granville Island. This took the form of making a gadget, for example, to accomplish a job that was frequently unnecessary and inevitably led to delays. The loss of concentration and manual dexterity was frustrating and tragic for a perfectionist like Reid.

Though Bill Reid obviously relished his superstar status, Parkinson's disease made him less and less able to create the well-made objects in which he, just like his mother Sophie Reid before him, took such pride. By 1997, Bill was taking thirty-five doses of medicine a day. He was largely confined to a wheelchair. He had registered nurses — along with Martine — caring for him twenty-four hours a day. "It seems," he told a reporter for the *Sun,* "like I spend half my day getting dressed and the other half getting undressed."[58]

Increasingly, he suffered a general discomfort, and ultimately he was afflicted with the serious memory failure and confusion that is often part of the late stages of Parkinson's disease. During the last few years of Reid's life, the writer David Watmough remembered that he surfaced from the shadows only momentarily.[59] There was an acute paradox between his fame and his infirmity. "What is being proud?" he commented to a reporter who had congratulated him on the successful arrival of the *Loo Taas* in Paris in 1989. "If you're looking at the sunrise behind the pyramids and you have a nail in your shoe, what you feel mostly is the nail in your shoe."[60]

Many of Reid's last public appearances were not joyful. But they did give the people who had moved in and out of the dying man's life an opportunity to bid him farewell. Peter Page and his wife, Louise Andrew, attended the installation of *The Spirit of Haida Gwaii* in Washington, D.C. "We got these visions of Bill in the crowd," Page recalled. On his way into the reception, Reid asked the man pushing his chair to stop. "I moved him over to a corner and we had a quiet talk. The next evening we said goodbye and I gave Bill a kiss and I thought, that is the last time."[61]

Shortly before Reid's death, Joe Plaskett visited his old friend during his annual visit to Vancouver. "His speech was so badly affected by his infirmity that even those with good hearing had difficulty following the conversation. Our communication became a sort of mime, I pretending to have heard and Bill pretending that I could make an intelligent response."[62] For another fellow artist from Reid's past, Tak Tanabe, communication during a hospital visit around the same time was impossible. But Reid was not immobile. As Tanabe sat by his bedside, Bill's arms reached out in the air and his hands were busy as though he were carving or drawing.[63]

On January 12, 1998, Bill Reid passed his seventy-eighth birthday. It was a long winter. On March 7 he took his leave from his wife. He placed a closed fist in Martine's hand as if to say "Here is my mind. Do what you want with it." Bill Reid was dead six days later.[64]

EPILOGUE

Farewell

Reid's ashes being carried into the Great Hall at the Museum of Anthropology

On March 24, 1998, almost two weeks after Bill Reid's death, upwards of a thousand people gathered on Musqueam land at the University of British Columbia's Museum of Anthropology in Vancouver. Some were personal friends, others were simply admirers. All were there to pay their last respects to Reid, who had died in his seventy-ninth year. During the course of the six-and-a-half-hour celebration, a recording of Reid's sonorous voice lamented that "today is not as it was," and his friends sang, gave speeches, danced, and recited poetry in his honour.[1] Every hour of prime-time viewing on Rogers Community Television that evening was devoted to "A Bill Reid Tribute." No figure in the history of Canadian art had been given such a send-off. But then, no other artist had touched the lives of so many people and fulfilled such a diversity of needs.

It was Reid's artistic legacy that people had come to celebrate that evening.[2] Until darkness descended, some of this legacy — the totem poles and dwellings comprising the Haida village that Reid, the Nimpkish Kwakwaka'wakw artist Doug Cranmer, and the Haida, Herman Collison, had constructed almost forty years earlier — could be seen through the plate-glass wall behind the lecture podium. When the totem poles and houses were covered in darkness, two of Reid's sculptures, a crouching bear and a sea wolf, stood guard over the proceedings, which took place in the Great Hall. In a nearby rotunda the raven in Reid's best-known carving, *Raven and the First Men,* cocked its head as if waiting, like the RCA Victor dog, to hear the sound of his master's voice. Hopping about the parking lot, flapping aloft among the cedar and fir trees surrounding the museum, while commenting in its mordant metallic voice on the sanctimony below, was the raven. As the evening progressed, it became clear that this greedy mischief-maker, this omniscient creator and transformer of all things, represented more than the Haida moiety to which Bill Reid belonged. By the end of the evening it seemed that Reid and the trickster raven were one and the same being.

∽০৩∽

The Vancouver businessman Herb Auerbach and Reid's widow, Martine, had less than two weeks following the artist's death to organize the tribute. They nevertheless gathered an impressive number of dignitaries and friends to help send Reid (as the Haida artist Robert Davidson put it) "on his journey." Museum and art gallery officials offered their praise: the director of the Canadian Museum of Civilization, George MacDonald; the president of the Vancouver Art Gallery, Michael Audain; and the founder (Harry Hawthorn) and former director (Michael Ames) of the Museum of Anthropology. Representatives from every level of government, from the prime minister to Vancouver's mayor, sent their respects. Boyhood chums, former colleagues, fellow artists, caregivers, and family members offered a personal touch to the more formal accolades. Reid's most recent friends were often the most loquacious speakers. The environmentalist David Suzuki recalled hearing Reid's powerful voice protesting against the logging of Lyell Island in South Moresby. The restaurateur John Bishop recited the menu of a "de-civilized dinner" that he had prepared for Reid at the University of British Columbia. (Served in the Haida House on the grounds of the Museum of Anthropology, the meal had consisted of wild salmon, bannock, clams, herring roe, and steamed potatoes slathered with oolichan oil.) And the president of the Vancouver International Airport Authority, Frank O'Neill, boasted of having awarded Reid the largest commission in the history of Canadian art.

The contingent of caregivers who helped Reid during the last, most painful years of his life, added a more sombre note to the occasion. Reid refused to be defeated by Parkinson's disease. His physician, Stanley Lubin, was still in awe of his patient, who had risen like Lazarus from his sick-bed to meet a friend, give a presentation, or to finish a work.

But it was the First Nations people, speaking for the other side of Reid's ancestry, who dominated the occasion. The proceedings began when a representative of the Musqueam Nation, Glen Garen, gave permission for the tribute to take place on Musqueam land. Then, to the beat of Gary Edenshaw's (Guujaaw's) drum and his mournful song, fourteen canoe bearers carried Reid's ashes into the Great Hall. The Musqueam elder Vincent Stogan read the opening prayer. Chief Chee-Xial, the hereditary chief of Skidegate, thanked Bill for bringing art back to the Haida Nation. Robert Davidson recalled Reid's Haida names — Iljuwas (Princely One), Yalth-Sgwansang (Solitary Raven), and Kihlguuline (One Who Speaks Well). He also confirmed Reid's ancestoral link to the famous late-nineteenth century Haida artist, Charles Edenshaw. Following Guujaaw's example, other Natives — Bob Baker and the Squamish singers, Alanis Obomsawin of the Abeneki Nation in Quebec, and Vancouver's Urban Haida Singers led by Terri-Lynn Davidson — sang to invoke the Haida spirits.

Reid's Native apprentices and co-workers got their chance on the podium too. As they spoke it became clear to the assembled mourners that Reid had taught them more than how to scale up his maquettes into monumental works. He had given them new standards of excellence for their own work. And he had taught them how to survive in the city. Above all, Bill Reid's influence, as the artist Don Yeomans noted, was felt beyond the studio: he had made "the world fall in love with what we do."

Of all the speakers who mounted the podium that evening, Miles Richardson stole the show. Adapting his oratorical skills to the role of master of ceremonies, Richardson provided a running commentary that linked the Native and non-Native participants, coordinated the aural and visual effects, and encouraged the guests, who had expected the tribute to last only three hours, "to hang on for food." He spoke of Reid's close association with the Haida people and of his attachment to the grandeur of the Queen Charlotte Islands. He often came home, Richardson recalled, then returned to Vancouver "with some profound thoughts and insights into the importance of our homelands."

Most of the speakers at the tribute agreed that Bill Reid had given Canadians a new appreciation of Haida culture. The sculptor George Norris told how Reid had done this by crossing back and forth between the Native and non-Native worlds, as conditions required, and by whatever means were at hand. Reid had never been shy about approaching a government official, a museum director, or a Native chief in order to get what he wanted. Yet, during the early years of his career, as Norris made clear, he had not always been successful: "Despite what we've heard this evening, he was not fully accepted by either of his worlds [even though] today each world would claim him as their own."

Everyone who mounted the podium to remember Reid staked out a claim in order to participate in his success: some in the creation and reception of his work; some in the formation of his non-Native aesthetic; some in his discovery, interpretation, and promotion of Native culture; some in his politicization of Native art; and others in his transformation from a Canadian WASP to a Haida Indian.

No one's claim was stronger than the anthropologists associated with the Museum of Anthropology. The museum's acquisition and documentation of

Native artifacts had, according to its director, Ruth Phillips, given Reid the building blocks that allowed him to revitalize Northwest Coast Native art. Their hiring of Reid to reconstruct a Haida village for the university had made it possible for him to quit his job at the CBC and devote his full time to the production of Native art. Their exhibition of Reid's work alongside that of his largely anonymous Native predecessors had linked his achievements to those of his Native ancestors. Their refusal to treat the exhibits in their collection as trade curios or museum artifacts had made it possible for Reid's work to be exhibited in art galleries and sold at fine-art auction houses. Finally, the installation of Reid's signature work, *Raven and the First Men,* in a special rotunda had given the Museum of Anthropology, in Ruth Phillips's words, its "beating heart."

The interplay between the Native and non-Native sides of Reid's personality, life, and work was evident in the speeches. But as the evening wore on, the division between the Native and non-Native participants became blurred. Frank O'Neill told how he had been adopted into Reid's Wolf clan and been given a Native name. The poet Robert Bringhurst recited part of his tribute to Reid in Haida (though it proved incomprehensible to at least one Haida speaker in the audience[3]). Other non-Natives wore Native clothing or donned the small frog brooch that Reid had designed in 1970 and later cast in multiple editions. The participants who were Native bore the names of the missionaries and early settlers who had a hand in dismantling their culture. They wore modified versions of traditional Native dress: button blankets, vests, and robes decorated with Native motifs. And they recited prayers that blended such Christian words as "blessed" with Hollywood-born phrases like "the great white father."

When the mischief-making Raven stopped hopping around the parking lot and entered the Great Hall, people were prompted to say things that revealed a different side of Reid's personality. He "would suck me up in his quests, his plans, and his dreams," lamented the artist Jim Hart. Over an eleven-year period of working for Bill, George Rammell had experienced a mixture of "awe, anger, envy, jealousy, compassion, rage and exhaustion." Reid had "intimidated the hell" out of David Suzuki. He had done the same to the vice-chancellor of the University of British Columbia, George Pederson, as well as to the publisher Scott McIntyre. Reid possessed a wicked sense of humour, which had an unsettling effect on many of his friends. David Suzuki said he could never figure out whether Reid was being mischievous or serious.

The raven was also at work in less obvious ways. Reid's old friends Robert Reid, Sherry Grauer, and Tak Tanabe were marginalized. Not invited to participate, they sat in silence on the fringes of the crowd. Bill's sister, Dr. Margaret Kennedy, did speak, though she was prohibited from wearing a button blanket, which Martine Reid felt to be her own prerogative.

⁓◦⌒

Standing over six feet, Reid had been an imposing figure. He spoke with so much authority and intelligence that it was impossible to separate the art from the man. Indeed, the former director of the Museum of Anthropology, Michael Ames, wondered if Reid's reputation would diminish without his presence. "He was famous . . . because of himself," Ames reflected two years after Reid's death. "Without the person himself around with that charisma how much of his work will carry on?"[4]

This was a good question. Less than a year after his death, Reid was attacked by a Toronto-based journalist in a popular magazine.[5] The sour and even hostile tone in which Jane O'Hara accused Reid of not doing his own work and of failing to give his assistants adequate recognition brought many letters to the editor in his defence.

In a millennium opinion poll, British Columbians deemed Bill Reid to be the second most influential person during the last hundred years of the province's history. And when the Bill Reid Foundation was unable to raise sufficient funds to allow it to acquire Martine Reid's personal collection of Bill's work, there was a public outcry when the Minister of Canadian Heritage, Sheila Copps, hesitated in making up the $500,000 shortfall. Copps annoyed the foundation's board members by referring to the collection as "incredible artifacts," by questioning the racial makeup of the board — according to Copps, there weren't enough Natives on it — and by questioning the foundation's plans to establish the Bill Reid Gallery in Vancouver. (Copps wanted the future gallery to be on the Queen Charlotte Islands, where it would enhance the economic development of the Haida people.) The press, the

Native peoples, Liberal MPs, and the public in general were outraged. Copps came up with the money. The Bill Reid Foundation now had the collection but not enough money to establish a gallery in which to display it.[6]

In the world of Northwest Coast Native art, Bill Reid was and remains the undisputed first. As the tribute at the Museum of Anthropology made clear, Reid influenced everyone who came within his ambit. He exposed his artistic and technical assistants to a new visual language and to new techniques. While looking at totem poles in Stanley Park, George Rammell was surprised to discover that, thanks to Reid, he was "visually bilingual." Another artist-assistant, Jim Hart, noted, a year after Reid's death, that there were "still some things he taught me that I haven't put into play yet."[7] The sheer quantity, calibre, and inventiveness of Reid's oeuvre made anthropologists and museum curators alike think about Native art in a new way. After Bill Reid, the words "decline" and "decay," which had been applied to Native culture throughout the twentieth century, were anachronistic.

Despite his critical outbursts against Native people, Reid nevertheless boosted the dignity, renown, and confidence of the Haida Nation. He gave them political clout when, in protest against the logging of South Moresby, he deliberately abandoned work on *The Spirit of Haida Gwaii*, and when he refused to accept the Order of Canada. Equally, he made the Haida Nation known beyond the shores of Haida Gwaii and of Canada itself, notably when he took *Loo Taas* to France. All this enabled Natives like Miles Richardson to be less defensive when they heard the childhood rhyme ending with the pejorative phrase: "Doctor, lawyer and Indian chief." "At first I used to get annoyed," Richardson recalled, "but after Bill, I am used to it."[8]

Reid had not, of course, been the first Native artist to combine western technology and western themes with traditional ways of carving, painting, and seeing. That process began in the late eighteenth century when the first Europeans visited the Queen Charlotte Islands. Nor was Reid necessarily the most accomplished Native artist in the history of Northwest Coast Native art. Tom Price, Captain Richard Carpenter, Charles Edenshaw, and many anonymous artists, whose work was so important to Reid during the formative years of his career, were equally capable of maintaining the tension between tradition and innovation. Reid's younger contemporary, Robert Davidson, was certainly the better designer of the two. Reid's assistant on the Haida village project at the University of British Columbia, Doug Cranmer, was more imaginative, as his series of abstract paintings shows. And the next generation of artists, from Don Yeomans, Ron Hamilton, and Jim Hart to Lawrence Paul (Yuxweluptun) and Susan Point, would take the Native art form further than anyone could have imagined during the height of Reid's career in the early 1980s.

Shortly after Reid's death, Don Yeomans wondered how many doors would slam "because there aren't the people left in the art community that are willing to go to the right parties, to be at the right place."[9] Yet Native art has become even more visible than it was during Reid's lifetime. Six new totem poles have been raised in Skidegate. Masks, rattles, and other ceremonial paraphernalia have continued to come alive through song, dance, and the dramatic presentation of the myths and stories at many feasts or doings. The Sto:lo artist Xwa-lack-tun is in the midst of carving thirteen totem poles in Scotland. (The organizers of the Totem Pole Project plan to have them erected across the Highlands by autumn 2004.) And the tail of a British Airways Boeing 757 has been painted with Joe David's *Whale Rider*. Even before Reid died, Susan Point's magnificent five-metre-high spindle whorl, along with the imposing welcome figures of Shane Pointe and the yarn weavings of Musqueam weavers, had joined *The Spirit of Haida Gwaii* at Vancouver International Airport.

Yet, unlike any other Native artist, Reid was better able to convey what Gitxan artist Doreen Jensen has called his creative vision.[10] A perfectionist who revelled in producing the well-made object, Reid helped raise non-Native awareness of Native art when he came on to the scene in the 1950s. He knew what would sell and how to make the right connections in order to get the best price. He possessed a gift for making the familiar appear to be new, thereby flattering his non-Native audience by giving them a sense of discovery. And, like the raven in Haida mythology, Reid was, above all, a transformer. What other artist would have seen the merit of scaling up a four-inch boxwood carving into a seven-foot-high sculpture? And who else possessed the confidence, the right connections, and the tenacity to see the project through, by getting his assistants to transform his grunts and his groans into *Raven and the First Men?*

ᄼᔆᄼ

Like the late nineteenth-century British prime minister Benjamin Disraeli, who claimed that he was the blank page between the Old Testament and the New, Bill Reid was a linchpin between artifact and art, between salvage and revival, between art and politics, and between the Native and non-Native communities. At various points in his career he justified the museum world's salvage, restoration, and reclassification of Native artifacts as works of art. He gave anthropologists, who had previously been concerned largely with the past, a new generation of Native artists to study. Above all, he made his own work, and that of other Native artists, become part of the artistic patrimony of the Canadian nation.

Reid's art arose not only from the tension between his Native and white artistic sensibility, but from his perception of himself as an artist who had transcended racial typecasting. This is what enabled him to produce work that spoke to Canadians regardless of whether they had Native blood flowing in their veins. Reid appreciated this point better than anyone else. "The dialogue between me as an urban twentieth-century product of this particular culture and this nineteenth-century thing has produced some quite remarkable pieces," he maintained in 1990. "What they symbolize or what their significance is, I don't know. They're just nice things — and that's all they have to be."[11]

Acknowledgements

E very biographer has encounters in their dreams with the people they are writing about. I dreamt about Bill Reid; about his elusive father, Billy Reid; about his stoic mother, Sophie, and her parents, Josephine and Charles Gladstone. I would ask them a question and, just as they were on the point of giving me a reply, I would wake up. My dreams about Bill Reid were frequent and intense. This was partly because he never, to my knowledge, confided his private thoughts to a diary or journal. He gave conflicting accounts of his life. And, while he had a brilliant way with words, he preferred the telephone to the letter as a means of keeping in touch with his friends. His work, which can be seen in institutions and public spaces across the country, presents another difficulty for the scholar. Under Canadian copyright law, only Reid's work that is on permanent public display may be reproduced for illustration without permission of the heirs.

Although Bill Reid does not serve the biographer well, many of his relatives, his artist-assistants, and his technicians, along with his dealers and his friends, allowed me or my assistant, Beverley Berger, to interview them. Among them are Richie Allen, Michael Ames, Louise Andrew, Thomas Berger, Dempsey Bob, Dr. Donald Calne, Toni Cavelti, Sophie Chevalier, Joe David, Robert Davidson, Beau Dick, Freda Diesing, Joanne Drake, Jean

Mackay Fahrni, Sherry Grauer, Walter Harris, Jim Hart, Audrey Hawthorn, Harry Hawthorn, Barry Herem, Robert Hinde, Bill Holm, Doreen Jensen, Dr. Margaret Kennedy, John Koerner, Professor Claude Lévi-Strauss, George F. MacDonald, Joanne MacDonald, Bill McLennan, Earl Muldoe, Joseph Murphy, Derek Norton, Peter Page, Duane Pasco, Joe Plaskett, Susan Point, Art Price, George Rammell, Barbara Reid, Martine Reid, Robert Reid, Douglas Reynolds, Larry Rosso, Miriam Shiell, Robert Smeriok, Ulli Steltzer, Vernon Stephens, Margaret Stott, Norman Tait, Takao Tanabe, Chief Saul Terry, Lucinda Turner, Einor Vinge, David Watmough, Anne Wood, and Don Yeomans.

I was determined not only to tell the story of Bill's life, but also to put his work in the context of Native art and contemporary jewellery-making. The publications and archival sources that helped me do this are cited in the notes and bibliography. Among the institutions and their representatives that gave me access to their oral, visual, and written collections are Art Gallery of Ontario, Larry Pfaff; Bowen Island Public Library; Burnaby Art Gallery, Karen Henry; Cambridge University Library; Canada Council Archives; Canadian Broadcasting Corporation Archives, Ken Puley, Roy Harris, Leon Earls, Bea Guttman, and Cathy Sprague; Canadian Museum of Civilization, Sylvie Régimbal, Louis Campeau, and Benoit Thoriault; Central Saint Martins College of Art & Design, Jane Rapley and Skilla Speet; Chilliwack Museum & Historical Society, Kelly Harms; Department of Indian and Northern Affairs, Doreen Vaillancourt; Emily Carr Institute of Art and Design, Michael Clark; Ethnographic Museum, Budapest, Tamås Hofer; Mary Hawkins Memorial Library, Salt Spring Island; Museum of Anthropology, University of British Columbia, Elizabeth Johnson, Krisztina Laszlo, Nancy Bergman, Karen Duffek, and Bill McLennan; Museum of Modern Art, New York, Jenny Tobias; National Archives of Canada, Joan Schwartz, Anne Goddard, and Jim Burant; National Gallery of Canada, Library, Sylvie Roy; National Library of Canada, Denis Robertie; Pacific Press Archives, Kate Bird; Provincial Archives of British Columbia, Kathryn Bridge and Frances Gundry; Public Record Office; Royal British Columbia Museum, Susan Hapsbury and Dan Savard; Ryerson Institute, Claude Doucet; Special Collections, University of British Columbia Library, George Brandak; Sto:lo Nation Archives, David Smith; Textual Archives, Ottawa, Nancy Bacon; Trinity Hall, David A. Thomas and Kay Arnold;

United Church of Canada, BC Conference Archives, Bob Stewart; University of Lethbridge Library, Alfred Youngman; University of Victoria Archives, Chris Petter; Vancouver Art Gallery, Library, Cheryl Siegel, Rose Emery, and Lynn Brockington; Vancouver Museum, Lynn Miranda; Victoria College Archives, Delphine Castles; and Victoria High School Archives, Peter Danby.

No biographer writes his or her work without the benefit of a helpful chance remark from friends and acquaintances. Among those who gave me their expertise, or a new angle, or challenged my views or checked my sources were Alistair McKay, Kate Bendall, Ann Cowan, Dan Curtis, David McNab, Diana Lary, Floyd St. Clair, Richard and Diana Lipsey, Isabel Nanton, Margaret Pegler, Jim Ironside, Jim Osborne, Margaret MacMillan, Marian Fowler, Norman Hilmer, Mona Holmlund, Pat Spiers, Richard Santo, Eric Tippett, Tony Pearse, Gordon and Helen Thom, Charlotte Townsend-Gault, Bill Young, Phillipe Bussey, and, especially, Beverley Berger.

There were also a number of long-suffering friends who took time out from their busy lives to read the manuscript. Fay Bendall and Diane Nelles contributed their editorial skills and Jim Miller and H.V. Nelles their knowledge of Canadian history. Peter Clarke, to whom this book is dedicated, was writing his own biography — *The Cripps Version* — while I was re-creating Bill Reid's life. Peter had full access to Stafford Cripps's voluminous archive, and the contrast between our situation as chroniclers made for good discussion when we read out a new chapter either at our home on the Gulf Islands in British Columbia or at the Master's Lodge in Cambridge, England. Peter proved to be more than what Emily Carr called a good "listening lady." When he read the text of my manuscript, he showed himself to be a good editor too. Finally, Anne Collins, Tanya Trafford, and Pamela Robertson at Random House Canada reminded me that I was not writing for an academic audience. To all of the above and to Churchill College, Cambridge University, the British Academy, and the Canada Council, who gave modest, but much needed financial assistance, I owe a big thank you.

Endnotes

Preface

1. Miro Cernetig, "Great Canadian Artist Led West Coast Native Art Renaissance," *Globe and Mail,* March 16, 1998.
2. Michael Scott, "A Tribute to Bill Reid, 1920–1998," *Vancouver Sun,* March 14, 1998.
3. "Bill Reid, 78, Sculptor in Indian Tradition," *New York Times,* March 22, 1998.
4. "Bill Reid," *The Times* (London), April 11, 1998.
5. David Silcox, "Lives Lived: William Ronald Reid," *Globe and Mail,* March 21, 1998.
6. Douglas Todd, "In the End, It's Just a Big Cosmic Joke," *Vancouver Sun,* Vancouver Art Gallery (hereafter VAG) clipping file.

PART I

Chapter One

1. Haida Gwaii is the Haida name for the Queen Charlotte Islands. Haida is the name for the Haida people and Gwaii means "the island home which is across the strait from Great Turtle Island," or to Euro-Canadians, the continent of North America.
2. Paula Brook, "At Home With Bill Reid," *Western Living* (September 1986), p. 39.
3. Charles Gladstone, "Notebook 1888–1895," No. 1991-012, Museum of Anthropology (hereafter MOA). The notebook has been mislabelled. The dates are 1888–1897 and it was the property of Josephine and William Wilson and, after 1895, of Josephine and Charles Gladstone.

4. Michael Roe, ed., *The Journal and Letters of Captain Charles Bishop on the North-West Coast of America, in the Pacific and in New South Wales 1794–1799* (Cambridge: Cambridge University Press, 1967), p. 77.

5. "Baptisms, Burials, Marriages, 1884–1916, Skidegate." The United Church of Canada, British Columbia Conference Archives, University of British Columbia. In Charles Gladstone, "Notebook 1888–1895," No. 1991-012, MOA, Sophie Gladstone's date of birth is given as January 8, 1895, and September 13, 1895. However since she was born in Port Simpson it seems likely that the September date is correct.

6. Doris Shadbolt, *Bill Reid: A Retrospective Exhibition* (Vancouver: Douglas & McIntyre, 1986), p. 14; Doris Shadbolt, "The Legacy of Bill Reid: A Critical Enquiry," conference, November 13, 1999, University of British Columbia.

7. Charles Edenshaw, *Thunderbird and Whale,* V11-B824 (S9468-17), Canadian Museum of Civilization, and Charles Gladstone, *Carving on Cedar of Dogfish,* No. J-241, Canadian Museum of Civilization.

Chapter Two

1. Claude Davidson interview with Susan Davidson, 1980, GNWC-T-048-A, Royal British Columbia Museum (hereafter RBMC).

2. *The Omineca Herald,* August 15, 1919.

3. Large, R. Geddes, *The Skeena: River of Destiny* (Vancouver: Mitchell Press, 1957), p. 44.

4. Marcia Crosby, "The Legacy of Bill Reid: A Critical Inquiry," conference, November 13, 1999, University of British Columbia.

5. *Portland Canal News* (Stewart), January 11, 1927.

6. Margaret Kennedy interview with Maria Tippett, July 28, 1998.

7. Charles W. Stokes, "Victoria, a Bit of England That Is Not England," *Canadian Magazine,* Vol. 53 (1919), p. 294.

8. R.C. Mayne, *Four Years in British Columbia and Vancouver Island* (London: J. Murray, 1862), p. 277.

9. Bill Reid to Norman MacKenzie, September 26, 1955, Audrey Hawthorn Collection 4-42, MOA.

10. Edith Iglauer, "The Myth Maker," *Saturday Night* (February 1982), p. 17.

11. Paula Brook, "At Home With Bill Reid," *Western Living* (September 1986), p. 39.

12. Brook, "At Home With Bill Reid," p. 39.

Chapter Three

1. Bill Reid, "Profile of Bill Reid," VAG, 1974, video. In 1955 Sophie Reid lent three bracelets to the *People of the Potlatch* exhibition at the VAG. Two gold bracelets

— *Dogfish* and *Eagle* — had been made by Charles Edenshaw and a silver bracelet by Charles Gladstone. *People of the Potlatch Exhibition,* VAG Archives.

2.   Bill Reid "Interview," University of British Columbia, film, 1961, F1990:124.1-2, Provincial Archives of British Columbia (hereafter PABC).

3.   Rhodi Lake, "A Modern Approach to Indian Jewelry," *Vancouver Sun,* July 25, 1953.

4.   Emily Carr, "Modern and Indian Art of the West Coast," *McGill News* (Supplement), June 1929, p. 4.

5.   Jack Shadbolt interviewed by Susan Feldman, "Bill Reid: Voyage through Two Worlds" CBC, January 1992.

6.   Bill Reid to D.H.E. Petch, University of Victoria Archives, n.d. (received March 5, 1979).

7.   Bill Reid's Application for a Canada Council Visual Arts Award, National Archives of Canada, Canada Council MG63 Vol. 545, October 17, 1967.

8.   Sid Baron, "A Bill Reid Tribute," MOA, March 24, 1998.

9.   Barbara Reid interview with Maria Tippett. July 15, 1998.

10.   Edith Iglauer, "The Myth Maker," *Saturday Night* (February 1982), p. 17.

11.   Bill Reid, "Curriculum vitae," *Bill Reid: A Retrospective Exhibition,* VAG catalogue, November 6 to December 8, 1974, n.p.

12.   *The Camosun* (Victoria, 1936).

13.   *The Craigdarroch* (Victoria College, 1927–28), p. 17.

14.   Iglauer, "The Myth Maker," p. 17.

15.   Baron, "A Bill Reid Tribute."

16.   Baron, "A Bill Reid Tribute."

17.   Reid, "Curriculum vitae."

18.   Margaret Kennedy interview with Maria Tippett, July 28, 1998.

Chapter Four

1.   "CKEY," *The Canadian Broadcaster,* January 20, 1945, p. 14.

2.   CBC Archives, Toronto, Bea Guttman, Human Resources to Maria Tippett, December 10, 1999. Reid worked at CKRN in Rouyn, Quebec, at CJKL in Kirkland Lake, Ontario, and from June 1943 to January 1945, Reid was back on the west coast, working for Vancouver's CKNX, before moving to Toronto. In Ontario's capital Reid worked at CKEY from August 1945 to March 1947, then moved to CKLW in Windsor. By November 1947, Reid was back in Toronto, where he worked at CHUM until June 1948.

3.   Catherine Bates, "Bauble-maker Supreme," *Star* (Montreal), October 16, 1971.

4.   Bill Reid, "Curriculum vitae," *Bill Reid: A Retrospective Exhibition,* VAG catalogue, November 6 to December 8, 1974, n.p. Without access to Reid's military

records, it is difficult to ascertain exactly when he was in the military. I have
used the dates Bill gave to the CBC for his record of employment.

5. Lloyd Dyck, "Arts and the Man," *Vancouver Sun*, August 16, 1983.

6. "The Announcer," *CBC Times* (Toronto), April 3–9, 1955, p. 5.

7. Diane Brown, "The Legacy of Bill Reid: A Critical Inquiry," conference,
    November 13, 1999, University of British Columbia.

8. Edith Iglauer, "The Myth Maker," *Saturday Night* (February 1982), p. 17.

9. Pat Lush, "A Transformer of Existing Things," *Ryerson Rambler*, No. 28 (Fall
    1985), p. 10.

10. Rhodi Lake, "A Modern Approach to Indian Jewelry," *Vancouver Sun*, July 25, 1953.

11. Lush, "A Transformer of Existing Things," p. 10.

12. "Interview in Burlington, Ontario, with James Green, retired British jeweller
    and Teacher," September 30, 1987, Ryerson University Archives, Toronto.

13. Bill Reid, *The Woman in the Moon*, brooch, silver, circa 1950, Nb1.688, MOA.
    There are two possible explanations for Reid's use of this motif. He may have
    lifted the drawing, which had been produced by John Wi'ha for Franz Boas,
    from Albert P. Niblack's "The Coast Indians of Southern Alaska and Northern
    British Columbia," *Annual Report for the Smithsonian Institute*, 1888, pp.
    225–386 or from Alice Ravenhill's *A Corner Stone of Canadian Culture: An
    Outline of the Arts and Crafts of the Indian Tribes of British Columbia*.
    (Occasional Papers of the British Columbia Provincial Museum, No. 5,
    Victoria, March 1944), where the motif appears as "The Man in the Moon,
    Haida," Plate 1 IV. It is interesting to note that Charles Gladstone produced a
    cruder version of the same motif, *Drawing* (1487/13, MOA). Reid made at least
    three brooches using the woman in the moon motif.

14. Ravenhill, *A Corner Stone of Canadian Culture*, Plate 1; *Killer Whale Earrings*,
    silver metal, 2.3 by 2.7 cm, 1955, Nbl.709 a-b, MOA.

15. Bill Reid, *Eagle Brooch*, gold metal, 6.9 by 3.7 by 8 cm, 1955, Nb1.703, MOA.

16. Lush, "A Transformer of Existing Things," p. 10; *Ryersonia 1951*, the Annual
    Publication of the Student Association of the Ryerson Institute of Technology,
    p. 111.

17. Robert Reid interview with Maria Tippett, June 8, 2000.

18. Lush, "A Transformer of Existing Things," p. 10.

PART II

Chapter Five

1. In 1952 the CBC announced that Reid took up his position at the Vancouver
    studios that year; Reid often stated that it was 1951 he and his family returned
    to Vancouver. See Bill Reid, "Curriculum vitae."

2. Bill Reid, *Beaver Bracelet,* silver metal, circa 1951, Nb1.743, MOA; Charles Gladstone *Sdast'aas, Two Bears Bracelet,* silver metal, 1951, Nb1.749, MOA.

3. Rhodi Lake, "A Modern Approach to Indian Jewelry," *Vancouver Sun,* July 25, 1953.

4. "Report of Conference on Native Indian Affairs, Acadia Camp, April 1–3 1948" (Victoria: Provincial Archives), p. 58.

5. "Report of Conference on Native Indian Affairs," pp. 12–13.

6. Bob Neel, interview with Elizabeth Johnson, 1988, tape, MOA.

7. Neel interview with Johnson.

8. Tom Merriman's "Village for Indians," *Victoria Daily Times,* January 6, 1954, and George Nicholson's "Native Indian Talents," *Victoria Daily Colonist,* February 7, 1954, would be followed up by Harold Weir's "More Totem Nonsense," *Vancouver Sun,* February 16, 1954. The totem motif was dropped that year from licence plates.

9. Bill Reid to Wilson Duff, February 22, 1954, GR111, Box 17, File 46, PABC.

10. P.C. Pineo, "Rounded Picture of Contemporary Life, Skidegate Mission," January 29, 1955, in Harry Hawthorn Papers, Box 27 File 1, Notes from June 1954, n.p. Special Collections, University of British Columbia.

11. Fergusson to Secretary, March 3, 1954, Box 107, VAG.

12. Franz Boas, "The Decorative Art of the Indians of the North Pacific Coast," *Bulletin of the American Museum of Natural History,* Vol. 9 (New York: American Museum of Natural History, 1897), pp. 123–76; Marius Barbeau, "The Canadian Northwest: Themes for Modern Painters," *Magazine of Art,* Vol. 24 (May 1932), pp. 331–38.

13. Karl Einstein, *Negerplastik* (Leipzig, 1915); Wolfgang Paalen, "Totem Art," *Dyn: The Journal of the Durham University Anthropological Society,* No. 4-5 (1943), pp. 7–39.

14. *Exhibition of Canadian West Coast Art: Native and Modern,* National Gallery of Canada and the Victoria Memorial Museum catalogue (December 1927), p. 2.

15. "Palette," "Indians of British Columbia Present Splendid Exhibition," *Province* (Vancouver), July 17, 1941.

16. Hattie Fergusson to J.A. Morris, January 26, 1953, Box 107, VAG.

17. Hattie Fergusson to J.A. Morris, November 13, 1954, Box 107, VAG.

18. George Swinton, *Sculpture of the Eskimo* (Toronto, McClelland & Stewart, 1971), p. 42.

19. Hattie Fergusson to J.A. Morris, July 25, 1954, Box 107, VAG.

20. Hattie Fergusson to J.A. Morris, July 7, 1954, Box 107, VAG.

21. Audrey Hawthorn Papers, Box 16, MOA; Renate Wilson, "Contemporary Indian Arts and Crafts," *Western Homes & Living* (1959).

22. Hattie Fergusson to J.A. Morris, November 13, 1954, Box 107, VAG.

Chapter Six

1. Audrey Hawthorn tape prepared for Maria Tippett, March 2000.
2. Rhodi Lake, "A Modern Approach to Indian Jewelry," *Vancouver Sun,* July 25, 1953.
3. Bill Reid quoted in Karen Duffek, "The Contemporary Northwest Coast Indian Art Market," M.A. Thesis, University of British Columbia, 1983, pp. 46–47.
4. Bill Reid, "Traditions of Northwest Coast Indian Culture," Museum of Anthropology, November 23, 1976, tape recording, MOA; Bill Reid, *Arts National,* CBC Radio, April 2, 1980.
5. Bill Reid, *Beaver Bracelet,* Charles Edenshaw, *Hummingbird Bracelet,* No. 9523, RBCM. A better comparison of Reid's and Edenshaw's work would be Reid's sea bear bracelet, *Tschumus,* 1953, A1500, MOA, which was based on Edenshaw's bracelet, illustrated in Karen Duffek's catalogue. However some time after the exhibition, Reid re-engraved the Edenshaw work, thereby making the comparison between the two works impossible.
6. Bill Reid, "A Fragment of Time Fades from the Forests to Mellow in Museums," *Radio* (March 1954), p. 10.
7. "Museum to Get 100-Year-Old Haida Totems," *Victoria Daily Times,* July 12, 1954.
8. Bill Reid, "lst Trailer, 2nd Beach, Skidegate Inlet, Q.C.I., August 3, 1976," *Vanguard* (October 1976), p. 17.
9. Bill Reid to Wilson Duff, June 2, 1954, GR111, Box 17, File 46, PABC.
10. Bill Reid to Wilson Duff, August 8, 1957, GR111, Box 17, File 46, PABC.
11. *Totems,* CBC Film, 1959, written and narrated by Bill Reid, film, PABC.
12. *Totems.*
13. Wilson Duff, "Mungo Martin, Carver of the Century," *Museum News,* Vol. 1 No. 1 (May 1959), p. 3.
14. Mungo Martin to Harry Hawthorn, March 15, 1952, Box 10-31, MOA; Audrey Hawthorn, *Kwakiutl Art* (Vancouver: Douglas & McIntyre, 1979), p. ix.
15. William Reid to Norman MacKenzie, September 26, 1955, Audrey Hawthorn Papers 4-42, MOA.
16. Reid to MacKenzie.
17. Tak Tanabe interview with Maria Tippett, July 13, 2000.
18. Susan Feldman, "Bill Reid: Voyage through Two Worlds," interview with Jack Shadbolt, January 1992, CBC Radio, produced March 1, 1994.
19. David Watmough to Maria Tippett, November 19, 1998.
20. George Rammell interview with Beverley Berger, November 13, 1998.
21. Robert Reid interview with Maria Tippett, July 22, 1999.
22. Bill Reid to Wilson Duff, July 17, 1956, GR111 Box 17 No 46, PABC.

23. Reid to Duff.

24. Norman MacKenzie to Harry Hawthorn, February 16, 1958, Audrey Hawthorn Papers, MOA.

Chapter Seven

1. In his interview with Rhodi Lake in the *Vancouver Sun* (July 25, 1953) Bill Reid told the remarkable story about purchasing two gold bracelets, which he later attributed to Edenshaw, in an antique shop in Toronto for sixty dollars.

2. Robert M. Hume, *100 Years of B.C. Art* (Vancouver: VAG 1958), n.p.

3. Doreen Jensen interview with Beverley Berger, November 26, 1998.

4. Lynn Harrington, "The Queen Charlotte Islands," *Canadian Geographical Journal*, VXXIX, No. 2 (August 1949), p. 59.

5. Scott Watson, "Art in the Fifties: Design, Leisure, and Painting in the Age of Anxiety," *Vancouver: Art and Artists 1931–1983*, VAG, 1983, p. 72.

6. J.L. Shadbolt, "Has B.C. Betrayed Its Heritage of Art?" *Vancouver Province Magazine* (November 6, 1954), pp. 10-11.

7. "B.C. Jewellery," *Western Homes & Living* (December–January 1955–56), p. 12.

8. Reid used *No.7* tattoo drawing by Charles Edenshaw of a dogfish to produce *Dogfish Gold Brooch*, circa 1959, MOA, A1499. Wi'ha's and Edenshaw's drawings were originally made for John Swanton's *Contributions to the Ethnology of the Haida: Memoirs of the American Museum of Natural History*, Memoir 8(1), New York, 1905.

9. Elizabeth Summer, "Have You Met Bill Reid?" *Radio Times* (September 1957), p. 24.

10. Mary Ann Lash, "New Life Is Given to the Craft of Haida Jewelry," *Canadian Art* (September 1957), p. 103.

11. Toni Cavelti interview with Maria Tippett, September 15 1999; Max Wyman, *Toni Cavelti: A Jeweller's Life* (Vancouver: Douglas & McIntyre, 1996), p. 38.

12. Bill Reid, *Silver Earrings*, abstract design, silver metal, circa 1956, Nb1.708 a & b, MOA.

13. Toni Cavelti in Bill Reid, *All the Gallant Beasts and Monsters* (Vancouver: Buschlen Mowatt, 1991), p. 28.

14. Jack Shadbolt and Susan Feldman, "Bill Reid: Voyage through Two Worlds," interview with Reid, January 1992, CBC Radio, produced March 1, 1994.

15. Tak Tanabe interview with Maria Tippett, July 13, 2000.

16. Bill Reid to Geoffrey Andrew, July 22, 1964, Special Collections, University of British Columbia, Geoffrey Andrew Papers Box 4-18.

17. Margaret Kennedy interview with Maria Tippett, July 23, 1998.

18. Robert Reid to Maria Tippett, July 9, 2000.

19. Tak Tanabe and Tom Berger have confirmed Robert Reid's recollection of Bill Reid's remarks about Natives (Robert Reid interview with Maria Tippett July 22, 1999; Tak Tanabe, July 13, 2000; and Tom Berger, January 9, 2000).

20. Tanabe interview with Tippett.

21. Reid interview with Tippett, July 22, 1999.

22. Harry Hawthorn to H.R. MacMillan, February 26, 1959, Box 12, Audrey Hawthorn Papers, MOA.

23. Wayne Suttles, "Report to Canada Council of Progress of Totem Carving Programme," Vancouver, 1960, p. 2, MOA.

24. *Radio Times,* May 21, 1959.

25. Edith Iglauer, "The Myth Maker," *Saturday Night* (Fall 1982), p. 19.

26. Bea Buttman to Maria Tippett, December 10, 1999, CBC Files, Record of Employment: date of resignation April 30, 1959.

27. Bill Reid, "Haida Means Human Being," draft typescript, 1979. Canadian Museum of Civilization.

28. Bill Reid interviewed by Peter Malkin, *Profile of Bill Reid,* video, VAG 1974; "Bill Reid Interview" (1961), CBC Film, F1990:12/41-1-2 PABC.

29. Bill Reid, *Sea Wolf Sculpture,* cedar wood painted, 142 by 247 by 70 cm, 1962, A50029, MOA.

30. Alfred Scow, "A Bill Reid Tribute," March 24, 1998.

31. Olive Dickason, "Of the Haidas," *Globe and Mail Magazine,* January 23, 1960.

32. H.B. Hawthorn to the Secretary, The Canada Council, November 15, 1961, Audrey Hawthorn Papers, MOA.

33. Audrey Hawthorn tape for Maria Tippett, March 2000.

Chapter Eight

1. See photo p. 145, Wolf, gold, 1962. UBC Museum of Anthropology, Nb1.719. Bracelet, Dogfish, silver, circa 1961. UBC Museum of Anthropology, Nb1.707. Bracelet, Grizzly Bear, gold, 1960. UBC Museum of Anthropology, Nb1.702.

2. Bill Reid, *Box,* bear and human design, silver metal, engraved 11 by 10 by 11 cm, circa 1961, A 1502, MOA.

3. Bill Reid, "The Indian as Artist," CBC Radio 1965, PABC.

4. Richard Wright, "The Spirit of Haida Gwaii," *En Route* (March 1991), p. 92.

5. Reid, "The Indian as Artist."

6. Bill Reid, *Panel Pipe,* 8.2 by 27.2 cm, argillite stone, lacquer, 1963, A2552, MOA; Reid, *Killer Whale and Raven,* 1962, Nb1.748, MOA.

7. Bill Reid quoted in "People of the Potlatch," *CBC Times* (May 13–19, 1956), p. 1.

8. Margaret Kennedy interview with Maria Tippett, July 23, 1998.

9. Bill Holm interview with Maria Tippett and Beverley Berger, November 9, 1999.

10. Audrey Hawthorn Papers, Box 16, MOA; Renate Wilson, "Contemporary Indian Arts and Crafts," *Western Homes & Living* (1959).

11. Dan Cranmer to Audrey Hawthorn, May 29, 1951, Audrey Hawthorn Papers Box 1-71, MOA.

12. Hawthorn Notebook 1950, Audrey Hawthorn Papers Box 1-71, MOA.

13. Wilson Duff to Sue VanValkenburgh, April 29, 1970, Wilson Duff Papers, MOA.

14. Bill Holm, *Northwest Coast Indian Art: An Analysis of Form* (Seattle: University of Washington Press, 1965). Holm's book was written at the beginning of the 1960s as a thesis for his University of Washington anthropologist-professor, Erna Gunther.

15. Earl Muldoe interview with Beverley Berger, August 18, 1999.

16. James Houston, *Eskimo Handicrafts* (Montreal: Canadian Handicrafts Guild, 1951).

17. Duff to Sue VanValkenburgh, Wilson Duff Papers.

18. Bill Reid, "The Box Painting by the 'Master of the Black Field,'" in Donald N. Abbott ed., *The World Is as Sharp as a Knife: An Anthology in Honour of Wilson Duff* (Victoria: RBCM, 1981), p. 300. Duff discovered among the papers of the Provincial Museum curator, C.F. Newcombe, that Charles Edenshaw had given him the names of various-sized templates: the female breast, the raven wing joint, the inner front of an ear, the tail joint of a whale, and a raven's wing, which charged anatomical parts for Duff with "iconic meaning." Drawing their vocabulary from nature showed Duff that Native artists were predisposed to basing their work on animal forms, just as Holm was content to invent a new nomenclature based on geometric design. Wilson Duff Papers, "undated, untitled notes," Box 4-8, MOA.

19. Doug Cranmer interview with Rosa Ho (transcribed by Eden Robinson), MOA.

20. Michael M. Ames, "Museum Anthropologists and the Arts of Acculturation on the Northwest Coast," *BC Studies,* No. 49 (Spring 1981), p. 13.

21. Bill Reid, "Traditions of Northwest Coast Indian Culture," lecture, November 23, 1976, MOA.

22. Bill Reid *Gold Eagle Box,* cast eagle on lid and bear motif on sides, 11 by 10 by 11 cm, 1967, Nb1.717, MOA; Charles Edenshaw, *Bear Mother,* 39.0 cm high, argillite compote, n.d., Sheldon Jackson Museum.

23. Bill Reid, "An Introduction to Northwest Coast Indian Art" typescript of audio-tape, February 6, 1979, p. 3, MOA.

24. Bill Reid, "A New Northwest Coast Art: A Dream of the Past or a New Awakening?" Issues and Images; New Dimensions in Native American Art History conference, Arizona State University, April 22, 1981.

25. Shell Oil, United Kingdom, has no record of this commission; the *Bear Sculpture* is in the Haida Gwaii Museum in Skidegate.

26. Bill Reid, "River of Clouds," CBC Radio, February 21, 1965, PABC.

27. Reid, "An Introduction to Northwest Coast Indian Art."

28. Einor Vinge interview with Maria Tippett, August 6, 1999.

29. Audrey Hawthorn tape prepared for Maria Tippett, March 2000.

30. Bill Reid to Bessie FitzGerald, June 13, 1965, Bessie FitzGerald Papers, MOA.

31. Bill McLennan interview with Beverley Berger, March 24, 2000.

32. Bill Reid to Bessie FitzGerald, June 13, 1965, Bessie FitzGerald Papers, MOA.

33. Bill Reid to Bessie FitzGerald, April 26, 1965, Bessie FitzGerald Papers, MOA, (received).

34. Bill Reid to Bessie FitzGerald, June 6, 1965, Bessie FitzGerald Papers, MOA.

35. Henry Speck exhibited ten multicoloured reproductions in an exhibition in the New Design Gallery (Vancouver) in 1964; Bill McLennan and Karen Duffek, *The Transforming Image: Painted Arts of Northwest Coast First Nations* (Vancouver: University of British Columbia Press, 2000), p. 258.

36. "Myth & Symbol," *Time* (September 28, 1962), p. 18.

Chapter Nine

1. Robert Davidson interviewed by Vicki Gabereau, September 13, 1989, CBC Radio; also see Hilary Stewart, *Robert Davidson: Haida Printmaker* (Vancouver: Douglas & McIntyre, 1979) and Joan Lowndes, "The Carvers' Sun," *Vancouver Sun*, February 19, 1971.

2. Audrey Hawthorn Papers, Box 16, MOA; Renate Wilson, "Contemporary Indian Arts and Crafts," *Western Homes & Living* (1959).

3. Constance Brissenden, "The Eagle Soars" (March 1990), p. 65, VAG clipping file.

4. Mary Lee Sterns to Wilson Duff, April 24, 1963, Wilson Duff Papers, Box 1-41, MOA.

5. Robert Davidson interview with Beverley Berger, February 7, 1999.

6. Einor Vinge, a student from the Vancouver School of Art who lived in Reid's Pender Street apartment-studio from 1962 to 1964 and, some years later, the jeweller Jeff Miller.

7. Jay Currie and Michèle Denis, "Hearing Old Songs: An Interview with Robert Bringhurst," *two chairs* (Vancouver), July 1999, p. 9.

8. Bill Reid, *Gold Box,* cast eagle on lid and bear motif on sides, 1967, No. Nb1.717, No 1.717, MOA; *Laminated Cedar Screen,* 1968, 213.0 by 190.3 by 14.6 cm, RBCM; Reginald Eyre Walters, ed., *British Columbia: A Centennial Anthology* (Toronto: McClelland & Stewart, 1958). For the book jacket, Reid had the assistance of his old friend Robert Reid.

9. Bill Reid quoted in Moira Johnston, "The Raven's Last Journey," *Saturday Night* (November 1998), p. 76.

10. Interview with Christie Harris, *30 From Vancouver*, CBC Television, 1972.

11. Jacqueline Hooper, "Raven's Cry Adds Stature to Our Literature" (1966). Vancouver Public Library Bill Reid clipping file.

12. The original illustration is housed in the MOA.

13. Harris, *30 From Vancouver*; Christie Harris, *Raven's Cry* (Toronto: McClelland and Stewart, 1966), p. 192. Great-great-uncle would be the correct relationship.

14. Franz Boas, *Primitive Art* (New York: Dover Publications, 1955, first published in Cambridge, Mass., 1927), fig. 287b, *The Box*, 19/1233, American Museum of Natural History.

15. "In a Clamb Shell," *Time*, June 16, 1967, p. 14.

16. Doris Shadbolt, "Our Relation to Primitive Art," *Canadian Art*, Vol. V No. 1 (Autumn 1947), pp. 14–16.

17. Doris Shadbolt in Wilson Duff, ed., *Arts of the Raven: Masterworks by the Northwest Coast Indians*, VAG catalogue, 1967, n.p.

18. Ian Wallace, "Arts of the Raven Opens at Gallery" (undated clipping, June 1967) VAG Archives; *New York Times*, September 3, 1967.

19. *Arts of the Raven.*

20. *Arts of the Raven.*

21. Jacqueline Hooper, "Arts of the Raven, B.C. Indian Art Is Something to Shout About," *Post-Intelligencer Weekender Magazine* (Seattle), July 22, 1967.

22. Marcia Crosby, "The Legacy of Bill Reid: A Critical Inquiry," conference, November 13, 1999, University of British Columbia.

23. In 1961 Reid had proposed "to observe and study drawing, craftsmanship, anatomy and sculpture in European countries." H.B. Hawthorn to Canada Council, November 15, 1961, Audrey Hawthorn Papers, 10-10, MOA.

24. Bill Reid's application for a Canada Council Arts Award, October 17, 1967 ("General Information" enclosed with the application form); Letter of Reference, Harry Hawthorn (received October 26, 1967); Letter of Reference, Wilson Duff, October 28, 1967; Letter of Reference, Walter Koerner, November 8, 1967, National Archives of Canada, Canada Council, MG63, Vol. 545.

25. Letter of Reference, R.N. Hume, December 7, 1967, National Archives of Canada, Canada Council, MG63, Vol. 5.

26. Press release, VAG 1967, and clipping file for *Arts of the Raven*, Vancouver Art Gallery Archives.

Chapter Ten

1. Bill Reid, *30 From Vancouver*, 1968, F1988.45/5.1, a Cable 10 Production, PABC.

2. The five Haida narratives involve the Bear Mother, Raven, Big Fisherman, Nanasimget, Sea Wolf, and Eagle-Frog.

3. Bill Reid, *30 From Vancouver*, 1968, F1988.45/5.1, a cable 10 production, PABC.

4. Bill Reid to David Silcox, March 2, 1968, National Archives of Canada, MG63 Vol. 545.

5. William Severini Kowinski, "Giving New Life to Haida Art and the Culture It Expresses," *Smithsonian*, Vol. 25 No. 10 (January 1995), p. 43.

6. Reid to Silcox, March 2, 1968.

7. Humphry Davy, "Sculpture Storm Blows," *Times* (Victoria), May 25, 1968.

8. Reid, *30 From Vancouver*.

9. Bill Reid to Donald Abbott, January 5, 1968, Donald Abbott Papers, RBCM.

10. Tak Tanabe interview with Maria Tippett, July 13, 2000.

11. William Reid, "Interim Report and Request for Second Installment," September 11, 1968, National Archives of Canada, MG63 Vol. 545.

12. Bill Reid, "Curriculum vitae," *Bill Reid: A Retrospective Exhibition*, VAG catalogue, 1974, n.p.

13. Bill Reid, *Necklace-Brooch* (also known as *The Milky Way Necklace*), 1968, 22-carat and 18-carat yellow and white gold and diamonds, diameter 6 inches, width 1/2 inch by 1 3/4 inches, Bill Reid Foundation.

14. Toni Calvelti quoted in Bill Reid, *All the Gallant Beasts and Monsters* (Vancouver: Buschlen Mowatt, 1991), p. 28.

15. David Thomas, *Gold and Diamond Bracelet*, Worshipful Company of Goldsmiths.

16. Karen Duffek, *Bill Reid, Beyond the Essential Form* (Vancouver: University of British Columbia Press, 1986), p. 16.

17. Joe Plaskett to Maria Tippett, February 11, 2001.

18. Peter Macnair's notebook, "Skedans," September 14, 1968, RBCM; "Indian Art Pieces Seized by RCMP," *Province* (Vancouver), September 13, 1968; Jack Brooks, "Totem Pole Rescuers Land in Queen Charlottes Court," *Vancouver Sun*, September 13, 1968.

19. Peter Macnair's notebook, "Skedans," September 14, 1968, RBCM.

20. Peter Macnair's notebook, "Skedans," September 14, 1968, RBCM.

21. Sherry Grauer interview with Maria Tippett, March 7, 2002; Grauer and Tippett, August 27, 1999.

22. United States District Court for the Northern District of New York, Judgment and Commitment (Rev 7-25 *United States of America v. William R. Reid*, No. 69CR119, February 16, 1970).

23. Robert Reid interview with Maria Tippett, July 22, 1999.

24. Sophie Reid to Bill Reid and Sophie Reid to Sherry Grauer, January 15, 1970, private collection.

25. *United States of America v. William R. Reid*, Criminal Docket, United States Court, No. 69-CR-119, February 16, 1970.

26. Sherry Grauer interview with Maria Tippett, August 27, 1999.

27. Bill Reid to Sherry Grauer, March 9, 1970, and March 12, 1970, private collection.

28. Bill Reid to Sherry Grauer, March 12, 1970, private collection.

29. Bill Reid to Sherry Grauer, April 1970, private collection.

30. Reid to Grauer, April 1970.

31. Bill Reid to Sherry Grauer, November 14, 1970, private collection.

32. Bill Reid, *Wasgo* or *Wolf Feast Dish,* 1970, A9325, MOA; Bill Reid *Mask, Woman,* portrait mask, wood, painted, human hair, 1970, 22 by 17.7 cm, A2617, MOA. This was not Reid's first mask. Listed in Reid's 1974 solo exhibition are previous masks: *Dogfish Mask,* 1959; *Bear,* 1960; *Dead Haida Woman,* 1960–61; and *Wolf,* 1963.

33. Robert Davidson interview with Beverley Berger, February 7, 1999.

34. Reid to Grauer, November 14, 1970; Sherry Grauer interview with Maria Tippett, August 27, 1999.

35. Peter Page interview with Maria Tippett, April 14, 1999.

36. Peter Page to Maria Tippett, December 7, 1999, and April 3, 1999.

37. *Gold Brooch with Abalone,* eagle motif, private collection; Peter Page interviewed by Maria Tippett, April 14, 1999.

38. *Gold Box,* No. 13902, RBCM; inscribed on the base, "Bill Reid, 1971"; Peter Page to Maria Tippett, December 7, 1999.

39. Reid to Grauer, November 14, 1970.

40. Reid to Grauer, November 14, 1970.

41. Bill Reid, *Horse Barnicle Necklace,* sterling silver and white gold, 15 cm diameter, circa 1970. Bill Reid Foundation.

42. Reid to Grauer, November 14, 1970.

Part III

Chapter Eleven

1. Peter Selz, "Vancouver Scene and Unscene," *Art in America,* Vol. 58 (January–February 1970), p. 122.

2. Bill Reid, "Traditions of Northwest Coast Indian Culture," November 23, 1976, MOA.

3. Gerry Marks interview with Susan Davidson, GNWC-T038 (1980), RBCM.

4. Bill Reid to Donald Abbott, curator, January 5, 1968, 'Ksan File, RBCM.

5. Larry Rosso interview with Beverley Berger, March 16, 1999.

6. Reid to Abbott, 'Ksan File, RBCM.

7. Lynn Maranda and Robert D. Watt, "An Interview with Bill Reid," *Canadian Collector* (May–June 1976), p. 34.

8. Bill Reid to Sherry Grauer, January 1971.

9.   Clive Cocking, "Indian Art Renaissance," *The Native Voice* (January 1972), p. 5.

10. Bill Reid, *Gold Box*, beaver and human design on the sides and killer whale on the lid, 1970–1971, No. 13902, RBCM.

11. Reid to Grauer, January 1971.

12. Harold Cardinal, *Unjust Society: The Tragedy of Canada's Indians* (Edmonton: M.G. Hurtig, 1969), p.17.

13. Sally M. Weaver, *Making Indian Policy: The Hidden Agenda 1968–1970* (Toronto: University of Toronto Press, 1981), p. 197.

14. Bill Reid to Sherry Grauer, March 12, 1970.

15. Bill Reid to Sherry Grauer, November 14, 1970.

16. Peter Macnair to Bill Reid, July 22, 1971, M20 Box 12, RBCM.

17. Bill Reid, *Bear Mother* gold box, 1972, Canadian Museum of Civilization; Charles Edenshaw, *Discovering Mankind*, compote, argillite, chest, PN106 22, RBCM.

18. Bill Reid, *Bear, Human and Wolf*, gold box, 1973, 3.5 cm high, 2.8 cm by 5.5 cm, Adelaide de Menil.

19. Toni Cavelti interviewed by Maria Tippett, September 1999.

20. Edith Iglauer, "The Myth Maker," *Saturday Night* (February 1982), p. 22.

21. Bill Reid, *Raven Discovering Mankind in a Clamshell*, signed 1970, 7 cm by 7 cm boxwood, Nb1.488, MOA.

22. Bill Reid, *The Raven and the First Men*, sterling bracelet, circa 1955, 6.3 cm by 2.5 cm, private collection.

23. Sculpture, Miniature, Flemish, 16th century, Bead Rosary, 2 1/8 inches high, No. 17.190.475, Metropolitan Museum of Art, New York.

24. Charles Edenshaw, *Chest, Discovering Mankind*, argillite, No. 10622, RBCM; Charles Edenshaw, *Argillite Dish Clamshell, Origin of Man*, circa 1904, 10 1/2 by 8 1/2 inches, argillite stone and bone, A2049, MOA.

25. See Claude Davidson's depiction of the creation myth in Leslie Drew and Douglas Wilson, *Argillite Art of the Haida* (North Vancouver: Hancock House, 1980), p. 114.

26. Ron Sudlow, "New Haida Indian Art No Longer Just a Hobby," *Regina Leader Post*, September 28, 1974.

27. *The Atlantic Reporter*, May 1, 1970.

28. Catherine Bates, "Bauble-maker Supreme," *Star* (Montreal), October 16, 1971.

29. Bill Reid, "Peddling the Ancestral Bones for Fun and Profit," *UAAC/AAUC Journal*, August 1974, typescript, VAG, p. 17.

30. Robert Reid interview with Maria Tippett, July 22, 1999.

31. Sherry Grauer interview with Maria Tippett, March 7, 2001.

32. Art Price to Maria Tippett, February 20, 2000.

33. Bill Reid to Harry Hawthorn (1972), Harry Hawthorn Papers, Special Collections, Box 8-25, University of British Columbia.

34. Audrey Hawthorn tape to Maria Tippett, March 2000. This account may be apocryphal because Reid told Harry Hawthorn a few months later that Koerner had just commissioned him to do the work. Bill Reid to Harry Hawthorn (January 1973), Special Collections, Box 8-25, University of British Columbia.

35. Bill Reid to Harry Hawthorn (autumn 1972), Box 8-25 Special Collections, University of British Columbia.

36. Bill Reid to Sherry Grauer, December 1970.

37. Audrey Hawthorn tape to Maria Tippett, March 2000.

38. Al Aranson, "Bill Reid Puts Focus on Disease," *Province* (Vancouver), September 30, 1985.

39. Iglauer, "The Myth Maker," p. 16.

40. *An Artist and Parkinson's Disease: A Portrait of Bill Reid,* April 1, 1985, a film by Nina Wasnicki.

41. R. Horowski, L. Horowski, S.M. Calne, and D.B. Calne, "From Wilhelm von Humboldt to Hitler — Are Prominent People More Prone to Have Parkinson's Disease?," in *Parkinson and Related Disorders* 6 (2000), 205–216; See also: John Marks, *The Treatment of Parkinsonism with L-Dopa* (New York: American Elsevier Pub. Co., 1974). I am grateful to Dr. D.B. Calne for his discussion of the disease.

42. Bill Reid, "Haida Artistry Superb," *The Native Voice* (November 1974), p. 2.

43. Johannes P.W.F. Lakke, "Art and Parkinson's Disease," in Gerald M. Stern, *Parkinson's Disease* (Philadelphia: Lippincott Williams and Wilkins, 1999), pp. 471–79.

44. Audrey Hawthorn tape to Maria Tippett, March 2000.

45. Harry Hawthorn to Bill Reid, November 3, 1972, Box 8-25, Harry Hawthorn Papers, Special Collections, University of British Columbia.

46. Art Perry, "New Haida Art Takes Form," *Province* (Vancouver), June 26, 1974.

47. Perry, "New Haida Art Takes Form."

48. Sudlow, "New Haida Art No Longer Just a Hobby."

49. Edmund Carpenter, Harry Hawthorn, and Claude Lévi-Strauss in *Bill Reid: A Retrospective Exhibition,* VAG catalogue, 1974, n.p.

50. Claude Lévi-Strauss in *Bill Reid: A Retrospective Exhibition.*

51. Wilson Duff in *Bill Reid: A Retrospective Exhibition,* VAG catalogue, 1974, n.p.

52. Joan Lowndes, "The Artist," *Vancouver Sun,* December 27, 1974.

53. William E. Taylor cited in "Continuing Exhibitions," *Vanguard,* Vol. 3, No. 10, (December 1974/January 1975), p. 7.

54. Bill Reid to Peter and Sandi Page, January 1975, private collection.

55.   Bill Reid quoted in Peter Malkin, "Bill Reid Retrospective," *Vanguard*, Vol. 3 No. 8 (November 1974), p. 3.

56.   "The Totem Carvers," *Radio Times*, May 21, 1959.

Chapter Twelve

1.   "Past Palls, So Totem Carver Prepares to Throw in the Chisel," *Toronto Star*, January 6, 1962.

2.   Joan M. Vastokas, "Bill Reid and the Native Renaissance," *artscanada* (June 1975), p. 15.

3.   Bill Reid to Peter Page, 1975, private collection.

4.   Bill Ellis, "Deserved Ceremony," *Province* (Vancouver), March 6, 1978.

5.   The University of British Columbia, the University of Victoria, York University, the University of Western Ontario, Trent University, Simon Fraser University, and the University of Toronto.

6.   Michael Ames interview with Beverley Berger, February 24, 2000.

7.   Bill Holm and William Reid, *Form and Freedom: A Dialogue on Northwest Coast Indian Art* (Houston: Institute for the Arts, Rice University, 1975); Roger Fry, *Vision and Design* (London: Chatto & Windus, 1920).

8.   Marjorie Halpin, "A Review Article," *BC Studies* (Spring 1978), pp. 48–59.

9.   Holm and Reid, *Form and Freedom*, pp. 170, 58.

10.   Bill Reid, "Traditions of Northwest Coast Indian Culture," November 23, 1976, MOA.

11.   Bill Reid to Russell Keiziere, August 10, 1982, Artist's File, VAG; Ian Mulgrew, "A Thin Renaissance in Western Native Art," *Globe and Mail*, June 23, 1982.

12.   Davidson interview with Katrin Sermat, 1981; Vickie Jensen, *Where The People Gather: Carving a Totem Pole* (Vancouver: Douglas & McIntyre, 1992), p. 9; Don Yeomans (1980) cited in Karen Duffek, "The Contemporary Northwest Coast Indian Art Market," M.A. Thesis, University of British Columbia, 1983, p. 107.

13.   Mulgrew, "A Thin Renaissance in Western Native Art."

14.   Reid, "Traditions of Northwest Coast Indian Culture."

15.   Reg Davidson interview with Susan Davidson, 1980, RBCM.

16.   Among the eight artists to participate were Earl Muldoe, Norman Tait, Nelson Cross, Gerry Marks, Francis Williams, and Russell Smith.

17.   Peter Page, "Goldsmiths Workshop," typescript (Vancouver 1977), private collection.

18.   Page, "Goldsmiths Workshop."

19.   Lloyd Dykk, "Arts and the Man," *Vancouver Sun*, August 6, 1983. "Reverent Homage to the Haida," *Province* (Vancouver), April 22, 1977.

20. Susan Feldman, "Bill Reid: Voyage through Two Worlds," interview with Reid, January 1992, CBC Radio.

21. Don Yeomans, Memorial Feast in Skidegate, July 3, 1998.

22. "Totem Poles Make a Comeback, Boosting Indians' Pride, Fortunes," *Wall Street Journal*, August 22, 1983, p. 10.

23. Tak Tanabe interview with Maria Tippett, July 13, 2000.

24. Thomas Hopkins, "The Happy Rebirth of an Intricate Art," *Maclean's*, April 14, 1980.

25. George Rammell interview with Beverley Berger, November 13, 1998.

26. Robert Davidson interview with Beverley Berger, February 7, 1999.

27. Joe David interview with Beverley Berger, October 20, 1998.

28. Gary Edenshaw, or Guujaaw, "The Legacy of Bill Reid: A Critical Enquiry," conference, November 14, 1999, University of British Columbia.

29. Dykk, "Arts and the Man."

30. Diane Brown, "The Legacy of Bill Reid: A Critical Inquiry," conference, November 13, 1999, University of British Columbia.

31. Peter Page interview with Maria Tippett, April 14, 1999; Don Yeomans interview with Maria Tippett, September 2, 1998; Davidson interview with Beverley Berger.

32. Gerry Marks interview with Susan Davidson, 1980, GN WCTO38, RBCM.

33. Ulli Steltzer and Catherine Kerr, "Coastal Icons: The Edge of the West," *The Canadian Province* (Vancouver), October 6–7, 1979, p. 18.

34. Steltzer and Kerr, "Coastal Icons," p. 18.

35. Steltzer and Kerr, "Coastal Icons," p. 18.

36. Duffek, "The Contemporary Northwest Coast Indian Art Market."

37. Clive Cooking, "Indian Art Renaissance," *The Native Voice* (January 1972), p. 5.

38. Diane Brown, "The Legacy of Bill Reid: A Critical Inquiry," conference, November 13, 1999, University of British Columbia.

39. Davidson interview with Berger.

40. Barry Herem interview with Maria Tippett, November 8, 1999.

Chapter Thirteen

1. Bill Reid, "1st Trailer, 2nd Beach, Skidegate Inlet, Queen Charlotte Islands, August 3 1976," *Vanguard* (October 1976), p. 17.

2. Wilson Duff to Peter Macnair, April 27, 1976, Macnair Correspondence, M20, Box 9, RBCM.

3. Tak Tanabe interview with Maria Tippett, July 13, 2000.

4. *Prince Rupert News*, August 26, 1976.

5. Margaret Kennedy interview with Maria Tippett, July 13, 1998.

6. Audrey Hawthorn tape for Maria Tippett, March 2000.

7. Moira Johnston, "The Raven's Last Journey," *Saturday Night* (November 1998), p. 79.

8. Lloyd Dykk, "Arts and the Man," *Vancouver Sun*, August 6, 1983.

9. Art Price interview with Maria Tippett, August 8, 2000.

10. Tak Tanabe interview with Maria Tippett, July 13, 2000.

11. Edith Iglauer, "The Myth Maker," *Saturday Night* (February 1982), p. 18.

12. *Boxwood Transformation Pendant with Detachable Mask*, 1982, Bill Reid Foundation Collection.

13. *Horse Barnicle Necklace*, Bill Reid Foundation Collection; Sherry Grauer to Maria Tippett, November 20, 2002.

14. Martine Reid interviewed on "Sunday Arts Entertainment," CBC Television, January 28, 1996.

15. Ron Sudlow, "Artist Wants to Repay Culture That Inspired Him," *Times-Colonist* (Victoria), July 13, 1990.

16. *An Artist and Parkinson's Disease: A Portrait of Bill Reid*, April 1, 1985, a film by Nina Wasnicki.

17. George Rammell interview with Beverley Berger, November 13, 1998; Rammell, "A Bill Reid Tribute," March 24, 1998.

18. Rammell interview with Berger.

19. Rammell interview with Berger.

20. Reg Davidson interview with Susan Davidson, 1980, RBCM.

21. Jim Hart interview with Beverley Berger, February 17, 1999.

22. Gerry Marks interview with Susan Davidson, 1980, RBCM.

23. Norman Tait interview with Beverley Berger, March 31, 1999.

24. Don Yeomans, "A Bill Reid Tribute," March 24, 1998.

25. Joe Plaskett to Maria Tippett, February 11, 2002.

26. Rammell interview with Beverley Berger.

27. Michael Ames interview with Beverley Berger, February 24, 2000.

28. Jim Hart to Stephen Inglis, February 3, 1990, Canadian Museum of Civilization.

29. Don Yeomans, "A Tribute to Bill Reid."

30. *UBC Reports*, Vol. 25 No. 3 (January 31, 1979), p. 1.

31. Moira Farrow, "Raven Carving Due to Move to Museum for Final Touching," *Vancouver Sun*, January 12, 1980; the same newspaper noted a few months later that Kim Kerrigan had also joined the team (April 26, 1980).

32. See, for example, *Western Living* (April 1980), p. 22, VAG clipping file.

33. "Reviews," *artscanada* (July/August 1981), p. 33.

34. After Jim Hart interview with Beverley Berger: Jim Hart to Stephen Inglis, February 3, 1990, Canadian Museum of Civilization

35. Jim Hart interview with Beverley Berger.

36. Moira Farrow, "Prince Unveils Sculpture During Visit to UBC and Has Go at TRIUMPH," *Vancouver Sun*, April 2, 1980.

37. Bill Reid, "The Haida Legend of the Raven and the First Humans as Retold by Bill Reid," *Museum Note* No. 8 (1980), MOA.

38. Brenda White, "Raven: How Two Cultures Came Together Under One Wing," *Vancouver Sun*, April 26, 1980.

39. Robert Williamson, "Sculptor Looks Anew at Haida Tradition," *Globe and Mail*, April 19, 1980.

40. Norman Tait interview with Beverley Berger.

41. Robert Davidson, "The Legacy of Bill Reid: A Critical Inquiry," conference, November 13, 1999, University of British Columbia.

42. Eve Johnson, "Revivalist Reid and the Indian Image," *Vancouver Sun*, August 9, 1986.

43. Susan J. Stewart, "The Chief of the Undersea World," *Canadian Collector* (July–August 1984), p. 19.

44. Bill Reid to Robert Reid, July 1978, private collection.

45. See illustration of Walter Russ's carving in Carol Sheehan, *Pipes That Won't Smoke; Coal That Won't Burn: Haida Sculpture in Argillite* (Calgary: Glenbow Museum, 1981), p. 121; Reid's gold box with cast three-dimensional *Killer Whale*, 1971, height 9 cm, RBCM; Reid's *Killer Whale*, 1983, 11.5 cm high, private collection.

46. Davidson, "The Legacy of Bill Reid: A Critical Inquiry."

47. See Reid's *Silver Brooch, Raven, Bear Frog* 2.6 cm by 7.9 cm, 1957; Reid would have seen the other source of inspiration, the argillite pipe, at the British Museum, but it was also illustrated in a work that was familiar to him: Robert Bruce Inverarity, *Art of the Northwest Coast Indians* (Los Angeles: University of California Press, 1950), Illustration No. 172.

48. *Mythic Messengers* (1984); A bronze cast of this work was installed for the opening of the Canadian Museum of Civilization in June 1989. The cast was made in the Jack Harman Foundry in Vancouver.

49. Robert Reid interview with Maria Tippett, July 22, 1999.

Chapter Fourteen

1. *Front Page Challenge*, January 11, 1986, CBC film (Vancouver), PABC. The panel was not able to identify Reid.

2. Christopher Hume, "The Spirit of Haida Art Holds His First Solo Show," *Toronto Star*, November 3, 1993.

3. Earl Muldoe interview with Beverley Berger, August 18, 1999.

4. Robert Davidson interview with Susan Davidson, 1980, GNWC-T-051, RBCM.

5. Miriam Shiell interview with Maria Tippett, November 17, 1999.

6. Ulli Steltzer interview with Beverley Berger, March 3, 1999.

7. Bill McLennan interview with Beverley Berger, March 24, 2000.

8. "Bill Reid, Archives Receives Funding," January 13, 1986, news release, University of British Columbia; See also: "Archive Honors Haida," *Vancouver Sun,* January 23, 1986.

9. Bill Reid, *Phyllidula, the Shape of Frogs to Come,* 45 cm high, 97 cm wide, 126 cm long, wood, stain finish, 1984–1985, VAG.

10. Bill McLennan interview with Maria Tippett, July 4, 2001.

11. Bill Reid, "The Haida Legend of the Raven and the First Humans," *Museum Note* No. 8 (1980), MOA.

12. *Bill Reid — Drawings,* Equinox Gallery catalogue, January 27 to February 26, 1983 (two-page statement by Reid).

13. Barry Herem, "UBC Has Major Exhibit By Bill Reid, to Oct. 5," *Northwest Arts,* September 16, 1986, p. 5.

14. Joe David interview with Beverely Berger, October 20, 1998.

15. Johannes P.W.F. Lakke, "Art and Parkinson's Disease," in Gerald M. Stern's *Parkinson's Disease* (Philadelphia: Lippencott Williams and Wilkins, 1999), p. 471.

16. *An Artist and Parkinson's Disease: A Portrait of Bill Reid,* a film by Nina Wasnicki, April 1, 1985 (Reid was filmed in August 1984).

17. The largest known Haida canoe is the 19.2-metre canoe held in the American Museum of Natural History in New York.

18. Bill Reid repainted the Shaw canoe in 1967 for the Museum of Anthropology. Bill Reid/David Shaw *Canoe,* circa 1934, cedar wood, paint, overall 80 by 90 by 504.5 cm, A1535, MOA.

19. Moira Farrow, "Bank of B.C. to Bail out Haida Canoe for Expo," *Vancouver Sun,* July 31, 1985.

20. Mark Hume, "Launching of War Canoe Moved Haida Elders to Tears," *Vancouver Sun,* June 17, 1987.

21. In a lecture at the Museum of Anthropology on February 6, 1979, Reid claimed that the ovoid "may be the origin of all the forms that you find in Northwest Coast art," though he made no reference to the canoe (typescript, MOA). "Haida Canoeists Paddle into Past," *Globe and Mail,* June 18, 1987.

22. "Invisible Artist Deserves Credit," *Vancouver Courier,* November 25, 1990, p. 27.

23. Stephen Godfrey, "Murphy's Romance," *Globe and Mail,* March 29, 1986.

24. Barbara Reid interview with Maria Tippett, July 15, 1998.

25. Rod Mickleburgh, "Haida Canoe's Trip up the Seine Native Artist's Fantasy Come True," *Globe and Mail,* September 30, 1989.

26. Ann Rees, "Lootaas Reaches Paris to Fulfill Artist's Dream," *Province* (Vancouver), October 3, 1989.

27. Mark Hume, "Lootaas' Journey Too Tough," *Vancouver Sun*, September 30, 1989.

28. French immigration officials allowed them into the country on their "Haida passports."

29. Mickleburgh, "Haida Canoe's Trip up the Seine Native Artist's Fantasy Come True."

30. "Native People Too Angry, Offended," *Vancouver Sun*, October 10, 1989.

31. Nicole Parton, "Haida Rejection of Flag a Cheeky Slap on Cheek," *Vancouver Sun*, September 23, 1989.

32. See, for example, "Mailbag," *Province* (Vancouver), October 5, 1989.

33. Stephen Hume, "Haida Had Reason for Flying Own Flag," *Vancouver Sun*, October 18, 1989.

34. Yvonne Rebeyrol, "Le Musée de l'homme rendre hommage à Claude Lévi-Strauss, le premier France ait introduit," *Le Monde*, October 18, 1989; Mark Hume, "Paddlers Enter Paris Flying Haida Flag," *Vancouver Sun*, October 2, 1989.

35. Peter Page interview with Maria Tippett, April 14, 1999.

36. Mickleburgh, "Haida Canoe's Trip up the Seine Native Artist's Fantasy Come True."

37. Mark Hume, "Haida Artist, Paddlers, War Canoe Bound for Paris Art Exhibition," *Vancouver Sun*, September 23, 1989.

38. Tom Price, *Canoe with People*, AA2326, and *Canoe with Figures*, anon., AA60, Centennial Museum.

39. Sarah Jennings, "Art at the Washington Embassy," *Canadian Art* (Fall 1987), p. 11.

40. Nicholas Jennings, "Haidas on the Seine," *Maclean's* (October 16, 1989), pp. 67–68.

41. See the photograph in Eve Johnson, "Revivalist Reid and the Indian Image," *Vancouver Sun*, August 9, 1986.

42. Bill Reid, "The Spirit of Haida Gwaii," Vancouver 1991 (mimeograph), VAG Archives.

43. Christopher Dafoe, "An Odyssey of Mythic Proportions: Bill Reid's *The Spirit of Haida Gwaii*," *Globe and Mail*, November 16, 1991.

44. See chapters 1 and 2 in James Tully, *Strange Multiplicity, Constitutionalism in the Age of Diversity* (Cambridge: Cambridge University Press, 1995), pp. 1–34.

45. Robert Davidson, "Voyage Through Two Worlds: The Sculpture of Bill Reid," *Border Crossings*, Vol. 11 No. 4 (December 1992), an adaptation of a radio documentary written and presented by Toronto radio producer Susan Feldman, September 7, 1992. CBC Radio.

46. See for example, Robert Bringhurst and Ulli Steltzer, *The Black Canoe: Bill Reid and the Spirit of Haida Gwaii* (Vancouver: Douglas & McIntyre, 1991); and Ulli Steltzer, *The Spirit of Haida Gwaii: Bill Reid's Masterpiece*, Introduction by Robin Laurence (Vancouver: Douglas & McIntyre, 1997).

Chapter Fifteen

1. Alan Bayless, "The Big Money in Native Art," *Financial Times,* August 28, 1993; See also "Northwest Indians Find Their Roots — Way Above Ground: A Totem-Pole Revival Brings Money; 'Why Let Our Culture Disappear?'" *Wall Street Journal,* August 22, 1983.

2. Bayless, "The Big Money in Native Art."

3. Don Yeomans interview with Susan Davidson, May 21, 1980, RBCM.

4. George Rammell interview with Beverley Berger, November 13, 1998.

5. A comparison of the Edenshaw-Reid bracelet, in the Bill Reid Foundation collection, with the original work makes me doubt whether Reid improved a work he told a journalist was incomplete before he "restored" it. Edith Iglauer, "The Myth Maker," *Saturday Night* (February 1982), p. 18.

6. Ron Hamilton quoted in Michael Kimmelman, "Indian Art vs Artifact: Problem of Ambiguity," *New York Times,* May 1, 1989.

7. Marnie Fleming, "Patrimony and Patronage: The Legacy Reviewed," *Vanguard* (Summer 1982), p. 18. "The Legacy Review Reviewed by Bill Reid," *Vanguard* (October/November 1982), p. 34. *The Legacy* was first mounted in 1971 by RBCM.

8. Tom Berger interview with Beverley Berger, January 9, 2000.

9. George Rammell interview with Beverley Berger, November 13, 1998.

10. Susan Feldman, "Bill Reid: Voyage through Two Worlds," CBC Radio, produced March 1, 1994.

11. Margaret Kennedy interview with Maria Tippett, July 23, 1998.

12. Don Yeomans interview with Maria Tippett, September 2, 1998; Merilyn Mohr, "The Bestiary of Bill Reid," *Equinox,* No. 53 (September–October 1990), p. 79.

13. Stephen Godfrey, "Murphy's Romance," *Globe and Mail,* March 29, 1986.

14. Limited bronze editions of nine were made of *The Dogfish Woman, The Bear Mother,* and *The Speaker Staff;* these were scaled-down replicas from *The Spirit of Haida Gwaii.* Reid's impressive wall relief bronze *Mythic Messengers* became the inspiration for a bracelet of the same name. *Mythic Messengers,* bracelet, cast gold, 18 cm diameter (1986), private collection.

15. Rammell interview with Beverley Berger.

16. Yeomans interview with Maria Tippett.

17. The extent to which the conception of *The Spirit of Haida Gwaii* changed can be seen by comparing a photograph of the original clay model — which has a non-Native central figure — to the finished work. (See Eve Johnson, "Revivalist Reid and the Indian Image," *Vancouver Sun,* August 9, 1986); Rammell interview with Berger.

18. George Rammell, "The Authentic Master, Bill Reid," *Vancouver Sun,* October 30, 1999.

19. Agnes Allen, *The Story of Michelangelo* (London: Faber and Faber, 1953), p. 84.

20. Michael Ames interview with Beverley Berger, February 24, 2000.

21. Wade Saunders, "Making Art, Making Artists," *Art in America* (January 1993), p. 70.

22. Robert Bringhurst on *Morningside*, November 19, 1991, CBC Radio.

23. Joe Plaskett to Maria Tippett, February 11, 2001.

24. Barry Herem, "UBC Has Major Exhibit by Bill Reid, to Oct. 5," *Northwest Arts*, September 16, 1986, pp. 5–6.

25. Eve Johnson, "Revivalist Reid and the Indian Image," *Vancouver Sun*, August 9, 1986.

26. Johnson, "Revivalist Reid and the Indian Image."

27. Miriam Shiell interview with Maria Tippett, November 17, 1999.

28. Eve Johnson, "Opportunity for Critical Evaluation of a Major Artist," *Vancouver Sun*, August 9, 1986.

29. The National Museum of Man — later the Canadian Museum of Civilization - — returned the ceremonial regalia that it had confiscated in 1922 from the potlatch on Village Island held in December 1921; the collection was divided between the Kwagiulth Museum at Cape Mudge and the U'Mista Cultural Centre at Alert Bay. The first National Native Indian Artists Symposium was held on Manitoulin Island in Ontario in October 1978 and the fourth at the University of Lethbridge in 1987.

30. Margaret Atwood, *Survival: A Thematic Guide to Canadian Literature* (Toronto: Anansi, 1972), p. 97.

31. "Just Another WASP: Haida Artist Bill Reid," *Province* (Vancouver), July 31, 1983.

32. Bill Reid, "Indian Equality Urged" (June 17, 1959), VAG clipping file; Bill Reid "Totem Pole is Epic in Carved Wood," *Vancouver Sun*, February 9, 1954.

33. Bill Reid, "The Enchanted Forest," *Vancouver Sun*, October 24, 1980.

34. Bill Reid, "These Shining Islands," in *Islands at the Edge: Preserving the Queen Charlotte Islands Wilderness* (Vancouver: Douglas & McIntyre, 1984), pp. 23–30.

35. Bill Reid, "Becoming Haida," in Robert Bringhurst, *Solitary Raven: Selected Writings of Bill Reid* (text of a talk Reid delivered on February 1, 1986, to the Wilderness Advisory Committee in Vancouver) (Vancouver: Douglas & McIntyre, 2000), p. 216.

36. *Vancouver Sun*, November 7, 1985.

37. Richard Wright, "The Spirit of Haida Gwaii," *En Route* (March 1991), p. 90.

38. "Stars Fight for Moresby," *Province* (Vancouver), October 24, 1985.

39. Yeomans interview with Tippett.

40. Suzanne Fournier, "Haida Artist Risks Arrest for Blocking Lyell Roads," *Province* (Vancouver), October 28, 1986.

41. *Adrienne Clarkson Presents*, CBC, September 2, 1992, had a film clip of this event; Yeomans interview with Tippett.

42. March 30, 1987, VAG clipping file; Tim Harper, "Artist Won't Give Art to Ottawa in Protest over Rights of Natives," *Toronto Star*, March 29, 1987.

43. See, for example, *Vancouver Courier*, April 1, 1987, p. 9.

44. Tom Berger interview with Beverley Berger.

45. Diane Brown, "The Legacy of Bill Reid: A Critical Inquiry," November 13, 1999, conference, University of British Columbia.

46. Yeomans interview with Tippett.

47. Ann Ross, "Paris Greets Haida," *Province* (Vancouver), October 3, 1989.

48. *The World of Bill Reid*, Canadian Embassy in Tokyo, March 5 to April 25, 1997; *Bill Reid*, Budapest Ethnographic Museum, The Budapest Spring Festival, March 12 to April 18, 1993.

49. Barbara Reid interview with Maria Tippett, July 15, 1998.

50. Karen Gram, "Artist Angry at Airport's Treatment of his Sculpture," *Vancouver Sun*, April 4, 1994; John O'Brian, "Art at the Airport" *Globe and Mail*, May 1, 1994.

51. Nicole Parton, "Art of the Raven," *Vancouver Sun*, 1991. Clipping file, Canadian Museum of Civilization; During Reid's memorial at the Museum of Anthropology, Robert Davidson referred to Reid as Kihlguuline. This name was not, however, engraved on Reid's tombstone.

52. Lloyd Dykk, "Arts and the Man," *Vancouver Sun*, August 6, 1983; Parton, "Art of the Raven."

53. Yeomans interview with Tippett.

54. Derek Norton interview with Maria Tippett, September 2, 1998

55. Rammell interview with Berger.

56. Jay Currie and Michèle Denis, "Hearing Old Songs: An Interview with Robert Bringhurst," *two chairs* (July 1999), p. 9.

57. Audrey Hawthorn tape for Maria Tippett, March 2000.

58. Pamela Fayerman, "Bill Reid Refuses to Say Die," *Vancouver Sun*, September 23, 1997.

59. David Watmough to Maria Tippett, November 19, 1998.

60. Nicholas Jennings, "Haidas on the Seine," *Maclean's*, October 16, 1989, p. 67.

61. Peter Page interview with Maria Tippett, April 14, 1999.

62. Plaskett to Tippett, February 11, 2001.

63. Tak Tanabe interview with Maria Tippett, July 13, 2000.

64. Martine Reid interview with Maria Tippett, June 1998.

Epilogue

1. Reid's contribution came from *Out of the Silence*, Photographs by Adelaide de Menil and Text by William Reid, The Amon Carter Museum, Fort Worth, Texas, 1971, p. 38. (This essay first appeared in *The Arts of the Raven*, VAG, 1967).

2. No fewer than ten speakers, including Doris Shadbolt, Toni Cavelti, George Rammell, Jim Hart, Don Yeomans, and Miles Richardson III, referred to Reid's legacy throughout "A Bill Reid Tribute," March 24, 1998, which is my source for further identified contributions below.

3. Adele Weder, "The Myths and the White Man," *Globe and Mail*, November 15, 1999.

4. Michael Ames interview with Beverley Berger, February 12, 2000.

5. Jane O'Hara, "Trade Secrets," *Maclean's*, October 18, 1999, pp. 20–29.

6. Peter O'Neil, John Mackie, Yvonne Zacharias, "Bill Reid Art 'Saved' for BC," *Vancouver Sun*, October 10, 2002.

7. George Rammell interview with Beverley Berger, November 13, 1998; Jim Hart interview with Beverley Berger, February 17, 1999.

8. Miles Richardson speaking at the memorial feast in Skidegate, July 3, 1998.

9. Don Yeomans interview with Maria Tippett, September 2, 1998.

10. Doreen Jensen interview with Beverley Berger, November 26, 1998.

11. Max Wyman, "Modest Artist Wins $100,000 Award," July 1990, VAG clipping file.

Selected Bibliography

Abbott, Donald N. ed. *The World Is as Sharp as a Knife: An Anthology in Honour of Wilson Duff.* Victoria, Royal British Columbia Museum, 1981.

A Bill Reid Tribute. Rogers Cable Television, March 24, 1998.

Adam, Leonard. "North-West American Indian Art and Its Early Chinese Parallels," *Man,* No. 2–3 (January 1936).

Ames, Michael M. "Museum Anthropologists and the Arts of Acculturation on the Northwest Coast," *BC Studies,* No. 49 (Spring 1981).

Ames, Michael M. *Museums, the Public and Anthropology: A Study in the Anthropology of Anthropology.* Vancouver: University of British Columbia Press, 1986.

An Artist and Parkinson's Disease: A Portrait of Bill Reid, April 1, 1985, film by Nina Wasnicki.

Atleo, Richard E. "Policy Development for Museums: A First Nations Perspective," *BC Studies,* No. 89 (Spring 1991).

Barbeau, Marius. "The Canadian Northwest: Themes for Modern Painters," *Magazine of Art,* Vol. 24 (May 1932).

Barbeau, Marius. *The Downfall of Temlaham.* Toronto: Macmillan, 1928.

Barbeau, Marius. *Haida Carvers in Argillite,* National Museum of Canada Bulletin No. 139, Anthropological Series No. 38 (Ottawa, 1957).

Barbeau, Marius. "Indian Silversmiths on the Pacific Coast," *Transactions of the Royal Society of Canada,* Section II, Vol. XXXIII, May 1939.

Barbeau, Marius. Lecture in "Editorial," *The Paint Box,* Vol. 11 (Vancouver, June 1927).

Barbeau, Marius. *Totem Poles, According to Crests and Topics,* Bulletin No. 119, Vol. I No. 36 (Ottawa, 1950).

Barbeau, Marius. *Totem Poles According to Location,* Vol. 11. National Museum of Canada, Bulletin No. 119, Anthropological Series No. 30 (Ottawa, 1950).

Barman, Jean. *The West Beyond the West: A History of British Columbia.* Toronto: University of Toronto Press, 1991.

Barnett, H.G. "Personal Conflicts and Cultural Change," *Social Forces,* Vol. 20 No. 2 (December 1941).

Bayless, Alan. "The Big Money in Native Art," *Financial Times,* August 28, 1993.

"B.C. Jewellery," *Western Homes & Living* (December–January, 1955–56).

Begg, Alexander. *History of British Columbia, from Its Earliest Discovery to the Present Time.* Toronto: W. Briggs, 1894.

Berlo, Janet C., and Ruth Phillips. *Native North American Art.* Oxford: Oxford University Press, 1998.

Beyond the Revival: Contemporary North West Native Art. Emily Carr College of Art & Design, July 25 to September 17, 1989.

Bill Reid. Budapest Ethnographic Museum catalogue, The Budapest Spring Festival, March 12 to April 18, 1993.

Bill Reid: A Retrospective Exhibition. VAG catalogue, 1974.

Blackman, Margaret. *During My Time, Florence Edenshaw Davidson, a Haida Woman.* Seattle: University of Washington Press, 1982.

Boas, Franz. "Art of the North Pacific Coast of North America," *Science,* Vol. IV No. 82, July 24, 1896.

Boas, Franz. "The Decorative Art of the Indians of the North Pacific Coast," *Bulletin of the American Museum of Natural History,* Vol. 9 (1897).

Boas, Franz. *Primitive Art.* New York: Dover Publications, 1955 (first published in 1927).

Boas, Franz. *Tsimshian Mythology.* Washington: Smithsonian Institution, 1916.

Boyd, Robert. "Smallpox in the Pacific Northwest: The First Epidemics," *BC Studies,* No. 101 (Spring 1994).

Bringhurst, Robert. *Morningside.* November 19, 1991, CBC Radio.

Bringhurst, Robert, and Ulli Steltzer. *The Black Canoe: Bill Reid and the Spirit of Haida Gwaii.* Vancouver: Douglas & McIntyre, 1991.

Bringhurst, Robert. *Solitary Raven: The Selected Writings of Bill Reid.* Vancouver: Douglas & McIntyre, 2000.

Brown, Steven C. *Native Visions: Evolution in Northwest Coast Art from the Eighteenth through the Twentieth Century.* Seattle: University of Washington Press, 1998.

Cabell, James Branch. *Jürgen: A Comedy of Justice.* New York: Grosset & Dunlap, 1919.

Cardinal, Harold. *Unjust Society: The Tragedy of Canada's Indians.* Edmonton: M. G. Hurtig, 1969.

Carr, Emily. "Modern and Indian Art of the West Coast," *McGill News* (Supplement), June 1929.

Clutesi, George. *Son of Raven, Son of Deer: Fables of the Tse-shaht People.* Sidney, BC: Gray's Publishing, 1967.

Cocking, Clive. "Indian Art Renaissance," *The Native Voice* (January 1972).

Coe, Ralph T. *Sacred Circles.* Exhibition organized by the Arts Council of Great Britain, London: Arts Council of Great Britain, 1976.

Cole, Douglas. *Captured Heritage.* Vancouver: Douglas & McIntyre, 1985.

Colnett, James. "Journal Aboard the Prince of Wales," October 16–November 7, 1788, Public Records Office, ADM 55/146.

Dalzell, Kathleen E. *The Queen Charlotte Islands.* Terrace, BC: Adam, 1968.

Davidson, Robert. "Voyage Through Two Worlds: The Sculpture of Bill Reid," *Border Crossings,* Vol. 11 No. 4 (December 1992).

Dixon, George. *A Voyage Round the World; but more particularly to the north-west coast of America performed in 1785, 1786, 1787, 1788 . . . in the "King George" and "Queen Charlotte."* Captains Peacock and Dixon, London: S. Goulding, 1789.

Downey, Roger. "Apprentice to a Lost Art," *Pacific Northwest* (October 1983).

Drew, Leslie, and Douglas Wilson. *Argillite Art of the Haida.* North Vancouver: Hancock House, 1980.

Duff, Wilson. "A Heritage in Decay — the Totem Art of the Haidas," *Canadian Art,* Vol. XI No. 2 (Winter 1954).

Duff, Wilson. *Images: Stone B.C., Thirty Centuries of Northwest Coast Indian Sculpture.* Seattle: University of Washington Press, 1975.

Duff, Wilson. "Mungo Martin: Carver of the Century," *Museum News,* Vol. 1 No. 1 (May 1959).

Duff, Wilson, Bill Holm, and Bill Reid. *The Arts of the Raven: Masterworks by the Northwest Coast Indian.* VAG catalogue, 1967.

Duffek, Karen. *Bill Reid: Beyond the Essential Form.* Vancouver: Museum of Anthropology, 1986.

Duffek, Karen. "The Contemporary Northwest Coast Indian Art Market." M.A. Thesis, University of British Columbia, 1983.

Duval, Paul. "Canadians Have Neglected Indian Art Heritage," *Saturday Night,* Vol. LXII (December 28, 1946).

Einstein, Karl. *Negerplastik.* Leipzig, 1915.

Exhibition of Canadian West Coast Art: Native and Modern. National Gallery of Canada and Victoria Memorial Museum catalogue (December 1927).

Feldman, Susan. "Bill Reid: Voyage through Two Worlds." Interview with Reid, January 1992, CBC Radio, March 1, 1994.

Fiske, Jo-Anne. "The Supreme Law and the Grand Law," *BC Studies* (Spring/Summer 1995), No. 105–106.

Fleming, Marnie. "Patrimony and Patronage: The Legacy Reviewed," *Vanguard* (Summer 1982).

Fleurieu, Charles Pierre Claret de. *A Voyage Round the World Performed during the Years 1790, 1791, 1792, Performed by Etienne Marchand.* London: T.N. Longman and O. Rees, 1801.

Foster, W. Garland. "The Graphic Art of the Haidas," *Museum Notes* (Art, Historical and Scientific Association, Vancouver), Vol. 111 No. 1 (March 1928).

Godfrey, Stephen. "Murphy's Romance," *Globe and Mail,* March 29, 1986.

Goodwin-Austen, R.B. *Parkinson's Disease, Day by Day.* London: Parkinson's Disease Society, circa 1995.

Gruber, Jacob W. "Ethnographic Salvage and the Shaping of Anthropology," *American Anthropologist,* Vol. 72 No. 6 (December 1970).

Haberland, Wolfgang. "The Bella Coolas in Germany," in Christian F. Feest ed., *Indians and Europe: An Interdisciplinary Collection of Essays.* Aachen: Edition Herodot, 1989.

Haeberlin, Herman K. "Principles of Esthetic Form in the Art of the North Pacific Coast," *American Anthropologist,* Vol. 20 No. 3 (July–September 1918).

"Haida Argillite Carver." *The Native Voice* (April 1962).

Haig-Brown, Celia. *Resistance and Renewal: Surviving the Indian Residential School.* Vancouver: Tillacum Library, 1988.

Halle, David. *Inside Culture: Art and Class in the American Home.* Chicago: University of Chicago Press, 1993.

Halpin, Marjorie. "A Review Article," *BC Studies,* No. 37 (Spring 1978).

Harris, Christie. *Raven's Cry.* Toronto: McClelland and Stewart, 1966.

Harris, Cole. "Editorial," *BC Studies,* No. 120 (Winter 1998–99).

Harris, Cole. *The Resettlement of British Columbia: Essays on Colonialism and Geographical Change.* Vancouver: University of British Columbia Press, 1997.

Harris, Nancy. "Reflections on Northwest Coast Silver," in Bill Holm's *The Box of Daylight: Northwest Coast Indian Art.* Seattle Art Museum catalogue. Seattle: University of Washington Press, 1984.

Harrison, Reverend C. "Masset 11 August 1886," *Church Missionary Society* (London 1886–87).

Harrison, J.D., et al. *The Spirit Sings, Artistic Traditions of Canada's First Peoples.* Toronto: McClelland and Stewart, 1987.

Hawthorn, Audrey. *Kwakiutl Art.* Vancouver: Douglas & McIntyre, 1979.

Hawthorn, Audrey. *People of the Potlatch.* VAG catalogue, 1956.

Hawthorn, Harry B., ed. *Report of Conference on Native Indian Affairs at Acadia Camp.* Victoria: Indian Arts and Welfare Society, 1948.

Henderson, John R. "Missionary Influences on the Haida Settlement and Subsistence Patterns, 1876–1920," *Ethnohistory,* Vol. 21 No. 4 (1974).

Henson, Alice Ernst. "Masks of the Northwest Coast," *Theatre Arts Monthly* (August 1933).

Herem, Barry. "UBC Has Major Exhibit By Bill Reid, to Oct. 5," *Northwest Arts,* September 16, 1986.

Herring, Frances E. *Among the People of British Columbia, Red, White, Yellow and Brown.* London: T.F. Unwin, 1903.

Highwater, Jamake. *Arts of the Indian Americans: Leaves from the Sacred Tree.* New York: Harper & Row, 1983.

Holm, Bill. *Northwest Coast Indian Art: An Analysis of Form.* Seattle: University of Washington Press, 1965.

Holm, Bill, and William Reid. *Form and Freedom: A Dialogue on Northwest Coast Indian Art.* Houston: Institute for the Arts, Rice University, 1975.

Hooper, Jacqueline. "Arts of the Raven: B.C. Indian Art Is Something to Shout About," *Post-Intelligencer Weekender Magazine* (Seattle), July 22, 1967.

Hopkins, Thomas. "The Happy Rebirth of an Intricate Art," *Maclean's,* April 14, 1980.

Horowski, R.L., S.M. Calne, and D.B. Calne. "From Wilhelm von Humboldt to Hitler — Are Prominent People More Prone to Have Parkinson's Disease?," in *Parkinson and Related Disorders* 6 (2000).

Hover, Alan L. "Charles Edenshaw: His Art and Audience," *American Indian Art Magazine* (Summer 1995).

Hume, Robert M. *100 Years of B.C. Art,* VAG catalogue 1958.

Hunter, Elizabeth. "The National Museum of Canada and the Promotion of 'Canadian' Art 1917–1935," Department of Art History, York University, April 21, 1987.

Hunter, Lynette. *Modern Allegory and Fantasy: Rhetorical Stances of Contemporary Writing.* New York: St. Martin's Press, 1989.

"The Indians Speak to Canada." CBC Radio (Ottawa 1939).

Inverarity, Robert Bruce. *Art of the Northwest Coast Indians.* Los Angeles: University of California Press, 1950.

Islands Protection Society. *Islands at the Edge: Preserving the Queen Charlotte Islands Wilderness.* Vancouver: Douglas & McIntyre, 1984.

Jamison, Kay Redfield. *Touched with Fire: Manic-Depressive Illness and the Artistic Temperament.* New York: Free Press Paperbacks, 1993.

Jensen, Doreen, and Polly Sargent. *Robes of Power: Totem Poles on Cloth.* Vancouver: University of British Columbia Press, 1986.

Jensen, Vicki. *Where the People Gather: Carving a Totem Pole.* Vancouver: Douglas & McIntyre, 1992.

Johnson, Eve. "Revivalist Reid and the Indian Image," *Vancouver Sun,* August 9, 1986.

Jonaitis, Aldona. *Chiefly Feasts: The Enduring Kwakiutl Potlatch.* Vancouver: Douglas & McIntyre, 1991.

Jonaitis, Aldona. *From the Land of the Totem Poles.* Vancouver: Douglas & McIntyre, 1988.

Karklins, Karlis. *Trade Ornament Usages Among the Native Peoples of Canada: A Source Book.* Studies in Archaeology, Architecture and History, Native Historic Sites Park Service, Environment Canada (Ottawa 1992).

Kowinski, William Severini. "Giving New Life to Haida Art and the Culture It Expresses," *Smithsonian,* Vol. 25 No. 10 (January 1995).

Lake, Rhodi. "A Modern Approach to Indian Jewelry," *Vancouver Sun,* July 25, 1953.

Lakke, Johannes P.W.R. "Art and Parkinson's Disease," in Gerald M. Stern, *Parkinson's Disease.* Philadelphia: Lippencott Williams and Wilkins, 1999.

Large, R. Geddes. *The Skeena: River of Destiny.* Vancouver: Mitchell Press, 1957.

Lash, Mary Ann. "New Life Is Given to the Craft of Haida Jewelry," *Canadian Art,* Vol. 24 (September 3, 1957).

Leechman, Douglas. "Native Canadian Art of the West Coast," *Studio,* Vol. XCVI No. 42 (November 1928).

Leechman, Douglas. "The 'Canadian Story,'" *The Canadian Bookman,* Vol. VII No. 7 (July 1925).

"The Legacy of Bill Reid: A Critical Enquiry." University of British Columbia conference, November 1999.

Lévi-Strauss, Claude. "Art of the Northwest Coast at the American Museum of Natural History," *Gazette des Beaux Arts,* Vol. 24 (1943).

Lewis, Hunter. "The Disappearing Totem Pole," *Canadian Art,* Vol. XI No. 2 (Winter 1954).

Lowndes, Joan. "Child of the Raven: Bill Reid," *Vanguard* (February 1982).

Lush, Pat. "A Transformer of Existing Things," *Ryerson Rambler,* No. 28 (Fall 1985).

MacDonald, George F. *Haida Art.* Vancouver: Douglas & McIntyre, 1996.

MacDonald, George F. *Haida Monumental Art: Villages of the Queen Charlotte Islands.* Vancouver: University of British Columbia Press, 1993.

Macnair, Peter L. "Inheritance and Innovation: Northwest Coast Artists Today," *artscanada* (December 1973/1974).

Macnair, Peter L. "Trends in Northwest Coast Indian Art 1880–1950: Decline and Expansion," in Gerhard Hoffmann, ed., *In the Shadow of the Sun: Perspectives on Contemporary Native Art.* Ottawa: Canadian Museum of Civilization, 1993.

Macnair, Peter L., Alan L. Hoover, and Kevin Neary. *The Legacy Continuing Traditions of Canadian Northwest Coast Indian Art.* Victoria: British Columbia Provincial Museum, 1980.

Mayne, R.C. *Four Years in British Columbia and Vancouver Island.* London: J. Murray, 1862.

McLennan, Bill and Karen Duffek. *The Transforming Image: Painted Arts of Northwest Coast First Nations.* Vancouver: University of British Columbia Press, 2000.

McNeil, Bill, and Morris Wolfe, eds. *Signing On: The Birth of Radio in Canada.* Toronto: Doubleday Canada, 1982.

Miller, J.R. *Shingwauk's Vision: A History of Native Residential Schools.* Toronto: University of Toronto Press, 1996.

Miller, J.R. *Skyscrapers Hide the Heavens.* Toronto: University of Toronto Press, 1989.

Mortimer, G.E. "Handicrafts Merit Protection," *The Native Voice* (January 1960).

"Myth & Symbol," *Time* (September 28, 1962).

Mowatt, Don, talking to Bill Reid, PABC, "Hornby Suite," CBC 1989.

Nemiroff, Diana, Roubert Houle, and Charlotte Townsend-Gault, eds. *Land, Spirit, Power: First Nations at the National Gallery of Canada.* Ottawa: National Gallery of Canada, 1992.

Niblack, Albert P. "The Coast Indians of Southern Alaska and Northern British Columbia," *Annual Report for the Smithsonian Institute* (Washington, 1888).

Nicks, Trudy. "Indian Handicrafts: The Marketing of an Image," *Rotunda* (Summer 1990).

Nuytten, Phil. *The Totem Carvers: Charlie James, Ellen Neel and Mungo Martin.* Vancouver: Panorama Publications, 1982.

O'Hara, Jane. "Trade Secrets," *Maclean's,* October 18, 1999.

Paalen, Wolfgang. "Totem Art," *Dyn: The Journal of the Durham University Anthropological Society,* Vol. 4–5 (1943).

"Palette," "Indians of British Columbia Present Splendid Exhibition," *Province* (Vancouver), July 17, 1941.

Pearce, J.M.S. *Parkinson's Disease and Its Management.* New York: Oxford University Press, 1992.

Peers, Frank W. *The Politics of Canadian Broadcasting 1920–1951.* Toronto: University of Toronto Press, 1969.

"People of the Potlatch," *CBC Times* (May 13–19, 1956).

Perry, Art. "Bill Reid: Master Sculptor of Contemporary Haida Art," *Artmagazine* (June 1978).

Pineo, P.C. "Rounded Picture of Contemporary Life, Skidegate Mission, 29 January 1955," Special Collections, University of British Columbia, Harry Hawthorn Papers No. 27-1.

Poole, Francis. *Queen Charlotte Islands: A Narrative of Discovery and Adventure in the North Pacific.* London: Hurst & Blackett, 1871.

Raban, Jonathan. *Passage to Juneau: A Sea and Its Meaning.* New York: Pantheon Books, 1999.

Raley, Reverend G.H. "Canadian Indian Art and Industries," *Journal of the Royal Society of Arts,* No. 4320 Vol. LXXXIII (September 6, 1935).

Ravenhill, Alice. *A Corner Stone of Canadian Culture: An Outline of the Arts and Crafts of the Indian Tribes of British Columbia.* Occasional Papers of the British Columbia Provincial Museum, No. 5 (Victoria, March 1944).

Ravenhill, Alice. "Photo Reproductions of Twenty Charts 36 x 80 Inches Prepared on Commission from Indian Affairs Branch 1940," RBCM Archives.

Reid, Bill. *All the Gallent Beasts and Monsters.* Vancouver: Buschlen Mowatt, 1991.

Reid, Bill. "Arts National," CBC Radio, April 2, 1980.

Reid, Bill. "Becoming Haida," Wilderness Advisory Committee, Vancouver, February 1, 1986.

Reid, Bill. *Bill Reid — Drawings.* Equinox Gallery catalogue, January 27 to February 26, 1983.

Reid, Bill. *The Carvers of the Totem Poles.* Film by Kelly Duncan, produced by Gene Lawrence, CBC, Pacific 8, Provincial Archives of British Columbia.

Reid, Bill. "Curriculum vitae," in *Bill Reid: A Retrospective Exhibition,* VAG catalogue, November 6 to 8 December 8, 1974.

Reid, Bill. "1st Trailer, 2nd Beach, Skidegate Inlet, Q.C.I., August 3, 1976," *Vanguard* (October 1976).

Reid, Bill. "A Fragment of Time Fades from the Forests to Mellow in Museums." CBC Radio (March 1954).

Reid, Bill. "The Haida Legend of the Raven and the First Humans," *Museum Notes* No. 8 (1980) MOA.

Reid, Bill. "The Indian as Artist,'" CBC Radio, 1965, PABC.

Reid, Bill. "Indian Equality Urged" (June 17, 1959), VAG clipping file.

Reid, Bill. "Interview." Film, UBC, 1961, PABC, F1990:124.1-2.

Reid, Bill. "An Introduction to Northwest Coast Indian Art," Talks on Northwest Coast Indian Art, typescript of audiotape, February 6, 1979, MOA.

Reid, Bill. Lecture in Northwest Coast Indian Artists in Dialogue series, MOA, March 27, 1984.

Reid, Bill. "The Legacy Review Reviewed by Bill Reid," *Vanguard* (October/November 1982).

Reid, Bill. "Mythic Messenger," *Sunday Arts Entertainment,* CBC Television, January 18, 1996.

Reid, Bill. "A New Northwest Coast Art: A Dream of the Past or a New Awakening?" Issues and Images; New Dimensions in Native American Art History conference, Arizona State University, April 22, 1981.

Reid, Bill. *Out of the Silence.* Fort Worth: Amon Carter Museum, 1971.

Reid, Bill. "Peddling the Ancestral Bones for Fun and Profit," *UAAC/AAUC Journal* (August 1974, typescript, Artist's File, VAG Library.

Reid, Bill. "A Personal Statement by Bill Reid." Reid File, Canadian Museum of Civilization, appended to Bill Reid, "Committee Members, the Canadian Crafts Council," March 29, 1986.

Reid, Bill. "Profile of Bill Reid." Video, VAG, 1974.

Reid, Bill. "River of Clouds," CBC Radio, February 21, 1965.

Reid, Bill. "The Spirit of Haida Gwaii," Vancouver, 1991, mimeograph, VAG Archives.

Reid, Bill, "Totem Pole is Epic in Carved Wood" *Vancouver Sun*, February 9, 1954.

Reid, Bill. "Traditions of Northwest Coast Indian Culture," Museum of Anthropology, November 23, 1976, tape recording, MOA.

Reid, Bill. Preface in *Bill Koochin,* Burnaby Art Gallery, 1980.

Reid, Bill. In *Visions: Artists and the Creative Process*, video recording (Toronto: TVOntario, 1983).

Reid, Bill. "Legacy dialogue," lecture, MOA, February 24, 1982.

Reid, Bill, and Robert Bringhurst. *The Raven Steals the Light.* Vancouver: Douglas & McIntyre, 1984.

"Report of Conference on Native Indian Affairs, Acadia Camp, April 1–3 1948," PABC.

Report of the Royal Commission on National Development of the Arts, Letters and Sciences 1949–51. Ottawa: King's Printer, 1951.

Richardson, Boyce. *People of Terra Nullius: Betrayal and Rebirth in Aboriginal Canada.* Vancouver: Douglas & McIntyre, 1993.

Roe, Michael, ed. *The Journal and Letters of Captain Charles Bishop on the North-West Coast of America, in the Pacific and in New South Wales 1794–1799.* Cambridge: Cambridge University Press, 1967.

Ryga, George. *The Ecstasy of Rita Joe.* Vancouver: Talonbooks, 1966.

Sapir, Edward. "Culture, Genuine and Spurious," *Dalhousie Review,* Vol. 11 (1922).

Sessional Papers, Department of Education Annual Reports (Victoria).

Sessional Papers, Department of Indian Affairs, Annual Reports (Ottawa).

Shadbolt, Doris. *Bill Reid.* Vancouver: Douglas & McIntyre, 1986.

Shadbolt, Doris. "Our Relation to Primitive Art," *Canadian Art,* Vol. V No. 1 (Autumn 1947).

Sheehan, Carol. *Pipes That Won't Smoke; Coal That Won't Burn: Haida Sculpture in Argillite.* Calgary: Glenbow Museum, 1981.

Shields, Carol. *The Republic of Love.* Toronto: Random House of Canada, 1992.

Smith, Harlan I. "Restoration of Totem-poles in British Columbia," *National Museum of Canada Annual Report for 1926,* Bulletin.

Smith, Harlan I. "Prehistoric Canadian Art as a Source of Distinctive Design," read by

L.J. Burpee, *Royal Society of Canada Proceedings and Transactions,* Third Series Vol. XII, 1918 (Toronto 1919).

Stearns, Mary Lee. *Haida Culture in Custody: The Masset Band.* Seattle: University of Washinton Press, 1981.

Steltzer, Ulli. *The Spirit of Haida Gwaii: Bill Reid's Masterpiece.* Vancouver: Douglas & McIntyre, 1997.

Stewart, Hilary. *Robert Davidson: Haida Printmaker.* Vancouver: Douglas & McIntyre, 1979.

Stewart, Susan J. "The Chief of the Undersea World," *Canadian Collector* (July–August 1984).

Stokes, Charles W. "Victoria, a Bit of England That Is Not England," *Canadian Magazine,* Vol. 53 (1919).

Swanton, John R. *Contributions to the Ethnology of the Haida.* American Museum of Natural History, Memoir 8 (1), New York, 1905.

Swanton, John R. *Haida Texts and Myths: Skidegate Dialect.* Washington: government print office, 1905.

Swinton, George. *Sculpture of the Eskimo.* Toronto: McClelland and Stewart, 1972.

Tennant, Paul. *Aboriginal Peoples and Politics: The Indian Land Question in British Columbia, 1849–1989.* Vancouver: University of British Columbia Press, 1990.

Tippett, Maria. *Between Two Cultures: A Photographer among the Inuit.* Toronto and London: Penguin, Hamish Hamilton, 1994, 1995.

Tippett, Maria. *Emily Carr: A biography.* Toronto: Oxford University Press, 1979.

Tippett, Maria. *Making Culture, Institutions and the Arts before the Massey Commission.* Toronto: University of Toronto Press, 1989.

"The Totem Carvers," *Radio Times,* May 21, 1959.

"Totem Poles Make a Comeback, Boosting Indians' Pride, Fortunes," *Wall Street Journal* (August 22, 1983).

Tully, James. *Strange Multiplicity: Constitutionalism in the Age of Diversity.* Cambridge: Cambridge University Press, 1995.

Vancouver: Art and Artists 1931–1983. VAG catalogue, 1983.

Vastokas, Joan M. "Bill Reid and the Native Renaissance," *artscanada* (June 1975).

Watt, Robert D., and Lynn Maranda. "An Interview with Bill Reid," *Canadian Collector* (May/June 1975).

Weaver, Sally M. *Making Indian Policy: The Hidden Agenda 1968–1970,* Toronto: University of Toronto Press, 1981.

The World of Bill Reid. Exhibition at Canadian Embassy in Tokyo, March 5 to April 25, 1997.

Wright, Richard. "The Spirit of Haida Gwaii," *En Route* (March 1991).

Index

A

Abbott, Donald, 156, 181
Aboriginal rights, 265
Academy of European Arts and
    Sciences, 237
acculturation, 25, 32, 126, 129
Adams, Victor, 241
Adrian, Johan, 20
American Museum of Natural History,
    145
Ames, Michael, 204, 225, 259, 261, 273,
    276
Andrew, Geoffrey, 167–8
Andrew, Louise, 270
Anglican Mission (Masset, Haida
    Gwaii), 14–15
anti-Native articles, 77–8
Apollinaire, Guillaume, 48
apprentices, 138–40
    See also assistants
appropriation of Native art and culture,
    30, 47–9, 53, 91

Art Gallery of Greater Victoria, 132, 205
Art Gallery of Ontario, 184
artistic legacy, 272
*Artist with Parkinson's Disease: A Portrait
    of Bill Reid, An* (film), 240–1
Asia-Pacific Festival (canoe launch), 243
assimilation, 183, 189
assistants, 154, 225, 227, 258
    See also Cranmer, Doug; Davidson,
        Robert
Atwood, Margaret, 262
Audain, Michael, 272
Auerbach, Herb, 272
authenticity, 257
autobiographical accounts, 5–6, 12–13,
    49, 85, 140, 196–7
awards, 110, 203–4, 237, 277
honorary degree, 49, 203, 262

B

Baez, Joan, 133
Baker, Bob, 273

Bank of British Columbia, 243–4

Barbeau, Marius, 22, 109
  influence on Native art, 79
  merits of Native art, 80–1
  removal of totem poles, 63, 91
  The Downfall of Temlaham, 142
  Haida Carvers in Argillite (1957), 154
  The Indian Speaks, 187

Baron, Sid, 49, 54–5

Bateman, Robert, 263

Bayless, Alan, 254

BC Association of Non-Status Indians,
  183, 228

BC Hydro, 109

Bella Coola performers, 20

Bentbox Gallery, 260

Berger, Tom, 255

Berton, Pierre, 52

Bibb, Leon, 227

Bill C-33 (Canada 1977), 202

Bill Reid Archive, 238

Bill Reid Endowment Fund, 236

Bill Reid Foundation, 221, 233,
  276–7

Bill Reid Gallery, 276

"Bill Reid Tribute," 272

Binning, Bert, 109

bipolar illness
  See manic depression

Bishop, Captain Charles, 16

Bishop, John, 228, 273

Black Man of the Woods (mask), 47

Boas, Franz, 20, 89, 95, 128, 139, 187,
  249
  aesthetic merits of Native art, 80
  The Kwakiutl of Vancouver Island, 242
  Primitive Art, 131, 145, 161

Bob, Dempsey, 181, 208, 261

Boggs, Jean Sutherland, 149

Bradford, Roark, 52–3

Brandtner, Fritz, 151

Brignall, Nancy, 258

Bringhurst, Robert, 141, 240, 269, 275

British Airways Boeing 757, 278

British Broadcasting Corporation, 142

British Columbia Cultural Fund, 208

British Columbia Indian Arts and
  Welfare Society, 74–5

British Museum, 158, 161, 171

Brodie, Steve, 59

Bronfman Award for Excellence in
  Crafts (1986), 237

Brown, Diane, 60, 212, 214

Brown, Eric, 80

Brown, Leah Alfonsine "Gogga," 33–4,
  39, 50

Brown, Tyson and Walker, 8

burial ceremony, 6–8

Burnaby Art Gallery, 222–3

Buschlen Mowatt Gallery, 239, 267

C

Cabell, James Branch
  Jürgen, 53

Calder, Ethel, 28

Calder, Frank, 107

Calne, Dr. Donald, 240

Cameron, Earl, 59

Campbell, Ronald
  The Story of the Totem, 187

Campbell, Tom, 149

Camus, Albert, 6

Canada Council, 151, 156, 158, 167, 197
  fellowship, 150, 218
  grant, 49, 115–16, 122–3

Canadian Conference for the Arts, 203

Canadian Constitution, Section 35, 262

Canadian Consul (New York), 167

Canadian Embassy (Washington), 3, 248, 265, 267

Canadian Guild of Crafts, 134

Canadian Heritage Gallery (Vancouver), 193

Canadian Jewellers Association, 64

Canadian Museum of Civilization (Ottawa), 225, 252, 261, 272

Canadian Native Prints, 202, 254

canoe making, 241–8

Canoe with Figures, 248

Canoe with People, 248

Capilano College, 210, 223

Caple, Kenneth, 91

Cardinal, Harold, 198
  Unjust Society: The Tragedy of Canada's Indians, 183

Carpenter, Edmund, 163–5, 194, 204

Carpenter, Captain Richard, 277

Carr, Alice, 37

Carr, Emily, 2, 48–9, 51, 54–5, 81, 125–6

Carson, Jack, 232, 244

Cartier, 65

carving demonstrations, 171
  Ellen Neel, in Stanley Park, 76–7

Cary, Joyce
  The Horse's Mouth, 203

Cassiar District (James Bay), 33–4, 40

Cavelti, Toni, 111–13, 134, 159, 186

CBC (Canadian Broadcasting Corporation), 140
  employment at, 58–61, 69, 109, 116–17, 209, 275, 288n5.1
  expedition to Haida Gwaii, 94
  listening to, 174
  Native art and culture, 197, 261
  Skeena River program, 241
  Explorations, 132
  Handbook for Announcers, 59

A Man and His Music, 70, 88, 101
  "River in Clouds" (radio documentary), 132
  Totems (film 1958), 96, 196

Cellini, Benvenuto, 202

Centennial Museum (Vancouver), 188, 193, 206, 231, 248

Central School of Art and Design (London), 3, 159, 161, 192, 197

Cernetig, Miro, 3

Chee-Xial, Chief, 267, 273

Chief of the Undersea (mask), 47

Chilliwack Valley, 28

Chirac, Jacques, 247

Chiriaeff, Ludmille, 203

Chrétien, Jean, 237

Clarke, Earl "Bunny," 50–2

Clarke Institute of Psychiatry (Toronto), 170, 190

Clifford, James, 261

Clutesi, George, 77, 81, 122, 148

Clyne, J.V., 227

Coast Salish, 2, 130, 139, 241

Cohen, Leonard, 170

Collison, Dempsey
  See Chee-Xial, Chief

Collison, Ellen, 28

Collison, Herman, 118, 272

Collison, Louis, 79

Colnett, Captain James, 15–16

commissions, 131–2, 142, 154, 175, 189–90, 194, 242, 252

Conceited Woman (mask), 47

Conference on Native Indian Affairs (1948), 75

Connally, Amelia, 31

Connor, Ralph, 48

conscription, 58

Cook, Captain James, 142, 157

Cooke, Jack Kent, 58
Cooking, Clive, 214
Copps, Sheila, 276
Coqualeetza Fellowship, 79
Coqualeetza Industrial Institute, 5, 25, 27–9
Council of the Haida Nation, 265
Craigdarroch Castle, 51
Cranmer, Daniel, 97, 126–7
Cranmer, Doug, 97, 101, 130, 140, 206, 261
  and *Arts of the Raven* exhibition, 146
  carving technique, 211
  cedar-plank house, 228
  Haida village project, 116, 118–21, 188, 272, 278
  The Talking Stick, 133
creation myths, 187
  George Rammell, 223
criminal charges, 5, 163, 166–9
Crosby, Mabel, 25, 28–9
Crosby, Marcia, 32, 150
Cross, Emma and Barney (second cousins), 28
Cross, James, 184
Cross, John, 4, 23, 32, 44–5, 61, 73, 105, 208
Cunningham, George, 45
"curios," 23, 30, 45–6, 53, 55, 75, 79

D
David, Joe, 208, 210, 240
  Whale Rider, 278
Davidson, Albert, 241
Davidson, Claude, 4, 28, 140, 188, 209
Davidson, Florence, 55, 241, 268
Davidson, Reg, 206, 224, 245
Davidson, Robert, 3, 180–1, 198, 201, 208, 224, 227–8, 252, 268, 272–3

  accomplishments of, 171–2, 254
  as an assistant, 225–6, 257
  apprenticeship of, 138–41
  and *Arts of the Raven* exhibition, 146
  compared to Reid, 193–4, 277–8
  critique of Reid, 229–30, 233, 236, 260–1
  totem pole carving, 154, 209–10, 213–15
  value of Native art, 205
Davidson, Robert Sr., 79, 140, 241
Davidson, Susan, 172
Davidson, Terri-Lynn, 273
Davidson canoe, 241–2
Davie, Alan, 65
Dawson, George M., 207
Deans, James, 14
Declusse, Leah
  See Brown, Leah Alfonsine "Gogga"
Dee, Miss, 83
de Menil, Adelaide, 163, 165–8, 185, 196
  Out of Silence: Totem Poles of the Northwest Coast, 164, 173, 204, 228
de Menil, John, 163, 204
Demerais, Lon, 246
Department of Anthropology (UBC), 88
Department of Indian Affairs, 138
de Patta, Margaret, 65–7, 160
design, 41, 67–8, 131, 161, 193
Dick, Simon, 243
Diesing, Freda, 181, 208, 210, 224
Dilworth, Ira, 109
Diplôme d'Honneur award, 203
Disraeli, Benjamin, 279
Dixon, Captain George, 15, 157
Dixon, Pat, 148, 180, 208
Dominion News, 59
Dorsey, Tommy, 54
Douglas, Sir James, 31

Drapeau, Mayor Jean, 172
Drew, Leslie, 248
Duff, Wilson, 101–3, 107, 128–9, 140, 182
    "artfakery," 195
    book with Reid, 156, 158
    essay for de Menil, 164
    expedition to Haida Gwaii, 90–8,
        265–6
    Mungo Martin memorial plaque, 132
    Reid exhibitions, 144, 146–7, 150
    rhetorical questions, 131
    suicide of, 217–18
    Images: Stone, BC, 204–5
    "Thoughts on the Nootka Canoe,"
        242
Duffek, Karen, 5, 160, 260–1
Dunsmuir, Honorable Robert, 51
Dupre, Paul, 244
Dwyer, Peter, 167
Dykk, Lloyd, 219
Dylan, Bob, 133

E
Edenshaw, Charles, 223
    ancestral relations, 138, 214, 221, 273
    drawings on paper, 193
    exhibitions of, 105, 147
    gold bracelets of, 64
    influence on Reid, 68, 89–90, 93,
        110–11, 114, 124, 143–4, 197, 255,
        277
    ivory walking stick finial, 157, 161
    repertoire of, 22–3, 45
    Bear Mother, 131
    Discovering Mankind, 185–8
    Hummingbird Bracelet, 90
    Thunderbird and Whale, 24
Edenshaw, Gary, 6, 8, 210, 212–13,
        222–3, 225, 243, 256, 268, 273

Edenshaw, Henry, 25
Edwards, Allen, 54
Einstein, Karl, 80
Elliot, P.H., 52
Ellis, Bill, 194, 203
Ellsworth, Fanny (great-aunt), 14, 17
Ellsworth, Josephine
    See Gladstone, Josephine (grand-
        mother)
Equinox Gallery (Vancouver), 239
Erickson, Arthur, 182, 222, 251, 267
Ernst, Max, 65
ethnographic motifs, 65
Ethnography Department of the British
        Museum, 157
exhibitions
    The Art of the American Indians
        (Galerie Mansart, Paris), 245
    Arts and Handicrafts Show
        (Vancouver Art Gallery), 80–5, 87,
        93, 106, 114, 151
    *Arts of the Raven: Masterworks by the
        Northwest Coast Indian*
        (Vancouver Art Gallery), 144–51,
        173, 248
    *Bill Reid: All the Gallant Beasts and
        Monsters* (1991), 267
    Bill Reid: A Retrospective Exhibition
        (1974), 194–9
    Bill Reid: Beyond the Essential Form
        (UBC Museum of Anthropology),
        5, 236, 260
    Canadian Designs for Living (1953
        Vancouver Art Gallery), 110
    *Exhibition of Canadian West Coast
        Art: Native and Modern* (1927), 80
    *Exhibition of Modern Indian Arts and
        Crafts* (annual exhibition,
        Provincial Museum), 81

Form and Freedom: A Dialogue on Northwest Coast Art (1975), 204–6, 231

Indians of Canada (Expo 67), 149

International Exhibition of Modern Jewellery 1890–1961, 159

Jewellery '71: An Exhibition of Contemporary Jewellery (Art Gallery of Ontario), 184

The Legacy: Continuing Traditions of Canadian Northwest Coast Indian Art (Provincial Museum), 182, 185, 255

Man and His World (Montreal 1970), 170–3, 193

New Brunswick's Handicraft Guild Centennial Exhibition, 110

100 Years of B.C. Art (Vancouver Art Gallery), 107, 111

People of the Potlatch (1970), 105–9, 111, 151, 171, 176, 193, 286n3.1

The Spirit Sings: Artistic Traditions of Canada's First Peoples (1987), 239

Treasures of London (1977 Centennial Museum Vancouver), 206–7

Expo 86, 228

F

Fabergé jewellery, 161

Falk, Gathie, 180

False Creek, 243

family ancestry, 21

fantasy and allegory (interest in), 52–3

Federation of Canadian Artists Exhibition, 110

Fergusson, Hattie, 80–1, 83–4

Financial Times, 253–4

first drawings, 67

First Nations House of Learning (UBC), 255

FitzGerald, Bessie, 133–5, 138

FLQ, 184

formalistic approach, 125

Forman, Werner
    North American Indian Art (1967), 158

Fort Victoria, 16

Fotheringham, Allan, 235

Fraser, Jack, 164

Freeman family, 29

friendships, 115, 141
    See also various individuals

Front Page Challenge, 235, 303n14.1

Fry, Robert, 204

Frye, Northrop, 109

G

Garen, Glen, 273

Gilhooly, David, 186, 188, 230

Gitanmaax School of Northwest Coast Indian Art, 180–1

Gitkun, Chief

Gladstone, Abraham, 22

Gladstone, Charles (grandfather), 12, 21–4, 29, 32, 41, 44–5, 60, 64, 70, 73, 78, 81, 88–9, 100, 105, 134, 197, 207, 209, 214, 266
    Carving on Cedar of Dogfish, 24
    Sdast'aas, Two Bears Bracelet, 74

Gladstone, Clayton, 210

Gladstone, Eleanor (aunt), 25, 41, 60

Gladstone, Ella, 79, 81, 83, 179

Gladstone, Ernie (uncle), 25, 41, 45

Gladstone, Irene (aunt), 25, 44

Gladstone, Josephine (grandmother), 5–6, 8, 11–16, 18–19, 25, 29, 44, 214, 265

Gladstone, Margaret (second cousin), 28–9

Gladstone, Percy (uncle), 25, 28, 41, 75, 88, 213

Gladstone, Sophie
  See Reid, Sophie (mother)

Gladstone, William (uncle), 22, 25, 28, 45

Glad Tidings (floating mission), 14

Glenbow Museum, 239

Godfrey, Stephen, 244

Goodman, Benny, 54

Gould, Glen, 203

Graham, Colin, 132

Graham, Isabelle, 228

Granville Island, 160, 268

Grauer, Sherry, 164–71, 173, 175–6, 179, 182–4, 186, 188–90, 220, 222, 276
  Dog Face Boy's Picnic, 164

Green, Jimmy, 64, 66–8, 70, 159

Greene, Lorne, 58

Gunn, Ella, 114, 133

Gunther, Erna, 130

Gwaii Haanas National Park, 265

H

Haeberlin, Herman, 128

Haida, 12–13, 15–18, 20–3, 45, 129, 138, 207, 209, 213, 246–7

Haida art, 66, 73, 99, 123, 156

Haida blockade, 264

Haida Carver (NFB 1963), 138

Haida flag, 246

Haida Gwaii, 11–12, 16, 73, 78–9, 114, 138, 143, 199, 207, 214, 241, 244, 267
  expedition to, 90–8, 256–66
  logging, 262

Haida Gwaii Watchmen, 8

Haida House, 228, 241, 273

Haida idenity, 262

Haida mythology, 123–4, 153, 249, 251, 278

Haida Nation, 228, 277

Haida people, 94, 141, 199, 204, 214–15, 274, 276

Haida screen, 192, 195, 202

Haida village project, 128, 131, 202, 207
  assistants' work on, 154, 192, 278
  carving for, 118–22
  construction techniques, 117
  continuing influence of, 138, 150, 164
  payment for, 115–17, 144
  Reid's proposal for, 99–101, 103
  and revitalization of Native art, 275

Haig-Brown, Roderick, 109

Hall, Rev. Joseph, 28

Halpin, Marjorie, 204, 256, 261

Halton, Matthew, 60

Hamilton, Ron, 181, 260, 278

Handel, George Frideric, 227

Harman, Jack, 250

Harrington, Lynn, 109

Harris, Christie
  Raven's Cry, 142–4

Harris, Walter, 181, 208

Hart, Jim, 224–6, 257, 259, 275, 278

Harvard Graduate School of Design, 164

Hawthorn, Audrey, 88, 91, 97, 106, 126–7, 133, 150, 190, 195, 269

Hawthorn, Harry, 88, 91, 97, 99, 103, 116, 122, 150–1, 189–90, 193–5, 272

Haydn, Joseph, 133

Helvey, Clinton, 163

Hepworth, Barbara, 259

Herem, Barry, 240, 260

Herrings, Frances, 48
Hitchcock, Sharon, 244
Hodgkin, Stephen, 175
Holgate, Edwin, 48, 81
Holm, Bill, 135, 139, 144, 146–8, 150,
    196, 204, 210, 229, 241–2
    Northwest Coast Indian Art: An
    Analysis of Form, 128–31
Hooper, Jacqueline, 142, 148
Hooper, Rev. L., 79
Hopkins, Rev., 17
Hotel Keith, 34, 39
Houston, James
    Eskimo Handicrafts, 129
Hudson's Bay Company, 134
Hume, R.N., 151
Hume, Stephen, 247
Hunt, Harry, 101
Hunt, Henry, 146, 208, 241
Hunt, Richard, 260–1
Hunt, Tony, 146, 180, 193, 198, 208, 229,
    257, 260–1

I
Illustrated London News, 25
Images exhibition, 193
impresario of Native art, 228
Indian Act, 91, 163, 256
Indian Affairs Branch in the
    Department of Citizenship, 183
Indian reserves (British Columbia), 14
Indians of Canada Pavilion (Expo 67),
    142
Inglis, Stephen, 225
International World's Fair in Brussels,
    110
Inverarity, Robert Bruce, 67, 74, 89
Ireland, 157
Irving, Tam, 219

Island Arts and Crafts Society's
    "Modern Room" (Victoria, British
    Columbia), 49, 51
Island Protection Society
    Islands at the Edge: Preserving the Queen
    Charlotte Islands Wilderness, 263
Italy, 158

J
Jackson, A.Y., 48, 81
Jacobsen, Fillip, 20–1, 23
James, Charlie, 96, 116
Janze, Phil, 257
Jarvis, Alan, 151
Jensen, Doreen, 108, 278
jewellery-making technique, 63, 65–8,
    90, 131, 186, 198
    See also Ryerson Institute (Toronto)
John, Jimmie, 77
Johnson, Eve, 230, 260–1
Johnson, Michael, 146
Johnson, Mr., 127
Jonaitis, Aldona, 261
Jones, Albert, 92
Jones, Clarence, 92
Jones, Jimmy, 92
Jones, Moses, 45
Jones, Roy, 92
Jones Beach, NY, 184
Julian, Alex, 148

K
Kaiser, Edgar F., 243
Kandinsky, Wassily, 49
Kelly, Rev. Peter, 138
Kelly, Tom, 45
Kennedy, Margaret "Peggy" (sister), 5,
    19, 32, 34, 37–8, 41, 43, 50, 55, 60,
    73, 124, 157, 219, 256, 276

Kennedy, Stewart, 161
Khyber-Gruber, Doris, 146
Kilkenny Design Workshops, 157
Kitwankul, 30
Koerner, John, 109, 180
Koerner, Joseph, 107
Koerner, Otto, 149
Koerner, Walter, 103, 107, 118, 149–50,
    182, 189, 192, 221, 255, 258
  bear sculpture for, 131–2
Kovach, Rudy, 170, 208
'Ksan, 180–1
Kwakwaka'wakw, 127–8, 138, 160, 207,
    218, 241
Kyooka, Roy, 180

L
Lake, Rhodi, 73, 78, 88
Lakke, Johannes, 240
land claims, 265
Laporte, Pierre, 184
Lash, Mary Ann, 111
Léger, Jules, 212
Leon and Thea Koerner Foundation,
    193, 238
Lévi-Strauss, Claude, 194–5, 218, 245,
    248
Lewis, Hunter, 91
Lindsay, Vachel, 53
Lippel Gallery of Tribal Arts (Montreal),
    185, 189
Liverpool, 157
logging, 3, 262–3, 265, 273, 277
Logging, Frank Beban, 264
London, England, 156–62
London's Central School of Art and
    Design, 150
London's Great Exhibition (1851), 23
Loo Plex, 7, 267

Loo Taas, 1, 6–7, 241, 243–7, 256, 266–7,
    269, 277
Lowndes, Joan, 196–7, 210
Lubin, Stanley, 267, 273
Lyell Island, 263–5

M
MacDonald, George, 163, 272
  Haida Monumental Art: Villages of the
    Queen Charlotte Islands, 239
Mackay, Jim, 45
MacKenzie, Larry, 108–9
MacKenzie, Norman, 99–101
MacMillan, Ernest, 48
MacMillan Bloedel, 243
Macnair, Peter, 164, 182, 185, 218, 260
Malpin, Marjorie, 227
manic depression, 6
  beginnings of, 102
  on a psychological high, 185
  and relationships, 115, 169, 173–5,
    218, 224
  treatment for, 170, 190, 198
  See also under Reid, Bill, health of
Mannis, Harry, 59
Mariposa Festival (Toronto, Ontario),
    170
Marks, Gerry, 113, 180–1, 210, 212, 224
marriage
  See romantic relationships
Martin, Abayah, 4, 97–8, 103
Martin, David, 98, 101, 103, 127, 148
Martin, Mungo, 2, 180, 193
  carving, 121, 154, 211
  compared to Reid, 150
  Cranmer as apprentice to, 116
  death of, 148
  donations to Provincial Museum,
    127–8

memorial plaque to, 132
Reid as apprentice to, 105, 110, 218,
    241
totem poles, 77, 96–9, 101, 103
Masset, 12, 14, 22, 24
    See also Old Masset
Massey, Geoffrey, 112
Matisse, Henri, 47, 81
McGill University (Montreal), 185
McGuire, Pat, 148, 180–1
McIntyre, Scott, 276
McLennan, Bill, 238–9
Melvin, Grace
    The Indian Speaks, 187
Methodists, 14–17, 22–5
Metropolitan Museum of Art (New
    York), 187
Michelangelo, Leonardo, 259
millennium opinion poll (British
    Columbia), 276
Miller, Jeff, 258
Miller, Rev. A.N., 17
Minifie, James, 60
Mintz, Bud, 256
Miriam Shiell Gallery (Toronto),
    239
mixed race, 36, 53
modernism, 55, 119, 161
Moholy-Nagy, László, 65
Molinari, Guido, 151
Molson Prize, 203
Le Monde, 248
Montreal (Quebec), 162–3, 169–70, 184,
    186, 189
Moody, Arthur, 78
Moody, Rufus, 79, 148
Moody, Rus, 83
Moody, Tom, 45
Moore, George, 64

Moore, Henry, 259
Morgan, Judith, 81
Morris, J.A., 106
Morriseau, Norval, 135
Mozart, Wolfgang Amadeus, 140, 227
Muldoe, Earl, 129, 236
Murray, Robert
    Cumbria, 268
Musée de l'Homme, 245, 248
Museum of Anthropology (UBC), 4, 13,
    67, 228, 236–9, 241–2, 271, 273–4,
    276–7
    See also under exhibitions
Museum of Modern Art (New York), 65,
    80
Musqueam Indian Reserve, 256
Musqueam nation, 273
Mythic Messengers, 233

N
Nabisco Brands, 268
Nash, Knowlton, 61
National Aboriginal Achievement Award
    for Lifetime Achievement (1994),
    237
National Art Gallery (Ottawa), 80
National Film Board (Canada), 138
National Gallery of Canada, 149, 165,
    261
National Museum of Canada, 63, 89,
    163, 241, 243, 261
National Museum of Man (Ottawa),
    185, 196, 242, 307n15.29
National Native Indian Artists
    Symposiums, 262
Native ancestry, 4–6, 12–13, 44, 49, 68,
    70, 73, 100, 256
Native ethnicity, 41, 49
Native Indian Brotherhood, 183

Native Voice, The, 192, 214
Native women (status of), 32–3
Neel, Ellen, 4, 75–8, 81–2, 84, 96–7, 148, 193, 205
Newcombe, C.F., 47
New Design Gallery (Vancouver), 135
Newman, Pauline (grandmother), 31
News Roundup, 59
New York, 169, 202
New York Times, 3, 146–7
Ngan, Wayne, 219
Nightmare Bringer (mask), 47
Ninstints Recovery Expedition, 95–6
non-status Native, 208
Norris, George, 222–3, 274
    Crab, 188, 231
Northwest Coast art, 2, 48, 128–9, 131, 139, 240, 277
North West Trade Fair (Seattle 1957), 110
Norton, Derek, 268
Nutter, John, 258
Nuu-chah-nulth carvers, 241
Nuxalk carvers, 241

O
obituaries, 3–4
Obomsawin, Alanis, 161, 170, 273
October Crisis, The (Canada), 184
O'Hara, Jane, 276
Old Masset, 79, 138, 140, 212–14, 227
    See also Masset
O'Neill, Frank, 273, 275
Onley, Toni, 180
Order of Canada, 277
O'Reilly, Peter, 14
Orpheum Theatre (Vancouver), 252

P
Paalen, Wolfgang, 80
Page, Peter, 170, 173–6, 182, 184, 186, 197, 202, 207, 247
Page, Sandi, 202
Pardon, Earl, 65
Paris, 245
Paris exhibition reviews, 248
Parkinson's disease, 2, 6, 190–2, 199, 209, 212, 221, 234, 240, 268–70, 273
Parry, Frank, 194
Pasco, Duane, 180, 210
patrons, 151, 185, 228, 257–8
Patterson, Pat, 64
Paul, Lawrence, 278
Paula Ross Dance Company, 227
Pearkes, George (Lieutenant-Governor), 149
Pearson, Tim, 78–9
Pederson, Vice Chancellor George, 275
Pérez, Juan Hernández, 15–16
Phillips, Arnold, 139
Phillips, Ruth, 275
Phillips, Walter J., 142
Picasso, Pablo, 12, 48–9, 81
Plaskett, Joe, 161, 219, 225, 260, 270
Platinum Art Company, 70
Point, Susan, 278
Pointe, Shane, 278
political statements and protest, 266
popularity, 254
potlatch, 207, 214, 228
Power Machinery Company, 121
preservation of wilderness, 263
Price, Art, 154, 186, 189, 219
Price, Tom, 23, 90, 277
Prince Charles, 227
Prince of Wales (ship), 15
Profile: Bill Reid (video 1974), 196

Prohibition Act (British Columbia), 34
promotion of Native culture, 202–3
Provincial Museum of Natural History
    (now the Royal British Columbia
    Museum), 2
  acquisition of artifacts, 182–3
  donations to, 127
  early influence on Reid, 46–7, 55, 241
  funding by, 208
  gold box with killer whale, 175, 232
  influence on Reid, 90, 120, 197
  memorial plaque to Mungo Martin, 132
  red cedar screen, 142, 153
  relocating totem poles, 96, 99
  See also under exhibitions
public persona, 1–2, 4, 56, 137, 201, 234,
    252

Q
Quintana, Rosa, 258

R
radio broadcaster, 55–8, 69, 85, 95,
    287n 4.2
  See also CBC (Canadian Broadcasting
    Corporation)
Radio Times, 111, 116
Rammell, George, 102, 210, 222–5, 230,
    254, 256–60, 267–9, 275, 277
  Pyrolith, 223
Ravenhill, Alice, 67, 74–5, 82, 89, 106, 128
  Corner Stone of Canadian Culture: An
    Outline of the Arts and Crafts of
    the Indian Tribes of British
    Columbia, 186
RCMP, 163–4, 167
Reid, Amanda (daughter), 69, 73, 114,
    156, 180, 208, 267
Reid, Barbara (sister-in-law), 267

Reid, Bill
  arrest of, 167
  birth, 33
  childhood, 38, 43–7, 53
  death, 3, 6–8, 270
  education, 49–51, 53, 55
  finances, 51, 167, 171, 173, 176, 197,
    208, 235–6, 253–4, 267
  Haida names, 55, 268, 273
  health of, 51, 94
    (See also manic depression;
    Parkinson's disease)
  relationship with father, 38, 56
  relationship with mother, 69
  reputation, 115, 137, 149, 227–8
  sound of voice, 55, 59–60, 270
  youth, 49–51, 53
  —ESSAYS
  for catalogue for Arts of the Raven,
    147–8
  for catalogue for Bill Reid: A
    Retrospective Exhibition, 196–7
  for Island Protection Society, 263
  for The Jade Canoe, 252
  letter to newspaper "Totem Pole is
    Epic in Carved Wood," 78
  for Out of the Silence: Totem Poles of
    the Northwest Coast, 173
  prologue to catalogue for Form and
    Freedom, 204
  for Raven and the First Men, 239
  for 100 Years of B.C. Art, 107–8
  —WORKS
  Bear Mother, 185
  bear sculpture (for Walter Koerner),
    131
  Beaver Bracelet, 74, 90
  Chief of the Undersea World (See Killer
    Whale)

Dogfish Gold Brooch, 110
drawings for *Haida Monumental Art: Villages of the Queen Charlotte Islands,* 239
Eagle Brooch (1955), 68
Gold Box, 142
Gold Eagle Box, 131
Horse Barnicle Necklace, 176
illustrations for *Raven's Cry,* 142
jacket design for *British Columbia: A Centennial Anthology,* 142
The Jade Canoe, 3, 252, 254
Killer Whale, 3, 221, 233, 256, 259
Killer Whale and Raven (platter), 124
killer-whale banners, 244
Killer Whale Earrings (1955), 68
killer-whale gold box, 182–3, 185
Laminated Cedar Screen, 142
Loo Plex, 7, 267
Loo Taas, 1, 6–7, 241, 243–7, 256, 266–7, 269, 277
medallion for Canadian Biographical Award, 88
mural for the Conference on Human Settlements (1976), 203
Peace Arch carving (BC-Washington border), 101
Phyllidula, the Shape of Frogs to Come, 239
Raven and the First Men, 1–3, 187–8, 192, 220, 222, 225–33, 238, 243, 251, 254, 256, 258–9, 268, 272, 275, 278
Raven Discovering Mankind in a Clamshell, 186–8, 221–3
The Raven Steals the Light, 240
Sea Bear, 248
Sea Wolf Sculpture, 120

The Spirit of Haida Gwaii, 1, 231, 248–50, 252, 254, 256–9, 265, 267–8, 270, 277–8, 306n15.17
totem poles, 55, 63, 77–8, 83, 91, 131–2, 208
Transformation Pendant with Detachable Mask, 220
Wolf Feast Dish, 171
The Woman in the Moon (brooch), 67, 88, 288n4.13
(*See also* Haida village project)
Reid, Charles (grandfather), 31
Reid, Mabel "Binkie" (wife), 58, 69, 73, 113–14, 141, 245
Reid, Margaret "Peggy"
See Kennedy, Margaret "Peggy" (sister)
Reid, Martine (wife), 1–2, 5, 218–20, 222, 229, 239, 245, 247, 256, 267, 269, 272, 276
Reid, Raymond ("son"), 103, 114, 141, 156, 180, 184, 190, 245
Reid, Robert (brother), 38–9, 167, 245
Reid, Robert (designer), 107, 115, 142, 163, 167, 170, 189, 193, 203, 259, 267, 276
Reid, Sophie (mother), 12, 20–1, 28–41, 53, 60, 65, 79, 110, 132, 140, 161, 168, 197, 204, 209, 219, 256, 269, 286n1.5
as Haida, 49–50
Reid, William "Billy" (father), 30–37, 39–41, 56, 60
Reid-Stevens, Amanda
See Reid, Amanda (daughter)
religious beliefs, 6
renaissance man, 203
renaissance of Native art, 1–3, 97, 182, 262
repatriation of native artifacts, 182

replication, 100, 181
repoussé, 186
restoration program, 99
Richardson, Colin, 248
Richardson, Miles III, 245–6, 264, 274, 277
Ridley, Robert, 207
Robinson, George, 15, 22
Robson, John, 23
Rodin, Auguste, 259
role models, 41, 53
romantic relationships, 58, 113–15, 158, 164, 175–6, 202, 218–20, 247
Rosso, Larry, 181
Royal Bank of Canada, 203, 239
Royal Museum of Ethnology, 20
Royal Ontario Museum, 63, 69, 211
Rubens, Peter Paul, 258
Ruddle, Bruce
    Spirit of Haida Gwaii, The (opera), 252
Russ, Walter, 232
Russian invasion of Czechoslovakia, 158
Ryersonia, 69
Ryerson Institute (Toronto), 61–70, 88, 197
Ryga, George
    The Ecstasy of Rita Joe, 149

S
salesman, 133
salvage operations, 108, 182, 198, 208
Sandberg, Carl, 251
Sargent, R.S., 30
Savage, Annie, 48
School of Design (Chicago), 65
School of Handicraft and Design (Victoria BC), 47–8
Scow, Alfred, 121
Scow, Peter, 133

Seaweed, Jimmy, 4
Seaweed, Willie, 107, 148
self-government, 262
Shadbolt, Doris, 21, 109, 146, 150
    Bill Reid, 6, 236
Shadbolt, Gordon, 109
Shadbolt, Jack, 49–51, 55, 102, 110, 112–13, 180, 194, 203
Shaughnessy, Arthur, 116
Shaw, David, 242
Shell Oil (London head office), 131
Shiell, Miriam, 237, 260
Sibert, Erna
    North American Indian Art (1967), 158
Silcox, David, 3, 154
Silent Ones, The (film), 96
Simms, Richard, 146
Skedans, 12, 90, 92–3, 101, 266
Skidegate Band Council Administration building, 208
Smith, Don Lelooska, 146
Smith, Gordon, 109, 112, 180
Smith, Leo, 48
Smithers, 31
Smithsonian Institution, 144–5, 167
Smyly, John, 95
Snow, Michael, 194
South Moresby, 263, 265
South Park Elementary School, 49
Speck, Henry, 135
Spence, Lois, 142
Squamish singers, 273
Stanley Park (Vancouver), 131, 249, 251, 277
Sta'stas clan, 22
status as Native, 256
Steinhouse, Herbert, 60
Steltzer, Ulli, 237

Stephens, A.M., 48
Stephens, James, 52
Stephens, Vernon, 181
Stevens, Raymond
    See Reid, Raymond ("son")
Stevens, William, 141
Stewart, 33–5, 38–41, 53
Stogan, Vincent, 273
Sumner, Richard, 7
Sun, Chang, 258
Suzuki, David, 263, 273, 275–6
Swan, James, 14
Swanton, John, 68, 249
Swinton, George, 83

T
Tait, Josiah, 208
Tait, Norman, 205, 208, 210, 229, 257
Talking Stick, The, 133
Tallix Foundry, 250, 259–60, 268
Tanabe, Takao "Tak," 101–2, 109,
    113–14, 158, 165, 210, 218–19,
    270, 276
Teleglobe Canada, 228, 233
Tennant Family, 18, 25, 33
Terasaki, George, 166
Thomas, David, 160
Thomas, Lionel, 154–5
Thomas, Lowell, 60–1
Thompson, Art, 260
Thompson River Native necklaces, 161
Thornton, Mildred Valley, 82
Thunderbird Park, 98–9, 127, 132, 241
tools, 120
Toronto Star, 236
Totem Park (Vancouver), 96–8, 103,
    119, 121
Totem Pole preservation Committee, 91
Totem Pole Project, 278

totem pole raising (Skidegate), 207–15,
    221, 228
Totems (1958), 196
Tousignant, Claude, 151
Treen, Gunilla, 160
Trudeau, Pierre Elliot, 183
Tully, James, 251

U
Union Club (Victoria), 134
Union of BC Indian Chiefs, 183, 228,
    246
University of Northern British
    Columbia, 236
University of Victoria, 49
University of Western Ontario, 262
Urban Haida Singers (Vancouver), 273

V
Van Boyen, Mabel
    See Reid, Mabel "Binkie" (wife)
Vancouver Art Gallery, 105–7, 110, 144,
    146, 148–9, 151, 194, 196–7, 203,
    239, 248, 272
    See also under exhibitions
Vancouver Art School, 141
Vancouver Bach choir, 254
Vancouver Courier, 244
Vancouver Foundation, 196
Vancouver International Airport, 252,
    254, 268, 273, 278
Vancouver Parks Board, 131, 203
Vancouver Public Aquarium, 3, 221,
    228, 232–3
Vancouver School of Art, 138–9, 222
Vancouver's international fair, Expo 86,
    242
Vancouver's Lifetime Achievement
    Award (1988), 237

Vancouver Sun, 3, 73, 78, 142, 146–7,
    225, 247, 260, 269
Vander Zalm, Premier Bill, 264–5
Vanguard, 217, 255
Vastokas, Joan, 210
Vickers, Roy Henry, 230
Victoria College, British Columbia,
    51–3, 55, 102
Victoria (Inner Harbour), 241
Victoria Memorial Museum (Ottawa),
    48, 80
Vinge, Einor, 133, 294n.9.6
Volkoff, Boris, 48
Volstead Act, 34, 39

W
Walker, Frank, 116
Wasnicki, Nina, 240
Watmough, David, 102, 269
Watson, James, 19
Watson, Luke, 45
Welsh, Anthony, 75
Wembley Exhibition (London), 80
Wesley, Rebecca, 28
Western Forest Products, 222, 243, 264
white establishment, 204
White Paper Canadian Federal
    Government (1969), 183
Widerspach-Thor, Martine
    See Reid, Martine (wife)
Wieland, Joyce, 151
Wi'ha, John, 68, 88
Wilderness Advisory Committee, 263
William Reid Ltd, 267
Williams, Howard, 148
Williams, Raymond, 148
Williams, Watson, 148
Wilson, Solomon, 45
Wilson, Douglas, 248

Wilson, Ernie, 213
Wilson, James, 92
Wilson, William, 16–18
Windy Bay, Lyell Island, 262
Wolfe, Louis, 168
Women's Missionary Society, 25
Woodcock, George, 109
Work, John, 15
workshop, 206–7
World's Fair (1974 Spokane,
    Washington), 194, 210
World War II, 58
Worshipful Company of Goldsmiths,
    159
Wynam, Jan, 222

X
Xwa-lack-tun, 278

Y
Yeltatzie,George, 214
Yeomans, Don, 7–8, 205, 209, 224–5,
    254, 257–8, 264–5, 268–9, 274, 278
Young, Allan, 92
Young, David, 260
Young, George, 79
Young, Henry, 45, 60